THE HUMAN PROSPERITY PROJECT

ESSAYS ON SOCIALISM AND
FREE-MARKET CAPITALISM
FROM THE HOOVER INSTITUTION

Foreword by Condoleezza Rice

Project Cochairs
Scott W. Atlas
Edward P. Lazear

Contributors
Terry L. Anderson, Scott W. Atlas, Michael R. Auslin,
Peter Berkowitz, Russell A. Berman, John F. Cogan,
Larry Diamond, Elizabeth Economy, Niall Ferguson,
Stephen Haber, Daniel L. Heil, Gregory Kearney,
Edward P. Lazear, Michael W. McConnell, Lee E. Ohanian,
Joshua Rauh, George P. Shultz, John Yoo

HOOVER INSTITUTION PRESS
Stanford University | Stanford, California

With its eminent scholars and world-renowned library and archives, the Hoover Institution seeks to improve the human condition by advancing ideas that promote economic opport unity and prosperity, while securing and safeguarding peace for America and all mankind. The views expressed in its publications are entirely those of the authors and do not necessarily reflect the views of the staff, officers, or Board of Overseers of the Hoover Institution.

hoover.org

Hoover Institution Press Publication No. 725

Hoover Institution at Leland Stanford Junior University, Stanford, California 94305-6003

First printing 2022
28   27   26   25   24   23   22   7   6   5   4   3   2   1

Manufactured in the United States of America
Printed on acid-free, archival-quality paper

Library of Congress Cataloging-in-Publication Data
Names: Hoover Institution | Human Prosperity Project (Hoover Institution on War, Revolution, and Peace)
Title: The Human Prosperity Project : essays on socialism and free-market capitalism from the Hoover Institution
Other titles: Hoover Institution Press publication ; 725.
Description: Stanford, California : Hoover Institution Press, Stanford University 2022. | Series: Hoover Institution Press publication ; no. 725 | Includes bibliographical references and index. | Summary: "Scholarly analyses of free-market capitalism, socialism, and hybrid systems from historical, economic, and public policy perspectives provide evidence on the effectiveness of each system in enhancing human prosperity and well-being"—Provided by publisher.
Identifiers: LCCN 2022011180 | ISBN 9780817925154 (paperback) | ISBN 9780817925161 (epub) | ISBN 9780817925185 (pdf)
Subjects: LCSH: Economic history—1918- | Socialism. | Capitalism. | Free enterprise. | Liberty—Economic aspects. | Economic policy.
Classification: LCC HC54 .H86 2022 | DDC 330.9—dc23/eng/20220316
LC record available at https://lccn.loc.gov/2022011180

THE HUMAN PROSPERITY PROJECT

Contents

III. The Contemporary Revival of Socialism and Its Prospects

IV. Social Democracy and Current Policy Debates

V. Afterword

Foreword

In his seminal work *Reflections on a Ravaged Century*, the late Hoover Institution research fellow Robert Conquest wrote: "In their inspirational aspect, the words 'socialism' and 'communism' convey an economy without sin." He continued:

> In the old days, and partly through Marxist jargon, the active definition [of socialism and communism] was easy—a society without capitalists. Unfortunately, since then a number of societies without capitalists have been created in various countries, and it would take a word fetishist of terrific obstinacy to maintain that these were indeed without sin.[1]

Indeed, history has shown that the principle "from each according to his ability, to each according to his needs" is a concept that works only at gunpoint. It has failed to inspire and motivate the populations subjected to it.

The Soviet experiment—the fullest expression to date of that principle—stood astride half of Europe for almost five decades. But its "internal contradictions," as George Kennan put it, were enormous. I saw firsthand, as a student in Moscow in 1979, that the Soviet Union was an economic and social shell, protected by propaganda, coercion, and prodigious military power. The population was dispirited and resigned and the leadership craven, corrupt, and entitled. The failures of the system and the gravitational pull of human freedom eventually proved to be too much, and the Soviet Union and its client states collapsed.

After those seismic events, it was widely believed that communism and socialism had fallen into the dustbin of history. The United States had prevailed in the Cold War, and it seemed that the principles of the free-market system would prove to be the only viable path toward human prosperity. However, over the ensuing decades, as barriers to trade withered away and nations became richer, economies remained vulnerable to global boom-bust cycles, while in some societies income disparities persisted and even widened. This led many critics to again challenge the precepts of free-market capitalism.

According to a Gallup poll released in November 2019, over the past decade favorability ratings about socialism among Americans ages eighteen to thirty-nine have hovered at around 50 percent. Meanwhile during that period, attitudes about capitalism in the same age group have deteriorated from a level of 66 percent to 51 percent.[2]

Capitalism certainly has its challenges. For many, the belief that hard work will lead to prosperity and upward mobility—in short, the American dream—is frayed. Educational opportunity is clearly shared unevenly. Many are undeniably left behind. To defend capitalism is not to ignore its flaws. Still, the experience with socialism, even its latest variant in China, is hardly one that would recommend it as the answer to these challenges.

As of late, arguments about socialism and capitalism boil down to axioms and passionately held beliefs. And, of course, there is an entire generation that does not remember the excesses of socialism and its failures. That is why it is incumbent on institutions like Hoover to produce volumes of scholarship like this one, which takes a close look at hard data that reflect the outcomes of these two conflicting economic and political systems.

Scott W. Atlas and the late Edward P. Lazear, the founding cochairs of Hoover's Human Prosperity Project, deserve our sincere gratitude for the compilation of this volume. They gathered and inspired an exceptional roster of scholars from the Hoover fellowship, who have produced richly researched and concisely argued essays from a diverse set of policy perspectives, including law, political and economic philosophy, technological innovation, health care, environmental progress, national security, income growth and inequality, individual liberty, and so much more.

In many ways, this deeply educational volume is a tribute to our extraordinary colleague Dr. Lazear, who was not only an exceptional teacher to generations of students at Stanford University but also an active convener of colleagues at Hoover, Stanford, and beyond.

It is especially appropriate that this volume end with words of wisdom from the late distinguished fellow George P. Shultz. Born three years after the fall of Russia to communism, Shultz lived to see these arguments play out as an academic and as a senior government official throughout the duration of the Cold War. As secretary of state in the 1980s, he had a front-row seat to the events that led to the collapse of the Soviet Union.

I hope you enjoy reading these essays as much as I did. They will enrich us with a deeper understanding of these economic and political systems that dominated life over the past century. Most importantly, they will inform us on how best to advance the human condition.

Condoleezza Rice

TAD AND DIANNE TAUBE DIRECTOR

THOMAS AND BARBARA STEPHENSON SENIOR FELLOW

HOOVER INSTITUTION, STANFORD UNIVERSITY

NOTES

1. Robert Conquest, *Reflections on a Ravaged Century* (New York: W. W. Norton, 1999), 53.
2. Lydia Saad, "Socialism as Popular as Capitalism Among Young Adults in the US," Gallup, November 25, 2019, https://news.gallup.com/poll/268766 /socialism-popular-capitalism-among-young-adults.aspx.

Preface

The Human Prosperity Project on Socialism and Free-Market Capitalism at the Hoover Institution represents a start at analyzing free-market capitalism and socialism in order to assess how these conflicting systems lead to social and economic prosperity.

Free-market capitalism with private ownership and market-determined allocation of goods and services is often credited with generating economic growth and high average income, but its critics argue that a market-based economy creates significant inequality and does not help the poor enough. Socialism and its variants, which couple government ownership of much of the means of production with substantial centrally determined allocation, are championed as being more benevolent than free-market capitalism.

The goal of this project is to provide objective and scholarly analyses of free-market capitalism, socialism, and hybrid systems and to provide evidence on the effectiveness of the various systems on outcomes that affect prosperity and well-being. The essays are written by renowned experts who cover a broad range of issues, including strictly economic subjects, like the impact of economic form on incomes and economic growth; important social goals, like providing broad access to quality medical care, promoting technological advancement, and sustaining our environment with rational priorities; and the political consequences of these systems, like ensuring individual liberty and freedom, enhancing strategic relations with other countries, and promoting long-term peace.

These evaluations aim to determine how well the various governmental and economic forms promote general well-being and prosperity. The project is particularly important and timely, given today's interest in policies that are quite radical from a US historical perspective, including many that are advocated by political and academic leaders. As in previous times in our nation's history when a sentiment toward more government control has swept the country, today's momentum toward more centralization of authority and away from individual empowerment is born out of disenchantment with current circumstances.

This project began with my short email to a handful of my colleagues at the Hoover Institution in 2019. In that email, I expressed concern that a confusing narrative was developing about capitalism and socialism. That narrative seemed steeped in politics. It involved strident views and opinion in the media, but it seemed notably absent of fact and historical context. Within hours, I heard a knock on my office door. It was my friend and colleague from down the hall, Eddie Lazear, one of the most esteemed economists among all the economists with high accolades at Hoover. Like me, Eddie was focused on empirical data as the best vehicle for exploring questions about policy. Eddie immediately agreed with the critical importance of a project setting the record straight on the historical data about capitalism and socialism, and the need to explore these systems with data and careful thought. He was, like me, eager to bring the project to fruition with the highest caliber of scholarship, and he offered to help develop and codirect what became known as the Hoover Institution's Human Prosperity Project on Socialism and Free-Market Capitalism.

With this volume, the Hoover Institution presents a set of essays based on scholarly research written by Hoover scholars participating in the Human Prosperity Project. This publication objectively investigates the historical record to assess the consequences for human welfare, individual liberty, and interactions between nations of various economic systems ranging from pure socialism to free-market capitalism. Each essay includes thoughtful and informed analysis from our top scholars. It is my distinct honor to have worked closely with Eddie Lazear in designing and constructing this important exploration. It is my hope, as it was his, that both the scope and the quality of the research will shed light on how the choice of government and economic structure affects the overall quality of life. This book is dedicated to the memory of my distinguished colleague and friend, Edward Paul Lazear.

Scott W. Atlas
ROBERT WESSON SENIOR FELLOW ON HEALTH POLICY
COCHAIR, HUMAN PROSPERITY PROJECT ON SOCIALISM AND
    FREE-MARKET CAPITALISM
HOOVER INSTITUTION, STANFORD UNIVERSITY

Acknowledgments

The Hoover Institution would like to thank the scholars who participated in this project, as well as their supporting researchers and assistants. We especially would like to acknowledge Policy Fellow Daniel Heil, who contributed to the introduction and organization of this volume, and Associate Director of Institutional Programming Denise Elson, who launched this project and developed the accompanying virtual speaker series.

Further thanks are given to Thomas Gilligan, former director of the Hoover Institution, under whose oversight the Human Prosperity Project was launched; and Christopher Dauer and Shana Farley in the Strategic Communications and Marketing department, who helped conceive the project and provided its forum in its original iteration as a series of essays on Hoover.org. Rachel Moltz produced the website.

The Hoover Institution Press, including Barbara Arellano, Danica Michels Hodge, and Alison Law, brought their expertise to the production of this publication, with the assistance of copy editor David Sweet and proofreader Nicole Cahill.

Scott W. Atlas, Robert Wesson Senior Fellow and cochair of the Human Prosperity Project, conceived the project and provided vital leadership.

Finally, we would like to acknowledge and honor Edward Lazear, Morris Arnold and Nona Jean Cox Senior Fellow, who cochaired this project and who passed away on November 23, 2020. A champion for economic freedom and prosperity, the Human Prosperity Project and this resulting compendium of essays could not have been accomplished without his intelligent observations and tireless research.

Introduction

The collapse of the Soviet Union was a triumphant moment for liberal democracy. Here was proof that command-and-control economies could not compete—economically, morally, or militarily—with nations devoted to limited government, free markets, and the rule of law.

The triumph was unexpected. In the years preceding the Soviet collapse, a pessimistic outlook animated the free world. Western prognosticators could readily see the disturbing trends in their own nations. They witnessed the persistence of poverty, stagflation, and increased political discord. Meanwhile, many of the same prognosticators naively accepted the Soviet assertion that widespread prosperity lay behind the Iron Curtain.

Seemingly overnight those assertions were proven wrong.

But the triumphant moment did not last. Global events quickly revealed weaknesses in liberal democracies. The 9/11 attacks demonstrated the vulnerabilities open societies face in an interconnected world. The Great Recession exposed cracks in the foundations of Western economies. And the slow recovery that followed brought renewed attention to poverty and economic inequality.

Today, pessimism is again pervasive. A growing and resilient China has reinvigorated a belief that central direction and state ownership—buttressed by some market mechanisms—can deliver broad prosperity.

Economic dynamism—a traditional hallmark of capitalism—is now used to describe the communist nation's economy. In contrast, decades of slow economic growth in the United States and Europe seem to weaken the case for free markets, while a muddled response to the COVID-19 pandemic in the United States and Europe has cast fresh doubts on the capabilities of their governments.

Once more the world is debating which economic system is best. The Hoover Institution's Human Prosperity Project is a substantial contribution to this debate. Composed of a series of essays by leading scholars, the project examines the effectiveness of free-market capitalism, socialism, and hybrid systems. It asks how these systems affect prosperity and human flourishing.

Properly understood, prosperity is far more expansive than material well-being. To flourish, humanity needs a bright outlook for the future, self-determination, a safe and secure society, and a clean and healthy environment. Because prosperity is multidimensional, the study of it demands a multifaceted approach. This compilation reflects that requirement. It is a multidisciplinary effort that features the efforts of economists, historians, legal experts, philosophers, and political scientists.

Part 1 of this compilation broadly summarizes the historical debate between capitalism and socialism. In chapter 1, Peter Berkowitz juxtaposes the political philosophies of John Locke and Karl Marx. The chapter assesses their arguments on political power, limited government, and property rights, and then considers the philosophers' predictions for the future. As Berkowitz highlights, both philosophers believed their system would promote human flourishing, but only Locke's prediction has come close to meeting this promise.

Why did Marx's promises go unfulfilled? Chapters 2 and 3 explore the economic and political incentives underlying these systems. The chapters focus on the institutions in liberal democracies that encourage innovation, hard work, risk taking, and investment. In chapter 2, Larry Diamond explores the disparate political and economic outcomes in different economic and political systems. He finds that nations with capitalism, democracy, and good governance are typically more prosperous than those that lack any of the three. Diamond explains that this "institutional formula ... weds two types of open and competitive markets: political competition between parties that seek the power to rule through regular, free, and fair elections and economic competition between private firms that seek profits through initiative, innovation, and improved productivity."

Steve Haber reiterates the importance of incentives in chapter 3. Why did the United States economy grow so much faster than the Chinese economy in the last two centuries? Haber points to a society that rewarded innovation and risk taking. He argues that "the key to the success of this process of innovation was the lack of centralized planning: people were free to pursue their self-interest through markets." Patent law and the invention of general incorporation played an important part in this process by aligning the incentives of individuals with the interests of the greater society.

Part 2 examines the wide gaps in outcomes between capitalism and socialism. In chapter 4, the late economist Edward P. Lazear analyzes the economic record of 162 nations, each with a unique political and economic history. He finds countries that adopted market-oriented reforms experienced growing economies and rising incomes. Perhaps more surprisingly, the economic gains are widespread. In China, India, and elsewhere, market reforms preceded wide gains in the standards of living of the poorest in these nations.

The effect economic systems have on prosperity extends far beyond material well-being, however. In chapter 5, Terry L. Anderson explores how environmental outcomes differ between liberal democracies and socialist economies. The differences are stark. Countries with fewer economic freedoms have worse environmental track records than capitalist nations. Socialist Venezuela is a clear example. The once-prosperous nation now "has the third-highest deforestation rate in South America, sewage pollution in its water supplies, soil degradation, and urban pollution." What explains this degradation? Anderson points to poor incentives embedded in socialist economies. In contrast, an economy with robust property rights "connects self-interest to resource stewardship by compelling resource owners to account for the costs and benefits of their actions and facilitate market transactions that create efficiency-enhancing gains from trade." The result is greater material prosperity *and* better environmental stewardship.

In chapter 6, Russell A. Berman explores the histories of West and East Germany. The divergent outcomes of these two nations serve as "a nearly textbook case of the difference between socialist and capitalist economic paradigms." Although East Germans were relatively wealthy compared to citizens of other Eastern bloc states, their standard of living fell far behind that of their western counterparts. Berman concludes with perhaps the best indication that West Germany's economic system offered superior outcomes. Namely, at the conclusion of the Cold War, "the East Germans chose to abandon socialism in order to pursue greater prosperity and political freedom through integration into the liberal democracy and social market economy of the Federal Republic."

Can modern-day socialist governments fare any better? Some point to the Chinese economy as proof that with the right policies and leaders, socialist countries can indeed thrive. In chapter 7, Elizabeth Economy challenges this notion. She finds that, contrary to the rhetoric of the Chinese Communist Party (CCP), their leaders have not "discovered a magical new formula for economic prosperity." Relative to economically similar developing nations that have embraced democratic reforms, China "does not stand out as providing more or better for the social welfare of its people."

Michael R. Auslin echoes these sentiments in chapter 8. He argues that recent authoritarian actions by the CCP have made life for the typical Chinese citizen "narrower and more brittle." There are additional indications that Chinese progress is illusive. For example, Chinese elites are increasingly buying property overseas and securing foreign passports as they hedge against any future domestic crisis. Casting further doubt on the Chinese economic model, Auslin points to the actions of developing nations in the Indo-Pacific. While perhaps envious and wary of China, these nations are not eager to adopt Chinese institutions or policies; instead these nations look to Japan as a template for the future.

Yet despite its dismal record, socialism is again in vogue in the Western world. Part 3 examines the reasons for its revival and whether it is likely to gain additional support.

In chapter 9, Niall Ferguson begins with an analysis of the Marxian belief that capitalism is doomed to fail. The belief extends far beyond Marx and his followers; countless twentieth-century scholars—including Joseph Schumpeter—were equally convinced that socialism would out-live capitalism. Where did they go wrong? Ferguson points to the inher-ent contradictions and failed predictions in Marxist ideology. In short, as we learn in part 2, "capitalism survived precisely because socialism did not work."

Ferguson, however, cautions that socialism is now attracting new fol-lowers. He points to the series of economic disruptions that have occurred in recent decades as the cause. The 2008 financial crisis and the slow re-covery that followed disproportionately affected certain groups who are now asking whether their nation's economic system works. Meanwhile, academics and politicians are increasingly advocating socialist policies "to soak the rich to fund new and bureaucratic entitlement programs." It is no wonder then that some people, particularly younger generations, are attracted to the promises of socialism. Still, Ferguson does not expect Western societies to adopt traditional socialism. He argues that political institutions such as the rule of law make it difficult to enact wholesale socialism in the United States and in Europe.

Chapters 10 and 11 highlight the particular US political institutions that would frustrate the efforts of any socialist reformer. In chapter 10, Michael McConnell explores the constitutional safeguards that "foster a free and prosperous society." Although the constitution is largely agnostic on particular economic policies, McConnell argues that the document "rests on a philosophy of individual rights that is most consistent with liberal democracy and private property." He points to the Constitution's separation of powers, its independent judiciary, and due process require-ments as barriers to socialism. These provisions would stifle socialist movements that must rely on the arbitrary and capricious actions of its leaders. Similarly, in chapter 11, John Yoo highlights the role federalism would play in preventing American socialism. The founders believed that the decentralization of power would be key to protecting liberty. After one hundred years of expansion, the federal government has centralized government power, but federalism remains a barrier to widespread assaults on liberty.

The risk of wholesale socialism in the United States is thus small. The Constitution's checks and balances, its protection of minority and individual rights, and its decentralization of power serve as significant obstacles to any socialist revolution. Moreover, as several of the essayists note, most modern-day supporters of socialism are not demanding state ownership of the means of production; rather they are largely interested in European social democracy. Peter Berkowitz (chapter 1) highlights the political wish list of this movement:

> Rather, they identify socialism with a progressive political agenda. They think of European social democracy. They tend to oppose the use of military force, favor fewer restrictions on immigration, and make a priority of addressing climate change. They seek reforms such as a higher minimum wage, national health care, stronger unions, and more robust communities grounded in shared values and mutual concern. They generally do not dream of abolishing private property or radically redistributing wealth but rather endeavor to expand government regulation for the public safety, health, and welfare and to use progressive taxation to reduce the gaps between rich and poor that have widened in recent decades.

Part 4 focuses on some of these policy ideas. Although they are a far cry from socialism, the following chapters reveal that these economic policies suffer from the same problems experienced in socialist countries. Specifically, the policies create disincentives to work, innovate, and invest; they weaken economies and rob future generations of economic opportunities.

In chapter 12, Lee Ohanian compares labor outcomes in the United States and Europe. Although the US labor market is not free of government interference, the nation's labor taxes and regulations are less burdensome than those of most European countries. As a consequence, the US economy is far more dynamic than Europe's, with lower levels of unemployment, stronger productivity rates, and higher wages. Ohanian points to better incentives in the United States as the explanation. The nation's labor market benefits from low labor tax rates, low minimum wages, fewer workplace regulations related to hiring and firing employees, and rules that limit the market power of private sector unions.

Scott W. Atlas completes a similar exercise for health outcomes in chapter 13. Although the US health care system is, again, not a paragon of a free market, it is far freer than its European counterparts. Atlas compares the performance of the US system to nations with single-payer health care systems. He finds the US system consistently delivers better health outcomes.

Expanding the social safety net is a key aim for advocates of social democracy, and for many, a universal basic income (UBI) would represent the culmination of their efforts. In chapter 14, John Cogan and Daniel Heil analyze the economic effects of a UBI that would provide a guaranteed income to all American adults. The authors highlight the many shortcomings in the existing American transfer system: it is costly, it poorly targets those in need, and it contains large disincentives to work. Nevertheless, they find that the UBI would exacerbate each of these problems, particularly if policy makers choose to layer the program on top of the existing welfare state.

In chapter 15, Joshua Rauh and Gregory Kearney analyze tax increases that often accompany proposals to expand government programs. In particular, they examine the economic effects of wealth taxes and tax hikes on high-income taxpayers. They find that past efforts to enact these types of taxes have raised little revenue while producing large economic distortions.

In the concluding chapter, the late George P. Shultz warns against the temptation to abandon the principles of limited government when new policy challenges arise. Failing to heed this warning led to the 1970s era wage and price controls and the economic damage that followed. Shultz concludes:

Markets generally work (even, or perhaps particularly so, in times of uncertainty), and excessive interventions by government in the operations of the economy or in personal decision making can cause problems, sometimes severe. Watch out for charges that the world has changed, or society has changed, or the economy has changed, as justifications for suddenly abandoning your principles.

* * *

The essays presented here are not the last word in the debate between socialism and capitalism. It is unlikely there will be a last word. As current experience reveals, new crises will inevitably revive past ideas about the optimal relationship between the government and the people. Nevertheless, these essays serve as important reminders of the stakes involved. Human flourishing depends on selecting and maintaining the institutions that create the right incentives for individuals, businesses, and governments. The last century was marked by repeated failures to appreciate this reality. The prosperity of future generations demands we not repeat that mistake again.

The compilation presented here is only a subset of the Human Prosperity Project essays. The entire series is available at https://www.hoover.org/publications/humanprosperityproject.

I
History and Background

1

Capitalism, Socialism, and Freedom

Peter Berkowitz

The classic distinction between capitalism and socialism is straightforward. In capitalism, private individuals make the major decisions about production, distribution, and consumption, and, under the rule of law, government protects a far-reaching right to private property. In socialism, the state makes the major decisions about production, distribution, and consumption and retains a direct say about who gets what property and how it is employed. Capitalism is compatible with the state's provision of a social safety net—that is, the guarantee of a material minimum below which citizens are not allowed to fall—but not with top-down management of economic life, which is the hallmark of socialism.

Despite the fundamental distinction between the two, misunderstandings of capitalism and socialism abound, and usually in favor of socialism. Indeed, socialism is seen especially among the young as a desirable political and economic arrangement. According to a Gallup poll from April 2019, 58 percent of US residents ages eighteen to thirty-four think "some form of socialism" would be good for the country, while only 37 percent think it would be bad.[1] In a Harris poll done the same month, nearly half of the eighteen- to forty-four-year-olds surveyed said they would rather live in a socialist country than a capitalist one.[2]

Most Americans who are well disposed toward socialism do not have in mind the classic definition: state ownership of the means of production and government planning of the economy. Rather, they identify socialism with a progressive political agenda. They think of European social democracy. They tend to oppose the use of military force, favor fewer restrictions on immigration, and make a priority of addressing climate change. They seek reforms such as a higher minimum wage, national health care, stronger unions, and more robust communities grounded in shared values and mutual concern. They generally do not dream of abolishing private property or radically redistributing wealth but rather endeavor to expand government regulation for the public safety, health, and welfare and to use progressive taxation to reduce the gaps between rich and poor that have widened in recent decades.

These concerns and aspirations are not identical to socialism. Some overlap with conservative apprehensions that advanced liberal democracies weaken traditional bonds of friendship and citizenship, unleash rampant individualism, and foster the unfettered pursuit of material wealth. But—as Friedrich Hayek argued in *The Road to Serfdom* (1944), his bracing analysis of the twentieth-century political and intellectual trends that favored central planning—socialism can come about indirectly, incrementally, and inadvertently. Acting on today's progressive agenda—most items of which tend to strengthen the central government's power over the economy—would undercut freedom by solidifying institutional foundations for, and conditioning citizens to acquiesce in, a form of government command of and control over the economy.

The prevalence of misconceptions about socialism obscures the dangers. Many Americans, especially younger ones, think the Nordic countries of northern Europe represent the triumph of socialism even though their economic systems owe much to the spirit of capitalism. Many Americans, especially younger ones, are unaware of the blatant failure of socialism as an organizing principle for politics and the economy—in the former Soviet Union, in Cuba, in Venezuela, and, indeed, everywhere else it has been tried. Many Americans, especially younger ones, are ignorant of the tens of millions who were slaughtered under communism—the most influential form of socialism—in the twentieth century in the name of an idyllic future that never arrived. Many Americans, especially younger ones, have scant understanding of the role of limited government in protecting individual freedom and market economies. Many Americans, especially younger ones, have little concrete appreciation of how wealth is produced. And many Americans, especially younger ones, are unacquainted with capitalism's stunning track record in lifting hundreds of millions around the world out of the grinding poverty that has been the typical lot of ordinary people throughout history and in creating prosperous middle classes across nations and civilizations.

In these circumstances, in which people speak with casual authority about capitalism and socialism but display a poor grasp of the two systems' premises and their implications for freedom, a return to the basics is warranted. The seventeenth-century writings of John Locke in defense of political and economic freedom and the mid-century critique by Karl Marx of political and economic freedom represent classics of the genre. Fresh examination of their ideas brings into better focus the case for freedom.

John Locke: The Foundations of Political and Economic Freedom

The publication of John Locke's *Two Treatises of Government* in 1689 followed fast on the heels of England's Glorious Revolution of 1688, but the work was conceived well before it. Although the book provides grounds for viewing the ascent of William of Orange and Mary II to the throne as a vindication of the nation's traditional rights and freedoms, Locke's argument in the *Two Treatises* focuses not on any particular political controversy but on the foundations of political legitimacy in individual freedom and human equality.

Locke's influence on ideas about freedom derives in large measure from the *Second Treatise*, the first chapter of which distills the *First Treatise's* devastating arguments against divine-right monarchy. At the time, the kings of England and elsewhere in Europe claimed title to rule on the grounds that, as direct descendants of Adam, they inherited dominion over their subjects and their kingdoms. Based on the biblical authority to which the kings appealed, Locke shows that Adam lacked dominion over his children and the world; that even if he possessed it, dominion did not transfer to his children and their heirs; that even if dominion did transfer to his children and their heirs, rules were lacking for determining which of the multiplying heirs inherited the right to rule; and that even if such rules existed, the passage of time hopelessly obscured the lines of descent that would allow for reliable application of the rules.[3]

Locke draws a stark conclusion: if political power rests exclusively on claims of divine-right monarchy, and if those claims are irredeemably flawed, then existing governments lack political legitimacy unless a satisfactory alternative can be discovered:

> He that will not give just occasion to think that all government in the world is the product only of force and violence, and that men live together by no other rules but that of beasts, where the strongest carries it, and so lay a foundation for perpetual disorder and mischief, tumult, sedition, and rebellion, (things that the followers of that hypothesis so loudly cry out against) must of necessity find out another rise of government, another original of political power, and another way of designing and knowing the persons that have it.[4]

The explicit purpose of Locke's *Second Treatise* is to define political power accurately and to determine the conditions under which it is appropriately exercised. Locke does not claim that existing governments are inherently illegitimate but rather that the standards for establishing their legitimacy had not been properly grasped.

Political power is, according to Locke, "a *right* of making laws with penalties of death, and consequently all less penalties, for the regulating and preserving of property, and of employing the force of the community, in the execution of such laws, and in the defense of the commonwealth from foreign injury; and all this only for the public good."[5] Locke understands property broadly; for him it includes the rights all human beings share. The protection of property so understood limits government power. Those limits, however, are subject to constant negotiation and renegotiation. The need to regularly reconsider and revise the boundaries of political power stems from the uncertainties and ambiguities that surround the crafting of appropriate rules and regulations; the various beliefs, habits, and associations that preserve property; and the mix of elements that advance the public good. The perpetual challenge of line drawing is consistent with Locke's view that the protection of property—which encompasses basic individual rights—is the central task of politics.

Locke's definition of political power is grounded in the all-important premise that human beings are by nature free and equal. By this Locke did not mean that human beings are free in every way and equal in all respects. We are naturally free in the politically relevant sense of the term, he contended, because no human being possesses an inherent right to control another's actions, dispose of another's property, or dictate another's beliefs. Hence, all human beings are naturally equal since none is born inherently subject to, or with right to rule over, another.[6]

Locke's account of "the state of nature"—through which he illuminates the moral, political, and legal significance of our natural freedom— is much maligned. It supposedly fails to supply a plausible historical account of the origins and development of political society, overlooks the social dimensions and psychological and spiritual complexity of human nature, and celebrates an untrammeled individual freedom. These objections rest on a misunderstanding of Locke's intention and a flawed reading of his analysis. Locke examines human beings in a pre-political context not because he believes that persons can prosper outside of political society but to illuminate the universal core of individual rights. His account of the state of nature, moreover, sheds light on political society's centrality to human flourishing. And it explains why reaping freedom's benefits depends on mutually agreed-upon political institutions that circumscribe natural freedom.

Although a pre-political condition, the state of nature is not a premoral one. According to Locke, "The *state of nature* has a law of nature to govern it, which obliges every one: and reason, which is that law, teaches all mankind, who will but consult it, that being all *equal and independent*, no one ought to harm another in his life, health, liberty, or possessions."[7] But what is the likelihood that those who dwell in the state of nature will consult the law of nature and that those who consult it will comply with it?

Over the intermediate term and long term, Locke believes, the likelihood is vanishingly small. In the state of nature each has a perfect freedom to decide for himself or herself what reason requires, permits, and forbids, and to act on such judgments. Such freedom, Locke maintains, subverts the security and stability that make freedom valuable. In the absence of settled laws issued by an agreed-upon authority, of recognized enforcement mechanisms, and of established authorities for resolving disputes, persons with the unconstrained right to act on their private judgment will tend to give priority to their own interests in interpreting what is just and proper and so will be inclined to resolve disputes in their own favor. The state of nature's perfect freedom gives rise to constant conflict among individuals while leaving them without a commonly recognized political authority for the peaceful resolution of their confrontations and clashes. As a result, the state of nature ineluctably deteriorates into what Locke called "the state of war"—a condition of "enmity, malice, violence, and mutual destruction." The absence of government, Locke shows, destroys the benefits that arise from natural freedom and equality.[8]

Although it is often asserted that Locke denies that human beings are by nature social and political animals, his analysis of the state of nature's swift collapse into a state of war shows that individuals were made for society and can flourish only in association with others. To enjoy the freedom that equally inheres in all persons, individuals must devise ways to limit under law the exercise of their shared right to make and enforce private judgments about justice and injustice.[9]

Locke maintains that to deserve obedience, laws—and the political institutions for making, enforcing, and adjudicating disputes about them—must be grounded in consent.[10] Consent is a prerequisite for law's legitimacy because of natural freedom and equality. Since none has the right to rule over another, an individual can only properly be subject to a law that issues from a set of basic procedures to which he or she has agreed. One needn't favor a particular law to have incurred an obligation to obey it. But consent to the larger framework from which laws emerge does give rise to an obligation to obey even the laws of which one disapproves.

Locke knows perfectly well that most individuals are seldom involved directly in legislation and rarely consent *expressly*—that is, explicitly and formally—to the larger lawmaking process. But he reasons that those who voluntarily live under laws that protect their property and keep government within its proper limits *tacitly* consent as long as they stay put and enjoy the laws' benefits while retaining the right to leave.[11] Individuals, Locke recognizes, are sure to disagree with this law or that. But if the disagreeable law has issued from a basic constitutional framework and settled governmental procedures that they can reasonably be seen to have accepted—explicitly or implicitly—then individuals are obliged to comply with it.

The doctrine of consent—express and tacit—is vulnerable to a variety of objections. But the core idea is a bedrock tenet of the modern tradition of freedom: law's legitimacy depends on the ability of persons to whom it applies to understand it as the result of fundamental political institutions that secure basic rights.

Political freedom for Locke is indissolubly bound up with economic freedom and religious freedom. Laws that infringe upon individuals' basic decisions about property—including the property one has in the fruits of one's labor—and about faith exceed the limits of political power and nullify the overriding purpose for which government is established.

In the *Second Treatise*, Locke highlights economic freedom. The right to property entails control, not subject to the arbitrary dictates of other human beings, over properly acquired land and objects as well as over oneself, including one's thoughts, actions, and body. It derives, according to Locke, from "the property every individual has in his own *person*; this nobody has any right to but himself." It follows, he argues, that "the labour of his body, and the work of his hands, we may say, are properly his."[12] With the invention of money, which serves as a recognized and enduring store of value, human beings acquire an incentive to produce more than they immediately need. This particularly advances the interests of "the industrious and rational,"[13] who earn more from cultivating the land and producing food, making clothes and tools, constructing physical infrastructure, and performing the multiplicity of functions and providing the vast array of services that others value. But everybody benefits because of the enormous increase in goods and services owing to the increasingly profitable division of labor and specialization of workers. The ability to exchange the fruits of one's labor and labor itself for money—accompanied by laws that protect private property—allows each to concentrate in one area and produce more of some good or service than would have been possible if each had to produce all the commodities he or she consumed.

In *A Letter Concerning Toleration* (1689), Locke focuses on religious freedom. Religion pertains to the supreme duty: the duty that an individual owes to God. Since faith cannot be coerced and remain faith, toleration of differences of opinion about religion and of varying forms of worship, argues Locke, is an imperative of faith as well as of reason. Consistent with Jesus's exhortation to give to Caesar the things that are Caesar's and to God those that are God's,[14] Locke holds that government has no business prescribing religious belief and practice just as the clergy has no authority to determine the civil law. Whereas government's job is to secure the rights all share, the proper purview of religion is to direct to salvation. Provided that individuals observe the generally applicable laws of the land—and on the assumption that these laws do not regulate beliefs and do not outlaw actions that, were they not performed as part of a religious ceremony, would be perfectly acceptable—individuals will enjoy wide latitude to believe and practice their faith in accordance with their conscience.

Locke recognizes that respect for private property along with the virtues of industry, rationality, and toleration does not develop automatically. They are the result of a specific kind of education: an education for freedom. Like every form of education, Locke's education for freedom involves the limitation of freedom and the discipline of the passions through the subordination of the student's whims and will to the teacher's superior knowledge. At the same time, such an education imposes restrictions on the restrictions imposed on students' freedom as well as on parents' duty to educate their children. In chapter VI of the *Second Treatise*, Locke emphasizes that the purpose of education, and the justification for parents' and teachers' authority over children, is to prepare students for the reasonable exercise of freedom. In his book-length treatment *Some Thoughts Concerning Education* (1693), Locke explores the many stages of an education for freedom, proceeding from infancy to young adulthood, and examines the wide range of virtues that go into the formation of free men and women.[15] For Locke, the exercise of parental authority is justified to the extent that it cultivates the virtues of freedom.

One critical exercise of the virtues of freedom is in the determination that government has lost its legitimacy. Although he is commonly thought of as setting forth a pioneering justification for revolution grounded in natural rights, Locke emphasizes the conditions under which governments, whose legitimacy depends on securing those rights, destroy the obligations that citizens owe them. He argues in chapter XIX of the *Second Treatise* that government's betrayal of citizens' trust through the protracted, systematic, and irreparable subversion of individual freedom terminates citizens' obligation to obey the law and throws individuals into a state of nature. The wise exercise of the perfect freedom into which the dissolution of government condemns individuals, Locke makes clear, consists in the first place in setting up new forms of government that will secure their rights by limiting the freedom of each and thereby protecting the rights of all.

A century later, such ideas about political and economic freedom exerted a decisive influence on those who declared American independence and drafted and ratified the US Constitution.

Karl Marx: The Critique of Political and Economic Freedom

Without acknowledging it, Karl Marx's critique of liberal democracy and of free-market capitalism presupposes a version of Locke's starting point—the freedom and equality of all. But whereas Locke concludes that limited government grounded in individual freedom and human equality provides the best security for private property and faith, Marx believes that by protecting private property and faith, limited government poisons the freedom and equality that is our birthright as human beings.

The crux of Marx's criticism is that political societies based on individual rights, the consent of the governed, and free markets enslave individuals to delusive ideas that provide popular justifications for unjust social and political arrangements that systemically oppress and entrench gross inequality. The extraordinary appeal that Marx's sweeping indictment of political and economic freedom has enjoyed around the world springs from genuine insights into the persistent discontents that free societies generate. Yet the historical record concerning free societies and Marxist regimes tells a dramatically different story than that told by Marx's followers: free societies have greatly reduced the gap between their promises of freedom and prosperity and the experience of their citizens, especially compared to the enormous gulf between the extravagant promises put forward by regimes based on Marxist ideas and the pervasive oppression and poverty such regimes have typically produced.

In the preface to *A Contribution to the Critique of Political Economy* (1859), Marx succinctly states his theory of ideology.[16] The key notion is that the dominant ideas and norms that emerge in societies are not objective and independent but rather reflect and rationalize existing economic practices and institutions. These modes of production, consumption, and distribution serve as the base on which an ideological "superstructure" arises. Individuals may believe that they deliberate about and choose their moral, political, and religious ideas. In reality, argues Marx, one's place in the division of labor dictates one's convictions about what is proper, just, and true: "It is not the consciousness of men that determines their existence," he asserts, "but their social existence that determines their consciousness." It follows, Marx teaches, that individual rights, the consent of the governed, private property, religious freedom—along with the other essential elements of free societies—do not proceed from a rational analysis of the human condition or reflect the imperatives of reason and justice. Rather, to maintain their positions of power, bourgeois beneficiaries of capitalism use the principles of political and economic freedom as intellectual weapons to persuade workers that their lowly place in society is appropriate and just.

In the first part of *On the Jewish Question* (1843), Marx identifies the chief ideological sleight of hand by which liberal democracies keep citizens in thrall.[17] Exemplified by the United States in the mid-nineteenth century, liberal democracy promises citizens what Marx calls "political emancipation"—that is, freedom from the authority of the state, particularly in matters of faith and private property. The protection individuals enjoy in their private homes and in their houses of worship to practice their faith and to pass their beliefs down to their children is, from Marx's point of view, a pernicious consequence of political emancipation. Religion, he believes, is an illusion that induces workers to accept tranquilly their degraded condition and prompts members of the bourgeoisie to believe arrogantly that they are entitled to their wealth and political power. He concludes, therefore, that liberal democracy delivers a fraudulent form of freedom. The separation of church and state—"the emancipation of the state from religion"—perpetuates human beings' subjugation to religion's degrading authority. The proper political goal, Marx insists, is to secure "the emancipation of the real man from religion." Similarly, when the state—consistent with the claims of political and economic freedom—abolishes the property qualification for voting, it does not eliminate the political significance of private property but instead entrenches it outside of state control. Thus, according to Marx, "the division of the human being into a *public man* and a *private man*" fostered by the right of private property and the consequent "*displacement* of religion from the state into civil society" do not form "a stage of political emancipation but its completion; this emancipation, therefore, neither abolished the *real* religiousness of man, nor strives to do so."

To free human beings from the dehumanizing grip of religion and private property is the aim of "human emancipation," the true and final form of emancipation. This occurs, however,

> only when the real, individual man re-absorbs in himself the abstract citizen, and as an individual human being has become a species-being in his everyday life, in his particular work, and in his particular situation, only when man has recognized and organized his "own powers" as social powers, and, consequently, no longer separates social power from himself in the shape of political power, only then will human emancipation have been accomplished.

Throughout his writings, Marx argues that the comprehensive reconciliation of the individual and the collectivity encapsulated in the idea of "human emancipation" depends on the replacement of the brutal economic relations that prevail under capitalism by new forms of economic life that satisfy the deepest and most widely shared human needs and the highest human aspirations.

In "Estranged Labor"—an extended fragment taken from a work Marx himself did not publish but which appeared in 1932 under the title "Economic and Philosophic Manuscripts of 1844"—Marx spells out four forms of the estrangement from, or alienation of, labor.[18] All, he claims, arise from the irresistible logic of capitalism's division of labor and modes of production. All reflect the exploitation of "propertyless workers" by wealthy "property owners." All, he will subsequently maintain, are overcome under communism. Underlying Marx's analysis is the belief that a political and economic system that fails to provide human beings the ability to satisfy their loftiest longings through the activities by which they earn a living is fundamentally unjust.

First, capitalism estranges workers from "the product of labor," which they experience as an "alien object." Instead of producing for their own use, workers participate in a single, isolated stage of the production process to create commodities that factory owners sell for their own profit and for someone else's use. Consequently, workers' labor represents "not the satisfaction of a need" but rather "a means to satisfy needs external to it."

Second, capitalism estranges workers from "the act of production." Tools, assembly lines, and factories' organizational structure do not give expression to workers' preferences and choices but rather curtail their responsibilities and erode their independence.

Third, capitalism estranges workers from "man's species-being," which, according to Marx, is "free, conscious activity." As he observes, "animals also produce"—for example, nests, hives, and dams. But such production is ingrained, automatic, and always more or less the same. Only human beings can transform nature based on ideas they develop and adjust, and in accordance with standards they adopt and revise. In depriving workers of the "spontaneous, free activity" that is at the root of individuals' shared humanity, capitalism cheats workers of what is most their own.

Fourth, capitalism estranges workers from fellow human beings: "What applies to a man's relation to his work, to the product of his labor and to himself, also holds of a man's relation to the other man, and to the other man's labor and object of labor." The inability to recognize one's own humanity results in the inability to recognize the humanity of others.

Despite this ghastly description of workers' experience under capitalism, Marx brings good news. In *The Manifesto of the Communist Party* (1848), he argues that the era of capitalist exploitation and estrangement is coming to an end, and with it the contradictions and injustices that have marked all previous eras.[19] This can be known rigorously, Marx contends, because history is determined by objective laws reflected in the "prevailing mode of economic production and exchange."

All history, according to Marx, has been characterized by class struggle, by the "constant opposition" of "oppressor and oppressed." His own epoch, "the epoch of the bourgeoisie," also pits the oppressed against the oppressors. But it has "simplified class antagonisms" and in the process brought out into the open the struggle between the comfortable bourgeois property owners and the debased and immiserated workers. It has also assigned to the bourgeoisie "a most revolutionary part."

The bourgeoisie are unwitting revolutionaries. By reducing economic and political life to the pursuit of self-interest, they create the conditions that make possible the overcoming of the traditional "religious and political illusions" that have tranquilized workers and induced them to accept their exploitation at the hands of the bourgeoisie as an expression of the way things ought to be. As a result, the bourgeois epoch is inherently unstable. Whereas all previous epochs were based on preserving inherited modes of production and the inherited justifications for them, "[c]onstant revolutionizing of production, uninterrupted disturbance of all social conditions, everlasting uncertainty and agitation distinguish the bourgeois epoch."

Although a prelude to the thoroughgoing elimination of oppression and alienation, the bourgeois epoch is not liberating in the manner intended by the bourgeoisie:

> All fixed, fast-frozen relations, with their train of ancient and venerable prejudices and opinions, are swept away, all new-formed ones become antiquated before they can ossify. All that is solid melts into air, all that is holy is profaned, and man is at last compelled to face with sober senses his real conditions of life, and his relations with his kind.

While enabling members of the proletariat to understand accurately the character and scope of their oppression, capitalism also produces a globe-covering market driven by breathtaking improvements in transportation and communications. The new mobility and the new capacity to exchange information across great distances transform workers around the world into a universal class whose members grasp their shared interests. These interests transcend state boundaries and cultural, national, and religious differences. Capitalism is "like the sorcerer who is no longer able to control the powers of the nether world whom he has called up by his spells." It prepares its own destruction by enabling workers to apprehend their common exploitation and to unite worldwide in opposition against their oppressors. "All previous historical movements were movements of minorities, or in the interest of minorities," Marx exults. "The proletarian movement is the self-conscious, independent movement of the immense majority, in the interest of the immense majority."

The fall of the bourgeoisie and the victory of the proletariat are, Marx writes, "equally inevitable." But notwithstanding his conviction that his conclusion carries the authority of science, Marx is notoriously vague on what the victory of the proletariat entails.

His most famous utterance on the shape of communist society appeared in "Critique of the Gotha Programme" (1875), which followed publication of the first volume of his magnum opus, *Capital* (1867–83).[20] Marx expresses in 1875 the same conviction as in his earliest philosophical writings: the all-embracing overcoming of conflict in politics and society is necessary, possible, and just around the corner. After emancipating individuals from private property and faith, repairing the split between physical and mental work, and reconciling individual development with social and economic cooperation, communism will replace the protection of rights with a form of social organization tailored to each individual's unique condition: "From each according to his ability, to each according to his needs!"

The implementation of such a formula would require a central authority of the highest wisdom, purest integrity, and most complete control. The gruesome consequences of communist rule across cultures and around the world testify to the folly of assigning to national governments and international politics such lofty capacities, exalted responsibilities, and unlimited powers.

The Dependence of Political and Economic Freedom on Liberal Education

Why did communism fail, and liberal democracy prosper?

In the nineteenth century, Marxism responded to genuine problems afflicting emerging liberal democracy and free-market capitalism. Factory owners exploited workers—men, women, and children—by subjecting them to debilitating working conditions and exhausting hours.

Notwithstanding the justice in this critique, Marxism—along with the many less influential varieties of socialism—suffered from several fundamental flaws.

First, Marx wildly underestimated the self-correcting powers of liberal democracies and free markets. He and his legions of followers failed to grasp the capacity of liberal democracies to acknowledge injustice, reform institutions to better serve the public interest, and pass laws that would bring the reality of political and economic life more in line with the promise of individual rights and equal citizenship. In addition, Marxism misjudged the enormous productive forces unleashed by capitalism. Free enterprise has not immiserated the working class as Marx insisted it must. To the contrary, undergirded by private property and the rule of law, free markets have proved history's greatest antidote to poverty and around the world have raised basic expectations concerning the material prerequisites of a decent life to levels unimaginable in Marx's time and even a few generations ago.

Second, Marx presumed to possess final and incontrovertible knowledge about the necessary unfolding of human affairs from the earliest forms of civilization to the present. Marx produced, and Marxists have routinely embraced, a one-dimensional account of history based exclusively on the conflict between oppressors and oppressed, as if no other factors significantly shaped morality, economics, and politics. Marxist history proceeds on the assumption that tradition, culture, faith, and justice are irrelevant, except as components of a code that, when properly deciphered, exposes the deceptions by which the powerful persuade the weak to acquiesce in their oppression.

Third, Marx succumbed to the utopian spirit. Despite his voluminous writings, he gave scant attention to the structure of politics or the habits and institutions that would organize the economy in the era that he maintained would follow the overcoming of liberal democracy and capitalism. He assumed that social and political disharmony of every sort would vanish with the setting aside of rights, the elimination of religion, and the abolition of private property. This extravagant conceit was in no small measure a consequence of his failure to reckon with the variety of passions and interests that motivate human beings, the rootedness of persons in particular traditions and communities, the limits of human knowledge, the enduring claims of faith, and the institutional arrangements that enable government to advance the public interest in individual freedom and human equality.

In each of these respects liberal democracy has demonstrated its manifest superiority. First, liberal democracies both limit and empower the people. Government's protection of individual rights sets boundaries on what majorities through their elected representatives can authorize even as the grounding of legitimate exercises of power in the consent of the governed gives majorities solid legitimacy and wide scope to enact laws, in accordance with changing circumstances and enduring principles, that serve the public interest.

Second, liberal democracy does not rest on a theory of history but rather on a conviction about human beings—that all are born free and equal and that equal rights inhere in every human being. Instead of reducing ideas to expressions of economic relations, liberal democracy affirms that economic relations should reflect the idea of individual freedom. Government secures individual rights by, in the first place, safeguarding private property and religious freedom. Twenty-first-century liberal democracies also defend an array of civil and political rights while, through a variety of institutional arrangements, providing protection against the inability to care for oneself and for one's family stemming from illness, unemployment, old age, poverty, and other forms of hardship. The state leaves the preponderance of decisions about work and consumption as well as religious belief and practice—and, in general, the pursuit of happiness—in the hands of individuals who, whatever the imperfections in their understanding, are likely to grasp their own interests better than would government bureaucrats.

Third, liberal democracy is grounded in the anti-utopian premise that the tendency to abuse power is more or less evenly distributed among human beings. This does not negate the belief in fundamental rights that all persons share or deny the need for, and the possibility of, decent character—and sometimes exemplary virtue—in citizens and officeholders. From the perspective of liberal democracy, each is endowed with the ability to reason and to take responsibility for oneself. Each is a mix of wants and needs, appetites and longings, fears and hopes that frequently distort judgment and defeat reason. And each can acquire at least a basic mixture of the virtues of freedom. Because of its understanding of the multiple dimensions of human nature, liberal democracy attaches great importance to the design of political institutions. Well-designed institutions secure individual rights by limiting government, playing officeholders' passions and prejudices against one another, tempering partisan preferences, providing incentives for deliberation and judgment, making space for the exercise of virtue, and keeping government ultimately accountable to the people.

Why are these basic notions about Marxism and liberal democracy so poorly understood today?

In *The Road to Serfdom*, Hayek suggests that a crucial step in the institutionalization of the central planning essential to socialism is a concerted attack on liberty of thought and discussion. To consolidate support for the one true state-approved economic plan, it is necessary to ensure that a uniform view prevails among the citizenry: "The most effective way of making everybody serve the single system of ends toward which the social plan is directed is to make everybody believe in those ends."[21] This requires, among other things, that universities—eventually the entire educational system—abandon the traditional goal of liberal education, which is to transmit knowledge, not least about the principles and institutions of freedom; cultivate independent thinking; and encourage the disinterested pursuit of truth. Instead, institutions of higher education must be conscripted into the cause. That involves the transformation of colleges and universities into giant propaganda machines for the inculcation and reaffirmation of the officially approved views.

The condition of higher education in America suggests that that transformation is well under way. It is increasingly rare, for instance, for colleges and universities to teach students the principles of individual liberty, limited government, and free markets along with the major criticisms of them, thereby both imparting knowledge to students and fostering their ability to think for themselves. Instead, our institutions of higher education often nurture an ill-informed enthusiasm for socialism and an ignorant disdain for political and economic freedom. In doing so, higher education builds on dogmas increasingly inculcated in K–12 schools.

To continue to enjoy the blessings of political and economic freedom, we must recover the practice of liberal education.

NOTES

1. Mohamed Younis, "Four in 10 Americans Embrace Some Form of Socialism," Gallup, April 17–30, 2019, https://news.gallup.com/poll/257639/four-americans -embrace-form-socialism.aspx.
2. Harris, April 16–18, 2019, https://documentcloud.org/documents/6145923 -Axios-Tabs-1.html.
3. John Locke, *Second Treatise*, Chapter I: Section 1, https://www.gutenberg.org/files /7370/7370-h/7370-h.htm. Hereafter, references to the *Second Treatise* are abbreviated to ST followed by chapter and section numbers.
4. ST I:1.
5. ST I:3.
6. ST II:4.
7. ST II:6.
8. ST III:19.
9. ST II:7–8, VII:87.
10. ST VII:87–89, VIII:95–99.
11. ST VIII:119–21.
12. ST V:27.
13. ST V:34.
14. Mark 12:17.
15. Locke emphasizes that generally and for the most part his advice for education of sons applies to the education of daughters. *Some Thoughts Concerning Education*, Section 6, https://oll.libertyfund.org/title/locke-the-works-vol-8-some -thoughts-concerning-education-posthumous-works-familiar-letters.
16. Karl Marx, *A Contribution to the Critique of Political Economy*, 1859, https://www .marxists.org/archive/marx/works/1859/critique-pol-economy/preface.htm.

17. Karl Marx, *On the Jewish Question*, 1843, https://marxists.org/archive/marx
/works/download/pdf/On%20The%20Jewish%20Question.pdf.

18. Karl Marx, "Estranged Labor," 1844, https://www.marxists.org/archive/marx
/works/1844/manuscripts/labour.htm.

19. Karl Marx, *The Manifesto of the Communist Party*, 1848, https://www.marxists
.org/archive/marx/works/1848/communist-manifesto.

20. Karl Marx, "Critique of the Gotha Programme," 1875, https://www.marxists.org
/archive/marx/works/download/Marx_Critique_of_the_Gotha_Programme.pdf.

21. Friedrich Hayek, *The Road to Serfdom: Text and Documents*, ed. Bruce Caldwell
(Chicago: University of Chicago Press, 2007), 171.

2

Political Freedom and Human Prosperity

Larry Diamond

One of the oldest and most important questions in the comparative study of nations is the impact of different economic and political systems on human prosperity. What is the secret to developmental success? Is it capitalism or socialism? Or what degree of market orientation? Democracy or dictatorship? What kind of democracy? And to complete the triangular relationship, what is the relationship between economic system and political system? Does democracy require capitalism?

I argue here four key points, the first two of which require little elaboration. To begin with, socialism cannot deliver countries to prosperity. Genuine and sustained developmental progress requires private property and a market economy. Second, socialism is equally antithetical to democracy, which also requires private property and reasonably free markets to limit the power of the state and protect civil liberties. Third, over the long run, democracy is the best system for delivering human prosperity, and almost all the world's most prosperous countries (save those that came upon a windfall of natural resource wealth) are democracies. But fourth, a crucial intervening variable in the relationship between democracy and prosperity is good governance: transparency, the rule of law, and a state regulatory environment that encourages investment and innovation. Singapore has managed to become rich by achieving good governance without democracy. Few (if any) other countries will be able to repeat that formula. For in the absence of open political and ideological competition, governments tend to go bad, abusing both civil rights and property rights.

Capitalism, Socialism, and Human Prosperity

The question of the relationship between economic structure and human prosperity can at a general level be fairly easily dispensed with. One need only compare the developmental performance of South Korea versus North Korea, or West Germany versus East Germany, to appreciate how much more successful market economies are at generating wealth. The key to creating wealth and human prosperity is to stimulate individual initiative, savings, investment, and technological innovation. Private enterprise, with limited government regulation, provides the incentives for individuals to work hard, take risks, invest, and innovate.

Expropriation of private property has disastrous consequences for productivity because it destroys incentives and misallocates resources. Witness the famines and human suffering in Stalin's Russia, Mao's China, and Kim's North Korea or the more recent economic catastrophes of Zimbabwe under Robert Mugabe or Venezuela (which had once been a relatively prosperous country) under Hugo Chavez's "Bolivarian Socialism." State socialism (which is the only kind of socialism that has existed in the modern world) stifles productivity and innovation and misdirects investment. At the end of the Korean War, in the early 1950s, South Korea was only about 1.3 times as rich (in per capita income) as North Korea. Four decades later, South Korean per capita income was estimated to be about seven times that of the North, and the South's economy (as measured by gross domestic product [GDP]) increased during those decades from three times that of the North to fourteen times.[1] In food production and other measures of human welfare, North Korea remains a basket case, with chronic shortages, human deprivation and malnutrition (including physical stunting), and underinvestment. The South's economy is now estimated to be fifty times that of the North, and the gap in per capita income has increased to a ratio of 23 to 1.[2] Though not as dramatic, there was also a radical divergence in the economic performance of West and East Germany from 1950 to unification in 1990, as West Germany vaulted into the ranks of advanced industrial democracies while per capita income largely stagnated in East Germany from the early 1970s to the end of communism.[3] It's not that Communist countries have been incapable of producing broad and sustained increases in human prosperity. Since Deng Xiaoping came to power in 1978, the People's Republic of China has lifted some 850 million people out of poverty and has reached annual GDP growth averaging nearly 10 percent. But such gains have largely come when—as with Deng's economic reforms in China and then later in Vietnam with *doi moi*—these regimes began to dismantle the socialist economic features of the communist system even while retaining the political apparatus of Leninist dictatorship.

Capitalism, Socialism, and Democracy

The second leg of the triangle is also fairly easily established. As Friedrich Hayek and Milton Friedman understood, economic and political freedom go together, economic freedom and private property being preconditions for political freedom.[4] There are few real laws in the social sciences, but this is one of them: true socialism—by which I mean a centrally planned economy that largely prohibits private property—is incompatible with democracy. This is true on its face empirically: there has never been a socialist democracy. There have been (mainly in northern Europe) successful "social democracies" with relatively high rates of taxation and redistribution, but these have not been socialist systems, because they are still based on market forces and private ownership of the means of production. As Peter Berger observed, "The welfare state, even in its Scandinavian apotheosis, continues to rest on a capitalist system of production; indeed only the affluence created by the latter makes this welfare state possible."[5]

In the moral or philosophical sense, the right to own and dispose of property is a fundamental individual right. When such a basic right is trampled on and the state is so engorged with power as to deny it, it is inevitable that other individual rights will be trampled on as well. Coercion in the economic realm suffuses the political realm as well, and, as Peter Berkowitz noted in his paper for this project, citing Hayek, it then further seeps into the intellectual realm, constricting freedom of thought and expression.[6] Private ownership of the means of production is a crucial bulwark against an overweening state and eventual political tyranny. The existence of private property constitutes a check on tyranny, and this is why so many incipient dictators seek to eliminate or politically subjugate it once they consolidate power. It is also why the Communist Party of China, under Xi Jinping—the country's most tyrannical leader since Mao Zedong—has recently launched a crackdown on wealthy independent-minded entrepreneurs in its high-tech sector. As Alexis de Tocqueville wrote a century before Hayek, private property is a crucial foundation of a vigorous civil society and a culture of liberty. In an 1848 speech to the French Constituent Assembly, he declared:

> [Common to] socialists of all schools and shades, is a profound opposition to personal liberty and scorn for individual reason, a complete contempt for the individual. They unceasingly attempt to mutilate, to curtail, to obstruct personal freedom in any and all ways. They hold that the State must not only act as the director of society, but must further be master of each man, and not only master, but keeper and trainer. For fear of allowing him to err, the State must place itself forever by his side, above him, around him, better to guide him, to maintain him, in a word, to confine him. They call, in fact, for the forfeiture, to a greater or less degree, of human liberty.[7]

Capitalism is thus a core condition for democracy, and still more so for that degree of democracy—liberal democracy—that ensures a high degree of liberty. The reverse is not true: democracy is not a precondition for successful capitalist development. It is possible to identify countries that have achieved rapid development under authoritarian rule. In fact, this has been closer to the norm for the early and middle stages of development in Asia, beginning with Meiji Japan (1868–1912) and then the post–World War II "Asian miracle" states of South Korea, Taiwan, and Singapore. But Japan, South Korea, and Taiwan all became democracies as they became middle-class societies, and a more recent developmental quasi-success story, Malaysia, has also experienced democratizing pressures. Moreover, beginning in the 1990s, South Korea and Taiwan continued their rise to the status of advanced industrial countries as democracies (as Japan did a generation before them). South Korea's economy grew at an average annualized rate of 5.9 percent between 1990 and 2015 and Taiwan's grew at 4.1 percent.[8] Since they completed their democratic transitions (Korea at the end of 1987, Taiwan in 1996) each country has sustained economic growth with only brief periods of downturn.[9]

Singapore stands alone as the one capitalist success story that has not become a democracy and does not show much sign of doing so soon. Its sustained success as a nondemocracy (lifting it from poverty to prosperity in the space of just two generations) is due to a governance formula that has been extremely difficult for other countries to reproduce on a sustained basis. In most countries, the political openness, electoral competition, and media freedom of liberal democracy have proved powerful mechanisms for controlling corruption and protecting property rights. Lacking the need to be transparent or to be held accountable by voters in regular, free, and fair elections, authoritarian regimes have all sooner or later fallen victim to venality and bad governance—except for Singapore. As a result of the founding developmental vision of former prime minister Lee Kuan Yew and the internal discipline and meritocracy of the ruling People's Action Party, Singapore has so far defied the odds. Singapore's top ranking on the Heritage Foundation's Index of Economic Freedom and its heavy investments in education and health have made it one of the ten richest countries in the world. This achievement of sustained good governance without democracy is, I believe, a feat that no large country—and certainly not China—could replicate.

Democracy, Governance, and Human Prosperity

Now on to the more challenging question: what is the relationship between democracy and human prosperity? Much historical and empirical research has demonstrated that democratic institutions constrain the arbitrary power of rulers and thus constitute a check against predatory behavior, leading to secure property rights and economic growth.[10] In these theories, the causal pathway from democracy to prosperity passes through the quality of governance. That is the first rationale for arguing that democracy promotes prosperity. It affirms the important overarching insight from John Cogan's contribution to this policy series: "Nothing is more important to sustained economic prosperity than rule of law, private property, limited government, and free markets."[11]

Three further arguments buttress the theoretical claims for the affinity between democracy and prosperity. The second rationale is that democracies are more responsive to the public and thus better able to deliver public goods such as education and health care, thereby increasing the accumulation of human capital and enhancing economic growth.[12] In addition, democracies provide mechanisms to moderate social conflicts and maintain political and economic stability.[13] Finally, democracies are more likely to facilitate technological progress and encourage innovation.[14] Open societies with freedom of speech are instrumental for generating and disseminating new ideas, which encourage innovation.

The features of governance that provide the enabling conditions for prosperity are closely related to democracy. The World Bank measures annually six different elements of the quality of governance based on the perceptions of thousands of informed experts and stakeholders in the private sector, NGOs, and public-sector agencies.[15] Three of these measures capture particularly well the conditions for sustained prosperity:

- Rule of law: "the quality of contract enforcement, property rights, the police, and the courts, as well as the likelihood of crime and violence."

- Control of corruption: "the extent to which public power is exercised for private gain, including both petty and grand forms of corruption, as well as capture of the state by elites and private interests."
- Regulatory quality: "the ability of the government to formulate and implement sound policies and regulations that permit and promote private sector development."[16]

Empirically, each of these three governance measures is strongly correlated with the other two and with the extent of democracy in a country (the figures that follow are for the Liberal Democracy scale of the Varieties of Democracy project).[17] By my calculation, the overall correlation between the rule of law and the extent of democracy is about .77. This means that a little over half of the variance among countries for the rule of law can be explained by the extent of liberal democracy. Democracy's correlation with regulatory quality is identical to the correlation with the rule of law (.77). The correlation with the World Bank's "control of corruption" measure is slightly lower (.70), but if we take instead Transparency International's measure of corruption control, the correlation is .76. Statistically, all these correlations are highly significant. Moreover, these associations are highly robust across different regions of the world. Although they are a little weaker within Asia (generally between .40 and .75), they are still mostly statistically significant, and within some regions they are especially strong (over .80 in Central and Eastern Europe). In most regions of the world (save the Middle East), the quality of governance is strongly positively related to the degree of democracy (see table 2.1).

We get a similar perspective if we examine the Heritage Foundation's 2020 Index of Economic Freedom, an aggregate score evaluating rule of law, government size, regulatory efficiency, and openness of markets.[18] Of the thirty-five countries rated free or mostly free, twenty-nine are democracies and two (Malaysia and Armenia) have had pluralistic and competitive political systems that have been approaching democracy. The four authoritarian regimes are mainly familiar by now: Singapore, United Arab Emirates (UAE), Qatar, and an ambitious African economic

Table 2.1. Correlations between the Quality of Governance and Liberal Democracy, 2019

Region	Rule of Law	Control of Corruption	Regulatory Quality
All countries	.77	.70	.77
Central and Eastern Europe	.83	.83	.84
East and Southeast Asia	.62	.45	.60
Latin America and the Caribbean	.78	.54	.73
Sub-Saharan Africa	.76	.69	.73

Sources: World Bank, Worldwide Governance Indicators, https://info.worldbank.org/governance/wgi; V-Dem Institute, Liberal Democracy Index, https://www.v-dem.net/en. Computation of correlations are the author's.

reformer, Rwanda. By contrast, most of the nineteen most economically repressed countries are politically authoritarian regimes such as Iran, Zimbabwe, and Venezuela. (The others are very poor, former war-torn states such as Liberia, Sierra Leone, and Timor-Leste). Five authoritarian regimes are not rated but probably fall in the latter category: Iraq, Libya, Syria, Yemen, and Somalia. Put differently, over 80 percent of the economically freest countries are democracies, and nearly 80 percent of the least economically free countries are authoritarian regimes. The world's most liberal democracies in political terms also generally have the freest economies.

Let's now look at the relationship between democracy and prosperity in two ways. One way to measure human prosperity is by per capita income—taking the annual income of a country and simply dividing it by the population. This is the single most common measure of the level of a country's economic development, but it doesn't tell us much about how it is distributed. The Human Development Index (HDI), produced annually by the United Nations Development Programme, provides an important additional measure of prosperity, because it controls somewhat for income inequality by averaging three measures: gross national income per capita (in purchasing power parity dollars); health, as measured by years of life expectancy; and education (an average of the current expected years of schooling for children at school-entry age and the mean

Table 2.2. Regime Type and Average Human Development Index, 2018

Regime Type	HDI Average	Number of Countries
Full democracy	.902	22
Flawed democracy	.786	53
Hybrid regime	.614	35
Authoritarian regime	.625	52

Sources: Economist Intelligence Unit (EIU), Economist Democracy Index 2018; United Nations Development Programme (UNDP), Human Development Index 2018, Human Development Report 2019, Table 1. Computation of correlations are the author's.

actual years of schooling of the adult population).[19] This produces a summary "human development" score that ranges from 0 (lowest) to 1 (highest). Because the HDI controls for inequality and tempers the artificial, distorting effect of oil wealth, it is more highly correlated with democracy. In fact, nearly half of the variance among countries in the 2019 HDI scores can be explained simply by the level of democracy in a country (as measured by the annual Democracy Index of *The Economist*).[20]

The Economist's Democracy Index summarizes democracy scores in four categories: full democracies, flawed democracies, hybrid regimes, and authoritarian regimes. The latter two nondemocratic regime types have significantly lower average scores (a little over .610) than do the democracies. As we see in table 2.2, even the flawed democracies score much higher (.786 on average), and the full (liberal) democracies perform by far the best (.902). By any measure, and over any period, democracies are more prosperous than authoritarian regimes—and when one looks at "real" human development, rather than just the average money income, the advantage increases. Table 2.3 averages scores on the HDI over the past decade (2010–18) according to the type of regime that has prevailed over the entire decade. The same pattern holds. The countries that have been continuously liberal democracies over the decade—with strong protections for rule of law, private property, and control of corruption—have achieved and maintained the highest levels of human development (.84 on average). Electoral democracies have performed better than hybrid regimes or continuous autocracies, but the difference is much smaller (.68 versus .62).

Table 2.3. Regime Type and Average Human Development Index, 2010–18

Type of Regime	Average HDI 2018	Average V-Dem Liberal Democracy Score
Continuously liberal democracy	.84	.74
Continuously electoral democracy	.68	.46
Oscillating or hybrid regimes	.62	.38
Authoritarian regimes	.62	.18

Sources: UNDP Human Development Index and author's calculations.

Table 2.4. Relationship between Gross National Income and Democracy, 2018

Rank on Gross National Income per Capita	Democracies (%)		Authoritarian (%)
	Liberal	Electoral	
Best 25 states	84	0	16
2nd best (26–50 rank)	76	4	20
3rd best (51–75)	56	16	28
4th best (76–100)	20	40	40
5th best (101–125)	32	28	40
2nd worst (126–150)	12	12	76
Worst 32 (151–182)	0	22	78

Sources: World Bank, https://data.worldbank.org/indicator/NY.GNP.MKTP.CD; and author's classifications of democracies.

Table 2.4 shows a clear step pattern in the relationship between per capita income and democracy. Only four of the twenty-five richest countries—Singapore, Qatar, Kuwait, and UAE—are nondemocracies. And only one of those, Singapore, became wealthy by its own entrepreneurial initiative, as opposed to the natural resource windfall of oil. With every step down the ladder of wealth, the percentage of authoritarian regimes rises. Only one-fifth of the fifty richest countries are authoritarian regimes, but more than three-quarters of the fifty-seven poorest countries are. The relationship between democracy and development is even more striking when we examine the HDI (table 2.5). Among the top twenty-five states in human development, only Singapore is not a democracy. In

POLITICAL FREEDOM AND HUMAN PROSPERITY 41

Table 2.5. Relationship between Human Development Index and
Democracy, 2018

Rank on Human Development Index	Democracies (%)		Authoritarian (%)
	Liberal	Electoral	
Best 25 states	96	0	4
2nd best (27–49 rank)	58	0	42
3rd best (51–75)	48	28	24
4th best (76–97)	28	40	32
5th best (101–123)	22	17	61
2nd worst (124–148)	27	12	61
Worst 38 (150–187)	3	18	79

Note: Skipped numbers in rankings are due to ties.
Sources: UNDP Human Development Index and author's classification of democracies.

the next twenty-five are several oil-rich states (and Russia and Belarus), but the step pattern then strikingly continues: with each step down the ladder of human development, there are fewer and fewer democracies.

There is another way of thinking about the relationship between prosperity and democracy, by looking at the most extreme deprivation of prosperity, namely famine. Table 2.6 lists the ten worst instances of humanitarian catastrophe (generally famine but also mass murder) in the last one hundred years. All these have occurred in authoritarian regimes, and almost all these have been communist or Marxist dictatorships. In fact, several occurred as part of an effort to establish, widen, or enforce the abolition of private property in the countryside. Other famines have occurred, for example, in Sudan in 1993 and 1998, killing tens of thousands of people. But none of these famines have ever occurred in a democracy. One of the great contributions of the Nobel Prize–winning economist Amartya Sen has been to demonstrate this point. He writes:

The process of preventing famines and other crises is significantly helped by the use of instrumental freedoms, such as the opportunity of open discussion, public scrutiny, electoral politics, and uncensored media. For example, the open and oppositional politics of a

Table 2.6. Great Famines of the Twentieth Century

Country	Regime Type	Years	Estimated Deaths
China (Great Leap Forward)	Communist dictatorship	1959–61	15 million–55 million
Soviet Union (Ukraine, Kazakhstan)	Communist dictatorship	1932–34	5 million–8 million
Soviet Union (Russia)	Communist dictatorship	1921–22	5 million
Northwest China	Authoritarian warlords	1928–30	3 million–10 million
Soviet Union (Ukraine and Russia)	Communist dictatorship	1946–47	1 million–1.5 million
Ethiopia	Marxist dictatorship	1983–85	1 million
North Korea	Totalitarian	1994–98	240,000–3 million
Cambodia	Marxist dictatorship	1975–79	500,000
Somalia	Authoritarian, civil war	1991–92	300,000
Somalia	Authoritarian, civil war	2011–12	285,000

Sources: Author's assessments of regimes; see, for example, Wikipedia, "List of Famines," last edited January 19, 2022, https://en.wikipedia.org/wiki/List_of_famines.

democratic country tends to force any government in office to take timely and effective steps to prevent famines, in a way that did not happen in the case of famines under nondemocratic arrangements— whether in China, Cambodia, Ethiopia or Somalia (as in the past), or in North Korea or Sudan (as is happening today [circa 1998]).[21]

Table 2.7 presents the countries with the best and worst economic growth rates in the immediate post–Cold War period, 1990–2015. We see that democracies were well represented among the countries with the most rapid economic growth, but the seven worst economic performers—with average annual growth rates in per capita income of less than half a percent for a quarter century—were authoritarian regimes. Studying African economic growth rates during the years 1996–2008, the development economist Steven Radelet found that the best economic performers were generally countries with democratic or at least somewhat pluralistic and competitive political systems. These seventeen countries achieved average annual growth rates in per capita income of over 3 percent, after per capita incomes

Table 2.7. Annual Rates of Economic Growth, 1990–2015

Fastest Growth Rates in Per Capita Income

Rank	Country	Regime Type	Growth Rate (%)
1	Equatorial Guinea (oil)	Authoritarian	14.3
2	China	Authoritarian	13.3
3	Vietnam	Authoritarian	12.9
5	Timor-Leste	Democratic	10.7
6	Cambodia	Authoritarian	10.7
7	Lebanon	Authoritarian	9.2
9	Myanmar	Authoritarian	9.1
11	Poland	Democratic	8.5
14	Costa Rica	Democratic	7.6
15	Tanzania	Authoritarian	7.5
16	Dominican Republic	Democratic	7.4
17	Armenia	Authoritarian	7.4
18	Panama	Democratic	7.3
23	Chile	Democratic	7.0

Worst Growth Rates in Per Capita Income

Rank	Country	Regime Type	Growth Rate (%)
176	Libya	Authoritarian	−3.7
175	Democratic Republic of the Congo	Authoritarian	−3.0
174	Iran	Authoritarian	−3.0
173	Gambia	Authoritarian	−0.5
172	Serbia	Authoritarian (later Democratic)	−0.1
171	Gabon	Authoritarian	0.3
170	Togo	Authoritarian	0.3

Sources: Growth rates are from the United Nations Statistics Division, as reported by Wikipedia, "List of Countries by GDP Growth 1980–2010," last modified October 26, 2020, https://en .wikipedia.org/wiki/List_of_countries_by_GDP_growth_1980%E2%80%932010.

had completely stagnated during the preceding two decades. Rational economic policies (such as the end of black markets, reductions in regulation and public debt, lower trade and investment barriers, and more incentives for business formation) were vitally important. But preceding and underlying these, Radelet found, was the rise of more accountable, democratic, and legitimate government, with associated improvements in the rule of law and transparency.[22]

Multivariate Analyses

The above statistical evidence is of course only correlative and suggestive, leaving open the question of whether democracy actually *generates* human prosperity more effectively than autocracy and, if it does, whether this is so at all stages of development and for all regions and all historical periods. The econometric literature on this subject is voluminous and somewhat conflicting. One of the most careful studies (of up to 135 countries from 1950 to 1990) did not find a clear statistical relationship between democracy and economic growth rate but rather concluded that autocracies were more likely to generate both spurts of extremely rapid growth and developmental catastrophes (as noted above).[23] Examining one hundred countries between 1960 and 1990, Robert Barro found a nonlinear relationship between democracy and economic growth: at its initial stage, democracy increased economic growth but began to inhibit growth once a moderate amount of democracy had been reached.[24] A study of 154 countries from 1950 to 2000 found that new democracies (within the first five years of democratization) have a positive effect on economic growth, whereas established democracies (more than five years after democratization) exert a small and negative effect on growth rate.[25]

More recent studies, however, have tended to affirm what is known as "the democracy advantage." An analysis of about 150 countries over the period 1960 to 2000 finds that democracy is associated with a .75 percentage point annual increase in economic growth.[26] In a similar fashion, an analysis of up to 166 countries during the 1960–2003 period shows that democratic transitions are associated with an increase of one percentage point in annual GDP per capita growth, and that the effect is relatively larger in "partial democratizations" and in the medium and long run.[27] Most recently (and exhaustively), Daron Acemoglu and his colleagues, drawing on a sample of 175 countries from 1960 to 2010, consistently find that democratization increases GDP per capita by approximately 20 percent in the long run (over more than twenty-five years).[28] In other words, the GDP per capita of the typical authoritarian regime would be 20 percent higher today had it democratized twenty-five years ago. Furthermore, the effect of democratic institutions is cumulative in the sense that democratic stock—a country's democracy history—is found to be robustly associated with economic growth rates.[29]

Conclusion

The institutional formula for human prosperity weds two types of open and competitive markets: political competition between parties that seek the power to rule through regular, free, and fair elections and economic competition between private firms that seek profits through initiative, innovation, and improved productivity. In each realm, competition generates responsiveness to the market and accountability. In each realm, low barriers to entry enhance competition and performance, while monopolistic or oligopolistic practices diminish the performance of the system and, ultimately, human welfare. In each realm, constitutional limits on the power of government protect freedom and enhance prosperity. In each realm, the rule of law, defended by neutral and independent courts and administered by a nonpartisan and independent civil service, prevents the abuse of power and ensures, respectively, civil rights and property rights. Political freedom and economic freedom are the symbiotic twin pillars of human prosperity and the indispensable foundations for enduringly successful nations.

NOTES

1. Namkoong Young, "A Comparative Study of North and South Korean Economic Capability," *Journal of East Asian Affairs* 9, no. 1 (Winter/Spring 1995), 6, table 2.

2. "South Korea vs. North Korea," Index Mundi, accessed November 12, 2020, https://www.indexmundi.com/factbook/compare/south-korea.north-korea /economy.

3. Daniel J. Mitchell, "Comparing the Economic Growth of East Germany to West Germany: A History Lesson," Foundation for Economic Education, May 11, 2019, https://fee.org/articles/comparing-the-economic-growth-of-east-germany -to-west-germany-a-history-lesson.

4. Friedrich Hayek, *The Road to Serfdom: Text and Documents*, ed. Bruce Caldwell (Chicago: University of Chicago Press, 2007; first published in 1944); Milton Friedman, *Capitalism as Freedom* (Chicago: University of Chicago Press, 1962).

5. Peter Berger, "The Uncertain Triumph of Democratic Capitalism," in *Capitalism, Socialism, and Democracy Revisited*, ed. Larry Diamond and Marc F. Plattner (Baltimore: Johns Hopkins University Press, 1993), 3.

6. Peter Berkowitz, chapter 1 of this volume.

7. "Tocqueville's Critique of Socialism," Online Library of Liberty, last modified April 13, 2016, https://oll.libertyfund.org/pages/tocqueville-s-critique-of -socialism-1848.

8. Wikipedia, "List of Countries by GDP Growth 1980–2010," last modified October 26, 2020, https://en.wikipedia.org/wiki/List_of_countries_by_GDP _growth_1980%E2%80%932010.

9. "South Korea GDP Growth Rate," and "Taiwan GDP Annual Growth Rate," Trading Economics, accessed January 22, 2022, https://tradingeconomics.com /south-korea/gdp-growth, https://tradingeconomics.com/taiwan/gdp-growth -annual.

10. Douglass North, *Institutions, Institutional Change and Economic Performance* (Cambridge: Cambridge University Press, 1990); Douglass North and Barry Weingast, "Constitutions and Commitment: The Institutions Governing Public Choice in Seventeenth-Century England," *Journal of Economic History* 49, no. 4 (December 1989): 803–32; Mancur Olson, "Democracy, Dictatorship and Development," *American Political Science Review* 87, no. 3 (September 1993): 567–76.

11. "John Cogan on the Factors That Promote Economic Prosperity," Hoover Institution, PolicyEd, November 3, 2020.

12. Bruce Bueno de Mesquita, Alastair Smith, Randolph Siverson, and James Morrow, *The Logic of Political Survival* (Cambridge, MA: MIT Press, 2003); Matthew Baum and David Lake, "The Political Economy of Growth: Democracy and Human Capital," *American Journal of Political Science* 47, no. 2 (April 2003): 333–47.

13. Dani Rodrik, "Participatory Politics, Social Cooperation, and Economic Stability," *American Economic Review* 90, no. 2 (May 2000): 140–44.

14. Morton Halperin, Joe Siegle, and Michael Weinstein, *The Democracy Advantage: How Democracies Promote Prosperity and Peace* (New York: Routledge, 2005); Helen Milner, "The Digital Divide: The Role of Political Institutions in Technology Diffusion," *Comparative Political Studies* 36, no. 2 (2006): 176–99.

15. Daniel Kaufmann, Aart Kraay, and Massimo Mastruzzi, "Governance Matters VIII: Aggregate and Individual Governance Indicators, 1996–2008," World Bank Policy Research Working Paper No. 4978, June 2009, 4, https://papers .ssrn.com/sol3/papers.cfm?abstract_id=1424591.

16. Kaufmann, Kraay, and Mastruzzi, "Governance Matters VIII," 6.

17. See the Varieties of Democracy project, https://www.v-dem.net/en/. The correlations with the annual Freedom House index of political rights and civil liberties are a bit lower but still quite high.

18. "2020 Index of Economic Freedom," Heritage Foundation, accessed November 12, 2020, https://www.heritage.org/index/ranking?version=468.

19. Max Roser, "Human Development Index," Our World in Data, revised 2019, accessed November 12, 2020, https://ourworldindata.org/human-development -index#.

20. "Democracy Index 2019," *The Economist*, accessed November 12, 2020, https:// www.eiu.com/topic/democracy-index. This correlation, which yields an R^2 of .49, is computed by excluding the five oil-rich Gulf states (Bahrain, Kuwait, Qatar, Saudi Arabia, and United Arab Emirates), whose artificial oil wealth relative to population distorts the results. If these are excluded, the R^2 drops to .42, which is still substantial.

21. Amartya Sen, *Development as Freedom* (New York: Alfred A. Knopf, 1999), 188.

22. Steven Radelet, *Emerging Africa: How 17 Countries Are Leading the Way* (Washington, DC: Center for Global Development, 2010).

23. Adam Przeworski, Michael E. Alvarez, José Antonio Cheibub, and Fernando Limongi, *Democracy and Development: Political Institutions and Well-Being in the World, 1950–1990* (Cambridge: Cambridge University Press, 2000).

24. Robert Barro, "Democracy and Growth," *Journal of Economic Growth* 1, no. 1 (March 1996): 1–27

25. Dani Rodrik and Romain Wacziarg, "Do Democratic Transitions Produce Bad Economic Outcomes?," *American Economic Review* 95, no. 2 (May 2005): 50–55.

26. Torsten Persson and Guido Tabellini, "Democracy and Development: The Devil in the Details," *American Economic Review* 96, no. 2 (May 2006): 319–24.

27. "Full" democratization is coded when both the Polity indicator is greater than +7 and the Freedom House status characterization is "free." Polity is another measurement scheme for regime type ranging from -10 (absolute monarchy) to +10 (consolidated democracy). Freedom House aggregates countries' freedom scores into three categories of regimes—free, partly free, and not free. All remaining democratization countries are coded as "partial." Elias Papaioannou and Gregorios Siourounis, "Democratization and Growth," *Economic Journal* 118, no. 532 (October 2008): 1520–51.

28. Daron Acemoglu, Suresh Naidu, Pascual Restrepo, and James A. Robinson, "Democracy Does Cause Growth," *Journal of Political Economy* 127, no. 1 (February 2019): 47–100.

29. John Gerring, Philip Bond, William Barndt, and Carola Moreno, "Democracy and Economic Growth: A Historical Perspective," *World Politics* 57, no. 3 (April 2005): 323–64; Torsten Persson and Guido Tabellini, "Democratic Capital: The Nexus of Political and Economic Change," *American Economic Journal: Macroeconomics* 1, no. 2 (July 2009): 88–126.

3

Innovation, Not Manna from Heaven

Stephen Haber

The United States is an outlier in the distribution of prosperity. As figure 3.1 shows, a small group of countries with per capita incomes above
$40,000 stand out from all the others—and the United States, with a
per capita income of roughly $62,000, stands out even within this small
group.

How can it be that the United States has a per capita income roughly
50 percent higher than that of Britain, its former colonizer? What explains why US per capita income is close to four times that of China,
which was one of the wealthiest societies on the planet when the first
British colonists arrived in Jamestown?

The short answer is that the United States is a highly innovative society that competes effectively in markets for high value-added products
and services. Some sense of the US innovative edge can be gleaned from
the PwC Global Innovation Study, which ranks the world's one thousand most innovative firms and provides information about the sectors in
which they compete, their revenues, and their spending on research and
development (R&D). In 2018, 34 percent of the world's one thousand
most innovative firms, accounting for 28 percent of total revenues and
42 percent of total R&D spending, were located in the United States.
Within the information technology sector—commonly referred to as

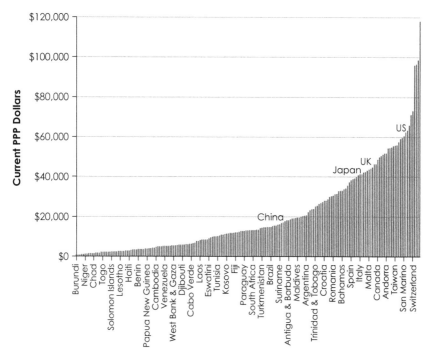

Figure 3.1. Distribution of Per Capita Gross National Income around the World in 2019. *Source*: International Monetary Fund, World Economic Outlook Database, October 2021.

high-tech—the results are even more striking. In 2018, 46 percent of the world's most innovative information technology firms, accounting for 48 percent of total revenues and 58 percent of R&D spending, were located in the United States.[1]

A somewhat more complete answer to the question of why the United States is uncommonly wealthy is that innovation is the creative act of seeing a demand curve that may not yet exist; imagining a product or service that will meet that demand; combining multiple technologies that already exist, while inventing others that do not yet exist, to build that product or service, recruiting people with the necessary skill sets; and persuading yet other people to risk their savings on the idea and the people. Innovation is, in short, about risk taking—but it is not about taking wild risks. It is about taking calculated risks—to start a company, to become an inventor, to invest in specialized skills, to deploy one's capital—in an environment in which it is common knowledge that lots of other people are taking complementary calculated risks. The key to innovation is therefore the maintenance of a social and institutional environment in which calculated risk taking is incentivized. The United States has an innovative society and economy because, at least until recently, risk taking has been rewarded with a share of the economic rents generated by a commercially successful innovation.

An even more complete answer to the question of how a former colonial backwater became one of the world's most innovative economies is that the social and institutional environment of the United States promoted calculated risk taking because, from the very start of the society, the United States was built around decentralized markets, not centralized political power. An innovative economy/society was not manna from heaven. It was the result of a complex combination of legal, financial, governance, transport, production, education, and warfare technologies—in which the word "technology" is understood to mean a way of carrying out a task that can be replicated.[2] No one chose this particular combination of technologies in any meaningful sense of the word. In point of fact, many of the technologies were initially conceived elsewhere and were then absorbed, modified, or improved on locally. These technologies had a powerful impact because of their interactions; each technology amplified the effects of the others.

The key to the success of this process of innovation was the lack of centralized planning: people were free to pursue their self-interest through markets. Some of those markets were economic, in which the currency was dollars. Some of those markets were political, in which the currency was votes. The net result is the equilibrium outcome we observe in figure 3.1: a society with an unusually high level of material prosperity.

To illustrate this idea, I draw on the historical records of the United States and China. Then I explain the challenge that faced societies at the beginning of the modern era, which is to say the eighteenth and nineteenth centuries. Next I focus on the history of innovation in the eighteenth- and nineteenth-century United States. I also focus on eighteenth- and nineteenth-century China in order to illustrate the concept that innovation is not simply production techniques but the outcome of a complex institutional environment. I conclude by discussing the implications of our findings.

The Challenge of Modernity

Most of human history has been characterized by stasis rather than innovation. The archaeological evidence indicates that from the emergence of *Homo sapiens* as a species roughly three hundred thousand years ago to the Neolithic Revolution (the domestication of plants and animals that took place roughly ten thousand years ago), there was little in the way of technological change. Innovation after the Neolithic Revolution tended to be slow. Thomas Malthus's *Essay on the Principle of Population* perhaps captures the pace and state of technological development. As of the essay's publication in 1798, the fundamental problem facing human societies had not really changed since the invention of agriculture: it remained how to avoid starvation under the constraints imposed by local soils and climates.

Beginning in the late eighteenth century, and then intensifying in the nineteenth and twentieth centuries, a suite of new legal, financial, educational, governance, production, transportation, communication, and warfare technologies that historians refer to as "modernity" began to emerge. It is beyond the scope of this essay to explain why those technologies emerged when they did. But suffice it to say that the new technologies did not emerge fully formed from any single society. Rather, the process was recursive, multicountry, iterative, and mutually reinforcing. That is, from the point of view of any society, modernity was an exogenous shock.

The challenge facing societies in the nineteenth and twentieth centuries was how to absorb the new technologies as a broad suite. Societies that were able to accomplish this task relaxed climatologic and geographic constraints on food availability, produced manufactured items on a scale previously unimaginable, conducted industrialized warfare, and built capacious nation-states. Those that were unable to do so were open to being dominated by, colonized by, or subsumed into those that had moved more quickly.

The United States

A social and institutional environment conducive to innovation began to emerge in the United States well before independence. The key to it was a decentralized and democratic political system.

This did not happen because anyone planned it. Quite the contrary. Stuart kings used the colonies to reward their family, friends, and political supporters by setting up proprietary colonies. A "lord proprietor" was essentially a monarch in his own realm, a prince who ran an outlying part of the kingdom with full authority to establish courts, appoint judges and magistrates, impose martial law, pardon crimes, call up the men of fighting age to wage war, grant land titles, levy duties, and collect tolls, so long as he agreed to maintain allegiance to the king.[3] Maryland, for example, was founded as a proprietary colony run by Cecil Calvert, the second Baron Baltimore, who had received a grant from Charles I in 1632. New York, to cite another example, was granted by King Charles II to his brother, James, the Duke of York, who would later become King James II. James, in turn, sold what is currently the state of New Jersey to two of his friends, Lord Berkeley and Sir George Carteret, as proprietors. Both Berkeley and Carteret were already proprietors of Carolina. Pennsylvania and Delaware were also granted as a proprietorship by Charles II to William Penn. In short, the Massachusetts Bay Colony, which was founded by Puritans and consumes so many pages in high school history textbooks, was an outlier.

The goal of the lords proprietors was not to create a democratic society of yeoman farmers that would one day throw off British rule. It was to re-create the manorial system, which had long since disappeared from England. The problem with this plan was that British North America contained neither a Potosí that produced piles of silver coins nor a Pernambuco that yielded prodigious quantities of highly valuable sugar. Cotton would play this role in the US South, but only much later, in the nineteenth century, after the cotton gin made it possible to process the short-staple varieties that could be grown in American soils. The one thing that the thirteen colonies did have, however, was seemingly endless expanses of farmland suitable for tobacco, corn, and wheat. Crucially, those crops share characteristics that allow them to be grown efficiently on family farms: they are highly storable and exhibit modest-scale economies in production.[4] Growing tobacco, corn, and wheat was not particularly attractive to the gentlemen that the lords proprietors hoped would establish rural manors, but it did prove attractive to small farmers who came as freemen and indentured workers to take advantage of the "headright system" that permitted them to obtain family-size tracts in fee simple.[5]

Much to the shock of the lords proprietors, the free farmers soon began to take advantage of the fact that many of the royal charters called for the establishment of colonial assemblies. The charters creating those assemblies had envisioned a system in which lords proprietors, or governors acting on their behalf, would decree laws, "with the advice, assent, and approbation of the freemen of the same province."[6] Rather than approving or suggesting changes to laws crafted by the lords proprietors, however, the assembled freemen began to draw up their own laws, challenged the lords proprietors to veto them, and gave one another proxies to represent them at assembly meetings.[7] That is, independent farmers created the right to vote for representatives endogenously in the seventeenth century; no one "granted" it. Even when formal restrictions on suffrage began to be established in the late seventeenth century, they were not onerous.[8] Suffrage was widespread, as typically 40 to 50 percent of early-eighteenth-century white male colonists were eligible to vote for colonial assemblies in the mid-Atlantic states.[9]

When the United States threw off British rule there was never any doubt that the political system would remain decentralized and, by the standards of the eighteenth century, would be democratic. When the founders crafted the Constitution they grafted two additional eighteenth-century governance technologies onto these native-born institutions: judicial independence, which was created by England's 1701 Act of Settlement through the stipulation that a judge's commission could be removed only by both houses of Parliament; and separation of powers, an institution whose benefits were first articulated, at least in the modern world, by Montesquieu in 1748 in *The Spirit of the Laws*.

One of the first acts of the new constitutional government was the creation of a patent system that was designed to encourage inventive activities by a broad cross section of American society.[10] As Sean Bottomley has shown, the legal concept that a patent of invention was not a monopoly, but was a temporary property right to something that did not exist before and that could be sold, licensed, or traded, emerged out of British jurisprudence over the period 1730 to 1780.[11] The United States Patent Acts of 1790 and 1793 were crafted with an eye to democratizing the British system by simplifying the application process, lowering the fees to 5 percent of the British level, requiring the patentee to be "the first and true inventor" anywhere in the world, and obliging the inventor to provide sufficient technical detail that the technology could be copied upon expiration or invented around prior to expiration.[12]

The legal technology of a patent of invention as a tradable property right interacted with the governance technology of judicial independence, thereby creating an institutional environment in which patents were enforceable. The perspective of nineteenth-century American courts about the patent system is perhaps best captured in the decision by Joseph Story, the acknowledged patent expert on the Supreme Court from 1812 to 1845, in Ex Parte Wood and Brundage (1824): "The inventor has a property in his invention; a property which is often of very great value, and of which the law intended to give him the absolute enjoyment and possession . . . involving some of the dearest and most valuable rights which society acknowledges, and the constitution itself means to favor."[13]

The response of the American public was even more enthusiastic than the authors of the patent acts had imagined. By 1810, the United States surpassed Britain in patenting per capita. From the 1840s through the 1870s, the per capita rate of patenting increased fifteen times. Many of these patents were taken out by ordinary citizens operating with common skills and represented technological improvements across a broad range of economic sectors.[14] As B. Zorina Khan and Kenneth Sokoloff show, they played a crucial role in incentivizing many of the key inventions of the nineteenth century.[15] Virtually all the great inventors of the nineteenth century made use of the patent system to appropriate returns to their efforts. In fact, rather than practicing their inventions themselves, more than half of them licensed or assigned their patents to other firms or individuals. Among these licensors were people whose names still adorn products today, such as Charles Goodyear, who invented the process for vulcanized rubber in 1839 but never manufactured or sold rubber products. Instead, Goodyear transferred his patent rights to other individuals and firms so that they could commercialize them.[16]

The US patent system was, in fact, a key input to the emergence of one of the most important breakthroughs of the nineteenth century, interchangeable parts manufacturing: components manufactured to specifications such that they will fit into any assembly of the same type. The idea of interchangeable parts was not new; it had been conceptualized in France in the 1760s and had then been employed in the manufacture of pulley blocks for sailing ships in Britain at the turn of the nineteenth century. The big jump came, however, out of the workshops of inventors and craftsmen in the United States in the 1810s, who developed the jigs and milling machines that made it possible to cut metal to precise tolerances, thereby allowing for the mass production of interchangeable metal components. These were then used in the manufacture of clocks and small arms and later in the manufacture of engines, electrical machinery, and automobiles. The combination of interchangeable parts and mass production came to be known as the "American system" and served as the model for late-nineteenth-century industrialization around the rest of the world.[17]

The legal technology of a patent of invention as a tradable property right and the governance technologies of federalism and judicial independence interacted with yet another American invention: general incorporation (the creation of a limited liability, joint stock company without a special act of a legislature or royal decree). The idea of the limited liability, joint stock company extends back to ancient Rome in the form of the *societas publicanorum*, which was used to mobilize capital for public works and services.[18] Cities, universities, and trading companies in medieval and early modern Europe were often organized as corporations operating under special charters. In eighteenth-century Britain, as a result of the treatment of patents by courts as property rights, joint stock companies were created, with inventors as shareholders, that specialized in commercializing patents by licensing them to manufacturers.[19] General incorporation built on these preexisting corporate forms, but it democratized access to incorporation by eliminating the need for a special act of a legislature or ruler. From the 1780s to the early 1800s, US states had used general incorporation for restricted purposes, such as religious congregations, colleges, libraries, and turnpikes. In 1811, the New York State Legislature, seeking to expand metal working and textile manufacturing in the state, extended general incorporation to manufacturing, so long as the company was capitalized at less than $100,000 and had no more than nine trustees.[20] New Jersey and Connecticut soon followed New York's lead. As each copied the others and sought to attract business enterprises to their states, they progressively reduced the restrictions on capital and business type that were part of the 1811 New York law.[21]

We cannot stress strongly enough that general incorporation, much like the patent system, was not a stand-alone technology: it could only mobilize capital efficiently in the context of a governance technology that prevented rulers or legislatures from arbitrarily amending or abolishing corporate charters. Thus, the spread of general incorporation depended on an independent judiciary that limited the power of the government to interfere with private charters, as the US Supreme Court did in *Trustees of Dartmouth College v. Woodward* (1819).[22]

The combination of these legal, financial, governance, and metalworking technologies yielded innovations whose products were greater than the sum of their parts. The railroad, perhaps *the* quintessential innovation of the nineteenth century, provides an example. The social returns to railroads were immense because they fed back into production, military, and governance technologies: food could be moved longer distances, making it possible to support larger populations devoted to non-agricultural activities; manufacturers could reach larger markets, allowing them to capture scale economies; and militaries could move troops and materiel rapidly, allowing governments to expand the scale and scope of the nation-state. Nevertheless, railroads did not diffuse around the planet at a uniform rate. While the technical innovations that underpinned the railroad were worked out in Britain during the first three decades of the nineteenth century, financing, building, and operating a railroad network required the absorption of numerous complementary technologies, such as electrical telegraphy to adjust schedules; metal cutting and joining to repair locomotives and cars; patents as property rights to incentivize improvements in locomotives, cars, brakes, and steel rail production; and general incorporation to mobilize capital to build trunk lines. The absorption of these technologies, in turn, required the absorption of additional complementary governance technologies, such as separation of powers, judicial independence, and electoral democracy, which prevented governments from amending corporate charters or patents arbitrarily.

In the United States all these complementary technologies predated the railroad. Thus, railway construction got under way in the 1830s, and by 1860—which is to say even before the transcontinental railroad—the United States already had a rail system with thirty thousand miles of track in operation. To give a sense of its extent, the US rail system was roughly three times the size of the British system, four times that of Germany, thirty times that of Spain, and 1,560 times that of Mexico—a difference that is all the more remarkable in light of the fact that the alternative to a railroad in the United States east of the Mississippi was a riverine barge, while the alternative to railroads in Mexico was a much less efficient two-wheeled wagon pulled by oxen.[23]

The innovation machine that emerged from America's underlying political and economic system did more than build railroads; it played a critical role in the emergence of new industrial centers. In the late eighteenth century, these centers were located in eastern Pennsylvania, New York, and

Connecticut, and the industries that flourished there were sawmills, grist-mills, paper mills, textile mills, breweries, distilleries, tanneries, and iron works.[24] Beginning in the 1820s, the fastest-growing industry was cotton textiles, and the new industrial centers had moved to Rhode Island and Massachusetts to take advantage of their abundant water power.[25] By the 1870s and 1880s, the innovation frontier had shifted to Cleveland, Ohio, which specialized in electrical machinery. Indeed, as Naomi Lamoreaux, Margaret Levenstein, and Kenneth Sokoloff have shown, from the 1880s to the 1920s Cleveland bore a strong resemblance to today's Silicon Valley, where local networks of firms and complementary educational, technological, and financial institutions helped to initiate and sustain waves of start-up enterprises.[26] Not only did Cleveland have a high rate of patenting, its manufacturing firms were intense users of those patented technologies—and, importantly, Cleveland was stunningly wealthy.

Successful as Compared to What?
A Chinese Counterpoint

Any statement about a process being fast or slow implies a counterfactual. Let us therefore draw a comparison to China during the same period to put the experience of the United States into stark relief.

China's political organization was almost the polar opposite of both the colonial and early national United States. Chinese dynasties since the Warring States period (475 to 221 BCE) had built immense bureaucracies to levy internal customs and directly tax farm output.[27] By the Qing dynasty (1644–1912), the system had become highly centralized. There were the emperor and his court, plus an immense, far-flung bureaucracy, headed by appointed governors, that reported to the court. There were no representative assemblies, nor was there voting of any kind.

This system had served China well, in the sense that it had allowed the territory of the realm to expand and had maintained social stability by using stocks of state-owned grain to normalize grain prices during periods of drought and flooding.[28] China was immense, in terms of both its territory and population size; circa 1800 it contained roughly 300 million people, as compared to a British population of roughly 10.5 million and a US population of 5.4 million.

China's centralized political structure proved, however, to be a major disadvantage in meeting the challenges posed by the new technologies of the modern era. Dynasties had long intervened in the commercial economy. In 1371, the first emperor of the Ming dynasty decreed that all foreign trade had to be conducted by official "tribute missions" and that private foreign trade was punishable by death. Between 1613 and 1684, the emperor prohibited coastal trade even among Chinese between the lands north and south of the Yangtze River, the goal being to force all north–south trade through the Grand Canal, where it could be monitored, restricted, or taxed.[29] In 1661, the government "ordered all people residing along the coast from Chekiang [roughly speaking, the present-day city of Hangzhou] to the border with Vietnam to move some seventeen miles inland. Troops constructed watchtowers and positioned guards on the coast to prevent anyone from living there."[30] In 1704, the emperor required all trade with the West to go through the port of Canton (Guangzhou), thereby allowing him to grant exclusive trading rights to a small number of merchant guilds, in exchange for which they forwarded an annual amount of customs revenue to the imperial government. Similar restrictions were imposed on mining and trade in salt.[31]

Restrictions on commercial activity during the Qing dynasty went beyond foreign trade, mining, and salt. Emperors and their courts worried that merchants might form coalitions with local officials that would weaken Beijing's power. To prevent that from happening, they throttled the commercial economy. The government required that merchants and brokers obtain licenses, set the fees for those licenses as a function of the value of trade moving through a town, and then limited the number of licenses. The net result was that by 1800, "few private organizations had achieved large scale size and complexity or been able to integrate different market activities."[32]

As a result of the humiliating defeats in the Opium Wars (1839–42 and 1856–60), Chinese elites took note of a broad suite of new technologies that comprised modernity—and then rejected them. The fundamental problem was that the emperor and his court understood those technologies to be a threat to the imperial system. Qing elites therefore sought to modernize militarily while maintaining the stable agrarian society that had been the basis for Chinese dynasties for the previous two millennia. The Self-Strengthening Movement of 1861–95 encouraged the domestic manufacture of Western armaments, but the production and distribution of commercial goods remained tightly controlled. Unlike Japan, which responded to the threat from the West by adapting the US patent system, the British banking system, German civil and corporate law, German military organization, and parliamentary government on the German model, China's bureaucrats chose only to build government-run armories, overseen by incompetent managers appointed on the basis of patronage, that made inferior copies of Western rifles and cannons.[33]

The limitation on the formation of private enterprises provides a sense of the restraints the Chinese political environment imposed on innovation. In the 1870s and 1880s, the government permitted some industrial enterprises to be founded, but only if they had active sponsorship *and supervision* from the government and its official bureaucrats. As William Goetzmann and Elisabeth Koll point out, these arrangements meant the private actors who put up the capital for the firms bore all the financial risks, while "they were required to work under the thumb of supervising government officials who often followed their own, not necessarily government-directed business agendas and who introduced bribes, corruption, and inflexible management into these enterprises."[34] When these restrictions were finally knocked down in 1895 it was not because the government sought to modernize the private economy. Rather, the Treaty of Shimonoseki, signed after the first Sino-Japanese war of 1894–95, required China to grant foreigners permission to engage in manufacturing operations in Chinese treaty ports. The government could not give foreigners this permission without also granting permission to its own nationals.[35]

It was not just that the government imposed restrictions; it was that the political and economic system that had emerged in China was not built around the idea of independent agents contracting with one another, as existed in the United States, but around the idea that business enterprises were the outgrowths of family lineages and guilds, which were regulated through patronage by state bureaucrats. Business did not exist apart from home and family. Until 1904, there was neither a commercial code nor a civil code. To the degree that there was a body of law that regulated business enterprise, it was through the penal code, which specified punishments for bribe taking by government officials.[36]

In 1904, the Chinese government finally made it legally possible to found an industrial enterprise as a limited liability, joint stock company. It did so, however, by cobbling together an abbreviated version of Japanese and English laws. Not surprisingly, the law had little impact. Only twenty-two of the 227 companies that registered were of any size, and much of the capital authorized for these firms was never raised. Given that the law was a transplant into a social and institutional context in which business was a family affair, regulated by patronage, in which disputes were adjudicated by custom, this should hardly be surprising. Chinese courts were not designed to handle disputes involving corporations. Thus, corporate disputes were referred to the Ministry of Commerce, an administrative, not legal, entity whose decisions had uncertain legal force.[37] The lack of legal force was, in fact, a reflection of a highly centralized political system; no force of law or countervailing political body could challenge a decision made by the bureaucrats in Beijing.

The educational system was similarly poorly designed to generate an innovative economy and society. It had been crafted in order to train young people to be imperial bureaucrats; the emphasis was preparation for an arcane examination on Confucian thought. The response of the government to the lack of engineers and factory managers was to send 120 students to study in the United States in 1872, but they were all called back by 1875 because of concerns about the students becoming overly familiar with Western political ideas.[38]

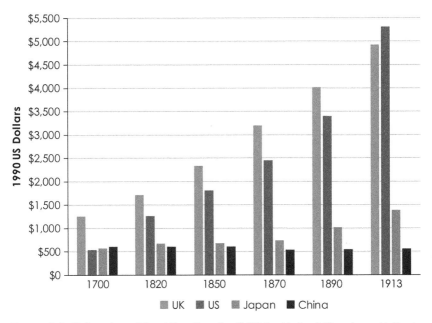

Figure 3.2. Estimates of Real Per Capita GDP for United Kingdom, United States, China, and Japan, 1700–1913 (in 1990 US dollars). *Source:* Angus Maddison, "Historical Statistics of the World Economy," 2010, https://www.rug.nl/ggdc/historicaldevelopment/maddison/releases/maddison-database-2010.

Some sense of the way that all these arrangements held back innovation can be garnered by looking at the growth of the railroad. Railway construction did not get under way in China until the 1890s. By 1910, the entire system had only nine thousand miles of track, which is to say that China had a rail system smaller than even that of Mexico and only 4 percent that of the United States.[39]

Some sense of the differences in equilibrium outcomes across China and the United States can be approximated using data on per capita GDP. We present the data covering the period from 1700 to 1913 in figure 3.2, as well as the data for two other societies we have mentioned in this essay, Britain and Japan. These figures should be taken with a grain of salt. Modern systems of national accounting were not developed until the 1950s; everything before that is a reconstruction. Generally speaking, the further back one goes, the less reliable the figures tend to be. Thus, the data points should be taken as statements of relative magnitude rather than as absolute values. That said, one does not have to squint to see the difference in relative magnitudes.

There are three salient patterns in figure 3.2, the first of which is that there was little difference in per capita income across the United States, Japan, and China circa 1700, while Britain was considerably more prosperous. The second is that the United States began to pull away from Japan and China in the early nineteenth century and began to close the gap with Britain. The third is that by the eve of World War I, the United States had outstripped Britain—at this point it had the highest per capita income in the world. Japanese growth had accelerated following the economic and political reforms of the Meiji Restoration, but the gap between the United States and Japan was on the order of four-to-one. Fourth, across the entire period of 1700–1913, Chinese per capita income had not grown at all.

Conclusion and Implications

We began this essay by inquiring into the question of why some societies are much more innovative than others, and thus much more prosperous. We hope that at least one implication is now fixed in the reader's mind: innovation is not an event, it is a process. It happens when individuals take risks because they know that risk taking will be rewarded. Without a common belief that individuals will share in the rents from innovation, the necessary complementary skills, laws, and technologies do not come into existence. We hope, as well, that at least one secondary implication is jostling about in the reader's mind: it is that innovation and the prosperity it brings are not manna from heaven. They are equilibrium outcomes of a complex combination of political structures, laws, judicial systems, stocks of human capital, and belief systems. As such, they are fragile plants.

NOTES

1. The most recent version of the dataset, covering 2012–2018, was retrieved from PwC's Business and Strategy website on September 8, 2020. Readers curious about the other countries highlighted in figure 3.1 may find it interesting that 160 of the one thousand most innovative firms, accounting for 15 percent of total revenues and 15 percent of R&D spending, were located in Japan; 133 firms, accounting for 14 percent of total revenues and 7 percent of R&D spending, were located in China; and thirty-seven firms, accounting for 4 percent of total revenues and 3 percent of R&D spending, were located in Britain. PricewaterhouseCoopers, "The Global Innovation 1000 Study: Investigating Trends at the World's 1000 Largest Corporate R&D Spenders," 2018, https://www.strategyand.pwc.com/gx/en/insights/innovation1000.html.

2. In this sense, a patent system is a legal technology that incentivizes invention by creating a tradable property right; a banking system is a financial technology that mobilizes capital by removing the need for savers and investors to know one another; public schools are an educational technology that promotes a broad distribution of human capital by giving all children the opportunity to study; and political correctness is a governance technology that reduces the ability of citizens to make up their own minds by shaming those who reject the orthodoxies promulgated by cultural elites.

3. David Galenson, "The Settlement and Growth of the Colonies: Population, Labor, and Economic Development," in *The Cambridge Economic History of the United States: Vol. 1, The Colonial Era*, ed. Stanley Engerman and Robert Gallman (Cambridge: Cambridge University Press, 1996), 135–208.

4. Hans Binswanger and Mark Rosenzweig, "Behavioural and Material Determinants of Production Relations in Agriculture," *Journal of Development Studies* 22 (1986): 503–39.

5. The lands were obtained as grants from the lords proprietors. Each grantee received fifty acres of land for each person they brought into the colony, whether as settler, indentured servant, or slave. The lords proprietors received an annual "quitrent" from the grantees. Aubrey Land, *Colonial Maryland: A History* (Millwood, NY: Kraus International Publications, 1981), 25.

6. Land, *Colonial Maryland*, 4.

7. In some colonies, such as Maryland, New Jersey, and Pennsylvania, the resistance of the colonial assemblies to the lord proprietor and his agents occurred almost

immediately. But even in New York, whose initial charter did not include a colonial assembly, the farmers agitated for one and were successful in their demands by 1691. Land, *Colonial Maryland*; John Murrin, "Political Development," in *Colonial British America: Essays in the New History of the Early Modern Era*, ed. Jack Greene and J. R. Pole (Baltimore: Johns Hopkins University Press, 1984), 443–44.

8. Edmund Morgan, *American Slavery, American Freedom* (New York: W. W. Norton, 1975), 145.

9. Alexander Keysaar, *The Right to Vote: The Contested History of Democracy in the United States* (New York: Basic Books, 2000), 7.

10. It is beyond the scope of this essay to explore every nuance of how patent systems work, but suffice it to say that most products are not themselves patented; what are patented are the technologies that make the products possible. You may, for example, be reading these words on a laptop computer, a tablet, or (eyesight permitting) a smartphone. However, there is no patent for a laptop, a tablet, or a smartphone. Rather, there are tens of thousands of patented technologies that allow you to download this essay, display the words on a screen, make notes in the margins, and share your thoughts about the essay's ideas with friends and colleagues—and do all these things regardless of the type and brand of the device you are using. Most of those patented technologies were not developed by the firm whose brand name appears on your device. They were developed by specialized firms, most of which you have never heard of. See F. Scott Kieff, "Coordination, Property, and Intellectual Property: An Unconventional Approach to Anticompetitive Effects and Downstream Access," *Emory Law Journal* 56 (2006): 327–438.

11. A patent can confer a monopoly in production only if there are absolutely no substitutes for a patented technology, the technology is itself being sold legally by the owner or her affiliates, and the patent owner declines to sell licenses. Put differently, a patent is only a right to exclude, not use. Any particular patented product or service may, and often does, compete with many substitutes in the market. Moreover, a patent requires that the invention be clearly specified such that a competitor can invent around it. This gives a patentee an incentive to sell others a license to the patent: either the patentee can get a royalty equal to some percentage of output or he can get zero; others have the choice between paying a royalty equal to some percentage of their output and bearing the costs of inventing around a patent. Writing a contract to license the patent therefore

makes both parties better off. In fact, if someone actually had a technology for which there were no substitutes and which could not be reverse-engineered by a third party at a lower cost than the R&D and other costs already incurred by the inventor, he would not patent it at all! He would instead take advantage of his proprietary knowledge to dominate the market. The result *would be* a monopoly—but it would have nothing to do with patents. Sean Bottomley, *The British Patent System during the Industrial Revolution 1700–1852: From Privilege to Property* (Cambridge: Cambridge University Press, 2014). See Jonathan Barnett, "Is Intellectual Property Trivial?," *University of Pennsylvania Law Review* 157 (2009): 1691–1742.

12. Patents were further strengthened by the Patent Act of 1836, which introduced the examination system still in use today, thereby reducing concerns third parties might have had about a patent's novelty. Britain, seeing the superiority of the US system at the Crystal Palace Exhibition of 1851, adopted many of the features of the US system in 1852. The US system also became the basis for Germany's 1877 patent law and Japan's 1888 patent law. The German system, in turn, influenced the patent systems of Argentina, Austria, Brazil, Denmark, Finland, Holland, Norway, Poland, Russia, and Sweden. Kenneth Sokoloff and B. Zorina Khan, "The Democratization of Invention During Early Industrialization: Evidence from the United States, 1790–1846," *Journal of Economic History* 50 (1990): 363–78; B. Zorina Kahn and Kenneth Sokoloff, "History Lessons: The Early Development of Intellectual Property Institutions in the United States," *Journal of Economic Perspectives* 15 (2001): 233–46; B. Zorina Kahn, "An Economic History of Patent Institutions," EH.Net Encyclopedia, ed. Robert Whaples, 2008, http://eh.net/encyclopedia/an-economic-history-of-pat ent-institutions/. Also see Adam Mossoff, "Rethinking the Development of Patents: An Intellectual History, 1550–1800," *Hastings Law Journal* 55 (2001): 1255–1322.

13. Joseph Story quoted in B. Zorina Kahn, "Property Rights and Patent Litigation in Early Nineteenth-Century America," *Journal of Economic History* 55 (1995): 58–97. Also see Adam Mossoff, "Patents as Constitutional Private Property: The Historical Protection of Patents Under the Takings Clause," *Boston University Law Review* 87 (2007): 689–724.

14. Sokoloff and Kahn, "The Democratization of Invention"; Kahn and Sokoloff, "Schemes of Political Utility: Entrepreneurship and Innovation Among 'Great Inventors' in the United States, 1790–1865," *Journal of Economic History* 53

(1993): 289–307; Kahn and Sokoloff, "History Lessons"; Kahn, *The Democratization of Invention: Patents and Copyrights in American Economic Development, 1790–1920* (Cambridge: Cambridge University Press, 2005).

15. Kahn and Sokoloff, "Schemes of Political Utility"; Kahn and Sokoloff, "Institutions and Democratic Invention in 19th-Century America: Evidence from 'Great Inventors,' 1790–1930," *American Economic Review* 94 (2004): 395–401.

16. The practice of patent licensing has a long history in the United States, and its emergence allowed for gains from specialization. But those gains could come only if an inventor could reap the returns from his or her investment through a well-defined and enforced property right. Kenneth Sokoloff, "Inventive Activity in Early Industrial America: Evidence from Patent Records, 1790–1846," *Journal of Economic History* 48 (1988): 813–50; Khan and Sokoloff, "Schemes of Practical Utility"; Naomi Lamoreaux, Kenneth Sokoloff, and Dhanoos Sutthiphisal, "Patent Alchemy: The Market for Technology in U.S. History," *Business History Review* 87 (2013): 3–38.

17. This history of the US patent system perhaps comes as a surprise to readers of this essay, who have in recent years been inundated with literature about patent trolls, patent failure, and patent holdup. Stanley Engerman and Kenneth Sokoloff, "Technology and Industrialization, 1790–1914," in *The Cambridge Economic History of the United States: Vol. 2, The Long 19th Century*, ed. Stanley Engerman and Robert Gallman (Cambridge: Cambridge University Press, 2000), 367–402. Also see, for example, James Bessen and Michael J. Meurer, *Patent Failure: How Judges, Bureaucrats, and Lawyers Put Innovation at Risk* (Princeton, NJ: Princeton University Press, 2008); Michele Boldrin and David K. Levine, *Against Intellectual Monopoly* (Cambridge: Cambridge University Press, 2008); Boldrin and Levine, "The Case Against Patents," *Journal of Economic Perspectives* 27 (2013): 3–22; Mark Lemley and Carl Shapiro, "Patent Holdup and Royalty Stacking," *Texas Law Review* 85 (2007): 1991–2049. For a critique of that literature, questioning its logic and evidence, see B. Zorina Khan, "Trolls and Other Patent Inventions: Economic History and the Patent Controversy in the Twenty-First Century," *George Mason Law Review* 21 (2014): 825–63; Alexander Galetovic, Stephen Haber, and Ross Levine, "An Empirical Examination of Patent Holdup," *Journal of Competition Law & Economics* 11 (2015): 549–78; Galetovic and Haber, "The Fallacies of Patent-Holdup Theory," *Journal of Competition Law & Economics* 13 (2017): 1–44; Jonathan Barnett, "Has the Academy Led Patent Law Astray?," *Berkeley Technology Law Journal* 32 (2017): 1313–80.

18. Ulrike Malmendier, "Law and Finance at the Origin," *Journal of Economic Literature* 47 (2009): 1076–1108.

19. Bottomley, *The British Patent System*.

20. Ronald Seavoy, "Laws to Encourage Manufacturing: New York Policy and the 1811 General Incorporation Statute," *Business History Review* 46 (1972): 85–95.

21. The concept proved so successful that it was gradually adopted by Britain in the 1840s and 1850s, by France in the 1860s, by Germany in the 1870s, and by Mexico, Brazil, and Japan in the 1880s. Leslie Hannah, "A Global Corporate Census: Publicly Traded and Close Companies in 1910," *Economic History Review* 68 (2014).

22. Even though general incorporation laws were later adopted by other countries, the extent to which they could mobilize capital varied widely. According to Haber, Razo, and Maurer, in settings in which connections to political elites were important to the success of an enterprise, general incorporation tended to be used only by those who were already well connected. Malmendier explores this point about the political basis for general incorporation, showing that the *societas publicanorum* was widely used during the Roman republic but fell into disuse after centralization of political power during the empire. Stephen Haber, Armando Razo, and Noel Maurer, *The Politics of Property Rights: Political Instability, Credible Commitments, and Economic Growth in Mexico, 1876–1929* (Cambridge: Cambridge University Press, 2003); Malmendier, "Law and Finance at the Origin."

23. Diego Comin and Bart Hobijn, "The CHAT Dataset," National Bureau of Economic Research Working Paper 15319, 2009.

24. Philip Scranton, *Proprietary Capitalism: The Textile Manufacture at Philadelphia, 1800–1885* (Cambridge: Cambridge University Press, 1983), 75–83.

25. Engerman and Sokoloff, "Technology and Industrialization, 1790–1914."

26. Naomi Lamoreaux, Margaret Levenstein, and Kenneth Sokoloff, "Mobilizing Venture Capital during the Second Industrial Revolution: Cleveland, Ohio, 1870–1920," *Capitalism and Society* 1 (2006): 1–61.

27. Pierre-Étienne Will and R. Bin Wong, *Nourish the People: The State Civilian Granary System in China, 1650–1850* (Ann Arbor: University of Michigan Press, 1991).

28. Will and Wong, *Nourish the People*.

29. Ramon Myers and Yeh-Chien Wang, "Economic Developments, 1644–1800," in *The Cambridge History of China, Vol. 9: The Ch'ing Dynasty to 1800, Part 1*, ed. Willard Peterson (Cambridge: Cambridge University Press, 2002), 587.

30. Myers and Wang, "Economic Developments, 1644–1800," 565.

31. Myers and Wang, "Economic Developments, 1644–1800," 589, 608, 625.

32. Myers and Wang, "Economic Developments, 1644–1800," 606, 644.

33. Kahn, "An Economic History of Patent Institutions"; Charles Calomiris and Stephen Haber, *Fragile by Design: The Political Origins of Banking Crises and Scarce Credit* (Princeton, NJ: Princeton University Press, 2014); William Kirby, "China Unincorporated: Company Law and Business Enterprise in Twentieth-Century China," *Journal of Asian Studies* 54 (1995): 43–63; Mark Ravina, *To Stand with Nations of the World: Japan's Meiji Restoration in World History* (Oxford: Oxford University Press, 2017); J. Mark Ramsayer and Frances Rosenbluth, *The Politics of Oligarchy: Institutional Choice in Imperial Japan* (Cambridge: Cambridge University Press, 1998).

34. William Goetzmann and Elisabeth Koll, "The History of Corporate Ownership in China: State Patronage, Company Legislation, and the Issue of Control," in *A History of Corporate Governance Around the World: Family Business Groups to Professional Managers*, ed. Randall Morck (Chicago: University of Chicago Press, 2005), 149–81.

35. Goetzmann and Koll, "The History of Corporate Ownership in China."

36. Kirby, "China Unincorporated."

37. Kirby, "China Unincorporated."

38. Ting Yee Kuo, "Self-Strengthening: The Pursuit of Western Technology," in *The Cambridge History of China, Vol. 10: Late Ch'ing 1800–1911, Part 1*, ed. John Fairbank (Cambridge: Cambridge University Press, 1978), 491–542.

39. Comin and Hobijn, "The CHAT Dataset."

II

Comparative Outcomes of Capitalism and Socialism

4

Socialism, Capitalism, and Income

Edward P. Lazear

Income is certainly among the most important metrics of societal success, but average income may mask much of what is important. A country that has a small proportion of very wealthy people coupled with a large group of very poor people is not what most would judge as a desirable society. Free-market capitalism with private ownership and market-determined allocation of goods and services often receives credit for generating economic growth and high average income. But critics argue that a market-based economy does not do enough to help the poor. Socialism, which combines government ownership of much of the means of production with substantial centrally determined allocation, is championed as being more benevolent than free-market capitalism.

Much of the literature analyzes relative well-being. Benevolence is often measured by inequality or how the rich do relative to the poor, but inequality is not a good measure of how well the poor fare in general.

China is perhaps the best case in point. Completely different inferences with respect to the welfare of the poor are likely to be drawn depending on the choice of measure. Figure 4.1 shows what happened to income inequality in China since 1980 as the economy moved from strict command to a more market-oriented one with significant private ownership and business flexibility. The increase in inequality is enormous. The

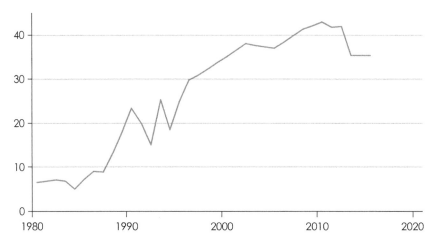

Figure 4.1. Income Inequality in China. *Note:* Income is monthly per capita at 2005 PPPs (purchasing power parity). *Source:* Rahul Lahoti, Jayadev Arjun, and Sanjay Reddy, "The Global Consumption and Income Project (GCIP): An Overview," *Journal of Globalization and Development* 7, no. 1 (June 2016): 61–108.

ratio of the average income of those in the top decile to the average income of those in the bottom decile went from eight in the 1980s to about forty, and only began to reverse in recent years. Presented alone, this fact suggests that although the move to the market has benefited the wealthy in China, it has not helped the poor.

Figure 4.2, which tracks the absolute monthly income of the lowest decile in China over time, suggests a different conclusion. Although it took a decade, in the mid-1990s income of the poorest in China began to grow and the growth rate picked up in the last decade. Today, the poorest Chinese earn five times as much as they did just two decades earlier. Before and throughout the 1980s, a large portion of the Chinese population lived in abject poverty. Today's poor in China remain poor by developed-country standards, but there is no denying that they are far better off than they were even two decades ago. Indeed, the rapid lifting of so many out of the worst state of poverty is likely the greatest change in human welfare in world history.

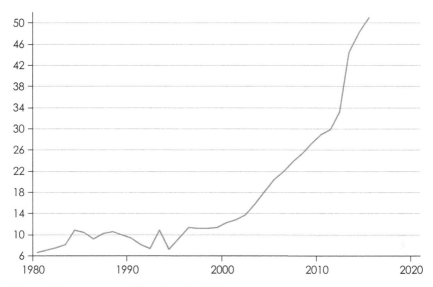

Figure 4.2. Income of the Poor in China. *Note:* Income is monthly per capita at 2005 PPPs (purchasing power parity). *Source:* Lahoti, Arjun, and Reddy, "The Global Consumption and Income Project (GCIP)."

China's experience is perhaps the most pronounced and most important because so many are affected. But it is not unique. India, with a population similar to China's, experienced a similar phenomenon, albeit to a lesser extent. The ratio of income of those in the top decile to those in the bottom decile went from sixteen to twenty over the past three decades. At the same time, the absolute income of the poorest decile approximately doubled (see appendix figures 4.A1 and 4.A2). Inequality rose, but the poor became substantially richer. India, too, adopted market reforms in the late 1980s and 1990s.[1]

Although surprising, the distinction between inequality and absolute income is an important one that is generally ignored in most of the literature. Almost all previously published analyses of economic systems and outcomes for income focus on mean income and income inequality, not how well the poor have fared under the various systems. It is possible to argue that both are relevant, but it is inappropriate to ignore the importance of poor people's income level as society moves from one system to another. It is doubtful that many earners in the lowest quartile of China would prefer to return to the situation that prevailed before the reforms of the 1980s, despite the dramatic rise in inequality.

Because the goal is to improve life for the typical individual and especially the poor, much of the focus in this essay is on the effects of governmental form on the standard of living of the rich and the poor, not on differences between them. Inequality receives attention below in large part to connect it to other literature and to make clear what happens to relative positions as societies change governmental and economic form.

A Brief Review of the Literature

General Discussion

The literature on economic systems is replete with theoretical justifications for one system over another. Karl Marx supplied the most historically important argument for the advantages of socialism over capitalism and the natural replacement of capitalism by socialism.[2] Capitalism brings about its own demise as technology creates more material goods for society and the abundance causes the rate of profit to decline, which results in depression, falling living standards, and the subsequent rise of the proletariat to overthrow the capitalist class.[3] More recently, Thomas Piketty presents a modern view of the doctrine that traces back to Marx.[4]

Piketty's work is both theoretical and empirical. The conceptual analysis builds on modern growth theory that begins with the Harrod-Domar model and incorporates the Solow growth model.[5] Piketty documents the rise in capital's share over time and argues that this will continue to happen unless action is taken to stop it. Concomitant increases in wage inequality are the inevitable result. There are a number of serious critiques of Piketty's analysis.[6]

On the other side, the notion that incentives matter is found throughout the economic literature and goes back to Adam Smith.[7] Perhaps most important" in the context of incentives is labor supply. Workers generally must be paid in order for them to provide labor hours and effort. The literature on how paying higher wages affects labor and effort goes back at least to the late nineteenth century.[8] More specifically, Harvey Rosen provides early estimates on the adverse effects of taxes on hours worked.[9] Higher taxes imply lower take-home wages, and Rosen finds that labor hours are diminished as a result. More recent work, including that of Steven J. Davis and Magnus Henrekson, finds a reduction in work hours occurs in response to higher taxes, based on data from OECD countries.[10] Edward Prescott's analysis of lower work hours among Europeans than among Americans attributes the majority of the difference to tax rates on labor income.[11] Barry Eichengreen also examines this and asks whether and why European leaders were naive about the effect of taxes on labor supply.[12] Additional analysis is provided by Richard Rogerson, who argues that it is important to understand how the tax revenue is spent because this affects the labor supply/tax elasticity.[13]

Ludwig von Mises and Friedrich A. Hayek separately argued that market prices are necessary and provide the best coordination in a world where no single consumer, worker, or firm can possess all the necessary information.[14]

A few authors have compared the performance of public and private firms within economies rather than attempting to compare entire economies under different systems. Early work by Anthony Boardman and Aidan Vining finds that state-owned or state-operated firms are less profitable and less efficient than their private counterparts.[15] Stephen Martin and David Parker examine eleven UK firms that transition from public to private ownership and obtain mixed results, concluding that "neither private nor public sector production is inherently or necessarily more efficient."[16] Clifford Winston examines the US transportation system and estimates that government involvement costs $100 billion per year in lost performance.[17] Arthur Comstock, Richard Kish, and Geraldo Vasconcellos analyze the long-term performance of privatized state-owned enterprises and find poorer stock returns that are about 50 percent below market performance for former state-owned enterprises.[18]

Transitions

Transitions from one form of government to another have been studied by a number of researchers in different contexts. János Kornai, who has a large body of work on transitions, examines the transition from socialism to capitalism in a series of essays.[19] Nina Bandelj and Matthew C. Mahutga find that income inequality in socialist Central and Eastern European countries was lower than in other countries at a similar stage of development. Furthermore, inequality increased substantially after the fall of communism.[20] In an earlier study, Adam Bergson estimates that income inequality was low in the 1970s Soviet Union.[21] This does not speak to whether the poorest Soviets earned more than the poor in other countries. Bergson finds that in the mid-1970s, inequality in the USSR, as measured by share of income earned by the highest and lowest quintiles, was comparable to that of Norway and the United Kingdom, but less than that in the United States and France.

Neither socialism nor capitalism guarantees or precludes democracy. As an empirical matter (using the data below), there is a negative correlation between legal rights and state ownership of capital. Certainly, the most important socialist societies, namely the Soviet Union (and its satellite states) and China, were far from democratic. Similarly, democracy does not ensure equality, and Daron Acemoglu et al. in their study find no clear relation of inequality to democracy.[22]

As made clear in the introduction, high inequality does not imply low wages for the poor. The ratio of wages of the rich to the poor may be rising at the same time that the poor's wage level is rising. There is little evidence on this. Instead, some have examined direct transfers and income redistribution and its relation to inequality. For example, Ostry, Berg, and Tsangarides find that richer and more unequal societies tend to engage in more redistribution.[23] They also find that growth is negatively correlated with inequality and that growth does not seem to suffer from efforts toward redistribution. Obvious well-known cases support this claim. Ireland, which experienced very high growth in average income and GDP over the past three decades, is also one of the most redistributive countries. A counterexample is New Zealand in the 1970s and 1980s, which had high redistribution and low growth both in GDP and income, especially for the poor. This led to the mid- to late-1980s "Rogernomics" reforms.

The connection between productivity and wages seems clear and has been documented recently by Anna Stansbury and Lawrence H. Summers and at a more disaggregated level by my own work on the subject.[24] If it is necessary to raise productivity in order to raise wages, particularly the wages of the poor, which systems are more likely to lead to productivity growth? Acemoglu and James A. Robinson argue that the Soviet Union was successful in producing economic and productivity growth by having a powerful central state that allocated resources toward industry.[25] The major failing, as a result of deficient incentives, was innovation in industry, which led to stagnation. Yet the Soviet Union used its command structure to direct resources to specific activities and innovated in both defense and space technology. In their book, Ladislav Rusmich and Stephen M. Sachs argue that the failings of the socialist system have to do with the lack of feedback mechanisms that allow inefficient organizations to fail.[26] The absence of the natural selection that capitalism ensures results in low growth, less change, slower productivity growth, and therefore stagnant wages.

China, another prominent socialist economy, is the best evidence for a successful transition from a complete command economy to a more market-oriented economy. During the twenty-five years between 1985 and 2010, average income rose at an unprecedented annual rate of 9.6 percent. The Fraser Institute's annual reports on the economic freedom of the world, described in more detail below, incorporate a variety of measures including private ownership, small government, low taxes, and property rights, which match the dictionary definition of capitalism given below. The highest-ranking countries in the 2019 report were Hong Kong, Singapore, New Zealand, Switzerland, the United States, Ireland, and the United Kingdom. At the low end are Venezuela, pre-reform China,

Libya, Sudan, Algeria, Angola, the Democratic Republic of the Congo, and Egypt. The index, which has a scale of 0 to 10 and a mean level of 6.54, rates China as 3.59 in 1980 and 6.42 in 2017.[27]

Several authors have examined the Chinese transition to middle-income status and have contrasted it with experiences in Eastern Europe. Peter Nolan focuses on the more gradual nature of the transition in China. Kellee S. Tsai discusses the ability of China to grow economically and to become capitalist without becoming democratic. Xiaogang Wu and Donald Joseph Treiman examine intergenerational mobility in China, which they argue is artificially high because the registration system in China has resulted in a small proportion of a large number of rural residents moving to the cities and obtaining higher incomes.[28]

Scandinavia

The Scandinavian experience is important and is sometimes viewed as a middle ground. Some proponents of socialism point to Scandinavia as what they have in mind. Indeed, Scandinavia has had high growth and has high standards of living, but it also has a large government sector, some-times viewed as a defining feature of socialism.[29] Scandinavia is known not only for the size of the state but also—and perhaps primarily—for its welfare programs like generous child care benefits in Sweden and "flexicu-rity" in Denmark.[30] The Scandinavian countries are in the top 20 percent of countries in terms of transfers and subsidy payments according to the Fraser Institute's Economic Freedom Report.[31] They share this charac-teristic with other wealthy European countries, the highest of which are Austria, Belgium, Germany, France, and the Netherlands, countries that rank even higher than Scandinavia on the amount of transfers and sub-sidies.[32] Others might deny that Scandinavia is socialist on a number of grounds. Non-Scandinavian countries, specifically, France, Belgium, Austria, Greece, and Italy, have comparable or larger state sectors as mea-sured by government expenditures as a share of GDP.[33] Sweden, Finland, and Denmark have less state ownership than the median country in the world, and all the Scandinavian countries rank high (in the top fifth of all countries) for general economic freedom.

The Scandinavian and larger European experience suggests that transfers are an important issue to consider when evaluating systems. It may be that inherently capitalist economies choose low transfers while inherently socialist ones choose high transfers. It might also be expected that transfers have effects on the distribution of living standards within a country as well as growth. That is studied below.

Data

There are two main sources of data. The primary dependent variables relate to the income distribution across countries and over time within a country. For this purpose, data from the Global Consumption and Income Project (GCIP) are used.[34] The data go back in some cases as far as the early 1960s and cover as many as 161 countries, although there are many missing observations for given countries in particular years. The income data harmonize national surveys to present real (2005 purchasing power parity or PPP) monthly income data for all deciles of the population.

Interpolation is used in years between national surveys to estimate the mean level of income for every decile in the country-year. In non-survey years, the income profile is estimated by using the appropriate per capita growth rate figures from the World Development Indicators. For the purposes here, only survey years are used to avoid understating the standard errors. The Global Income Dataset draws on several sources of data, mainly the EU-SILC database, the Luxembourg Income Study, the SEDLAC database, and the UNU-WIDER World Income Inequality Database. All measures of income are per capita.

A few checks suggest that the income data are reasonable. A ranking of countries by median income makes sense. The richest countries in 2015, in order, are Luxembourg, Norway, Hong Kong, Switzerland, Canada, New Zealand, the United States, Sweden, Austria, and Iceland.

The poorest countries are Madagascar, Malawi, Congo, Mozambique, Zambia, Nigeria, Mali, Senegal, Niger, and Tanzania. Internal inequality measures are also consistent with other sources. Of the ten richest countries, the United States has one of the highest levels of inequality as measured by the difference in the log of top decile income and the log of bottom decile income. Iceland, Norway, and Sweden have the lowest levels of inequality.[35]

The other key data component relates to measures of governmental form, the primary source being the Fraser Institute's annual reports on economic freedom, which include ratings for 162 countries. Datasets for most of these countries are available at least from 1980 through 2017 through the Fraser Institute's website. Many metrics are provided, ranging from those that most directly define capitalism and socialism, namely state ownership of capital, to regulatory structure. The measurement of economic freedom has five major categories: (1) size of government, (2) legal system and security of property rights, (3) sound money, (4) freedom to trade internationally, and (5) regulation. Within each of the major areas are forty-two subcomponents, which come from various third-party sources such as the International Country Risk Guide, the Global Competitiveness Report, and the World Bank's Doing Business project. The subcomponents are scaled from zero to ten to reflect the distribution of the underlying data. Within each major category, components are then averaged to give a rating within the category. These ratings are again averaged to arrive at the overall economic freedom rankings, with values closer to ten representing more open and free economies. The five major components are similarly weighted equally to obtain the summary economic freedom ranking.

A similar measure used to validate some of the findings is compiled by the Heritage Foundation: the Heritage Index of Economic Freedom.[36] It is based on twelve quantitative and qualitative factors, broadly grouped into four categories: (1) rule of law, (2) government size, (3) regulatory efficiency, and (4) open markets. After being graded from zero to one hundred on each factor, a country receives an overall score equal to the unweighted average of the twelve indicators. A higher score indicates a higher level of economic freedom. The data are available annually between 1995 and 2019 and cover around 180 countries. Because the Heritage Foundation's index covers a shorter period that sometimes misses important changes from one government form to another, the Fraser Institute's data is used as the primary measure in this paper. Appendix table 4.A1 compares results obtained using the Fraser Institute's rankings to those using the Heritage Foundation's index and shows that they are qualitatively similar.

There are other indexes that might be used to define capitalism and socialism. The World Economic Forum compiles an index of business competitiveness that covers the period from 2007 through 2018 for more than one hundred countries.[37] Also available, roughly biannually starting in 2012, is the Rule of Law Index, produced by the World Justice Project.[38] It covers about one hundred countries. Except for checking for consistency, neither index is used as a primary part of the analysis because the time of availability does not cover the relevant period.

Defining Capitalism and Socialism

A key to exploring the relation of system to income is settling on common definitions of socialism and capitalism. Merriam-Webster defines socialism as "any of various economic and political theories advocating collective or governmental ownership and administration of the means of production and distribution of goods" and secondarily as "a. a system of society or group living in which there is no private property" and "b. a system or condition of society in which the means of production are owned and controlled by the state." Conversely, capitalism is defined by the same source as "an economic system characterized by private or corporate ownership of capital goods, by investments that are determined by private decision, and by prices, production, and the distribution of goods that are determined mainly by competition in a free market."

A variety of measures of free-market capitalism are used. Initially, and most frequently, the metric that is closest to the dictionary definitions given above is the Fraser Institute's variable that measures state ownership of capital on a ten-point scale, where ten is the highest degree of private ownership and the lowest level of state ownership.[39] Countries with zero values include the Soviet bloc countries before the fall of the Soviet Union, China in 1970, Vietnam and Laos in 1980, and Mozambique in 1975 and 1980. The countries with the least state ownership include the United States, Switzerland, Germany, and modern-day Lithuania.

Also corresponding to the dictionary definitions of socialism and capitalism is the way the Fraser Institute measures economic freedom, using an average of a number of other indicators, including those that measure state ownership, rule of law, the size of government, and the amount of transfers. The Fraser Institute provides information for most countries over a significant period. The data go back as far as 1970 for over fifty countries, but there is information on more than one hundred countries from 1980 to the present.

The Heritage Foundation Index also corresponds to Webster's definitions of socialism and capitalism but is available over a shorter period than covered by the Fraser Institute. The correlation between the two indexes is .85 over all countries and all years for which both are available.

The World Justice Project (WJP) Rule of Law Index, used only for verification purposes, is not necessarily related to capitalism or socialism per se because a country with state ownership of capital and government-administered prices could adhere to the rule of law and protect individual civil liberties. As an empirical matter, however, the WJP index correlates strongly with having low state ownership. The World Economic Forum Business Competitiveness Index, also used primarily as a check on other indexes, purports to measure the openness of business to market forces and the absence of government interference in markets, which conforms to Webster's definition of capitalism. It is strongly correlated with both the Fraser Institute and Heritage Foundation assessments of overall economic freedom as well as with the WJP Rule of Law Index.

Taken as a whole, these sets of indexes, their correlations and definitions, support the view that the Fraser Institute's state ownership ratings and economic freedom rankings are good summary measures of capitalism and socialism. High values of these components correspond to private ownership and free markets and low values correspond to state ownership and government-controlled markets.

Results

The panel income and rankings data are used to analyze the relation of income to economic form. The analysis separates lowest-decile, median, and highest-decile incomes. Most of what follows examines the levels of those measures, taken independently, but there is some analysis of the relation of the various income deciles to one another, which is more closely related to inequality per se.

Income Variations and State Ownership

A number of measures of free-market capitalism and socialism have been suggested. The analysis starts by examining the metric that most closely matches the dictionary definition of socialism, namely, the amount of state ownership of capital as measured by the Fraser Institute, described above. Recall that a high number refers to high levels of private ownership and a zero value implies complete state ownership. The rankings seem to capture significant variation in countries in a consistent way. For example, in 1980 a value of 4.26 was reported for Poland and zero for Russia. It is well known that Poland had a significant amount of private ownership, even as part of the Soviet bloc.[40] But in Russia, the state nationalized virtually every activity outside of the black market.

The basic approach in this section is to examine the relation of income of three groups to state ownership. The three dependent variables are the log of mean income of the lowest decile, the log of median income, and the log of mean income of the highest decile. The data consist of an unbalanced panel so that the results use information on 147 countries for a period potentially as long as 1970 through 2015. Standard errors are clustered at the country level.

There are three sets of regressions for each dependent variable, shown in table 4.1 as columns 1–3, 4–6, and 7–9, respectively. The dependent variable is income ten years in the future rather than contemporaneous income.[41] There are at least two reasons for relating future income to state ownership at a point in time. First is a concern about reverse causation. It is possible, for example, that as countries get wealthier, they demand less state involvement. This argument makes more sense in the context of human rights and rule of law, analyzed later, but it is worth considering even here. One way to reduce that concern is to exploit the timing. If state ownership changes first, say, ten years earlier, then it is unlikely that it changed in response to income changes that occurred the next decade. Of course, even that is a possibility were the future income changes anticipated, but that is much more of a stretch.

Additionally, from a logical point of view, it makes sense that it would take some time for changes in state ownership to show up in incomes. That provides another reason to relate income ten years in the future to levels today.

Columns 1, 4, and 7 show the relation of income ten years hence to state ownership of capital for the poorest, median, and wealthiest members of the economy. Higher values reflect more private ownership and less state ownership. All coefficients on state ownership are positive, strong, and statistically significant. For example, using the coefficient in column 4, a one standard deviation increase in private ownership increases median income by about 19 percent of the mean value of the log of median income. Also interesting is that the lowest-income groups benefit as much or more from private ownership as the highest-income groups (compare coefficients in columns 1, 4, and 7).

An obvious concern is that other omitted factors may be correlated with state ownership and that the state ownership ratings may pick up the effect of those other factors on income. The inclusion of country fixed effects addresses some of those worries. Results from regressions that include country fixed effects are contained in columns 2, 5, and 8. Qualitatively, the results are similar to those without fixed effects, but the magnitudes of the coefficients are generally lower when country fixed effects are included.

Table 4.1. Income and State Ownership

Variables	1	2	3	4	5	6	7	8	9
	Log lowest decile income 10 years ahead	Log lowest decile income 10 years ahead	Change in log lowest decile income over future 10 years	Log median income 10 years ahead	Log median income 10 years ahead	Change in log median income over future 10 years	Log top decile income 10 years ahead	Log top decile income 10 years ahead	Change in log top decile income over future 10 years
State Ownership Component of the Fraser Institute Economic Freedom Index (high values imply more private, less state ownership)	0.195* (0.0548)	0.0556 (0.0367)	0.0776‡ (0.0433)	0.191* (0.0447)	0.0742* (0.0215)	0.0544† (0.0241)	0.129* (0.0323)	0.0793* (0.0194)	0.00169 (0.0120)
Constant	2.807* (0.383)	3.735* (0.243)	−0.272 (0.287)	4.102* (0.311)	4.878* (0.143)	−0.126 (0.160)	6.171* (0.231)	6.499* (0.129)	0.212* (0.0797)
Observations	517	517	517	517	517	514	517	517	517
R-squared	0.079	0.964	0.458	0.113	0.972	0.570	0.100	0.945	0.694
Notes	Clustered at country level	Clustered at country level; country fixed effects	Clustered at country level; country fixed effects	Clustered at country level	Clustered at country level; country fixed effects	Clustered at country level; country fixed effects	Clustered at country level	Clustered at country level; country fixed effects	Clustered at country level; country fixed effects

Note: * $p < 0.01$, † $p < 0.05$, ‡ $p < 0.1$. Unit of observation is a country-year. Robust standard errors in parentheses. Unbalanced panel. Earliest income data are from 1962. Income source: Rahul Lahoti, Arjun Jayadev, and Sanjay Reddy, "The Global Consumption and Income Project (GCIP): An Overview," *Journal of Globalization and Development* 7, no. 1 (June 2016): 61–108.

Columns 3, 6, and 9 use an alternative specification to examine whether today's level of state ownership affects the income growth of the various groups over the subsequent ten years. Country fixed effects are included to allow for different levels of development and other factors that might affect income growth directly. The effect of low state ownership on income growth is marginally positive for the lowest decile, positive for the median, and essentially zero for the highest decile.

The cross-country correlation between private ownership and income ten years in the future is positive and strong. It is also true that median income seems to rise over time within a country as the country moves toward more private ownership and less state ownership. The results are less clear-cut for bottom and top deciles within a country over time. The within-country intertemporal effects are less clear-cut for the lowest- and highest-decile incomes.

Income Variation and Other Measures of Economic Form

As described in the data section, a large number of measures might be construed as relating to capitalism and socialism. The measures tend to be highly correlated with one another, both within a given index compiler and for similar named measures across index compilers.[42] For example, the correlation between the WJP Rule of Law Index and the Fraser Institute's ratings for law and rights is .91. Already mentioned is that the Fraser Institute's summary measure correlates strongly with the Heritage Foundation Economic Freedom Index.

Neither the Fraser Institute's nor the Heritage Foundation's measure of economic freedom is a measure of capitalism or socialism per se, but the separately rated components tend to use metrics that are consistent with the dictionary definition of capitalism. The United States has a mean level as measured by the Fraser Institute over all years equal to 8.24. The corresponding value for the four Scandinavian countries is 7.5 and the mean across all countries is 6.54. The value for pre-1985 China was 3.59 and the value from 1985 on is 5.95. At least in relative terms, the report's ranking system seems to correspond closely to intuitive definitions of free-market capitalist and socialist economies.

Both the Fraser Institute and the Heritage Foundation "scores" are averages of all the individually rated components tracked by the organization. The Fraser Institute's rankings are based on all the subcomponents; but a regression of the index on the subcomponents reveals that variation in the summary measure is driven primarily by the ratings of state ownership, law and rights, and a limited regulatory environment. For the Heritage Foundation Index, the most important drivers are measurements of well-defined property rights (there is no Heritage ranking of state ownership, per se), low government spending, and a free monetary regime.

There is simply insufficient power to include every possible metric of free-market capitalism and socialism so some choices must be made. In this section, the summary measure provided by the Fraser Institute is used. It is chosen over the Heritage Foundation because it covers a longer period and appears to have higher explanatory power. Appendix table 4.A2 compares results from using the two sources. Qualitatively, conclusions are the same, independent of the choice between the Fraser Institute and Heritage Foundation data.

Table 4.2 shows a pattern that is very similar to that of table 4.1. Table 4.2 uses the same specifications as found in table 4.1 but simply replaces the state ownership ratings with the summary economic freedom rankings. The results with the summary measure are parallel—but stronger than—those found using the state ownership alone.

It is particularly important to look at effects today on income in the future as opposed to contemporaneous income when relating income to economic freedom. In this case, reverse causation is a potentially serious issue. It is reasonable that citizens of wealthier countries will demand more personal rights. As countries become wealthier, the demand for personal rights, reflected in the Fraser Institute economic freedom ranking, might well increase. Using the future value of income and relating that to changes that occur today is helpful in that regard. It is possible, but

Table 4.2. Income and Fraser Institute Economic Freedom Index

Variables	1 Log lowest decile income 10 years ahead	2 Log lowest decile income 10 years ahead	3 Change in log lowest decile income over future 10 years	4 Log median income 10 years ahead	5 Log median income 10 years ahead	6 Change in log median income over future 10 years	7 Log top decile income 10 years ahead	8 Log top decile income 10 years ahead	9 Change in log top decile income over future 10 years
Fraser Institute economic freedom index (higher implies more economic freedom)	0.718* (0.0724)	0.190* (0.0368)	0.124† (0.0604)	0.632* (0.0611)	0.186* (0.0292)	0.0752* (0.0273)	0.414* (0.0492)	0.141* (0.0412)	0.00392 (0.0280)
Constant	−0.525 (0.486)	2.968* (0.244)	−0.581 (0.400)	1.308* (0.417)	4.256* (0.193)	−0.271 (0.181)	4.378* (0.345)	6.185* (0.273)	0.159 (0.185)
Observations	433	433	433	433	433	431	433	433	433
R-squared	0.374	0.971	0.427	0.434	0.980	0.542	0.374	0.956	0.602
Notes	Clustered at country level	Clustered at country level; country fixed effects	Clustered at country level; country fixed effects	Clustered at country level	Clustered at country level; country fixed effects	Clustered at country level; country fixed effects	Clustered at country level	Clustered at country level; country fixed effects	Clustered at country level; country fixed effects

Note: * $p<0.01$, † $p<0.05$, ‡ $p<0.1$. Unit of observation is a country-year. Robust standard errors in parentheses. Unbalanced panel. Earliest income data are from 1962. Income source: Lahoti, Jayadev, and Reddy, "The Global Consumption and Income Project (GCIP)."

less likely, that changes in economic freedom occur in anticipation, but not yet the realization, of high income in the future. The country fixed effects regressions provide further comfort that other omitted characteristics are not driving the correlation between the economic freedom score and income.

Columns 2, 5, and 8, as well as 3, 6, and 9, of table 4.2 provide evidence on how within-country changes in freedom affect the incomes of various groups. Using the country fixed effect regressions of column 2, each change in the economic freedom ranking raises the income of the poor by .19 log points. In 2015, Mexico is the median country and Singapore is the most free according to the ranking. Changing freedom from the Mexico level to the Singapore level is predicted to raise the income of the poor by about 40 percent. All income groups benefit from the change, but the change typically helps the poor more than other income groups as reflected in the higher coefficient in column 2 than in column 8.

One additional measure of socialism was used: specifically, words in the country names that denote socialism. Not all socialist countries have names that indicate socialism, but some do, including the words "socialist," "democratic," or "people" in the country's name. A dummy was created for whether, at each point in time, the country self-declared itself as socialist by including one of these terms in its name. About 15 percent of the sample has a socialist name by this criterion. The levels regressions shown in table 4.2 with and without country fixed effects were repeated, but the economic freedom ranking was dropped and replaced by a dummy for having a socialist name. The results are shown in appendix table 4.A3. Having a socialist name is negatively associated with all income levels but, unsurprisingly, the existence of a socialist name is most pronounced on its relation to the highest-income group. The fixed effects regressions, which exploit within-country changes in the name over time, show an increase in income of .18 log points for the lowest decile and almost .49 log points for the highest decile when changing the name from socialist to nonsocialist, which happens thirty-nine times across countries and over time, or in the opposite direction, which happens eighteen times.

Rule of Law

Others, for example, Robert J. Barro, Robert E. Hall and Charles I. Jones, and Acemoglu and Robinson, have found a more complex relation of institutions to growth.[43] That literature is related to this research but not the same for two reasons. First, economic growth is not the same as income levels or growth and especially not the same as income of the lowest decile. Second, the literature concerns itself with a variety of institutions—for example, institutions formed under colonialism—and usually not the direct comparison of socialism and capitalism. Still, it is instructive to pay attention to the lessons of this sophisticated and extensive literature and to heed its findings. A primary finding is that the rule of law is a key determinant of growth.

Once again, there is nothing that precludes a socialist country from having the rule of law or guarantees that a capitalist country possesses or adheres closely to the rule of law. Chad in the 2000s, Guatemala in the 1980s, and Haiti and Madagascar now are characterized by high levels of private ownership, consistent with capitalism, but very low adherence to the rule of law as measured over time by the annual Fraser Institute rankings.

It is possible to provide some generalizations. One approach is to compare countries that self-declare themselves as socialist by having a socialist name to those without socialist names. The Fraser rankings and World Justice Project Rule of Law Index are negatively related to socialist names—statistically so in the case of the World Justice Project index. Additionally, the correlation between the Fraser Institute's low state ownership rankings and law and rights values is positive and statistically significant. Countries and periods that have less state ownership also rank higher in adherence to the rule of law.

Because of the attention the rule of law has received in the prior literature, it is treated separately from other indicators here. Unfortunately, there is almost no overlap between the income data and the World Justice Project index so only the Fraser Institute's law and rights measure is used. Table 4.3 contains the results of both the state ownership index used in table 4.1 and the Fraser Institute law and rights rankings.

Table 4.3. Income, State Ownership, and Rule of Law

Variables	1 Log lowest decile income 10 years ahead	2 Log lowest decile income 10 years ahead	3 Change in log lowest decile income over future 10 years	4 Log median income 10 years ahead	5 Log median income 10 years ahead	6 Change in log median income over future 10 years	7 Log top decile income 10 years ahead	8 Log top decile income 10 years ahead	9 Change in log top decile income over future 10 years
Rating of state ownership (high values imply more private, less state ownership)	0.0875† (0.0412)	0.0952* (0.0323)	0.103† (0.0422)	0.0899* (0.0309)	0.0904* (0.0204)	0.0663* (0.0222)	0.0424 (0.0327)	0.0704† (0.0269)	0.0101 (0.0244)
Index of strong legal system (high values imply better functioning system)	0.522* (0.0308)	0.0605† (0.0305)	0.0198 (0.0371)	0.438* (0.0246)	0.0480† (0.0240)	−0.0120 (0.0232)	0.271* (0.0224)	0.0372 (0.0249)	0.00596 (0.0273)
Constant	0.705† (0.351)	3.218* (0.269)	−0.587 (0.372)	2.418* (0.251)	4.586* (0.165)	−0.173 (0.160)	5.310* (0.285)	6.418* (0.237)	0.0837 (0.173)
Observations	438	438	438	438	438	436	438	438	438
R-squared	0.590	0.969	0.434	0.646	0.977	0.561	0.481	0.955	0.596
Notes	Clustered at country level	Clustered at country level; country fixed effects	Clustered at country level; country fixed effects	Clustered at country level	Clustered at country level; country fixed effects	Clustered at country level; country fixed effects	Clustered at country level	Clustered at country level; country fixed effects	Clustered at country level; country fixed effects

Note: * $p<0.01$, † $p<0.05$, ‡ $p<0.1$. Unit of observation is a country-year. Robust standard errors in parentheses. Unbalanced panel. Earliest income data are from 1962. Income source: Lahoti, Jayadev, and Reddy, "The Global Consumption and Income Project (GCIP)."

Interesting here is that when country fixed effects are excluded, the law and rights coefficient is very large and significant. But when country fixed effects are included, the coefficient shrinks and is sometimes insignificant, and the relative importance of state ownership increases. This suggests that reverse causation is an issue as it affects rule of law. Those countries that are wealthy demand more rights. There is, however, some support of causation running from rule of law to income growth found in the country fixed effects regressions in columns 2, 5, and 7. However, those results are not supported by specifications that examine changes in income over the subsequent ten years and relate that to rule of law today, which finds no effect. Decreases in state ownership are more closely associated with higher incomes ten years later than is the rule of law.

Transfers and Taxes

Some might define socialist economies as merely being those that have high levels of redistribution, meaning high taxes and transfers. This definition is most consistent with thinking of the Scandinavian countries as socialist. It is certainly true that the Scandinavian countries have higher taxes and transfers than non-Scandinavian countries over the period measured according to the Fraser Institute rankings. They are not alone. Other high-transfer countries include Belgium, France, Germany, and Austria, all countries that have values for other metrics of socialism, namely private ownership of capital, that are inconsistent with standard definitions of socialism. In each of these countries—Belgium, France, Germany, and Austria, plus the four Scandinavian countries (Denmark, Finland, Norway, and Sweden)—the state ownership and economic freedom rankings, where high values correspond to more private ownership and less state involvement, have above-country-average readings. Figure 4.3 shows that the Scandinavian countries all have low state ownership values (taken over the entire period) and high values of economic freedom. The values for Scandinavia look much more like those for the United States than they do for pre-1985 China or post-2000 Venezuela. At the same time, figure 4.4 shows that Scandinavian countries have low values for low top tax

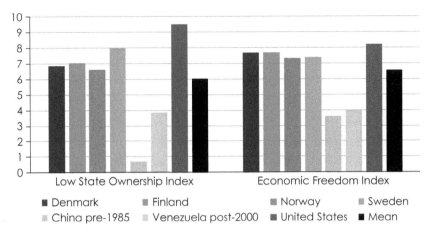

Figure 4.3. Low State Ownership and Economic Freedom Indexes.
Source: James Gwartney, Robert Lawson, Joshua Hall, and Ryan Murphy,
Economic Freedom of the World: 2019 Annual Report, Fraser Institute,
2019, http://www.fraserinstitute.org/studies/economic-freedom.

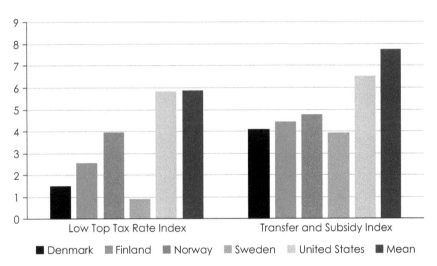

Figure 4.4. Low Top Tax Rate and Low Transfers and Subsidies Indexes.
Source: Gwartney, Lawson, Hall, and Murphy, *Economic Freedom of the
World: 2019.*

rate and on the low transfers and subsidies measures (again, taken over the entire period).[44] Perhaps a more accurate description of Scandinavia is that the countries rely primarily on private ownership and markets but have chosen to have a large government transfer program, which implies not only high transfers but also high taxes. Evidently, having private capital, rule of law, and other aspects of economic freedom is not inconsistent with having high levels of transfers and taxes.[45]

The relation of income to transfers and taxes is somewhat complex. Forces work in two directions, particularly as transfers for the lowest decile. For a given country at a point in time, increasing transfers to the poor must result in higher incomes (after transfers) among the poor, almost definitionally. In the long run, however, it is possible that the adverse general effects on the economy more than outweigh the effects of transfers and the poor end up worse off. This is investigated here.

Richer countries have higher transfers in general. The correlation between the average transfers ratings value for a given country (where a high value is a low transfer) and median income (averaged for a given country over the entire period) is -.70. Countries having the lowest transfers are Myanmar, Burkina Faso, Chad, Sierra Leone, Tanzania, and Swaziland, all of which are among the world's lowest-income countries. Countries having the highest transfers are Belgium, France, Austria, Germany, the Netherlands, and Sweden, all of which are high-income countries. The average level of the low transfer ratings for the poorest 20 percent of countries (as measured by average median income over all survey years) is 2.1 below that for nonpoor countries on a scale with an overall mean of 7.8. The ability to generate revenue and redistribute to the poor seems to be a luxury that only rich countries can afford or are willing to undertake.

Among high-income countries, defined as in the top quintile by median income, transfers tend to be positively related to income over time. For a given country, transfers tend to be low when those countries are poorest and high when those countries are richest.[46] Median income in countries that rank in the top half for transfers is about 2.5 times as high as median income in countries that rank in the bottom half for transfers.

With that in mind, table 4.4 presents some results that bear on the issue. Columns 1 through 3 examine the contemporaneous relation of income of the lowest decile, median, and highest decile to transfers as measured by the Fraser Institute's transfers and subsidies component. A high value corresponds to low transfers. The coefficients on transfers and subsidies are negative for all three groups, although the magnitude declines as income rises. Low-income individuals are helped more by transfers than are high-income individuals, which makes sense given that transfers are generally redistributive. The surprise is that high-income individuals are helped at all. It is possible that high-transfer countries transfer to all and simply tax at high rates to pay for it. Child care in Sweden is an example of this kind of subsidy. Although possible for some countries like those with generous benefits at all income levels, the interpretation of reverse causation is at least as plausible. High-income countries, as measured by income of the lowest-decile, median, or highest-decile individual, tend to engage more in large transfers and subsidies. The same pattern was observed before and is seen here again with respect to adherence to rule of law. Richer countries tend to demand more rule of law and also tend to have larger amounts of redistribution.

Columns 4, 5, and 6 report the same analysis but include country fixed effects. As before, the specification used relates values of the independent variables today to income ten years in the future. The results are similar across the three income groups but tend to be stronger for the top income group than for the bottom. Within a given country, low taxes today relate to higher income in the future. As reported above, stronger adherence to the rule of law today is associated with higher income in the future. The amount of transfer today does not relate to income of any group in the future. Because of the lag structure, the reverse causation running from income to the independent variables is less of a concern.

Table 4.4 implies that the poor benefit from higher transfers at a point in time.[47] That is the point, of course. Nor does it appear that transfers today have lasting effects on the economy independent of the taxes that are required to finance the transfers. It is possible that a transfer environment is so detrimental to work incentives that future income growth is

Table 4.4. Income, Transfers, and Taxes

Variables	1	2	3	4	5	6
	Log lowest decile income	Log median income	Log top decile income	Log lowest decile income 10 years ahead	Log median income 10 years ahead	Log top decile income 10 years ahead
Index of state ownership (high values imply more private, less state ownership)	0.0728† (0.0323)	0.0708† (0.0306)	0.0395 (0.0292)	0.0984† (0.0414)	0.0758† (0.0322)	0.0531 (0.0369)
Index of top marginal tax rate (high value implies lower top rate)	-0.0159 (0.0216)	0.000565 (0.0199)	0.00205 (0.0172)	0.0164 (0.0161)	0.0269† (0.0122)	0.0233† (0.0112)
Index of government transfers and subsidies (high value implies fewer transfers and subsidies)	-0.249* (0.0330)	-0.185* (0.0257)	-0.0683* (0.0196)	0.00677 (0.0307)	0.00239 (0.0259)	-0.0168 (0.0243)
Index of strong legal system (high values imply better functioning system)	0.370* (0.0497)	0.340* (0.0359)	0.248* (0.0291)	0.0361 (0.0326)	0.0241 (0.0228)	0.0331 (0.0231)
Constant	3.405* (0.493)	4.318* (0.390)	5.872* (0.353)	3.375* (0.415)	4.836* (0.300)	6.669* (0.312)
Observations	927	927	927	373	373	373
R-squared	0.724	0.741	0.546	0.975	0.982	0.965
Notes	Clustered at country level	Clustered at country level	Clustered at country level	Clustered at country level; country fixed effects	Clustered at country level; country fixed effects	Clustered at country level; country fixed effects

Note: * p<0.01, † p<0.05, ‡ p<0.1. Unit of observation is a country-year. Robust standard errors in parentheses. Unbalanced panel. Earliest income data are from 1962. Income source: Lahoti, Jayadev, and Reddy, "The Global Consumption and Income Project (GCIP)."

adversely affected. There is little evidence that the effect of transfers is adverse for any income group. However, high taxes generally go along with transfers, the correlation between the two being .37. It is also true, as columns 5 and 6 imply, that most income earners see lower future income when a country adopts high top tax rates today.

There is evidence elsewhere that having a larger government sector reduces growth.[48] This is true even for quite successful countries like Denmark and Finland during the past decade. To the extent that lower growth reduces the income of all, the poor of the future may be adversely affected by large transfers made to today's poor.

There is nothing that precludes a country that would be defined as capitalist by other measures from having significant transfers. For example, Germany is a high-transfer country, ranking fourth out of 150 countries in the transfer and subsidy rankings over all years and above all of the Scandinavian countries. Yet Germany ranks about as high as the United States, Japan, and Switzerland for lack of state ownership and an abundance of economic freedom. None of those three countries have high transfers given their income levels. The United States, Japan, Switzerland, and Germany have among the lowest values in the state ownership rankings and highest levels of economic freedom. Nor does a regression of the country-mean levels of the transfer rankings on median income, state ownership, and economic freedom index produce a significant coefficient for anything other than median income, the strong result being that richer countries have higher transfers. Some rich and otherwise capitalist countries, like the United States, have chosen low transfers and subsidies, while others, like Germany and the Scandinavian countries, have chosen high transfers and subsidies despite having economic freedom and state ownership levels that align them more closely with otherwise capitalist countries.

Income of the Poor and Inequality

The introduction made the point that China, and India to a lesser extent, have experienced large increases in inequality while at the same time witnessing dramatic growth in the incomes of a substantial fraction of the poor. Is this specific to those countries? Or is it generally the case that income growth among the poor is correlated, positively, with growing inequality? This seems unlikely because inequality is the difference between the (log) incomes of the rich and the poor so an exogenous shock to the income of the poor would seem to imply a reduction in inequality unless that same shock increased the incomes of the rich by more.[49]

It is possible that the general pattern resembles that of China, where growing inequality is also associated with growing incomes of the poor. It is also possible that the reverse is true and that China (and India) are anomalies. Although conceptually straightforward, this is a statistical challenge because any error that is incorporated into measurement of the income of the lowest decile will be reflected, negatively, in the measure of inequality since inequality is measured as log (income of top decile) minus the log of (income of bottom decile). Nor is there a ready instrument available to address this issue.

Instead, a more indirect approach is taken. Evidence has already been presented that bears on this question. Tables 4.1 and 4.2, in particular, provide estimates of what happens differentially to income when state ownership or economic freedom changes. The comparisons among columns 2, 5, and 8 and among 3, 6, and 9 show the relation of various groups' income to changes in metrics of socialism and capitalism within a country. There is no clear pattern one way or the other. Neither high-income nor low-income groups unambiguously benefit more from moving to less state ownership or more economic freedom. Inequality may be a consequence of some rapid development, as in the case of China, but as a general phenomenon, movements toward more capitalism as indicated by the two measurements do not clearly favor the rich over the poor or vice versa.

Table 4.5 relates income of the lowest and highest deciles to median income across countries and over time in columns 1 and 2 and within countries over time in columns 3 and 4, which include country fixed effects. Incomes of both the lowest and highest deciles tend to move with the median across countries and within countries over time. The movement of the lowest decile with the median tends to be greater than the movement of the highest decile with the median.

Table 4.5. Incomes Move Together

Variables	1 Log lowest decile income	2 Log top decile income	3 Log lowest decile income	4 Log top decile income	5 Log lowest decile income	6 Log lowest decile income
Log median income	1.145* (0.0280)	0.676* (0.0195)	1.047* (0.0519)	0.889* (0.0621)		
Log top decile income					1.233* (0.0715)	0.541* (0.0482)
Constant	-1.985* (0.139)	3.298* (0.115)	-1.481* (0.270)	2.191* (0.322)	-4.434* (0.496)	0.273 (0.328)
Observations	1,985	1,985	1,985	1,985	1,985	1,985
R-squared	0.911	0.782	0.966	0.947	0.617	0.931
Notes	Clustered at country level	Clustered at country level	Clustered at country level; country fixed effects	Clustered at country level; country fixed effects	Clustered at country level	Clustered at country level; country fixed effects

Note: * p<0.01, † p<0.05, ‡ p<0.1. Unit of observation is a country-year. Robust standard errors in parentheses. Unbalanced panel. Earliest income data are from 1962. Income source: Lahoti, Jayadev, and Reddy, "The Global Consumption and Income Project (GCIP)."

Columns 5 and 6 address whether incomes of the top and bottom deciles are complements or substitutes. It is clear that in both specifications, with and without fixed effects, the bottom tends to prosper when the top prospers.[50] It may be the case that the top can enhance its income at the expense of the bottom, but the data provide no support for that view. Columns 5 and 6 are more consistent with a rising tide lifting all boats, although not necessarily at the same rate.

Inequality and income growth are addressed directly in table 4.6. Column 1 simply regresses inequality (the difference in the log incomes of top decile and bottom decile) on median income and includes country fixed effects so that the focus is on within-country changes. The coefficient is negative, implying reduced inequality with income growth, but is not statistically significant. The second column uses an instrumental variables approach, forecasting the log of median income using a first stage that regresses log of median income on the Fraser Institute economic freedom rankings. The sign of the coefficient changes, but again the relationship is not statistically significant. Columns 3 and 4 repeat the exercise but use per capita GDP as the measure of economic growth rather than median income. The coefficients are positive but again not statistically significant. The message of table 4.6 is that there is no obvious, strong, and country-invariant relation of inequality to income growth over time. As will be shown in the next section, there are some countries where growth was accompanied by large increases in incomes of the poor but, at the same time, large increases in inequality.[51] There are other countries where substantial income growth occurred during the move from socialism to capitalism without much permanent change in inequality.

Transitions

Not all transitions are alike. Compare figure 4.5 to figure 4.2. In China, shown in figure 4.2, the transition toward a market economy was marked by almost uninterrupted upward progress in the income of the lowest decile. In contrast, figure 4.5 shows the average income in Soviet bloc countries during the 1980s and the 1990s transition to the market. Both the richest

Table 4.6. Income and Growth

Variables	1	2	3	4
	Difference between log 10th and log 1st decile income	Difference between log 10th and log 1st decile income IV	Difference between log 10th and log 1st decile income	Difference between log 10th and log 1st decile income
Log median income	−0.158 (0.108)			
Log median income predicted by economic freedom index		0.228 (0.314)		
Log GDP per capita			0.170 (0.109)	
Log GDP per capita predicted by economic freedom index				0.164 (0.226)
Constant	3.671* (0.563)	1.667 (1.704)	1.440 (0.951)	1.436 (2.022)
Observations	1,985	1,028	1,790	1,028
R-squared	0.803	0.905	0.832	0.905
Notes	Clustered at country level; country fixed effects	Clustered at country level; country fixed effects	Clustered at country level; country fixed effects	Clustered at country level; country fixed effects

Note: * $p<0.01$, † $p<0.05$, ‡ $p<0.1$. Unit of observation is a country-year. Robust standard errors in parentheses. Unbalanced panel. Earliest income data are from 1962. Income source: Lahofi, Jayadev, and Reddy, "The Global Consumption and Income Project (GCIP)."

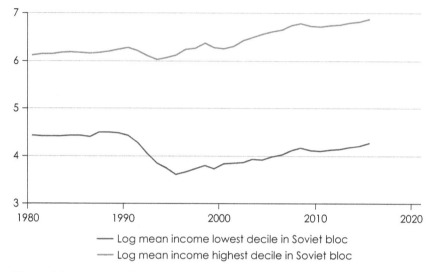

Figure 4.5. Income of the Highest and Lowest Deciles during the Soviet Bloc Transition. *Source:* Lahoti, Arjun, and Reddy, "The Global Consumption and Income Project (GCIP)."

and the poorest suffered substantial declines in income, but the lowest decile's fall was much larger than that of the highest decile. The Eastern European transition was particularly hard on the poor. There were a number of ways that this came about. One mechanism involved pensioners. In the late 1990s, Russia's finances were in ruins, which led to defaults and non-payment of pension obligations. Pensioners are creditors. They exchange their labor for current wages and a promise of future pension flows, which is implicitly a loan to the government. When Russia defaulted on creditors during its financial crisis, pensioners were among them, which imposed significant hardship as Penka Kovacheva and Xiaotong Niu document.[52]

Chile provides an interesting example of a transition from an elected socialist government to a market economy. Salvador Allende, a Marxist physician, became president in 1970 and was ousted in a military coup in 1973. He was succeeded by the controversial and eventually indicted Augusto Pinochet. Pinochet's economic advisers were University of Chicago–trained market-oriented economists (the "Chicago boys"). Inflation fell from over

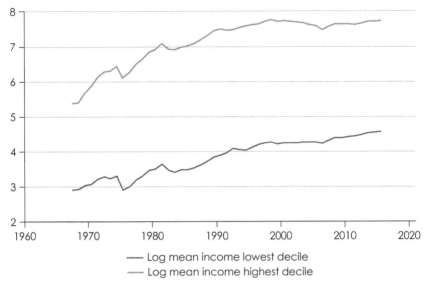

Figure 4.6. Income of the Highest and Lowest Deciles in Chile.
Source: Lahoti, Arjun, and Reddy, "The Global Consumption and
Income Project (GCIP)."

500 percent in Allende's last year to below 10 percent by 1981.[53] It is well
known that Chile had an extremely successful growth period with GDP
growth averaging over 5 percent annually from 1977 to 2000.[54] Figure 4.6
displays income growth for the lowest and highest deciles. There was a
transition period, immediately after the coup, where income for both
groups declined. That was reversed around 1977, and by 1978 income of
the lowest decile reached its previous peak.

Income declined again in the early 1980s but always remained above
1973 levels and then grew, virtually uninterrupted, throughout the following period. Inequality, measured as the difference in the log of top
decile income to the log of the bottom decile income, grew initially but
declined from the mid-1990s on. Inequality is now slightly greater than
it was during the Allende period. The difference in log of top and bottom
income deciles is 3.16 now and was 3.0 in 1972.

Chile's transition was more gradual than China's and inequality did
not rise very much during the transition, in contrast to the Chinese

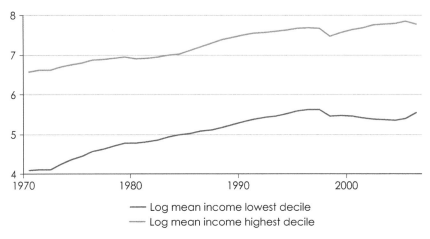

Figure 4.7. Income of the Highest and Lowest Deciles in the Republic of Korea. *Source:* Lahoti, Arjun, and Reddy, "The Global Consumption and Income Project (GCIP)."

situation, where the level of income of the poor rose dramatically but at a substantially lower rate than for the top decile. The rate of income growth of the poor during Chile's transition was about 60 percent as rapid as that of the poor in China. In Chile, however, the rate of growth of the upper decile was just slightly higher than that of the lowest, while in China, the top grew 65 percent faster than the bottom.

China, the Eastern European transition, and the Chilean experience mark moves from socialism toward capitalism, but not all transitions are of that form. Incomes in South Korea, a successful Asian tiger, grew dramatically in the late twentieth century as figure 4.7 shows. South Korea did not move from socialism to capitalism, but the nation improved its openness over time. The Fraser Institute now ranks its level of economic freedom ahead of Italy and about even with Sweden, Norway, and Austria. The score rose from 5.74 in 1970 to 7.59 in 2017. Much of this was driven by reforms that improved the business climate and provided incentives for investment and innovation.[55] Over the 1970 and 2007 period (the first and last survey years), median income rose almost fivefold. South Korea's inequality declined as economic freedom grew,

similar pattern exists with respect to rule of law. The contemporane-
relation of rule of law to income is strong, but this seems to reflect
fact that countries that are wealthy demand rule of law rather than
reverse. Low state ownership at a point in time is a more consistent
dictor of income growth within a country over the following decade
is rule of law at that same point in time.

inally, not all transitions are alike. The Eastern European countries
the former Soviet Union saw large transitory declines in incomes for
groups during their transition to the market and the poor were more
ersely affected than the rich. In China, and to a lesser extent India,
ket reforms brought about almost uninterrupted income growth.
ezuela provides an opposite example, moving from a more market-
nted economy to a socialist one. Inequality fell slightly, but income
wth was low for all groups and the poor have not regained the income
ls that they had at the peak during the 1990s. The evidence suggests
it is economic shocks rather than transitions that disproportionately
ct the poor. Transition from a command structure to the market is but
example of such a shock.

n sum, most income groups benefit from moves away from socialist
mand structures to free-market capitalism, but transfers can at least
he short run improve the well-being of those worst off.

and income inequality was somewhat lower in the last year than in the
first year of the survey period.

One feature that South Korea shares with the Soviet bloc economies
is worth noting. As figure 4.7 shows, the 1990s Asian financial crisis and
subsequent recession hurt the lowest decile more than it did the top decile
and it took longer for the poor to recover from that shock. This suggests
that it is not transitions per se but economic shocks that have adverse
consequences on the lowest-income earners, the Soviet bloc transition being but one example. This same phenomenon is commonly observed in
developed economies like the United States. During the recession that
followed the 2008 financial crisis, unemployment rates about tripled for
those with less than a high school education but only doubled for those
with college or more.[56] Chile's experience was similar. The mid-1980s was
a recession period. The lowest decile's income fell by more than that of the
upper decile's and recovery was slower for the lowest decile. Transitions
are more likely to be associated with shocks. But it appears to be the shock,
not the transition per se, that affects low-income earners most negatively.

Venezuela represents a transition, one of the few in recent times, that
goes in the other direction. Socialist Hugo Chavez was elected president in
February 1999. The country quickly launched into a regime of increased state
ownership and control, nationalizing major industries in oil, agriculture, finance, gold, steel, telecom, communications, and power.[57] Private ownership
declined from 5.9 in 1995 to 2.0 today as measured by the Fraser Institute's
rankings of state ownership while economic freedom fell from 4.3 to 2.6.
Chavez's stated goal was to bring about the democratization of Venezuela
and improve the conditions of the poor.[58] By the inequality measure, he
was slightly successful. The difference in the log of the top decile's income
and the log of bottom decile's income was 3.2 in 1999 and now is 2.8. But
income of the poor has not grown, as figure 4.8 shows. The transition under
Chavez brought declining income across the board and the poor suffered
more than the rich, again suggesting that shocks are borne disproportionately by low-income groups. The rise in oil prices in the late 2000s helped
Venezuelan income, but neither today's poor nor rich have reached the peak
level of income that they had attained in the 1990s. The poor are just slightly

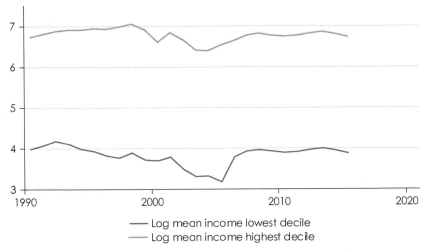

Figure 4.8. Income of the Highest and Lowest Deciles in Venezuela.
Source: Lahoti, Arjun, and Reddy, "The Global Consumption and Income Project (GCIP)."

better off than they were in 1998, just before Chavez took power, while the top decile's income today is 72 percent of what it was in 1998. Venezuela has succeeded in bringing income of the top group down but has not succeeded in bringing income of the bottom group up.

Conclusion

The past century witnessed transitions from capitalism to socialism and back again. The historical record provides evidence on how countries have fared under the two extreme systems as well as under intermediate cases, where countries adopt primarily private ownership and economic freedom but couple that with a large government sector and transfers. The general evidence suggests that both across countries and over time within a country, providing more economic freedom improves the incomes of all groups, including the lowest group. As countries liberalize their economic environment, incomes, including those of the lowest decile, grow. The

evidence supports the view that moves away from socialism ▮ free-market capitalism may affect the rich and poor differen▮ are some examples of this, the most important of which is ▮ the 1980s, where income of the poor rose dramatically, but in▮ rocketed at the same time.

The Chinese case is evidence that growing inequality do▮ falling incomes among the poor. Beyond China, there is gen▮ on the issue derived from many countries and over a number ▮ results of that analysis can be summarized.

First, there is no evidence that, as a general matter, high-in▮ benefit more from a move toward capitalism than low-incom▮ effect of changing state ownership and economic freedom ▮ is not larger for the rich than for the poor. Second, incon▮ positively correlated across deciles. The situation is closer to ▮ lifting all boats than to the fat man becoming fat by mak▮ man thin. Finally, there is no consistent evidence across the ▮ of countries and periods examined of any strong and wic▮ between income growth and inequality. There are example▮ where income growth was coupled with large increases in i▮ others like Chile, where strong income growth came about v▮ change in inequality, and South Korea, where inequality dec▮ as economic freedom and income grew over time.

Transfers and redistribution present the most complex p▮ involvement. Transfers from rich to poor through the tax▮ luxury that only rich countries seem to be able to afford ▮ product of socialism per se. There is a very high correlation ▮ between contemporaneous median income and the low-tra▮ across countries. High-transfer countries like those in Sc▮ other rich parts of Europe have primarily private ownership ▮ freedom more like what prevails in the United States th▮ countries. The poor definitely—and unsurprisingly—seem t▮ higher transfers at a point in time. But the high taxes tha▮ along with transfers do result in low income growth for ▮ high-income groups within a given country over time.

and income inequality was somewhat lower in the last year than in the first year of the survey period.

One feature that South Korea shares with the Soviet bloc economies is worth noting. As figure 4.7 shows, the 1990s Asian financial crisis and subsequent recession hurt the lowest decile more than it did the top decile and it took longer for the poor to recover from that shock. This suggests that it is not transitions per se but economic shocks that have adverse consequences on the lowest-income earners, the Soviet bloc transition being but one example. This same phenomenon is commonly observed in developed economies like the United States. During the recession that followed the 2008 financial crisis, unemployment rates about tripled for those with less than a high school education but only doubled for those with college or more.[56] Chile's experience was similar. The mid-1980s was a recession period. The lowest decile's income fell by more than that of the upper decile's and recovery was slower for the lowest decile. Transitions are more likely to be associated with shocks. But it appears to be the shock, not the transition per se, that affects low-income earners most negatively.

Venezuela represents a transition, one of the few in recent times, that goes in the other direction. Socialist Hugo Chavez was elected president in February 1999. The country quickly launched into a regime of increased state ownership and control, nationalizing major industries in oil, agriculture, finance, gold, steel, telecom, communications, and power.[57] Private ownership declined from 5.9 in 1995 to 2.0 today as measured by the Fraser Institute's rankings of state ownership while economic freedom fell from 4.3 to 2.6. Chavez's stated goal was to bring about the democratization of Venezuela and improve the conditions of the poor.[58] By the inequality measure, he was slightly successful. The difference in the log of the top decile's income and the log of bottom decile's income was 3.2 in 1999 and now is 2.8. But income of the poor has not grown, as figure 4.8 shows. The transition under Chavez brought declining income across the board and the poor suffered more than the rich, again suggesting that shocks are borne disproportionately by low-income groups. The rise in oil prices in the late 2000s helped Venezuelan income, but neither today's poor nor rich have reached the peak level of income that they had attained in the 1990s. The poor are just slightly

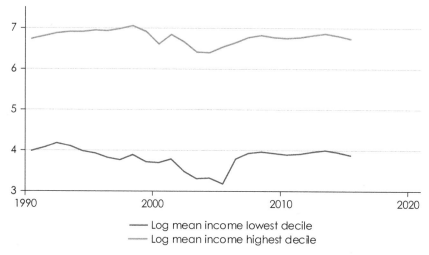

Figure 4.8. Income of the Highest and Lowest Deciles in Venezuela. *Source:* Lahoti, Arjun, and Reddy, "The Global Consumption and Income Project (GCIP)."

better off than they were in 1998, just before Chavez took power, while the top decile's income today is 72 percent of what it was in 1998. Venezuela has succeeded in bringing income of the top group down but has not succeeded in bringing income of the bottom group up.

Conclusion

The past century witnessed transitions from capitalism to socialism and back again. The historical record provides evidence on how countries have fared under the two extreme systems as well as under intermediate cases, where countries adopt primarily private ownership and economic freedom but couple that with a large government sector and transfers. The general evidence suggests that both across countries and over time within a country, providing more economic freedom improves the incomes of all groups, including the lowest group. As countries liberalize their economic environment, incomes, including those of the lowest decile, grow. The evidence supports the view that moves away from socialism and toward free-market capitalism may affect the rich and poor differentially. There are some examples of this, the most important of which is China since the 1980s, where income of the poor rose dramatically, but inequality skyrocketed at the same time.

The Chinese case is evidence that growing inequality does not imply falling incomes among the poor. Beyond China, there is general evidence on the issue derived from many countries and over a number of years. The results of that analysis can be summarized.

First, there is no evidence that, as a general matter, high-income groups benefit more from a move toward capitalism than low-income groups. The effect of changing state ownership and economic freedom on income is not larger for the rich than for the poor. Second, income growth is positively correlated across deciles. The situation is closer to a rising tide lifting all boats than to the fat man becoming fat by making the thin man thin. Finally, there is no consistent evidence across the large number of countries and periods examined of any strong and widespread link between income growth and inequality. There are examples, like China, where income growth was coupled with large increases in inequality, but others like Chile, where strong income growth came about without much change in inequality, and South Korea, where inequality declined slightly as economic freedom and income grew over time.

Transfers and redistribution present the most complex picture of state involvement. Transfers from rich to poor through the tax system are a luxury that only rich countries seem to be able to afford and are not a product of socialism per se. There is a very high correlation (-.67 in 2010) between contemporaneous median income and the low-transfer rankings across countries. High-transfer countries like those in Scandinavia and other rich parts of Europe have primarily private ownership and economic freedom more like what prevails in the United States than in socialist countries. The poor definitely—and unsurprisingly—seem to benefit from higher transfers at a point in time. But the high taxes that generally go along with transfers do result in low income growth for median- and high-income groups within a given country over time.

A similar pattern exists with respect to rule of law. The contemporaneous relation of rule of law to income is strong, but this seems to reflect the fact that countries that are wealthy demand rule of law rather than the reverse. Low state ownership at a point in time is a more consistent predictor of income growth within a country over the following decade than is rule of law at that same point in time.

Finally, not all transitions are alike. The Eastern European countries and the former Soviet Union saw large transitory declines in incomes for all groups during their transition to the market and the poor were more adversely affected than the rich. In China, and to a lesser extent India, market reforms brought about almost uninterrupted income growth. Venezuela provides an opposite example, moving from a more market-oriented economy to a socialist one. Inequality fell slightly, but income growth was low for all groups and the poor have not regained the income levels that they had at the peak during the 1990s. The evidence suggests that it is economic shocks rather than transitions that disproportionately affect the poor. Transition from a command structure to the market is but one example of such a shock.

In sum, most income groups benefit from moves away from socialist command structures to free-market capitalism, but transfers can at least in the short run improve the well-being of those worst off.

Appendix

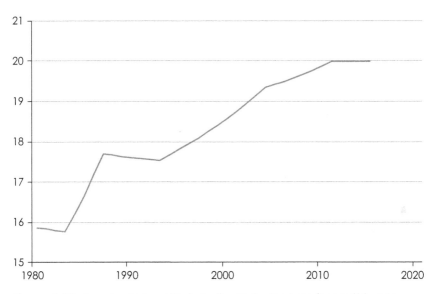

Figure 4.A1. Income Inequality in India. *Note:* Income is monthly per capita at 2005 PPPs (purchasing power parity). *Source:* Lahoti, Arjun, and Reddy, "The Global Consumption and Income Project (GCIP)."

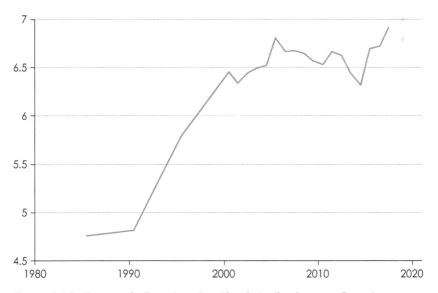

Figure 4.A2. Economic Freedom Ranking in India. *Source:* Gwartney, Lawson, Hall, and Murphy, *Economic Freedom of the World: 2019.*

Table 4.A1. Summary Statistics

Variables	N	mean	sd	min	max	Sources
Income						
Mean income of decile 1	8,805	80.72	131.8	0.282	1,293	Lahoti et al. (2016)
Median income	8,805	216.7	289.2	2.917	1,668	Lahoti et al. (2016)
Mean income	8,805	308.7	364.7	8.136	2,690	Lahoti et al. (2016)
Mean income of decile 10	8,805	1,068	1,812	16.90	27,312	Lahoti et al. (2016)
Log mean decile 1 income	8,805	3.282	1.568	-1.266	7.165	Lahoti et al. (2016)
Log median income	8,805	4.600	1.273	1.071	7.419	Lahoti et al. (2016)
Log mean income	8,805	5.149	1.088	2.096	7.897	Lahoti et al. (2016)
Log mean decile 10 income	8,805	6.436	0.993	2.827	10.22	Lahoti et al. (2016)
Log median income predicted from economic freedom index	3,132	5.361	0.201	4.569	5.807	Lahoti et al. (2016)
Log GDP per capita (2010 USD)	9,592	8.351	1.582	4.431	12.16	United Nations (2018)
Log GDP per capita predicted from economic freedom index (2010 USD)	3,132	8.861	0.279	7.761	9.481	United Nations (2018); Lahoti et al. (2016)
1-year change in log 1st decile income	8,644	0.0137	0.146	-2.697	3.183	Lahoti et al. (2016)
1-year change in log top decile income	8,644	0.0174	0.0971	-1.414	1.342	Lahoti et al. (2016)
Change in log 1st decile income over future 10-year period	7,225	0.120	0.493	-3.959	3.195	Lahoti et al. (2016)
Change in log median income over future 10-year period	7,210	0.149	0.351	-2.291	1.940	Lahoti et al. (2016)
Change in log top decile income over future 10-year period	7,225	0.170	0.346	-2.291	2.368	Lahoti et al. (2016)
Ratio of mean 10th decile earnings to mean 1st decile earnings	8,805	42.51	78.48	2.739	1,090	Lahoti et al. (2016)
Log top decile income minus log bottom decile income	8,805	3.154	1.048	1.008	6.994	Lahoti et al. (2016)

Economic Indexes

Economic freedom summary index	3,132	6.544	1.154	1.990	9.110	Fraser Institute (2018)
Mean of economic freedom index across years for a given country	8,863	6.526	0.891	4.105	8.828	Fraser Institute (2018)
Lack of state ownership of assets index	3,671	6.026	2.234	0	10	Fraser Institute (2018)
Average of state ownership index for a given country	9,233	6.057	1.834	1.548	9.512	Fraser Institute (2018)
Stronger legal system index	3,097	5.268	1.768	0.956	9.278	Fraser Institute (2018)
Lack of transfers and subsidies index	2,924	7.703	2.108	0	10	Fraser Institute (2018)
Average of transfers and subsidies index for a given country	8,707	7.817	1.956	2.893	9.965	Fraser Institute (2018)
Low top marginal tax rate index	2,806	5.849	2.635	0	10	Fraser Institute (2018)
Mean of low top marginal tax rate for a given country	9,183	6.003	2.101	0.896	10	Fraser Institute (2018)
Heritage economic freedom index	4,029	59.50	11.75	1	90.50	Heritage Foundation (2019)
Rule of law index (1 is highest)	633	0.565	0.141	0.280	0.900	World Justice Project (2019)
Global competitiveness index (1 is lowest, 7 is highest)	1,492	4.211	0.668	2.577	5.858	Schwab (2019)
Socialist name dummy (=1 if country has "people," "democratic," or "socialist" in name during year)	9,439	0.158	0.365	0	1	Wikipedia

Note: All income variables are per capita in monthly 2005 PPPs (purchasing power parity) unless otherwise indicated. *Sources:* Lahoti, Jayadev, and Reddy, "The Global Consumption and Income Project (GCIP)"; United Nations, National Accounts Data, 2018, https://unstats.un.org/unsd/nationalaccount/data .asp; Fraser Institute, *Economic Freedom of the World: 2018 Annual Report*, https://fraserinstitute.org/studies/economic-freedom-of-the-world-2018-annual -report; Heritage Foundation, *2019 Index of Economic Freedom*, https://www.heritage.org/index/about; World Justice Project, *WJP Rule of Law Index 2019*, https://worldjusticeproject.org/our-work/research-and-data/wjp-rule-of-law-index-2019; Klaus Schwab, ed., *The Global Competitiveness Report 2019* (Cologny/Geneva: World Economic Forum, 2019).

Table 4.A2. Income and Fraser Index versus Heritage Index of Economic Freedom

Variables	1 Log lowest decile income 10 years ahead	2 Log lowest decile income 10 years ahead	3 Log median income 10 years ahead	4 Log median income 10 years ahead	5 Log top decile income 10 years ahead	6 Log top decile income 10 years ahead
Fraser Institute economic freedom index (higher implies more economic freedom)	0.718* (0.0724)		0.632* (0.0611)		0.414* (0.0492)	
Heritage Foundation economic freedom index (higher implies more economic freedom)		0.0652* (0.0111)		0.0607* (0.00939)		0.0458* (0.00746)
Constant	0.525 (0.486)	0.190 (0.690)	1.308* (0.417)	1.739* (0.591)	4.378* (0.345)	4.293* (0.476)
Observations	433	642	433	642	433	642
R-squared	0.374	0.217	0.434	0.276	0.374	0.314
Notes	Clustered at country level	Clustered at country level	Clustered at country level	Clustered at country level	Clustered at country level	Clustered at country level

Note: * p<0.01, † p<0.05, ‡ p<0.1. Unit of observation is a country-year. Robust standard errors in parentheses. Unbalanced panel. Earliest income data are from 1962. Income source: Lahoti, Jayadev, and Reddy, "The Global Consumption and Income Project (GCIP)."

Table 4.A3. Income and Socialist Country Name

Variables	1	2	3	4	5	6
	Log lowest decile income 10 years ahead	Log lowest decile income 10 years ahead	Log median income 10 years ahead	Log median income 10 years ahead	Log top decile income 10 years ahead	Log top decile income 10 years ahead
Socialist name dummy (=1 if "people," "democratic," or "socialist" in country name in year i)	-0.227 (0.226)	-0.175† (0.0839)	-0.469* (0.177)	-0.294* (0.0729)	-0.806* (0.110)	-0.490* (0.0936)
Constant	4.023* (0.137)	4.015* (0.0133)	5.311* (0.114)	5.283* (0.0115)	6.999* (0.0799)	6.949* (0.0148)
Observations	1,347	1,347	1,347	1,347	1,347	1,347
R-squared	0.003	0.946	0.021	0.953	0.109	0.905
Notes	Clustered at country level	Clustered at country level; country fixed effects	Clustered at country level	Clustered at country level; country fixed effects	Clustered at country level	Clustered at country level; country fixed effects

Note: * p<0.01, † p<0.05, ‡ p<0.1. Unit of observation is a country-year. Robust standard errors in parentheses. Unbalanced panel. Earliest income data are from 1962. Income source: Lahoti, Jayadev, and Reddy, "The Global Consumption and Income Project (GCIP)."

NOTES

1. The Fraser Institute's economic freedom rating for India rises from 4.7 in the late 1980s to almost 7 in the most recent data. (Data over time available at http://www.fraserinstitute.org.)

2. Karl Marx, *Das Kapital* (Hamburg: Otto Meissner, 1867).

3. Schumpeter, who is known for his analyses of entrepreneurship and creative destruction, also believed that capitalism would fail because monopolies would prevent the entrepreneurship necessary to drive the capitalist economy. Joseph Schumpeter, *Capitalism, Socialism and Democracy* (New York: Harper and Brothers, 1942).

4. Thomas Piketty, *Capital in the Twenty-First Century* (Cambridge: Harvard University Press, 2014).

5. R. F. Harrod, "An Essay in Dynamic Theory," *Economic Journal* 49, no. 193 (March 1999): 14–33; Evsey D. Domar, "Capital Expansion, Rate of Growth, and Employment," *Econometrica* 14, no. 2 (April 1946): 137–47; Domar, "Expansion and Employment," *American Economic Review* 37, no. 1 (March 1947): 34–55; Robert M. Solow, "A Contribution to the Theory of Economic Growth," *Quarterly Journal of Economics* 70, no. 1 (February 1956): 65–94.

6. Most important is the point that the rate of return to capital has not exceeded the growth rate of the economy. Indeed, many (e.g., Summers; and Eggertsson, Mehrotra, and Summers) argue that the low real rate of interest is evidence of secular stagnation. Acemoglu and Robinson and Feldstein take issue with measures used and claim that the evidence used on wages and profits is either misleading or incorrect. Auten and Splinter dispute the findings on rising income share of the top 1 percent that Piketty and Saez reported. Lawrence H. Summers, "Demand Side Secular Stagnation," *American Economic Review* 105, no. 5 (May 2015): 60–65; Gauti B. Eggertsson, Neil R. Mehrotra, and Lawrence H. Summers, "Secular Stagnation in the Open Economy," *American Economic Review* 106, no. 5 (May 2016): 503–7; Daron Acemoglu and James A. Robinson, "The Rise and Decline of General Laws of Capitalism," *Journal of Economic Perspectives* 29, no. 1 (Winter 2015): 3–28; Martin Feldstein, "Piketty's Numbers Don't Add Up," *Wall Street Journal*, May 14, 2014; Gerald Auten and David Splinter, "Income Inequality in the United States: Using Tax Data to Measure Long-term Trends," http://davidsplinter.com/AutenSplinter-Tax_Data_and_Inequality_2017.pdf; Thomas Piketty and Emmanuel Saez, "Income Inequality in the United States, 1913–1998," *Quarterly Journal of Economics* 118, no. 1 (February 2003): 1–41.

7. Adam Smith, *The Wealth of Nations* (London: W. Strahan and T. Cadell, 1776).

8. Alfred Marshall, *Principles of Economics* (London: Macmillan, 1890).

9. Harvey Rosen, "Tax Illusion and the Labor Supply of Married Women," *Review of Economics and Statistics* 58, no. 2 (May 1976): 167–72.

10. Steven J. Davis and Magnus Henrekson, "Tax Effects on Work Activity, Industry Mix and Shadow Economy Size: Evidence from Rich-Country Comparisons," National Bureau of Economic Research Working Paper 10509, 2004.

11. Edward Prescott, "Why Do Americans Work So Much More Than Europeans?," National Bureau of Economic Research Working Paper 10316, 2004.

12. Barry Eichengreen, *The European Economy since 1945: Coordinated Capitalism and Beyond* (Princeton, NJ: Princeton University Press, 2008).

13. Richard Rogerson, "Understanding Differences in Hours Worked," *Review of Economic Dynamics* 9, no. 3 (July 2006): 365–409; Rogerson, "Taxation and Market Work: Is Scandinavia an Outlier?," *Economic Theory* 32, no. 1 (July 2007): 59–85.

14. Ludwig von Mises, "Die Wirtschaftsrechnung im sozialistischen Gemeinswesen," *Archiv für Sozialwissenschaft und Sozialpolitik* 47, no. 1 (April 1920): 86–121; Friedrich A. Hayek, "The Use of Knowledge in Society," *American Economic Review* 35, no. 4 (1945): 519–30.

15. Anthony Boardman and Aidan Vining, "Ownership and Performance in Competitive Environments: A Comparison of the Performance of Private, Mixed, and State-Owned Enterprises," *Journal of Law and Economics* 32, no. 1 (April 1989): 1–33.

16. Stephen Martin and David Parker, *The Impact of Privatization: Ownership and Corporate Performance in the United Kingdom* (London: Routledge, 1997).

17. Clifford Winston, *Last Exit: Privatization and Deregulation of the US Transportation System* (Washington, DC: Brookings Institution Press, 2010).

18. Arthur Comstock, Richard Kish, and Geraldo Vasconcellos, "The Post-Privatization Financial Performance of Former State-Owned Enterprises," *Journal of International Financial Markets, Institutions and Money* 13, no. 1 (February 2003): 19–37.

19. János Kornai, *From Socialism to Capitalism: Eight Essays* (Budapest: Central European University Press, 2008).

20. Nina Bandelj and Matthew C. Mahutga, "How Socio-Economic Change Shapes Income Inequality in Post-Socialist Europe," *Social Forces* 88, no. 5 (July 2010): 2133–61.

21. Abram Bergson, "Income Inequality under Soviet Socialism," *Journal of Economic Literature* 22, no. 3 (September 1984): 1052–99.

22. Daron Acemoglu, Suresh Naidu, Pascual Restrepo, and James A. Robinson, "Democracy, Redistribution, and Inequality," chapter 21 in *Handbook of Income Distribution*, vol. 2B, ed. Anthony B. Atkinson and François Bourguignon (Oxford/Amsterdam: Elsevier/North-Holland, 2015), 1855–1966.

23. Jonathan D. Ostry, Andrew Berg, and Charalambos G. Tsangarides, "Redistribution, Inequality, and Growth," International Monetary Fund, Staff Discussion Note, 2014.

24. Anna Stansbury and Lawrence H. Summers, "Productivity and Pay: Is the Link Broken?," National Bureau of Economic Research Working Paper 24165, 2017; Edward P. Lazear, "Productivity and Wages: Common Factors and Idiosyncracies Across Countries and Industries," National Bureau of Economic Research Working Paper 26428, 2019.

25. Daron Acemoglu and James A. Robinson, *Why Nations Fail: The Origins of Power, Prosperity, and Poverty* (New York: Crown Books, 2012).

26. Ladislav Rusmich and Stephen M. Sachs, *Lessons from the Failure of the Communist Economic System* (Lanham, MD: Lexington Books, 2004).

27. James Gwartney, Robert Lawson, Joshua Hall, and Ryan Murphy, *Economic Freedom of the World: 2019 Annual Report*, Fraser Institute, 2019, http://www.fraserinstitute.org/studies/economic-freedom.

28. Peter Nolan, *China's Rise, Russia's Fall: Politics, Economics and Planning in the Transition from Stalinism* (London: Palgrave Macmillan, 1995); Kellee S. Tsai, *Capitalism without Democracy: The Private Sector in Contemporary China* (Ithaca, NY: Cornell University Press, 2007); Xiaogang Wu and Donald Joseph Treiman, "Inequality and Equality under Chinese Socialism: The Hukou System and Intergenerational Occupational Mobility," *American Journal of Sociology* 113, no. 2 (September 2007).

29. Barth, Moene, and Willumsen argue that success hinges on a strong complementarity between Scandinavian nonmarket institutions and capitalist dynamics. Kumlin and Rothstein document the high level of social capital in Scandinavia and suggest that the welfare-state institutions have the ability to create as well as destroy social capital. Einhorn and Logue claim that Scandinavian firms are not disadvantaged by high tax burdens because, at the same time, they face low health insurance costs and benefit from a well-trained, flexible labor force. Erling Barth, Karl O. Moene, and Fredrik Willumsen, "The Scandinavian Model: An Interpretation," *Journal of Public Economics* 117 (2014): 60–72; Steffan Kumlin and Bo Rothstein, "Making and Breaking Social Capital: The Impact of Welfare-State Institutions," *Comparative Political Studies* 38, no. 4 (May 2005): 339–65; Eric S. Einhorn and

John Logue, "Can Welfare States Be Sustained in a Global Economy? Lessons from Scandinavia," *Political Science Quarterly* 125, no. 1 (Spring 2010): 1–29.

30. "Flexicurity" is a term coined in the 1990s by then Danish prime minister Poul Nyrup Rasmussen. It allows for employment flexibility, which gives employers rights to hire and fire freely but protects workers with training and generous benefits during periods of unemployment.

31. Scandinavian countries as defined here include Denmark, Finland, Norway, and Sweden. Some references to Scandinavia exclude Finland and some include Iceland, the latter having a population that is less than one-tenth of the smallest of the other four.

32. James Gwartney, Robert Lawson, and Joshua C. Hall, *Economic Freedom of the World: 2012 Annual Report.* Fraser Institute, 2012, http://www.fraserinstitute .org/studies/economic-freedom.

33. Organisation for Economic Co-operation and Development (OECD), "Revenue Statistics 2018," 2018, https://www.oecd.org/publications/revenue-statistics -2522770x.htm; "OECD Compendium of Productivity Indicators 2019," 2019, https:www.//oecd.org/sdd/productivity-stats/oecd-compendium-of-productivity -indicators-22252126.htm; OECD National Accounts Statistics (database), 2019, https://www.oecd.org/sdd/na.

34. Rahul Lahoti, Jayadev Arjun, and Sanjay Reddy, "The Global Consumption and Income Project (GCIP): An Overview," *Journal of Globalization and Development* 7, no. 1 (June 2016): 61–108.

35. One concern is that monetary indexes of income, even after adjusting for purchasing power parity, may not accurately reflect living standards. Jones and Klenow show the importance of including leisure time and life expectancy in adjusting real incomes. These adjustments are important cross-sectionally but are less likely to be important over a short time span within a country. Charles I. Jones and Peter J. Klenow, "Beyond GDP? Welfare Across Countries and Time," *American Economic Review* 106, no. 9 (September 2016): 2426–57.

36. Heritage Foundation, *2019 Index of Economic Freedom*, https://www.heritage .org/index/about.

37. Klaus Schwab, ed., *The Global Competitiveness Report 2019* (Cologny/Geneva: World Economic Forum, 2019).

38. World Justice Project, *WJP Rule of Law Index 2019*, https://worldjusticeproject .org/our-work/research-and-data/wjp-rule-law-index-2019.

39. The Fraser Institute creates the state ownership ratings based on data from the Varieties of Democracy project (V-Dem.net), which constructs a measure by having

a group of five or more experts with deep knowledge of a country and political institutions code responses to a particular question, in this case the degree to which the state directly owns or controls important sectors of the economy. Fraser's description of the state ownership variable follows: This component is based on ratings from the Varieties of Democracy (V-Dem) database on "State Ownership of the Economy," which "gauges the degree to which the state owns and controls capital (including land) in the industrial, agricultural, and service sectors. It does not measure the extent of government revenue and expenditure as a share of total output; indeed, it is quite common for states with expansive fiscal policies to exercise little direct control (and virtually no ownership) over the economy." The rating for this component is designed to mirror the actual distribution of the raw data but on a zero-to-10 scale. The rating is equal to (Vi-Vmin)/(Vmax-Vmin) multiplied by ten. The Vi is the country's state ownership score while the Vmax and Vmin were set at 2.5 standard deviations above and below the average, respectively. The 1990 data were used to derive the maximum and minimum values for this component. Countries with greater government ownership of assets get lower scores.

40. Giovarelli and Bledsoe report that approximately three-fourths of agriculture was privately owned in Poland during the Soviet-dominated period. Renee Giovarelli and David Bledsoe, *Land Reform in Eastern Europe: Western CIS, Transcaucuses, Balkans, and EU Accession Countries* (Seattle: Rural Development Institute, 2001).

41. Results are generally qualitatively similar when the dependent variables in columns 1, 2, 4, 5, 7, and 8 are replaced by their contemporaneous values.

42. See Fraser Institute, *Economic Freedom of the World: 2018 Annual Report*, https://www.fraserinstitute.org/studies/economic-freedom-of-the-world-2018-annual-report; and Heritage Foundation, *2019 Index of Economic Freedom*.

43. Robert J. Barro, "Economic Growth in a Cross Section of Countries," *Quarterly Journal of Economics* 106, no. 2 (May 1991): 407–43; Robert E. Hall and Charles I. Jones, "Why Do Some Countries Produce So Much More Output Per Worker Than Others?," *Quarterly Journal of Economics* 114, no. 1 (February 1999): 83–116; Acemoglu and Robinson, *Why Nations Fail*.

44. Data for top tax and transfers were not available for pre-1985 China. Venezuela and China are so much poorer than Scandinavia and the United States that they are not appropriate comparisons, as is discussed in the text.

45. To see the positive correlation between transfers and high taxes across OECD countries and over time, see Edward Lazear, "Government Spending Discourages Work," *Wall Street Journal*, February 26, 2018.

46. A regression of the low-transfer ranking on log of median income with country fixed effects for the richest quintile countries yields a negative and statistically significant coefficient.

47. Lazear, "Government Spending Discourages Work."

48. This result parallels that of Squire, who finds that countries with high levels of expenditure growth saw sharp declines in poverty head count. Similarly, Van de Walle for Indonesia and Hammer, Nabi, and Cercone for Malaysia find that allocating more resources to health and education has beneficial effects on the poor. Additionally, Nelson finds that for six wealthy countries, social insurance provided to the middle class also increases welfare of poorer deciles of the population. Lyn Squire, "Fighting Poverty," *American Economic Review* 83, no. 2 (May 1993): 377–82; Dominique van de Walle, "The Distribution of the Benefits from Social Services in Indonesia, 1978–87," World Bank Policy Research Working Paper 871, 1992; Jeffrey Hammer, Ijaz Nabi, and James Cercone, "Distributional Impact of Social Sector Expenditure in Malaysia," World Bank, 1992; Kenneth Nelson, "Mechanisms of Poverty Alleviation: Anti-Poverty Effects of Non-Means-Tested and Means-Tested Benefits in Five Welfare States," *Journal of European Social Policy* 14, no. 4 (November 2004): 371–90.

49. Some cross-country and cross-state analysis within the United States suggests that health and social problems are positively correlated with income inequality. See Richard G. Wilkinson and Kate E. Pickett, "Income Inequality and Social Dysfunction," *Annual Review of Sociology* 35 (2009): 493–511.

50. The coefficient being less than one in the fixed effects specification may be meaningful but also reflects measurement error that biases the coefficient toward zero.

51. This evidence is consistent with Bourguignon and Verdier's review, which concludes that there is no uncontroversial finding for or against the idea that equity and growth are complements. Berg and Ostry reach a contrary conclusion; they find that longer growth spells are associated with more equality in income. François Bourguignon and Thierry Verdier, "Can Redistribution Accelerate Growth and Development?," *Annual World Bank Conference on Development Economics* (2000): 26–28; Andrew G. Berg and Jonathan D. Ostry, *Inequality and Unsustainable Growth: Two Sides of the Same Coin?*, International Monetary Fund, Staff Discussion Note, 2011, www.imf.org

52. Penka Kovacheva and Xiaotong Niu, "The Mental Cost of Pension Loss: The Experience of Russia's Pensioners during Transition," in *Research in Labor Economics*, vol. 36, ed. Solomon W. Polachek and Konstantinos Tatsiramos (Bingley, UK: Emerald Publishing, 2012): 191–240.

53. Inflation.eu, "Inflation Chile 1981," 2019, https://inflation.eu/inflation-rates /chile/historic-inflation/cpi-inflation-chile-1981.aspx.

54. World Bank, "GDP Growth (annual %)—Chile," 2019, https://data.worldbank .org/indicator/NY.GDP.MKTP.KD.ZG?locations=CL.

55. Ana Maria Santacreu and Heting Zhu, "How Did South Korea's Economy Develop So Quickly?," *On the Economy* (blog), Federal Reserve Bank of St. Louis, March 20, 2018, https://www.stlouisfed.org/on-the-economy/2018/march/how -south-korea-economy-develop-quickly.

56. US Bureau of Labor Statistics, "Unemployment Rates for Persons 25 Years and Older by Educational Attainment," https://www.bls.gov/charts/employment -situation/unemployment-rates-for-persons-25-years-and-older-by-educational -attainment.htm.

57. Reuters, "Factbox: Venezuela's Nationalizations under Chavez," October 7, 2012, https://www.reuters.com/article/%20us-venezuela-election-nationaliza tions/factbox-%20venezuelas-nationalizations-under-%20chavez-idUSBRE 89701X20121008.

58. Jones reports Chavez's swearing-in statement: "I swear before God and my people that upon this moribund constitution I will drive forth the necessary democratic transformations so that the new republic will have a Magna Carta befitting these new times." Bart Jones, *Hugo! The Hugo Chavez Story from Mud Hut to Perpetual Revolution* (Hanover, NH: Steerforth, 2007).

5

Environmental Markets versus Environmental Socialism

Capturing Prosperity and Environmental Quality

Terry L. Anderson

It is hard to date the beginning of environmentalism. It might have started when the Reverend Thomas Malthus in 1798 penned *An Essay on the Principle of Population*. Therein he postulated that humans would continue to reproduce until the population demands exceed their ability to produce food, after which famine, disease, and pestilence would check population growth in a "Malthusian trap." His postulate continues to permeate environmental thinking. For example, in the 1970s, the Club of Rome, armed with data and computers, predicted precise years when we would reach the limits of the world's resources.[1] Their predictions of disaster for humankind called for regulations to restrict use and consumption of resources and thereby restrict economic progress.

Despite the fact that we have avoided the trap, this pessimism persists, cloaked in romantic views of nature without human beings. Henry David Thoreau's *Walden* provided a more romantic or transcendental view from his window and John Muir used wilderness as his environmental pulpit, but both were not sanguine about human beings' ability to respect and preserve nature. Aldo Leopold's *Sand County Almanac* continued the romantic tradition of the nineteenth century, calling for a "land ethic" to encourage resource stewardship.[2]

Malthus's ghost set the stage for modern environmental policies, emphasized in books such as Rachel Carson's *Silent Spring* and Paul Ehrlich's *The Population Bomb*.[3] Like earlier predictions, the books forecast famine, pestilence, and wild species endangerment if we did not limit population growth and resource use.

Both of these books paved the way for the environmental movement that gave us a regulatory alphabet soup—the WA (Wilderness Act, 1964), the CAA (Clean Air Act, 1970), the CWA (Clean Water Act, 1972), and the ESA (Endangered Species Act, 1973), to mention a few. This legislation is based on the premise that private individuals and companies will not be good environmental stewards, thus making command and control at the federal level necessary to ensure environmental quality. The classic example of the need for regulation, especially the Clean Water Act, was the Cuyahoga River fire in 1969, allegedly caused by chemicals in the water but actually resulting from a railroad spark that ignited logs and other debris that had accumulated at a trestle.

To be sure, some of the environmental regulations have had a positive effect on the environment. For example, endangered species such as the bald eagle are no longer routinely shot or poisoned, and populations of bald eagles have increased enough to reduce them from "endangered" to "least concern." Similarly, sulfur emissions have been reduced significantly to reduce the threat of acid rain.

The record of environmental regulation, however, is not an upward trend. To the contrary, many regulations—environmental, energy, trade, health and safety, and so on—have thwarted environmental and economic progress.[4] A book titled *Political Environmentalism: Going Behind the Green Curtain* documents several examples.[5] The Endangered Species Act has succeeded in protecting iconic species such as the grizzly bear, whales, and the bald eagle, but it has also made many species the enemy in a war of "shoot, shovel, and shut up." Recall the spotted owl that was the poster child of protectionists wanting to stop logging in the Pacific Northwest in the late 1990s. Listing the spotted owl as endangered virtually halted logging on almost all the nation's national forests, but it also stopped private forestland owners from wanting the owls on their property and it encouraged, because timber prices increased, more logging on private lands. Similarly, listing the red-cockaded woodpecker in the Southeast has led to harvesting pine trees at a younger age before they become old-growth trees suitable for woodpecker habitat.[6]

Fishery management focused on season, catch, and equipment regulations led to more intensive fishing during the season, greater bycatch (fish that weren't targeted for markets but were killed in the process), and fewer—but bigger and more efficient—boats. As a result, such regulated fisheries declined rather than improved.[7]

Finally, the century-old Jones Act, which prohibits foreign ships from carrying goods from one US port to another, has regulated US marine shipping in ways that have increased greenhouse gas emissions. The US commercial fleet is powered by far less efficient engines with higher emissions than less regulated foreign fleets. And, because of the reduced efficiency, it takes more ships to carry the same goods. As University of Chicago economist Casey Mulligan reports, "A sizable amount of the cargo that, without the Jones Act, would be shipped on coastal waters ends up on trucks congesting our highways and polluting our atmosphere, especially near large cities where many people live and breathe."[8]

Despite the detrimental effects of regulations and the gloom and doom from environmentalists, all the evidence suggests, as the Beatles song put it, "It's getting better all the time," and the improvement is closely linked to human ingenuity, prosperity, and economic growth. In response to "neo-Malthusians," the late Julian Simon was fond of saying, "With every mouth comes two hands and a mind." Harnessing the power of the hands and mind is the key to economic and environmental progress.

One of the more systematic analyses of the relationship between prosperity and the environment is the environmental sustainability index (ESI) developed by the joint effort of the World Economic Forum, the Yale University Center for Environmental Law and Policy, and the Columbia University Center for International Earth Science Information Network.[9] The group measured 145 nations based on twenty indicators and sixty-eight related variables in order to place a sustainability score on each nation. On the ESI scale for 2002, Finland came in first, with a score of 73.9, and Kuwait came in last, with a score of 23.9.

The most significant finding derived from the ESI study compares each nation's ESI score with its gross domestic product (GDP) per capita and shows that a strong positive relationship exists between wealth and environmental quality. The data follow the pattern of what economists call the environmental Kuznets curve, named after Nobel laureate Simon Kuznets.[10] Generally, environmental quality declines in the early stages of growth and then increases after a certain threshold, where the turning point varies with the environmental goods in question. As incomes rise people shift their focus from obtaining the basic necessities of life to other goods and services. For a person living at subsistence, setting aside land for wildlife or reducing carbon emissions to reduce the potential for global warming is unfathomable. With higher incomes, people demand cleaner water, cleaner air, and other ecosystem services. The higher demand for environmental amenities stimulates environmental entrepreneurship.[11]

More recent data on the ESI for 2015–17 show that environmental quality is rising for 114 of the 135 nations for which data are available and that the world median ESI is growing slightly. The United States experienced a year-on-year average growth rate of 2.39 percent for the period 2015 to 2017.[12] Lesotho had the highest year-on-year average growth rate at 21.56 percent.[13] And Uruguay had the lowest year-on-year average growth rate at −16.78 percent.[14]

Institutions Matter

Whether economic growth occurs and whether it is positively correlated with environmental quality depend mainly on the institutions—especially secure property rights and the rule of law—within each country. Economic growth creates the conditions for environmental improvement by raising the demand for improved environmental quality and makes the resources available for supplying it. Whether environmental quality improvements materialize or not, when, and how depend critically on government policies, social institutions, and the completeness and functioning of markets.

Institutions that promote democratic governments are a prerequisite for sustainable development and enhanced environmental quality. Where democracy dwells, constituencies for environmental protection can afford to exist without people fearing arrest or prosecution. The democratization of thirty-plus countries in the last thirty-five years has dramatically improved the prospects for environmental protection.[15] In the other direction, dictatorships and warlords burden people and environments in many regions of the world such as China and much of Africa.

Seth Norton calculated the statistical relationship between various freedom indexes and environmental improvements. His results show that institutions—especially property rights and the rule of law—are key to human well-being and environmental quality. Dividing a sample of countries into groups with low, medium, and high economic freedom and similar categories for the rule of law, Norton showed that, except for water pollution, countries with low economic freedom are worse off than the countries with moderate economic freedom. Moreover, countries with high economic freedom are better off in all cases than the countries with medium economic freedom. A similar pattern is evident for the rule-of-law measures.[16]

On the other hand, countries with lower freedom index scores, mainly founded on socialism, have less environmental quality and less prosperity. Consider Venezuela, one of the world's more repressed economies. It ranks only above North Korea in the Heritage Foundation's economic freedom index. It has one of the ten most biodiverse environments in the world and was a prosperous nation at the beginning of the twenty-first century. After decades of socialism, however, environmental quality has declined along with prosperity. Just how much the environment has deteriorated is difficult to say because the government restricts collection and dissemination of data. It has the third-highest deforestation rate in South America, sewage pollution in its water supplies, soil degradation, and urban pollution.

Venezuela's record follows that of its socialist guiding light, the former Soviet Union. The *Huffington Post* reported that attendees of the Sochi Olympics faced signs in hotel rooms telling them not to use the tap water "because it contains something very dangerous."[17] The condition of Sochi's water "is an example of the massive environmental degradation in the former Soviet Union that began in the 1920s when Joseph Stalin ordered industrialization at all costs to catch up with the West. An irony is that although the USSR took hundreds of thousands of environmental shortcuts while industrializing, it never did catch up."[18]

These two examples of socialistic, top-down control of the environment give credence to the saying, "No one washes a rental car." The antidote is private property and free markets, which explain why the exception to the rule of not washing rental cars is that rental car companies always wash the rental cars they own.

Free-Market Environmentalism

The connection between property rights and markets is the basis for the idea of "free-market environmentalism."[19] The combination of markets and property rights connects self-interest to resource stewardship by compelling resource owners to account for the costs and benefits of their actions and facilitate market transactions that create efficiency-enhancing gains from trade. To be sure, some people may act with enlightened self-interest if they are motivated by what Aldo Leopold called a land ethic.[20] However, good intentions are often not enough to produce good results, which is why Leopold, the pragmatic environmentalist, declared, "Conservation will ultimately boil down to rewarding the private landowner who conserves the public interest."[21]

Markets based on secure property rights provide a decentralized system for enhancing the value of resources. They generate information in the form of prices that gives demanders and suppliers objective measures of subjective values. Resource stewardship will occur as long as private owners are rewarded for the benefits they generate from resource use while being held accountable for any costs they create.

To be sure, governments play a critical role in clearly specifying and recording ownership claims, establishing liability rules, and adjudicating disputed property rights. That said, well-defined and enforced property rights impose discipline on resource owners by holding them accountable for the damage they do to others and rewarding them for improving resource use. Property rights incentivize owners to protect the value of their environmental assets.

Trade encourages owners to consider not only their own values in natural resource use decisions, but also the values of others who are willing to pay for the use of the resource. When rights are transferable in the marketplace, owners, be they individuals, corporations, nonprofit organizations, or communal groups, have an incentive to evaluate long-term trade-offs because their wealth is at stake. In short, property rights align self-interest with society's environmental interests.

Market forces based on demand and supply of environmental goods and services stimulate human ingenuity to find ways to cope with natural resource constraints. Producers improve productivity and find substitutes to conserve in the face of resource scarcity, while consumers reduce consumption and redirect their purchases in response to changing prices.

In addition to promoting gains from trade, free-market environmentalism embraces the free enterprise market system as a proven engine for economic growth, which, in turn, is an important driver of environmental quality. Since the fall of the Soviet Union, economists have devoted an untold number of pages and statistics showing the correlation between the institutions of free societies and economic development.

Moreover, the new technology and innovation that stimulate growth in other sectors can be applied to the environment, thus reducing the cost of producing environmental quality. For example, computer technology can be applied to transportation to improve fuel efficiency, reduce congestion, and decrease automobile emissions. Global positioning satellites and geographic information systems can better define land boundaries, track land use, and monitor water supplies.

Markets, like Mother Nature, hold no guarantees, but then no institution, private or public, does. Forces in the natural world are complex and therefore difficult to model and predict. Just when we think there is a pattern in nature, a volcano blows, sunspots erupt, or a fault slips, and the pattern is disrupted. Similarly, forces in the human world are complex and difficult to model and predict. When we think there is a pattern to consumption habits, preferences shift or nature changes resource scarcity, and the pattern is disrupted.

For the most part, the best that we humans can do is sense the changes in our surroundings and adapt to them. When the first human touched fire, she undoubtedly pulled her hand back and said to herself, "Don't do that again." Similarly, when whales were overharvested, leading to whale oil shortages, consumers and producers searched for substitutes and the first "oil boom" occurred. When the owner of a beachfront house realizes that waves are lapping at his doorstep, he wonders whether he should build a seawall or move farther from the beach. These are individual responses to what Friedrich Hayek called the "special circumstance of time and place."[22]

In assessing the success of any human response to these special circumstances, we must continually recall that nature and people are dynamic and ask whether and how people will respond. Throughout the history of the world, both nature and humans have shown remarkable resilience. As science writer Emma Marris puts it, we live in a "rambunctious garden" that seems to survive despite human action.[23]

This conclusion raises the question of whether human action can make the "rambunctious garden" even more "uncontrollably exuberant" (as the dictionary defines it). This requires an institutional system capable of determining what the human demands are for environmental goods and services and what natural capabilities there are for meeting them. Doing so requires getting the incentives right to collect information on both sides of the demand and supply equation.

The central theme of free-market environmentalism is that property rights and markets are institutions that do this. Property rights create incentives for owners to know what they have, know what environmental goods they can produce, and know what demands there are for environmental resources. Environmental markets create information on all these dimensions in the form of prices.

Between these two institutions—property rights and markets—are environmental entrepreneurs who reduce the frictions that economists call transaction costs. These "enviropreneurs" observe when natural conditions or human demands change, discover new environmental resources, see new opportunities for existing resources, discover demands for environmental goods, and find ways to get demanders to pay suppliers. All these entrepreneurial actions work best when property rights are well defined, enforced, and marketable. When they are not, institutional entrepreneurs have an incentive to create or improve upon the property rights to environmental assets.

If human action can be linked to our dynamic natural environment through property rights, markets, and prices, the rambunctious garden will not just survive, it will thrive. Free-market environmentalism offers optimism for future generations.

Environmental Markets at Work

Since the 1970s, when environmental regulations helped solve a myriad of environmental problems by picking the low-hanging fruit—stopping the killing of endangered species such as the bald eagle, designating over one hundred million acres of wilderness where not even pedal bikes are allowed, and restricting emissions into the air and water—environmentalists have begun looking for better ways to achieve environmental goals. As the Environmental Defense Fund's motto puts it, they are "finding the ways that work."

Environmental markets are one of those ways. From the early days when "free-market environmentalism" was considered an oxymoron, markets have proved an effective tool for environmental protection. Water markets have thrived, creating higher prices for water and encouraging conservation. Where water has a higher value left instream, environmental groups have negotiated with diverters—farmers and municipalities—to leave more water instream for fish and wildlife. By owning land or conservation easements that restrict land use, environmental groups such as the Nature Conservancy have been able to allow environmentally friendly energy production and protect grizzly bear habitat where there can be predation on livestock. Transferable fishing quotas have given fishermen a stake in ocean fishery management and efficiently improved fish stocks and allowable catches. Finally, emission trading programs for sulfur dioxide have virtually eliminated acid rain at far lower costs than regulatory mandates.

None of these examples are meant to say that markets can solve all environmental problems. Rather, they suggest how property rights incentivize owners to take account of the value of owned resources and the costs of using them in alternative ways.

Perhaps the hardest of all environmental issues to deal with using markets is climate change. The benefits of reducing the rise in global temperatures are diffuse across the world and across time, the benefits accrue over dozens or hundreds of years, and the costs accrue and are concentrated on companies that produce hydrocarbons and economies that depend on them. Couple this with the impossibility of defining and enforcing property rights to the atmosphere, and market solutions seem impossible.

That is why many economies resort to calls for "market-like" solutions that are really political solutions disguised as markets. A carbon tax is at the top of the list of these solutions. A governmentally imposed tax on carbon emissions equal to the social cost of carbon associated with global warming would encourage producers to reduce their use of hydrocarbons. Of the many problems associated with this solution, the difficulty of establishing the proper tax, the difficulty of enforcing it across nations, and the politics of distributing the tax proceeds make it a pipe dream.

The good news is that asset and financial markets are already responding to climate change. Increased rainfall raises the value of land for crops, lower snowfall reduces the value of ski resorts, and rising sea levels and storm surge lower the value of beachfront properties. The result is that asset owners and investors facing higher variance in their returns are adapting.

Even if the atmosphere is a greenhouse gas sink and greenhouse gas emissions themselves are not priced, prices correlated with the effects of climate change will induce adaptation. For example, if climate change reduces the productivity of land for certain wheat production, the price of land will be high relative to its productivity. This generates an incentive for wheat farmers to seek new places for wheat production where land prices are lower. Hence, the 2012 Bloomberg News headline "Corn Belt Shifts North with Climate as Kansas Crop Dies."[24] As Hoover Senior Fellow Edward Lazear puts it, "Economic incentives will induce people who are setting up new households, businesses, and farms to move to areas that are less severely harmed by warming temperatures."[25]

There is evidence that property owners who experience increased coastal flooding due to slowly rising sea levels are moving to higher ground. A paper in the journal of *Environmental Research Letters* by three Harvard University professors tested the hypothesis "that the rate of price appreciation of single-family properties in MDC [Miami-Dade County] is positively related to and correlated with incremental measures of higher elevation."[26] Using the value of 107,984 properties between 1971 and 2017, they found a positive relationship between price appreciation and elevation in 76 percent of the properties (82,068) in the sample.

A similar study by economists at the University of Colorado and Penn State found that beachfront homes in Miami exposed to rising sea levels sell at a 7 percent discount compared to properties with less exposure to coastal flooding.[27] Moreover, the discount has risen significantly over the past decade. Comparing rental rates to selling prices of coastal homes, they found that the discount in selling prices "does not exist in rental rates, indicating that this discount is due to expectations of future damage, not current property quality."

Though not armed with large datasets and sophisticated regressions, Massachusetts real estate agents are coming to the same conclusions. According to Jim McGue, a Quincy real estate agent, the nor'easter that "happened here in March [2018] certainly underscores what a 100-year flood map is all about." Another broker, Maureen Celata from Revere, said a home that included a private beach sold for 9 percent less than its list price of nearly $799,000 and took fifty-five days to sell, which she called an "eternity."[28]

Wine producers in California, Bordeaux, and Tuscany beware. A study by Conservation International published in the Proceedings of the National Academy of Sciences forecasts that wine production in California may drop by 70 percent and regions along the Mediterranean by as much as 85 percent over the next fifty years.[29] The silver lining is that vintners will adapt by moving their grape production north, some predicting it will even move to places such as Montana, Wyoming, and Michigan, noted for their severe winters.[30]

In the future you may also see more signs on fruit saying, "Country of Origin—Canada." Canadian biologist John Pedlar sees more people in southern Ontario "trying their hand at things like peaches a little farther north from where they have been trying." This is consistent with the US Department of Agriculture's Plant Hardiness Zone Map, which shows tolerant zones moving north.[31]

The conclusion is simple—property rights encourage prosperity and environmental stewardship.

NOTES

1. Donnela H. Meadows, Dennis L. Meadows, Jørgen Randers, and William W. Behrens III, *The Limits to Growth: A Report for the Club of Rome's Project on the Predicament of Mankind* (New York: Universe Books, 1962).

2. Aldo Leopold, *A Sand County Almanac: With Essays on Conservation from Round River* (New York: Oxford University Press, 1966).

3. Rachel Carson, *Silent Spring* (Boston: Houghton Mifflin, 1962); Paul Ehrlich, *The Population Bomb* (Cutchogue, NY: Buccaneer Books, 1968).

4. Terry L. Anderson and Donald R. Leal, *Free Market Environmentalism for the Next Generation* (New York: Palgrave Macmillan, 2015).

5. Terry L. Anderson, ed., *Political Environmentalism: Going Behind the Green Curtain* (Stanford, CA: Hoover Institution Press, 2000).

6. Dean Lueck and Jeffrey A. Michael, "Preemptive Habitat Destruction under the Endangered Species Act," *Journal of Law and Economics* 46, no. 1 (April 2003): 27–60.

7. Donald R. Leal, ed., *Evolving Property Rights in Marine Fisheries* (Lanham, MD: Rowman & Littlefield, 2005).

8. Casey Mulligan, "How the Maritime Industry Is Sunk by Prohibition," *Washington Times*, June 3, 2020.

9. World Bank, TCdata360, WEF Environmental Sustainability, https://tcdata 360.worldbank.org/indicators/tour.comp.env?country=BRA&indicator=3554 &viz=bar_chart&years=2017.

10. Tejvan Pettinger, "Environmental Kuznets Curve," *Economics Help* (blog), September 11, 2019, https://www.economicshelp.org/blog/14337/environment /environmental-kuznets-curve.

11. Bruce Yandle, Madhusudan Bhattarai, and Maya Vijayaraghavan, *Environmental Kuznets Curves: A Review of Findings, Methods, and Policy Implications*, Property and Environment Research Center Study 02-1, April 16, 2004.

12. World Bank, TCdata360, https://tcdata360.worldbank.org/countries/USA ?indicator=1541&countries=BRA&viz=line_chart&years=1970,2018&coun try=USA.

13. World Bank, TCdata360, Lesotho, https://tcdata360.worldbank.org/countries /LSO?indicator=1541&countries=BRA&viz=line_chart&years=1970,2018 &country=LSO.

14. World Bank, TCdata360, Uruguay, https://tcdata360.worldbank.org/countries /URY?indicator=1541&countries=BRA&viz=line_chart&years=1970,2018 &country=URY.

15. Asayehgn Desta, *Environmentally Sustainable Economic Development* (Westport, CT: Praeger, 1999).

16. Seth W. Norton, "Population Growth, Economic Freedom, and the Rule of Law," in *You Have to Admit It's Getting Better: From Economic Prosperity to Environmental Quality*, ed. Terry L. Anderson (Stanford, CA: Hoover Institution Press, 2004), 143–72.

17. "Sochi Hotel Warns Reporter to Not Let 'Very Dangerous' Water Touch Her Face," *Huffington Post,* February 5, 2014.

18. Armine Sahakyan, "The Grim Pollution Picture in the Former Soviet Union," *Huffington Post*, February 19, 2016.

19. Anderson and Leal, *Free Market Environmentalism*.

20. Leopold, *A Sand County Almanac*.

21. Aldo Leopold, "Conservation Economics," in *The River of the Mother of God and Other Essays by Aldo Leopold*, ed. Susan L. Flader and J. Baird Callicott (Madison: University of Wisconsin Press, 1934), 202.

22. Friedrich A. von Hayek, "The Use of Knowledge in Society," *American Economic Review*, 35, no. 4 (September 1945): 521.

23. Emma Marris, *Rambunctious Garden: Saving Nature in a Post-Wild World* (New York: Bloomsbury, 2011).

24. Alan Bjerga, "Corn Belt Shifts North with Climate as Kansas Crop Dies," *Bloomberg News*, October 15, 2012.

25. Edward P. Lazear, "The Climate Change Agenda Needs to Adapt to Reality," *Wall Street Journal*, September 2, 2014.

26. Jesse M. Keenan, Thomas Hill, and Anurag Gumber, "Climate Gentrification: From Theory to Empiricism in Miami-Dade County, Florida," *Environmental Research Letters*, April 23, 2018, https://iopscience.iop.org/article/10.1088/1748 -9326/aabb32.

27. Asaf Bernstein, Matthew Gustafson, and Ryan Lewis, "Disaster on the Horizon: The Price Effect of Sea Level Rise," *SSRN Electronic Journal*, May 3, 2018.

28. Katheleen Conti, "Homes Near Ocean Risk Losing Value, Even in a Hot Market," *Boston Globe*, April 23, 2018.

29. Lee Hannah, Patrick R. Roehrdanz, Makihiko Ikegami, Anderson V. Shepard, M. Rebecca Shaw, Gary Tabor, Lu Zhi, Pablo A. Marquet, and Robert J. Hijmans, "Climate Change, Wine, and Conservation," *Proceedings of the National Academy of Sciences*, April 23, 2013, https://doi.org/10.1073/pnas.1210127110.

30. Akshat Rathi, "The Improbable New Wine Countries That Climate Change Is Creating," *Quartz*, November 10, 2017.

31. Dan Charles, "Gardening Map of Warming U.S. Has Plant Zones Moving North," National Public Radio, January 26, 2012.

6

Leaving Socialism Behind

A Lesson from German History

Russell A. Berman

The well-known images of East Germans eagerly pouring into West Berlin on the night of November 9, 1989, have become symbols of the beginning of the end of the Cold War and, more specifically, evidence of the failure of Communist rule in the German Democratic Republic (GDR, or East Germany) and its socialist economic system. Yet that historic moment was only the final dramatic high point in the long history of dissatisfaction with living conditions in the eastern territory of Germany, first occupied by the Red Army during the defeat of Nazi Germany in 1945 and, four years later, established as the GDR when, in Winston Churchill's words, the Iron Curtain fell across the continent.

Between the formal political division of Germany in 1949 and the final hardening of the border with the construction of the Berlin Wall in 1961, a constant population flow from east to west took place, a movement away from Soviet-style socialism and toward Western capitalism. East Germans stopped voting with their feet only when the construction of the wall in Berlin made it impossible to leave; outside the capital, prohibitive barriers already had stretched across the whole country. Nonetheless, many continued to try to escape, and hundreds lost their lives, shot by border guards in brave attempts to "flee the republic," as the crime was cynically designated. To state the obvious: there are no similar accounts of throngs of westerners clamoring to enter East Germany. Between 1950 and 1989, the GDR's population decreased from 18.4 million to 16.4 million, while that of West Germany (the Federal Republic of Germany, or FRG) grew from 50 million to 62 million.[1] This tally is an indisputable judgment on the failure of socialism. The GDR system was unable to provide sufficient grounds to convince its population to remain willingly. Only the wall and the rifles of the border guards prevented East Germans from departing.

Several distinct, if interrelated, factors contributed to the economic limitations of the GDR. As noted, it emerged from the Soviet Occupation Zone, and the Soviet Union's treatment of its defeated wartime adversary was harsh. Extensive manufacturing capacity was systematically dismantled and moved to the Soviet Union, further undermining an industrial base already reduced through wartime destruction, although this phenomenon declined by the early 1950s. In contrast, West Germany was benefiting from the very different American occupation and the positive effects of the Marshall Plan. While the West German economy profited from access to the world economy, East German trade remained largely constrained to the Soviet bloc. In addition, from 1949 to 1961, the population flight to the west disproportionately involved middle-class and relatively wealthy East Germans, who took with them skill sets and amplifying capital flight. Each of these elements on its own arguably put East German economic performance at a relative disadvantage.

Yet in addition to these distinct factors, the primary difference between East German underperformance and the West German "economic miracle" involved the antithetical organization of the countries' economic systems and the philosophical assumptions underpinning them. Jaap Sleifer writes:

> The difference between the two systems may be characterized by the structure of ownership and the degree of centralization in decision-making. West Germany, as a capitalist country, mainly relies on private and individual ownership and control of the business enterprise, whereas in East Germany, as a socialist country, state

enterprises were predominant. Regarding the degree of centralization, capitalism provides wide areas of discretion for freedom of
individual choice, which leads to decentralization of economic decisions, whereas socialism shows a more centralized approach towards
economic decisions.[2]

The comparative performance of the East and West German economies therefore provides a nearly textbook case of the difference between
socialist and capitalist economic paradigms. To be sure, other factors
played a role, such as the countries' differing treatments by occupation
forces and the ongoing migration from east to west. Yet each of these
two potentially mitigating circumstances was also simultaneously symptomatic of the opposed economic systems: the East German economy
was disadvantaged precisely because the Soviet Union imposed its
model of socialist planning, while the brain drain (and capital drain) to
the west was a function of and response to the effects of the socialist
model. In contrast to the imposition of the Soviet model—a derivative
of the Marxist ideological legacy—in the GDR, the FRG benefited from
the free-market vision of thinkers such as Walter Eucken and Ludwig
Erhard, who steered it toward its successful model of a social market
economy: that is, a capitalist economy tempered by a social safety net and
restrictions on monopolies.

As a result, the contrast between East and West German economic
performance became a set piece in representations of the Cold War. In
1960, Bellikoth Raghunath Shenoy, a prominent classical economist
from India, provided a journalistic account of his visit to the city, not yet
divided by the wall, which includes these trenchant observations:

The main thoroughfares of West Berlin are nearly jammed with
prosperous looking automobile traffic, the German make of cars,
big and small, being much in evidence. Buses and trams dominate
the thoroughfares in East Berlin; other automobiles, generally old
and small cars, are in much smaller numbers than in West Berlin.
One notices cars parked in front of workers' quarters in West

Berlin. The phenomenon of workers owning cars, which West Berlin shares with the U.S.A. and many parts of Europe, is unknown in East Berlin. In contrast with what one sees in West Berlin, the buildings here are generally grey from neglect, the furnishings lack in brightness and quality, and the roads and pavements are shabby, somewhat as in our [Indian] cities.[3]

This description pertains to differences in productivity, consumer culture, and standards of living, but Shenoy also proceeds from these economic data points to more subjective and qualitative evaluations of the culture:

Visiting East Berlin gives the impression of visiting a prison camp. The people do not seem to feel free. In striking contrast with the cordiality of West Berliners, they show an unwillingness to talk to strangers, generally taking shelter behind the plea that they do not understand English. At frequent intervals one comes across on the pavements uniformed police and military strutting along. Apart from the white armed traffic police and the police in the routine patrol cars, uniformed men are rarely seen on West Berlin roads.[4]

Evidently more is at stake than contrasting consumer cultures or access to privately owned cars. East Berlin is, in Shenoy's view, symptomatic of a repressive society in which the inhabitants fear authority and shy away from contact with outsiders lest they draw attention to themselves. Hence his conclusion:

The main explanation lies in the divergent political systems. The people being the same, there is no difference in talent, technological skill and aspirations of the residents of the two parts of the city. In West Berlin efforts are spontaneous and self-directed by free men, under the urge to go ahead. In East Berlin effort is centrally directed by Communist planners. . . . The contrast in prosperity is convincing proof of the superiority of the forces of freedom over centralized planning.[5]

Today it is especially important to remember both objective economic differences between the two Germanys and these subjective experiences: that is, the dynamic excitement Shenoy felt in the west as opposed to the timidity of the east. Preserving these insights is vital because of current attempts to idealize socialism retrospectively by pointing to allegedly positive aspects of the East German performance. Although socialist-era statistics are notoriously unreliable, it is likely that East German standards of living were in fact consistently the highest in the Eastern bloc, that is, better than in the other satellite states and certainly superior to the Soviet Union. Yet that comparative claim hardly proves the success of GDR socialism, since the difference reflects a historic pattern: Germany long had been wealthier than its eastern neighbors. GDR standards of living also reflected the political pressure on East German leadership to attempt to keep up with the standard of living in the west, of which the East German population was well aware. This constant comparison with the Federal Republic is one unique feature of East German socialism; Poland never had to compete with a West Poland, or Hungary with a West Hungary. Yet artificially propping up the standard of living in East Germany contributed to the indebtedness of the state and its ultimate fragility, and in any case, the GDR's living standards never came close to matching what West Germans grew to expect. The GDR could afford less than the FRG; its per capita GDP has been measured at only 56 percent of GDP in the west.[6]

Nonetheless, one can hear apologists for the GDR and its socialist system argue that the East German state provided social goods such as extensive child care, correlating to a relatively higher degree of participation by women in the workforce. In post-unification debates, such features are sometimes taken as evidence of the positive accomplishments of the GDR. Yet in fact they represented instances of making a virtue out of necessity: in light of migration to the west and the dwindling population, raising labor force participation through the inclusion of women became unavoidable.

Such retrospective considerations of the notionally positive accomplishments of the GDR are, however, less a matter of substantive examinations of the socialist system than they are functions of rosy false memories in the context of post-unification reality. The past may look attractive to those who do not have to relive it. Yet there is in fact no evidence of any significant interest on the part of former GDR citizens in returning to the socialist regime. Of course, it is true that parts of the so-called Left Party (die Linke), an opposition party represented in the Bundestag, maintain some positive evaluation of the socialist past—which explains why that party to date has not been viewed as acceptable for participation in any governing coalition on the national level. A full-fledged endorsement of the socialist past is simply not an appealing political program in contemporary Germany. However, one can observe some dissatisfaction in the former East Germany with the character of the unification process for various reasons, including a perceived condescension on the part of West Germany. East Germans at times experience the western critique of the GDR as offensively triumphalist, and, worse, they believe that the western critique of the socialist system simultaneously belittles their own personal lives within the system. This dynamic can generate defensiveness on an individual level, but it rarely turns into a reactive identification with the former regime.

A further aspect affects the character of memories of the GDR. The abrupt transformation of life contexts through the unification of 1990, the economic disruption as East German enterprises collapsed, and the GDR's sudden integration into a West German and, more broadly, cosmopolitan world have produced the phenomenon of *Ostalgie*, a nostalgia for the east. Sometimes it is expressed merely as a yearning for the (few) consumer products of one's childhood, and sometimes it is a more complex psychological orientation toward a remembered youth in an allegedly simpler past. Such diffuse idealizations of the East German past follow a certain cultural logic, but they fall far short of any systematic program for a return to socialism, and they certainly do not include any positive evaluation of the repressive aspects of the system. Yet for just that reason, the repressive aspects—the role of the Stasi, the secret police, the extensive surveillance network, the lack of a free press—are minimized or absent in the *Ostalgie* discourse, which therefore evades undertaking a critical examination of the repression. The psychological appeal of *Ostalgie*—of succumbing to the glow of a wrongly remembered past—therefore can be instrumentalized by left-of-center politicians to conjure the illusion of a better past in order to advocate for statist policies in the present, such as the recent effort to impose an across-the-board rent freeze in Berlin.

Yet there is more to the German example than the familiar comparison of the FRG and its economic miracle on the one hand with the dismal track record of the GDR and its gray socialism on the other. As Shenoy points out, the alternative economic systems dovetail with political and cultural phenomena. Therefore, the failure of GDR socialism to establish its legitimacy by maintaining the loyalty of its population—who, given the chance, evidently would have largely decamped to the west—was a matter of economics but not only of economics. At stake is instead a broader infringement on human freedom that made life in the GDR undesirable. This broader perspective on quality of life within the German experience with socialism, which began well before the founding of the GDR, can tell us why socialism is incompatible with liberty and stands in the way of what, in the American tradition, is termed "the pursuit of happiness." It is not only in terms of material prosperity that socialism fails.

To understand this broader failure of the GDR's system, it is useful to explore its roots and the incompatibility of socialism and liberty at three pivotal moments in the history of German Communism, which also shed light on the substance of socialism internationally: (1) the origin of communist doctrine in the 1840s, when Karl Marx and Friedrich Engels jointly authored *The Communist Manifesto*; (2) the revolutionary moment at the end of World War I, when Kaiser Wilhelm was forced out and a republic was proclaimed in 1918 in Berlin, against the backdrop of the Russian Revolution; and (3) the end of World War II, when the GDR was established, as well as the first workers' uprising against the dictatorship in 1953. When East Germans fled to the west or when they took the first opportunity to visit after the wall opened, they were not only leaving behind an inefficient economy. They were leaving a dictatorship in order to encounter the opportunities that only a free society can offer. Socialism precludes that freedom.

The Roots of Socialist Repression in *The Communist Manifesto*

Communist politics played out in many countries during the twentieth century, but they have a particular relationship to the intellectual history of Germany, the land where the theory of socialism initially emerged. Its central thinker was Karl Marx, born in western Germany in the city of Trier in 1818. Initially a student of Hegelian philosophy, he began a career as a radical journalist and eventually spent much of his mature life in London, where he wrote *Das Kapital*. As Marx's worldview took shape during the 1830s and 1840s, he worked under the various influences of utopian thinkers in France and political economists in England, where the Industrial Revolution was in full force, well ahead of a still-backward Germany. Marx attempted to amalgamate these diverse sources within the framework of German idealist philosophy. For our purposes, however, what is crucial is that Marx, like others in his generation of young liberals and radicals, found a key historical point of reference in the French Revolution of 1789, which, so it was widely argued, amounted to a bourgeois or middle-class revolution that successfully ended the feudal ancien régime but was fundamentally insufficient. That first revolution therefore was expected to be followed by a second revolution, one that could surpass bourgeois civil society in order to replace it with an ultimately communist order. This worldview combined a teleological view of history (i.e., the assumption that society was moving toward an inevitable endpoint); an agonistic understanding of society as being always characterized by internal struggles or contradictions; and a deep suspicion of individual liberty, the specifically bourgeois legacy of the French Revolution.

These tenets generated the core Marxist narrative that the development of society must proceed through class struggle and requires the coercive elimination of individualism in the name of the collective good. This repressive outcome formed part of the socialist program from the start and cannot be attributed, as apologists sometimes do, to alleged misunderstandings of some pure core of socialism or to extrinsic factors that are said to have hindered a genuine and correct socialist order. With regard to the GDR, therefore, an evaluation of the dismal character of its social relations should not be explained away as consequences of competition from the west or the character of Soviet exploitation of East German productivity in the context of the Cold War. Such factors did, of course, contribute to the particular character of life in the GDR. Yet it was not these contextual elements that rendered the GDR a dictatorship. Its police-state character was no accident. On the contrary, the dictatorial outcome was integral to the program of socialist economics as it initially germinated in Marx's work, and then through subsequent ideologues, always involving an explicit mandate to suppress individuality and to restrict liberty.

Marx and Engels, coauthors of *The Communist Manifesto,* are explicit on this point, linking the abolition of private property, the attack on individualism, and the elimination of freedom as parts of a single, unified agenda: "The theory of the Communists may be summed up in the single sentence: Abolition of private property.... And the abolition of this state of things is called by the bourgeois, abolition of individuality and freedom! And rightly so. The abolition of bourgeois individuality, bourgeois independence, and bourgeois freedom is undoubtedly aimed at."[7] For Marx, the sort of freedom that developed in the wake of the French Revolution remained fundamentally flawed because it was "bourgeois" in several senses. It was a bourgeois freedom because it involved the rights of isolated individuals, defined by their separation from others rather than through their commonality. Furthermore, the immiserated population outside the middle class, the workers, was seen as having little access to, and frankly little interest in, such freedom; that is, it was a liberal rather than a democratic good. Finally, bourgeois freedom pertained only to civil and political society, with little or no ramifications on social and economic matters. Marx and Engels relied on a teleological world-view, based on Hegelian philosophy, that predicted that the progress of history would inevitably suppress this freedom because of its limitations and replace it with an emancipated and socialized society: ending bourgeois freedom was the precondition of socialism.

In a separate text from the same period, *The Poverty of Philosophy*, Marx used his characteristically predictive voice to claim that "the working class, in the course of its development, will substitute for the old civil society an association which will exclude classes and their antagonism, and there will be no more political power properly so called, since political power is precisely the official expression of antagonism in civil society."[8] For Marx, the heroic role of the working class had little to do with its economic disadvantage, its presumed impoverishment, which might be addressed through a different economic organization; rather, he assigned to it a world-historical mission of redeeming the world through the elimination of the bourgeoisie and all class distinctions. With the disappearance of distinctions, he foresaw the end of civil society, politics, or political power. It was this repressive agenda that was at the heart of the project rather than, for example, an amelioration of poverty.

The passage testifies to the political deficiency of Marx's theory in general: he made extensive room for philosophical speculation, and, in *Das Kapital*, he postulated laws of economic development, but rarely did he give consideration to a relatively autonomous political sphere in which citizens, members of a political community, could work through disputes and come to decisions. Such politics are at best, in Marxist terminology, epiphenomenal, merely secondary effects of underlying economic forces. Yet the elimination of politics means the end of distinctive institutions of governance; not, however, in the spirit of an anarchist paradigm—on the contrary, Marx would do polemical battle with anarchist competitors among late-nineteenth-century radicals—but because he foresaw and welcomed coercion and violence as alternatives to the political sphere of bourgeois civil society. Thus, for example, in a commentary on the anarchist Mikhail Bakunin, Marx emphatically endorsed the use of force against class enemies:

> So long as other classes continue to exist, the capitalist class in particular, the proletariat fights it (for with the coming of the proletariat to power, its enemies will not yet have disappeared, the old organization of society will not yet have disappeared), it must use measures of *force*, hence governmental measures; if it itself still remains a class and the economic conditions on which the class struggle and the existence of classes have not yet disappeared, they must be forcibly removed or transformed, and the process of their transformation must be forcibly accelerated.[9]

The statement is a chilling anticipation of what would take place in Russia—the extermination of Vladimir Lenin's and Joseph Stalin's various class enemies—and similar processes in the GDR, elsewhere in Eastern Europe, and in China today. The brutality with which groups would be "disappeared" demonstrates the centrality of violence to the socialist project. To evaluate the legacy of GDR socialism, one certainly may dwell on its relative inability to generate a successful consumer economy, but there is a much deeper and ominous current of violence that pulses through the socialist legacy. The failure of socialism was not only a matter of too few cars.

Criticism of Bolshevism from the Left: Rosa Luxemburg

A fascinating aspect of the history of labor radicalism is that some of the most trenchant criticism of repressive currents in socialism came from within the movement itself, from self-identified radicals with otherwise impeccably radical credentials. Pointing out the terror inherent in socialism is hardly a monopoly of anti-Communists on the right. Consider now the second moment in the history of German Communism: after *The Communist Manifesto*, written on the eve of the Revolution of 1848, which swept across Europe, we turn to early November 1918, the last weeks of

World War I, which came to an end as mutinies spread through the German military, igniting demonstrations and strikes in the cities to protest the continuation of a war effort many recognized as fruitless.

On the morning of November 9, the imminent abdication of Kaiser Wilhelm was announced, and that same afternoon two separate announcements of a parliamentary republic were made: one on a balcony of the Reichstag by the centrist Social Democrat Philipp Scheidemann, and the other, declaring a Soviet republic, by the leader of the far-left Spartacus Group, Karl Liebknecht, in front of the Royal Palace. These double declarations set the stage for subsequent violent conflict, especially in January, between the new, Social Democratic–led Weimar Republic and the Communists, who developed out of the Spartacus Group. Liebknecht founded the Communist Party in December together with the formidable writer and activist Rosa Luxemburg. On January 15, 1919, both Liebknecht and Luxemburg were arrested by right-wing paramilitary forces and murdered. As they were the assassinated founders of the party, their memories came to be honored throughout the history of German Communism, including during the four decades of the GDR. They were revered as symbolic martyrs to the cause.

Given Luxemburg's undisputed commitment to revolutionary radicalism, it is remarkable to read her text *The Russian Revolution*, published posthumously in 1922, a critical judgment by the leading German activist on the Bolshevik Revolution playing out contemporaneously in Russia. We find her expressing a stringent criticism of Bolshevik politics, especially of Lenin's and Leon Trotsky's decisions to suppress democracy and free speech. First, however, she cushions this criticism with remarks that repeatedly emphasize her admiration for the leaders of the Russian Revolution, her identification with their cause, and her own full commitment to a "proletarian revolution." Nowhere does she indicate any sympathy for the other political parties in Russia with which the Bolsheviks were competing. Her remarks firmly establish her partisan loyalties, which makes her subsequent critiques of the Communist leadership all the more stunning.

In fact, her claim to radicalism is amplified by some initial critical points, which position her to the left of even Lenin and Trotsky, more revolutionary than the revolutionary leaders themselves. She argues that their policy of distributing land to the peasants would eventually backfire and have the effect of expanding the principle of private property ownership, therefore increasing the power of antirevolutionary parties. Her programmatic alternative on this point would have involved expropriations of large estates and their transformation into state-owned—that is, socialist—enterprises. Similarly, she criticizes Lenin for his policy on those nationalities that had been included in the Russian Empire and his willingness to allow for their self-determination and potential departure. Here, too, Luxemburg foresees the potential for a counterrevolutionary consequence. In both cases, however, she stakes out a more radical stance, while criticizing Lenin and Trotsky for making opportunistic choices that may have seemed to serve the short-term purpose of winning political support but undermined long-term goals.

Given her flaunted radicalism, it is all the more surprising that she proceeds to criticize the Russian revolutionaries precisely for their curtailing of democracy and civil rights, including freedom of speech and opinion. In her account, every revolution depends on the expansion of democratic participation, not its limitation. Yet whenever the Bolsheviks saw democratic institutions opposing their program, they were prepared to suppress them. For Luxemburg, this antidemocratic inclination toward repressive strategies was characteristic of the Bolshevik tendencies in the Russian Revolution that she hoped to prevent from gaining a foothold in German Communism. (In fact, by the mid-1920s, most communist parties around the world had become "bolshevized"; i.e., brought under the influence of Moscow, and they participated in the same kind of internal repressive discipline.) She also regarded this tendency as ultimately inimical to the revolutionary enterprise. In her own words: "It is true that every democratic institution has its limitations and flaws, a feature shared with every human institution. But the solution that Lenin and Trotsky found—the elimination of democracy in general—is worse than the problem it is supposed to fix: it seals off the living source that alone can correct the congenital deficiencies of all institutions: the active, unhampered, and energetic political life of the broadest masses of the people."[10] Similarly, she accuses the Bolsheviks of "blocking off the source of political experience and development progress by their crushing of public life."

The passage makes Luxemburg's approach clear, especially her vitalism, which valorizes popular spontaneity against efforts by any party leadership to impose its will from above. For this reason, during the subsequent decades of communism, authoritarian orthodox Marxists often denounced popular initiatives "from below" as "Luxemburgist" threats to party rule. Luxemburg's achievement is to have recognized this inherent hostility toward freedom as constitutive of the Bolshevik position, despite her own de facto radicalism on a range of specific policy points. She articulates this understanding in the passage immediately following the initial citation with a clarion defense of free speech against authoritarian rule: "Freedom only for the supporters of a government, or only for the members of one party—no matter how many that may be—is not freedom. Freedom is always the freedom of those who think differently. Not because of the fanaticism of 'justice,' but because all the instructive, wholesome, and cleansing potential of political freedom depends on this feature, and it will be ineffective if 'freedom' becomes a privilege." Luxemburg's insistence on the importance of respect for "the freedom of those who think differently"—that is, for the freedom of the critic of the powers that be, the outsider, the freethinker—became the phrase with which she would be most often associated over the decades. Yet it is precisely her emphatic underscoring of the importance of this freedom *against* the Bolshevik leadership that indicates she had come to recognize the repression at the heart of the socialist revolution. Her insight into how socialism displays a predisposition toward extirpating freedom goes a long way toward understanding the anxiety and trepidation that Shenoy observed in the streets of East Berlin.

As one follows Luxemburg's argument, it is impossible to resist the conclusion that her dystopic predictions for the outcome of the bolshevization of the Russian Revolution presciently anticipate the dictatorial character of the Soviet-style socialism that came to prevail in East Germany. She begins with a rejection of what would become the priority of planning in the GDR: "The implicit precondition of the Lenin-Trotsky theory of dictatorship is that the revolutionary party has a finished recipe in its pocket for the socialist upheaval, and that one only needs to apply the recipe energetically: this is unfortunately, or rather fortunately, not the case." She explains that the standard socialist presumption of the capacity to plan with accuracy rests on an untenable epistemological dogmatism, the heir to Marx's non-fallibilistic claim to predictive capacity. Instead of the illusion that theory predicts history, she points to an alternative modality of knowledge, empirical experience and genuine events. "The socialist society can and must only be a historical product, born out of its own school of experience.... Only experience is capable of corrections and identifying new paths. Only unconstrained, effervescent life finds its way to thousands of new forms, and improvisations, shedding light on creative power and correcting all mistakes." For that reason, the importance of evidence based in experience, socialism cannot be simply "decreed by a dozen intellectuals." A robust democracy is required because it alone allows for the full participation of the population, which could bring with it the full richness of its own historical experience. Dictatorship by definition precludes that participation and therefore suffers from a knowledge deficit that necessarily prohibits the success of planned economies.

While Luxemburg invokes the image of a robust democracy perpetually incorporating new experience, the strength of her account lies in her ominously prescient worry concerning the character of political life that would develop in the Soviet Union and that would then be exported to its Eastern European satellites. The passage is worth citing at length because it anticipates with uncanny accuracy what would play out again and again in the subsequent decades of socialism, especially in Russia but throughout the Communist bloc, including in the GDR:

Without general elections, unlimited freedom of the press and assembly and a free competition of ideas, the life of public institutions withers away into a pseudo-life, in which bureaucracy is the only active element. Gradually public life falls asleep, while a few dozen party leaders, with inexhaustible energy and unlimited idealism, direct and rule, a dozen exceptional heads are truly in charge, and the elite of the working class is convened now and then at meetings, in order to applaud the leaders' speeches and unanimously approve the resolutions put forward: ultimately rule by a clique, a dictatorship, but instead of the dictatorship of the proletariat, the dictatorship of a handful of politicians, i.e., a dictatorship in the bourgeois sense, like the Jacobin dictatorship.... And more: such conditions must end up with a brutalization of public life: assassinations, executions of prisoners, and so forth.

Party Leadership, the Working Class, and the End of East German Socialism

The Communist Manifesto announced the program of ending civil liberties and eliminating enemies by force. Luxemburg watched that process play out in the early years of the communist revolution in Russia. The consequences in the GDR show how the failings of East German socialism went much deeper than bad economic results. Two pieces of literary and historical evidence testify to the indigenous flaws in the mind-set of the East European satellite countries and especially the GDR, where patterns of subordination, obsequiousness, and obedience worked against the disruptive capacities of individuality, creativity, and spontaneity that drive change and growth. Instead, the "really existing socialism," as it was labeled, entailed a systemic bias against the recognition of any signals that might allow for processes of auto-correction. Infallibility and determinism, hallmarks of socialist thought, systematically eliminate opportunities to undertake modifications on the basis of experience.

The first piece of symptomatic evidence is the poem "Song of the Party" (*Lied der Partei*), which became the anthem of the Socialist Unity Party, the official name of the ruling Communist Party of the GDR. (It was the "unity" party because it emerged from the forced unification of the Social Democrats with the Communists at the outset of the GDR, in a sense resolving the duality of the doubled announcement of a republic in November 1918.) The anthem was written by German-Czech Communist poet Louis Fürnberg. Before World War II, he was active as a journalist in Prague, fleeing when the Germans invaded. He was eventually apprehended by the Gestapo and tortured. Reportedly thanks to a bribe, he was able to escape through Italy to Palestine and after the war returned to Prague as well as to the GDR. Despite a prolific literary career, he is primarily remembered for this one song, written in 1949, and particularly for its repeated line that conveys the core message "the Party is always right." The refrain sums up the poem and provides an accurate description of the intellectual expectations of participants in the cultures of Soviet-style socialism:

The Party, the Party, it is always right!
And Comrades, may it stay that way;
For whoever fights for the right
Is always in the right.[11]

The original version even included some praise for Stalin, which was eliminated after 1961, but the substance of the poem did not change. It conveys an unironic insistence on absolute obedience to the organization, which in turn is regarded as all-defining for the existence of its members. Even worse, the song propagates a radical consequentialism: if one is fighting for the right, one is necessarily in the right; that is, the end justifies the means. No room remains for any ethical limitation on the instruments one employs to reach a goal. As a document of the psychology and values of GDR socialism, the "Song of the Party" helps considerably in understanding the widespread suppression of individuality: this was, after all, the party anthem, a sort of ethical catechism for party members and society as a whole. The problems with GDR socialism went far beyond the indisputable quantitative failings of the economy; Fürnberg's ethos, as expressed in the "Song of the Party," is exactly the opposite of the spontaneity that Luxemburg envisioned, but it gives clear expression to the desiccation of political life that she foresaw as a result of the essence of the Bolshevik program and the socialist enterprise.

In the summer of 1953, four years after Fürnberg wrote the song, the East German Central Committee declared an increase in production quotas in response to worsening economic conditions. The mandate involved an expectation that workers achieve 10 percent greater output for the same wage, while simultaneously facing price hikes for food and various services. Spontaneous protests erupted across the country, reaching a high point on June 17, 1953, with strikes in all major industrial areas. The Soviet occupation forces suppressed the uprising quickly, as protestors were shot and executions followed.

Poet and playwright Bertolt Brecht responded to the suppression of the 1953 uprising with a poem that has been repeatedly cited as an account of the mismatch between statist governance and democratic legitimation. Brecht, who had achieved world fame in the 1920s with his *Threepenny Opera*, had to flee Germany in 1933, after Hitler's accession to power, eventually traveling through Scandinavia and Russia and then sailing across the Pacific to reach Los Angeles, where he joined the large German exile community. After the war, Brecht returned to settle in East Berlin, one of the celebrated authors of the communist world. His bitter response to the suppression of the June 17 uprising is recorded in his poem "The Solution" (*Die Lösung*), in which he describes how the Communist writers' organization handed out flyers criticizing the workers for disappointing the government. He concludes with bitter irony and the laconic suggestion that the government should "dissolve the people and elect another."[12]

The poem captures what must have appeared to Brecht and many others as the absurdity of the socialist condition in East Germany, with the Communist government, allegedly the party of the proletariat, using violence against striking workers. More generally, the poem focuses attention on the distortion of political life inherent in the expectation that the people are obligated to win the confidence of the government, a complete inversion of normal democratic processes. In addition, Brecht's scene-setting reference to the role of "the Secretary of the Writers' Union" conveys both animosity toward the propagandistic instrumentalization of literature in the communist world and a subtle invocation of the labor issues at stake in the uprising, in which the official unions, normally the vehicle of workers' interests, failed to take action. Yet the overriding point of "The Solution" is the counterintuitive suggestion in the final quatrain, the darkly humorous contradiction of the government electing the people. (Brecht elsewhere builds part of his aesthetics around the notion of the "humor of contradiction.") In the final analysis, the poem corroborates the prediction in Luxemburg's critique of the Bolsheviks: the hollowing-out of democracy and the elimination of rights, consistent with Marx and Engels's animosity to "civil society" and merely bourgeois liberty, produces dictatorship as the defining feature of socialism.

Such was communist culture in the early years of the GDR. Yet later, just before the end of the socialist regime, matters had begun to change. There is evidence that servility and subordination were giving way to different personality types no longer consistent with authoritarian rule. In a fascinating document from November 21, 1988, less than one year before the opening of the Berlin Wall, the director of the Youth Institute, Walter Friedrich, composed an internal memorandum for Egon Krenz, at that point head of the official youth organization, the Freie Deutsche Jugend. (Between October and December 1989—around the time of the opening of the wall—Krenz would serve briefly as general secretary of the party.) In the report, Friedrich describes the emergence of a shift in attitudes, especially among the youth of the GDR. He points, for example, to "a shift in people's self-confidence to a higher level of self-esteem, a stronger sense of self-determination and self-fulfillment."[13] These greater aspirations for oneself, he goes on to explain, turn into a more critical and less obedient attitude toward social authority:

Sometimes this results in exaggerated anti-authoritarian behavioral patterns. The consequences are as follows: conflict with authority figures of all type (parents, teachers, self-righteous functionaries, and media or media actors who lack credibility and offer slogans rather than realistic information); rejection of the adulation of politicians, artists, athletes (unfortunately also [two-time Olympic gold-medal winner] Katarina Witt!), and other people; general rejection of all forms of know-it-all behavior and the cult of personality.

The consequences include expectations of greater freedom in personal lives and in relationships, such as "the demand for freedom in choosing a partner, and surely also the phenomenon of cohabitation and the high divorce rates here. The greater demands by women, especially younger ones, for self-determination should also be regarded from this perspective—right up to feminist postulates." He goes on to report on how changes in personality characteristics were also leading to greater engagement in organizations such as church groups and the environmental movement. Despite these significant shifts, Friedrich complained that the leadership of the country, the political leaders as well as the social scientists, were paying too little attention to these cultural-psychological developments, which were running against the established behavioral patterns for socialist society. A protest potential was growing.

One year later, the East Germans were pushing their way into West Berlin. The end of the socialist regime was approaching rapidly, although it was not immediately apparent to all. Even after the border opened, some continued to harbor illusions that the GDR might remain a separate state. Parts of the East German intelligentsia and cultural elite promoted this idea; after all, they had often benefited from relatively privileged positions in GDR society and continued to identify with aspects of socialist ideology, even if in a spirit of moderate reform. There were also a few voices in West Germany who were against unification, notably the 1999 Nobel Prize winner Günter Grass, author of *The Tin Drum*. For Grass, the division of Germany was punishment for the Holocaust, although none of the occupying powers ever justified the division of the country in those terms. This was solely Grass's perspective, but his argument implied that it was up to the population of the GDR, not the West Germans, to pay the price for the crimes of the Hitler era. (Later, in 2006, Grass's own World War II–era participation in the Waffen-SS came to light, a bizarre twist at the end of his long literary career.)

It was, however, in the voices of the demonstrators during the fall of 1989, especially in Leipzig, where a series of "Monday demonstrations" unfolded, and then in Berlin, that an important transition took place. The crowds expressed aspirations to end not only the dictatorship but also

eventually the division of Germany. Before the opening of the wall, in
October and early November, the demonstrators regularly chanted, "*Wir
sind das Volk*" (We are the people); that is, they asserted the democratic
claim on popular sovereignty against a regime that had never achieved legitimacy through a free election. "We are the people" was, in effect, a call
for a realization of the democracy that had been consistently denied due
to the dictatorial character of GDR socialism, precisely as Luxemburg
had predicted would develop out of Lenin's pattern of suppressing of
elections and civil rights: as in Russia, so too in Germany.

That democratic chant was, however, sometimes accompanied by another sentence: "*Wir sind ein Volk*" (We are one people). There is evidence
that this variant was initially intended as an appeal to the police and the
military to refrain from using force against the demonstrations. The historical setting is crucial for this understanding of the phrase: in the fall
of 1989, the events at Tiananmen Square in Beijing, where the Chinese
Communists used the military to attack demonstrators, were barely
three months old. The prospect that the GDR leadership might similarly
choose to use violence was plausible. It certainly had not shied away from
the use of force in 1953; it had used violence against people trying to
escape; and it might turn the military against the demonstrators, hence
the demonstrators' slogan.

Yet simultaneously there was a degree of semantic ambiguity in the
insistence on "*ein Volk*," a shared peoplehood. The terminology was also
taken to convey an assertion of a single German national identity, a protest against the division and therefore against the separate existence of
the GDR. There are also reports of demonstrators, as early as October,
carrying signs with the words "*Deutschland, einig Vaterland*" (Germany,
unified fatherland), a verse from the original East German national anthem, authored by poet Johannes R. Becher. Becher's text had been sung
regularly until 1973, when the GDR gave up on the political vision of
achieving unification with the west, and thereafter only the music of
the anthem was played and hummed without any singing of the lyrics,
which had grown politically obsolete. The reappearance of the verse in
October 1989 indicated that the prospect of ending the division of the

country had begun to circulate. After the opening of the wall, the call for "one people" spread rapidly, promoted by the Alliance for Germany, the East German partner of the Christian Democratic Union in the west.[14] The end of the GDR and its socialist system was rapidly approaching.

On October 3, 1990, East Germany—or, more precisely, the five *Länder* in the territory of East Germany—joined the Federal Republic, leading to the formation of a single German state and the end of the post–World War II division. Whether this unification was inevitable is now a matter of, at best, academic speculation. The West German constitution, or Basic Law, had always foreseen a unification, although unification had long ceased to be a realistic goal for West German politicians or public sentiment. On the contrary, during the 1970s and 1980s, a gradual accommodation to the division into two states had developed. Ultimately, the conditions for unification were arguably driven less by indigenous German developments than by global politics in the final decade of the Cold War, the pressure of the Reagan administration's arms buildup, and the reform initiatives unleashed by Mikhail Gorbachev. Without that larger context, especially Russian acquiescence, it is difficult to imagine the division of Germany coming to an end. Might the GDR have survived as an independent but post-socialist state? One could point to an inexact analogy, Austria, which, after its annexation into the Third Reich and its postwar four-power occupation, achieved national independence on conditions of neutrality in 1955. With some imagination, one could dig further into the past to posit an independent GDR as the heir to the long-gone kingdoms of Prussia and Saxony. Yet such musings are just implausible counter-histories. What one can instead say with certainty is that the specifically socialist character of the GDR—its poor economic performance and its constitutively repressive character that precluded political processes of democratic legitimation—made the continuity of an independent state deeply unappealing. In the end, the East Germans chose to abandon socialism in order to pursue greater prosperity and political freedom through integration into the liberal democracy and social market economy of the Federal Republic. There are few regrets.

NOTES

1. Jaap Sleifer, *Planning Ahead and Falling Behind: The East German Economy in Comparison with West Germany, 1936–2002* (Berlin: Akademie Verlag, 2006), 53.

2. Sleifer, *Planning Ahead and Falling Behind*, 18.

3. Bellikoth Raghunath Shenoy, "East and West Berlin: A Study in Free vs. Controlled Economy," *Indian Libertarian*, August 15, 1960, http://www.libertarianism.org /publications/essays/east-west-berlin-study-free-vs-controlled-economy.

4. Shenoy, "East and West Berlin."

5. Shenoy, "East and West Berlin."

6. Sleifer, *Planning Ahead*, 52.

7. Karl Marx and Friedrich Engels, *Manifesto of the Communist Party*, in *The Marx-Engels Reader*, 2nd ed., ed. Robert C. Tucker (New York: W. W. Norton, 1978), 484–85.

8. Marx and Engels, "The Coming Upheaval," from *The Poverty of Philosophy*, in *The Marx-Engels Reader*, 218–19.

9. Marx and Engels, "After the Revolution," in *The Marx-Engels Reader*, 542–43.

10. Rosa Luxemburg, *Die Russische Revolution*, in *Politische Schriften*, vol. 3 (Frankfurt am Main: Europäische Verlagsanstalt, 1968), 106–41, http://www.mlwerke.de /lu/lu3_106.htm. Translations of Luxemburg's writings are the author's own. Subsequent quotes are from the same text.

11. "Lied der Partei," YouTube, April 14, 2018, https://www.youtube.com/watch?v =865Sn8JrMvY. English lyrics are the author's translation.

12. Bertolt Brecht, "The Solution," 1953, https://www.poemhunter.com/poem/the -solution.

13. Walter Friedrich, "The Director of the Youth Institute Comments on the Progressive Alienation of the Youth of the GDR," German History in Documents and Images, November 21, 1988, http://germanhistorydocs.ghi-dc.org/sub _document.cfm?document_id=1178. Subsequent Friedrich quotes in this essay are drawn from the same source.

14. Vanessa Fischer, "Wir sind ein Volk: Geschichte eines deutschen Rufes," *Deutschlandfunk Kultur*, September 29, 2005, http://www.deutschlandfunkkultur .de/wir-sind-ein-volk.1001.de.html?dram:article_id=155887.

7

The China Model

Unexceptional Exceptionalism

Elizabeth Economy

At the 19th National Congress of the Chinese Communist Party (CCP) in October 2017, CCP general secretary Xi Jinping startled international observers by claiming that "the banner of socialism with Chinese characteristics is now flying high and proud for all to see ... blazing a new trail for other developing countries to achieve modernization. It offers a new option for other countries and nations who want to speed up their development while preserving their independence, and it offers Chinese wisdom and a Chinese approach to solving the problems facing humanity."[1]

Xi's assertion marked the first time since Mao Zedong that a Chinese leader had advanced the notion that the Chinese system was worthy of emulation. For his part, Mao preached about China's approach to revolution: building support among rural poor as the base for communist revolution in societies that lacked Marx's prerequisite of an industrial base and proletariat. Mao's own efforts to leapfrog the early stage of communism and economically surpass the United Kingdom by simultaneously developing agriculture and industry resulted in the Great Leap Forward campaign (1958–62) that devastated the Chinese economy and led to the death of an estimated twenty million Chinese from starvation.[2] And his notion of continuous revolution inspired the Cultural Revolution that convulsed the country politically and disrupted economic growth through the mid-1960s and early 1970s. At the time of Mao's death in 1976, per capita GDP stood at US$165.[3] This was an unremarkable increase from almost a quarter century earlier in 1952, when the country's GDP per capita stood at US$54.[4] China's abject poverty notwithstanding, Mao also provided material support for communist revolutionary efforts throughout the 1960s and 1970s in Kenya, Indonesia, Zimbabwe, Cambodia, and elsewhere.[5]

The death of Mao in 1976, however, marked an important inflection point in the conceptualization of China's development model. Maoist ideals of continuous revolution gave way to an overriding preference for stability. Mao's successor, Deng Xiaoping, advanced the notion of "socialism with Chinese characteristics," a vague descriptor that provided space for experimentation with a range of state-directed and market-based reforms. Every Chinese leader—beginning with Deng and continuing on to Jiang Zemin, Hu Jintao, and Xi Jinping—has sought to correct what he believed were the shortcomings of his predecessors. Most often, these efforts have involved enhancing or diminishing both the role of the state in the economy relative to the market and the openness of the economy to the outside world.

Xi Jinping's assertion that China has a model worthy of emulation raises several distinct questions. After more than four decades of "socialism with Chinese characteristics," is there a definable China model? Does it differ significantly from that of other countries? Does it provide substantially more social welfare benefits than other countries at a comparable level of GDP per capita? This paper reflects briefly on each of these issues and offers some preliminary thoughts to encourage further conversation and research. Before the world draws battle lines around the notion of a China model and the challenge it poses to market democracy, it is worth exploring the assumptions inherent in Xi's claims.

Mapping the Evolution of the China Model

In defining the Chinese economic model before a group of Japanese visitors in 1984, Chinese leader Deng Xiaoping argued:

Some people ask why we chose socialism. We answer that we had to, because capitalism would get China nowhere. If we had taken the capitalist road, we could not have put an end to the chaos in the country or done away with poverty and backwardness. That is why we have repeatedly declared that we shall adhere to Marxism and keep to the socialist road. But by Marxism we mean Marxism that is integrated with Chinese conditions, and by socialism we mean a socialism that is tailored to Chinese conditions and has a specifically Chinese character.[6]

Deng's stretching of the concepts of Marxism and socialism to include "Chinese conditions" and "Chinese character" provided the Chinese leadership with the ideological space necessary to experiment with different forms of state relations to the market and to society. Over the next forty years, "the China model" has never been static; instead, it has reflected long periods where the state has appeared to be in retreat, as well as those when the state is clearly assuming greater dominance in managing the economy and society.

Deng characterized his own approach as one of "reform and opening." He introduced market principles into the domestic economy and opened the country's economy to the outside world. In practical terms he moved to open the countryside, where 80 percent of all Chinese lived at the time, and to open large and medium-size coastal cities to foreign investment and "advanced techniques." Deng believed that China's economy had suffered most when it was closed to the rest of the world—both at the time of the Industrial Revolution and during Mao's tenure. He anticipated some difficulties in opening the country to foreign investment, but he argued that its benefits in accelerating Chinese economic development would outweigh the "slight risk" it might entail.[7]

The results of Deng's reform and opening were dramatic. In 1979–80, China opened four special economic zones (SEZs) in the southern coastal cities of Shenzhen, Zhuhai, Shantou, and Xiamen. The Chinese government permitted these regions to reduce corporate income tax for foreign investors who set up joint ventures in a bid to gain access to foreign capital, technology, know-how, and earnings. In 1981, the four zones accounted for 59.8 percent of total foreign direct investment (FDI) in China. From 1980 to 1984, Shenzhen grew at an annual rate of 58 percent, Zhuhai at 32 percent, Xiamen at 13 percent, and Shantou at 9 percent; the country overall averaged 10 percent.[8]

These zones were not without their detractors. Politically conservative leaders such as Chen Yun believed that the zones resembled concession zones granted to foreign powers during China's "century of humiliation."[9] There was concern that foreign investment would lead to China "being exploited, having sovereignty undermined, or suffering an insult."[10] In 1982, these officials launched a "strike hard" campaign that targeted economic crimes related to the SEZs.[11] The economic success of the SEZs, however, was indisputable. In 1983, Premier Zhao Ziyang reaffirmed their importance: "Special Economic Zones are not being developed for solving the employment problem, nor should they go solely after increases in output. Rather they are areas demarcated for attracting enterprises of high technological and knowledge content through the offer of preferential treatment. They are to serve as windows of advanced production technology and management methods of the world."[12] And during 1984–85, China established fourteen additional "open coastal cities" or "open economic zones."[13]

Deng's opening in the agricultural sector began with the Household Responsibility System. Arguably an even more important contributor than the SEZs to China's dramatic growth in the early 1980s, this reform allowed families in collectivized communes to divide land among themselves, establish contracts to lease their land, and keep their excess crops to sell on the market. By 1984, 98 percent of rural households had joined this system. Agricultural productivity skyrocketed and the average income of farm households increased by 166 percent. The country's GDP growth reflected the shift, jumping from 8.9 percent in 1982 to 15.1 percent in 1984.[14]

Elements of competition and free enterprise entered the Chinese economy in myriad other forms as well. Universities reintroduced competitive exams for entrance, abandoning the Maoist emphasis on political rectitude and class background. Importantly, in 1984, as Yasheng Huang has explained, Beijing redefined township and village enterprises, which had traditionally been the provenance of communes and then local governments, to include firms established by peasants and individual entrepreneurs.[15] The government legalized entrepreneurs, and small-scale township and village enterprises that manufactured chemicals, textiles, and low-cost goods for export rapidly began to populate rural communities, serving as important engines of employment and economic growth. As Barry Naughton has described, the period of the 1980s was one of "reforms without losers." The reforms were designed to give the Chinese people the opportunity to "act entrepreneurially and meet market demands" through "pockets of unregulated and lightly taxed activity."[16]

China Takes Flight

Deng's successor Jiang Zemin continued down the path Deng had set out. Like Deng, he advocated that remuneration should be "according to one's work" and that the country must "allow and encourage some areas and individuals to grow rich first, so that more and more areas and individuals will do so until common prosperity is eventually achieved."[17] Jiang also reinforced the notion that the country's economic progress would benefit by welcoming talented individuals no matter their class background—a factor that had prevented many talented individuals from advancing in society post-1949. In a February 2000 speech in Guangdong province, he announced the "Three Represents," which, among other things, were designed to ensure that the CCP opened its door to private entrepreneurs.[18] In a bold statement at the 16th Party Congress in 2002, he called on the party to avoid "scrutinizing individuals' pasts" and advocated: "We must respect work, knowledge, competition, people, and creation." He further identified "entrepreneurs, managers, overseas funded enterprise employees and freelance professionals" as "all builders of socialism with Chinese characteristics."[19]

Together, Jiang Zemin and Premier Zhu Rongji also adopted several measures that enhanced the role of the market in the Chinese economy. First, they opened the country further to foreign investment. By the mid-1990s, China was second only to the United States in inbound FDI and had become one of the top ten trading countries in the world.[20] In 2001, they effected China's accession to the World Trade Organization (WTO). As China's chief global trade negotiator Long Yongtu stated, "Countries with planned economies have never participated in economic globalization. China's economy must become a market economy in order to become part of the global economic system, as well as to effectively participate in the economic globalization process."[21] Underpinning the decision to join the WTO was in part the Chinese leaders' realization that the country's large state-owned firms resembled those of the Soviet Union: they were inefficient, losing money, burdened with substantial pension and social welfare obligations, and producing substandard goods.[22] WTO accession produced a dramatic shift in China's economy. The number of state-owned enterprises (SOEs) fell from 2,024 to 476.[23] The value of China's exports accelerated sharply from the period preceding WTO accession: from $195 billion in 1999 to $593 billion in 2004.[24]

Jiang, who took the helm of the CCP in the aftermath of the 1989 Tiananmen Square massacre, also oversaw a gradual reopening of the political system beginning in the mid-1990s, adopting a motto of "small government, big society."[25] The government allowed Chinese citizens to establish nongovernmental organizations to help address issues such as environmental protection, the education of migrant children, and poverty alleviation.[26] Journals, such as the *Hundred Year Tide*, published articles lauding the 1980s political reformer Hu Yaobang and blaming the Korean War on North Korean aggression as opposed to US imperialism. And some CCP members openly called for political reform, arguing, "China is successful in economic reform, but at a certain stage, it needs the corresponding political reform. The economic rules demand the reform of the political system."[27]

Reevaluating the China Model

In his 2008 speech marking the thirtieth anniversary of Deng's period of reform and opening, CCP general secretary and president Hu Jintao uttered the phrase *bu zheteng* (don't rock the boat). It was a fair characterization of his tenure as China's leader (2002–12). Hu shut the door on the preceding era of bold economic reform. As Carl Minzner details, "After a bout of reform in the 1990s, a silent counterrevolution had occurred in which state-owned enterprises saw their financial and political privileges reconfirmed. By 2006, Beijing was openly promulgating policies to help state-owned national champions compete with the foreign firms that had arrived to do business in China during the reform period."[28] The government established two categories of SOEs: strategic industries that were entirely controlled by the state, including telecommunications, power generation, and aerospace; and pillar industries, such as autos, steel, and chemicals, that were required to be majority state-owned. The independent Unirule Institute of Economics—which was shuttered in 2014 under Xi Jinping's assault on reform-oriented think tanks and organizations—estimated that over the course of the 2000s, SOEs amassed more than $800 billion in profits. However, if the various advantages provided SOEs—including subsidies, cheap land and utilities, and low interest rates—were deducted from the profits, the average return on equity was negative 6.29 percent.[29]

Hu Jintao's priority was to redress the imbalances that had emerged as a result of three decades of "go-go" economic growth through the creation of a harmonious society. At the March 2007 National People's Congress, Premier Wen Jiabao warned that China's development path was "unstable, unbalanced, uncoordinated, and unsustainable."[30] This meant addressing environmental pollution and degradation, imbalances in regional development, income inequality, health care, and the lack of a social welfare safety net.

One of the signal achievements of the Hu-Wen era was rebalancing investment away from coastal areas to the interior provinces of the country: nearly two-thirds of state-financed national infrastructure projects were designated for the inland region.[31] And during 2008–11, inland provinces averaged 13 percent real GDP growth while the wealthy coastal provinces averaged 11.5 percent. Progress was less notable across Hu and Wen's other priorities. Environmental pollution skyrocketed; the level of inequality stabilized but did not decline.[32] And although China achieved universal health care coverage in 2011, the quality of coverage, particularly in rural areas, remained poor.[33]

For much of the Hu-Wen decade, civil society activism and media openness increased dramatically. The issues they identified as critical social challenges became fodder for tens of thousands of protests annually. In 2010, China experienced 180,000 protests and mass demonstrations around issues such as illegal land expropriation, environmental degradation, and exorbitant health care costs.[34] These protests were often facilitated by the internet, which allowed Chinese citizens to create a virtual political community and to connect across geographic boundaries in new ways. Online protests also proliferated as citizens pushed political boundaries and explored new opportunities to hold government officials accountable. Real estate tycoons, such as Pan Shiyi and Ren Zhiqiang, amassed tens of millions of online followers as they called for the government to do a better job protecting the environment and opening the door to political reform, respectively.[35] And the world was captivated as the small village of Wukan, in Guangdong province, protested against illegal land expropriation, forced out the local party leadership, and elected the protest leaders to the local village committee.[36] Both Wukan and the Arab Spring in 2011, in which several Middle Eastern countries experienced mass, often violent, demonstrations in support of political change, contributed to a significant political crackdown in China. The government rounded up well-known political activists, canceled international conferences, and began to exert new controls over the internet, such as disrupting the ability of Chinese citizens to access news from overseas via virtual private networks.[37] Over the next two years, as a new Chinese leadership under Xi Jinping assumed power, the role of the CCP and the state in political life would be cemented and expanded in significant new ways.

The Party-State Roars Back

The economic reform agenda issued after the November 2013 Third Plenum of the 18th Party Congress had something for everyone. It pledged that the market would play a "decisive role" in the allocation of resources and, at the same time, that the government would "persist in the dominant position of public ownership, give full play to the leading role of the state-owned sector, and continuously increase its vitality, controlling force, and influence."[38] In the following seven years, the CCP resolved any contradiction in its early plans in favor of enhancing the state at the expense of the market. Xi Jinping and the rest of the Chinese leadership moved decisively, for example, to buttress the role of state-owned enterprises in the Chinese economy. As Nick Lardy has noted, under Xi, the country has resumed state-led growth in which an increasing share of resources has flowed into lower-productivity state firms.[39] SOEs that had been broken up during the days of Zhu Rongji reconstituted themselves. Xi also viewed SOEs as important extensions of Chinese state interest abroad. As former head of China's State-owned Assets Supervision and Administration Commission, Xiao Yaqing said that SOEs are a "major force" in China's "going out" strategy (Chinese enterprises investing and operating abroad) and for the Belt and Road Initiative.[40]

According to Lardy, Xi's reliance on SOEs and his determination to make them bigger through multiple mergers of larger enterprises has resulted in "reduced competition, weakening the incentive for innovation and cost control." Lardy also notes that during 2013–19 the share of bank lending to the far more efficient private sector shrank by 80 percent.[41] In addition, SOEs are poor generators of jobs and technological innovation relative to private firms. In fact, the importance of the private sector to the Chinese economy is reflected by Chinese people's use of the number 56789 to reflect the fact that private firms contribute 50 percent of tax revenue, 60 percent of output, 70 percent of industrial modernization and innovation, 80 percent of jobs, and 90 percent of enterprises.[42]

The China model under Xi has also advanced the role of the CCP within private enterprises, further blurring the line between the state and private sectors. In March 2012, before becoming general secretary of the Communist Party later that year, Xi called for party committees within firms (the formal grouping of all party members within a work unit) to play a larger role in supervising the work of the company, even calling for the party secretary to participate in company decisions.[43] The CCP followed with a series of regulations in the mid-2010s granting party committees an enhanced position in firms. In response, multinationals in joint ventures with Chinese firms complained that CCP members were undermining the role of companies' boards.[44] In Hangzhou, a hub of Chinese technological innovation, the local government announced in 2019 that it would place local officials in one hundred companies to help align the companies' interests with those of the local government.[45] And in September 2020, the CCP Central Committee issued a new set of guidelines that noted: "With the expansion of the private economy there has been a clear increase in risks and challenges, while the values and pursuit of interests of private entrepreneurs are also diversifying, which has posed a new situation and tasks for the party's work."[46] Alongside the new guidelines, Xi Jinping delivered a speech in which he stressed that the party needed to "educate and guide" entrepreneurs to ensure that they "unswervingly listen to and follow the steps of the party." In particular, officials have called for the party committees to have control over the personnel decisions of enterprises and allow them to carry out company audits, including monitoring personal behavior.[47]

Together with Chinese government subsidies and regulations that seem-ingly require Chinese firms to turn over all information requested by the government, the growing role of the party committees has caused the inter-national community to question whether Chinese firms can ever be con-sidered truly private.[48] In spring 2021, Xi further launched a wholesale regulatory attack on many of the sectors where private companies had thrived, such as financial technology, private tutoring, and gaming, among others, leading many prominent Chinese CEOs to resign from their positions.

In addition, in 2020, Xi advanced a dual-circulation theory to guide Chinese economic development over the coming years. The centerpiece of the theory is the creation of a closed loop of Chinese innovation, manu-facturing, and consumption. The plan builds on the CCP's 2015 Made in China 2025 initiative that called for China to manufacture domestically 70 percent or more of the components involved in ten critical cutting-edge areas of technology, such as artificial intelligence, new materials, and new energy vehicles. The plan harkens back to Mao Zedong's doctrine of self-reliance. At the July 1960 Beidaihe Central Committee Work Conference, in an atmosphere of growing tensions with the Soviet Union, Mao stated that China had to rely on itself in pursuit of technological modernity and socialism.[49] Xi's efforts are designed to protect the Chinese economy—in particular, areas with foreign technological dependence—from any potentially deleterious impacts of globalization and reliance on other countries for critical technologies. Within this framework, China will still engage with the international community in order to acquire needed know-how, technology, and capital and to promote exports. For example, in late 2020, China undertook a series of measures to open its bond market to foreign investors to make it easier for them to invest in yuan-denominated bonds and help raise money for further Chinese government investment needs.[50] Despite these selective openings, Xi's vision for the Chinese economy is one in which the party and the state remain firmly in control.

Xi Jinping's emphasis on the party and the state in the Chinese economy has been matched by a growing intrusion of the party into the daily lives of the Chinese people. China boasts more than half of all surveillance cameras in the world and possesses the most advanced facial recognition technology.[51] It also is in the process of implementing a social credit system designed to evaluate the political and economic trustworthiness of individual Chinese citizens and multinationals and reward and punish them accordingly.[52] Xi has called for the media to be in service of the party.[53] Broader censorship of internet content sharply limits the ability of the Chinese people to share ideas and mobilize politically. Contact between members of Chinese civil society and their foreign counterparts has also diminished sharply during Xi's tenure. The passage of the Law of the People's Republic of China on Administration of Activities of Overseas Nongovernmental Organizations in the Mainland of China in January 2017 resulted in the number of foreign NGOs operating in China falling from over seven thousand to fewer than six hundred.[54] The market now plays a much smaller role both in the Chinese economy and in the world of ideas and political debate.

The China Model: What Does It Offer?

The evolution of the China model since 1979 reflects different leaders' understandings of the appropriate balance between the role of the market and the role of the state in China's economic and political system. Over time, the model has embraced both bold moves to diminish the state's role and subsequent efforts to enhance it. Although particular initiatives, such as the social credit system, may represent a form of Chinese policy innovation, most scholars of China, such as Yuen Yuen Ang, understand the China model as a type of authoritarian or state capitalism—a single-party state whose polity is characterized by extensive state control over political and social life, including the media, internet, and education, and whose economy reflects a mix of both market-based practices and the strong hand of the state in core sectors of the economy.[55] Suisheng Zhao adopts a similar notion, writing, "The China model is often described as a combination of economic freedom and political oppression." But Zhao notes that although China has established in large measure a free-market economy, it is only "selectively free." The state maintains ultimate control over strategic sectors of the economy and a large range of core industries. The characteristics of economic governance in democracies, such as transparency, independent courts, enforceable property rights, and free information, are absent.[56]

Scholars, including Zhao, also liken China's development model to that of the fast-growing Asian economies of Singapore, Taiwan, Hong Kong, and South Korea in the 1970s and 1980s.[57] As William Overholt has suggested, China is "the latecomer in a group of 'Asian miracle' economies—Japan, South Korea, Taiwan, and Singapore—that exhibit common characteristics."[58] (The latecomer status is reflected in the fact that although the GDP per capita of Taiwan and South Korea was roughly equivalent to that of China in the early 1950s, the two Asian tigers now boast GDP per capita that is two-and-a-half and three times that of China, respectively.[59]) Overholt points to single-party rule, as well as gradual opening to foreign trade and investment and the import of best practices from Western economies, as defining features of the development path. In addition, China has followed in the footsteps of these other Asian economies by focusing on industrial policy, reforming the agricultural sector to support land rights and mechanization, and committing to export-oriented industrialization, as opposed to import substitution. The opportunities for China to learn from these economies were present at the very start of the economic reform program: many of China's earliest investors in the SEZs were overseas Chinese from Taiwan, Hong Kong, and Singapore. And over the years, more than twenty-two thousand Chinese officials traveled to Singapore to learn from its model of economic growth and limited political freedoms.[60]

Xi Jinping's claim to a China model that others might emulate also holds within it an implicit assertion that it has managed to meet the needs of its people better than market democracies. Former World Bank president Jim Yong Kim celebrated China's poverty alleviation successes, for example, in remarks before the 2017 annual meetings of the International Monetary Fund (IMF) and World Bank, noting, "This is one of the great stories in human history" and there are "lessons to be learned" from China.[61] Certainly China's economic growth over forty years has been impressive, including sixteen years of double-digit growth; 2019 GDP per capita stood at $10,262.[62] Inequality, however, is persistent. A 2019 Chinese central bank report revealed that among thirty thousand urban families surveyed, 20 percent held 63 percent of total assets while the bottom 20 percent owned just 2.6 percent.[63] During 1990–2015, inequality in China grew at more than twice the rate of the next most unequal region of the world, emerging and developing Europe. The IMF points to educational disparities and continued limits to freedom of movement, as well as technological changes that increased the wages of higher-skilled workers, as the sources of the disparity.[64] Thomas Piketty, Li Yang, and Gabriel Zucman suggest that China's development model appears "more egalitarian than that of the United States, but less than that of European countries."[65] But in a study comparing the Gini coefficients of China with those of European Union countries, researchers from Shijiazhuang University of Economics suggest that the level of China's inequality "does not conform to the nature of socialism and is higher than market capitalism countries in North America, and even more unequal than [the] most typical market capitalism country—the United States."[66] Even more striking, Premier Li Keqiang announced in his speech before the May 2020 National People's Congress that six hundred million people, nearly half the population of the country, earned just $141 per month. It was news that shocked the broader Chinese public and prompted an investigation that later confirmed the number's accuracy.[67]

By many other measures of the provision of social welfare, China finds itself unexceptional among its peer countries as defined by GDP per capita. Across measures of life expectancy at birth, mortality from heart or respiratory disease, cancer and diabetes, and maternal mortality, China sits well in the middle of peer countries, such as Argentina, Mexico, and Malaysia. It excels in its ability to prevent infant mortality and provide primary education but falls short by a significant measure in the percentage of students attending secondary school through college: 24 percent of Mexicans, 40 percent of Argentinians, and 24 percent of Malaysians received tertiary education while only 18 percent of Chinese have attained this level.[68] And despite significant efforts in recent years to clean up the environment, China nonetheless ranks 120th out of 180 countries in Yale University's Environmental Performance Index, as compared to Mexico (51st), Argentina (54th), and Malaysia (68th).[69] Even China's 2020 unemployment rate, a figure many economists believe the government underreported, exceeded that of Mexico and Malaysia.[70] Only Argentina posted a higher rate of unemployment.[71]

In acknowledgment of the vast income disparities that had emerged, as well as the challenges with affordable housing and education for the middle class, in 2021, Xi renewed a call by Mao for "common prosperity" to rectify the economic inequities. At the outset, "common prosperity" targeted China's billionaires and their firms, calling on them to share their wealth voluntarily. Billions of dollars, particularly from the country's highly successful technology firms, poured forth in response. Looking forward, however, Xi has pledged to institutionalize greater income equality through significant tax reform.

Conclusion

In the aftermath of Xi Jinping's assertion that China presented an alternative model to that of Western market democracy, senior Chinese diplomat He Yafei made explicit the notion of the model's competition with the United States. In an opinion piece he penned for the *China Daily*, he wrote: "That China has blazed a different trail has made the U.S. realize it overestimated its capability to lead China's strategic orientation. And the success of the 'Chinese model,' which offers other developing countries an option different from the 'American model' for economic development, has made the U.S. blind to China's remarkable contributions to the world and U.S. economies."[72] Merrimack College political science professor He Li concurs with He Yafei as to the China model's attraction for others. She notes that a growing number of countries are looking at China as a model for "growth with stability." She argues, "Given a choice between market democracy and its freedoms and market authoritarianism and its high growth stability, improved living standards, and limits on expression, a majority in the developing world and in many middle-size non-Western powers prefer the authoritarian model."[73] Yet the very nature of the China model—in terms of the relationship between the state on the one hand and the economy and society on the other—has changed over the course of successive Chinese leaders, making it difficult to determine what precisely the model represents beyond a broad categorization of state capitalism or market authoritarianism.

In "socialism with Chinese characteristics," Chinese leaders do not appear to have discovered a magical new formula for economic prosperity; they have simply sought, as all countries do, to determine the right balance between the role of the state and the role of private enterprise in contributing to economic growth and the provision of social welfare. The broad contours of the China model do not appear to differ in significant measure from the Asian tiger economies that came before it. And measured against other countries whose per-capita GDP is roughly equivalent to that of China, and which have transitioned from authoritarian to democratic forms of government, China does not stand out as providing more or better for the social welfare of its people. Thus far, the development path that China has followed, as well as its successes and shortcomings, do not appear to be exceptional. What is distinctive and challenging, however, is the determination of the current Chinese leadership not to follow the Asian tigers further down the path to transition away from its authoritarian system to become a democracy and its belief that such an end state is a worthy alternative to market democracy for other countries.

NOTES

1. Xi Jinping, "Secure a Decisive Victory in Building a Moderately Prosperous Society in All Respects and Strive for the Great Success of Socialism with Chinese Characteristics for a New Era," speech delivered in Beijing, October 18, 2017, printed in Xi Jinping, *The Governance of China*, vol. 3 (Beijing: Foreign Language Press, 2020), 12.

2. The Great Leap Forward was an economic and social campaign that aimed to boost Chinese industrial and agricultural output to surpass the United Kingdom and eventually the United States. Under Mao's direction, the CCP collectivized rural agriculture into people's communes and oversaw the development of inefficient backyard steel furnaces. Local party officials seeking to impress their superiors vastly overstated crop yields and industrial output leading to widespread famine and economic collapse. The overwhelming failure of the Great Leap Forward caused Mao to temporarily cede power to other party leaders.

3. World Bank, "GDP Per Capita (Current US$)—China," https://data.worldbank .org/indicator/NY.GDP.PCAP.CD?locations=CN.

4. PricewaterhouseCoopers, "China Economic Quarterly Q2 2019," August 2019, http://pwccn.com/en/research-and-insights/publications/ceq-q2-2019/china -economic-quarterly-q2-2019.pdf.

5. Isabel Hilton, "Politics with Bloodshed: How Maoism Changed the World," *Prospect*, May 4, 2019, https://www.prospectmagazine.co.uk/magazine/politics -with-bloodshed-how-maoism-changed-the-world.

6. Deng Xiaoping, "Build Socialism with Chinese Characteristics," excerpt from a talk with the Japanese delegation to the second session of the Council of Sino-Japanese

Non-Governmental Persons, Wellesley College, June 1984, http://academics
.wellesley.edu/Polisci/wj/China/Deng/Building.htm.

7. Deng, "Build Socialism with Chinese Characteristics."

8. Douglas Zhihua Zeng, "Building Engines for Growth and Competitiveness
in China," World Bank, 2010, http://documents1.worldbank.org/curated/en
/294021468213279589/pdf/564470PUB0buil10Box349496B01PUBLIC1.pdf.

9. Zhao Ziyang, *Prisoner of the State: The Secret Journal of Premier Zhao Ziyang*
(New York: Simon and Schuster, 2009), 101.

10. Zhao, *Prisoner of the State*, 107.

11. Zhao, *Prisoner of the State*, 101.

12. Lai Har Rebecca Chiu, "Modernization in China: The Experiment of Shenzhen
Special Economic Zone 1979–1984" (PhD thesis, Australian National
University, 1986), 28, https://core.ac.uk/download/pdf/156719637.pdf.

13. "Special Economic Zones and Open Coastal Cities," China in Brief, http://
www.china.org.cn/e-china/openingup/sez.htm.

14. "China GDP Growth Rate 1961–2020," MacroTrends, 2020, https://www
.macrotrends.net/countries/CHN/china/gdp-growth-rate.

15. Yasheng Huang, "China Boom: Rural China in the 1980s," MIT Sloan School
of Management, July 1, 2020, 6, https://rucore.libraries.rutgers.edu/rutgers-lib
/42167/PDF/1/play.

16. Barry Naughton, *The Chinese Economy: Transitions and Growth* (Cambridge,
MA: MIT Press, 2007), 87.

17. "Full Text of Jiang Zemin's Report at 14th Party Congress," *Beijing Review*,
March 29, 2011, http://www.bjreview.com/document/txt/2011-03/29/content
_363504_2.htm.

18. Raviprasad Narayanan, "The Politics of Reform in China: Deng, Jiang and Hu,"
Strategic Analysis 30, no. 2 (April–June 2006): 335.

19. "Full Text of Jiang Zemin's Report at the 16th Party Congress," China Through a
Lens, November 17, 2002, http://www.china.org.cn/english/2002/Nov/49107.htm.

20. Harm Zebregs and Wanda Tseng, "Foreign Direct Investment in China," IMF
eLibrary, February 2002, https://www.elibrary.imf.org/view/IMF003/02587
-9781451974171/02587-9781451974171/02587-9781451974171_A001.xml
?language=en&redirect=true#:~:text=By%20the%201990s%2C%20China%20
became,flows%20to%20all%20developing%20countries.

21. Nicholas R. Lardy, "Issues in China's WTO Accession," Brookings Institution,
May 9, 2001.

22. Lardy, "Issues in China's WTO Accession."

23. Ryuhei Wakasugi, "Asymmetric Impacts of the WTO Accession on Chinese Exporters," *Vox EU*, June 2, 2015, https://voxeu.org/article/china-s-wto-accession-and-exports-impact-firm-ownership.

24. World Integrated Trade Solution, "China Export to World in US$ Thousands 1999–2004," https://wits.worldbank.org/CountryProfile/en/Country/CHN/StartYear/1999/EndYear/2004/TradeFlow/Export/Partner/WLD/Indicator/XPRT-TRD-VL.

25. Deyong Yin, "China's Attitude toward Foreign NGOs," *Washington University Global Studies Law Review* 8, no. 3 (January 2009).

26. Chen Jie, "The NGO Community in China: Expanding Linkages With Transnational Civil Society and Their Democratic Implications," *China Perspectives* 68 (November–December 2005).

27. Steven Mufson, "China Tolerates Talk of Reform," *Washington Post*, August 10, 1997.

28. Carl F. Minzner, "China After the Reform Era," Fordham Law Archive of Scholarship and History, 2015, https://ir.lawnet.fordham.edu/cgi/viewcontent.cgi?article=1653&context=faculty_scholarship.

29. James McGregor, "No Ancient Wisdom for China," YaleGlobal Online, October 8, 2012, https://yaleglobal.yale.edu/content/no-ancient-wisdom-china.

30. "Wen Confident in Maintaining Economic Growth," *China Daily*, March 16, 2007, https://www.chinadaily.com.cn/business/2007-03/16/content_8298 15.htm.

31. Ryan Rutkowski, "A Legacy of Inland Development," Peterson Institute for International Economics, November 27, 2020, https://www.piie.com/blogs/china-economic-watch/legacy-inland-development.

32. World Bank, "Gini Index (World Bank Estimate)—China," https://data.worldbank.org/indicator/SI.POV.GINI?locations=CN.

33. Lua Wilkinson, "Universal Rural Healthcare in China? Not So Fast," *The Atlantic*, September 6, 2013.

34. Max Fisher, "How China Stays Stable Despite 500 Protests Every Day," *The Atlantic*, January 5, 2012.

35. Heng Shao, "Arrest of Venture Capitalist Brings Back Question of Chinese Entrepreneurs' Civic Responsibility," *Forbes*, September 18, 2013.

36. Echo Hui, "Grass Roots Leader Withdraws from Politics as Wukan Loses Faith in Democracy Experiment," *South China Morning Post*, January 16, 2014,

https://www.scmp.com/news/china/article/1406766/grass-roots-leader-with draws-politics-wukan-loses-faith-democracy.

37. James Fallows, "Arab Spring, Chinese Winter," *The Atlantic*, September 2011.

38. "Decision of the Central Committee of the Communist Party of China on Some Major Issues Concerning Comprehensively Deepening the Reform," China.org.cn, January 16, 2014, http://www.china.org.cn/china/third_plenary _session/2014-01/16/content_31212602.htm.

39. Nicholas Lardy, *The State Strikes Back: The End of Economic Reform in China?* (Washington, DC: Peterson Institute for International Economics, 2019).

40. "China's SOEs Speed Up Going Abroad: Report," *China Daily*, July 1, 2016, http://www.chinadaily.com.cn/business/2016-07/01/content_25927534.htm.

41. Nicholas Lardy, "Xi Jinping's Turn Away from the Market Puts Chinese Growth at Risk," *Financial Times*, January 15, 2019.

42. George Magnus, "Meaningful Reform in China? Don't Hold Your Breath," GeorgeMagnus.com, January 8, 2019.

43. Richard McGregor, "How the West Got Xi Jinping Wrong on Business," *Financial Review*, July 11, 2019, https://www.afr.com/world/asia/how-the-west -got-xi-jinping-wrong-on-business-20190709-p525n0.

44. Richard McGregor, "How the State Runs Business in China," *The Guardian*, July 25, 2019.

45. Josh Horwitz, "China to Send State Officials to 100 Private Firms Including Alibaba," *Reuters*, September 23, 2019.

46. "[The General Office of the CCP Central Committee issued the 'Opinions on Strengthening the United Front Work of Private Economy in the New Era']," Central Committee of the People's Republic of China, September 15, 2020, http://www.gov.cn/zhengce/2020-09/15/content_5543685.htm.

47. You Shu, "They're Coming for the Private Sector," *Credible Target* (blog), September 20, 2020, http://credibletarget.net/notes/YeQing.

48. Yuan Yang, "Is Huawei Compelled by Chinese Law to Help with Espionage?," *Financial Times*, March 4, 2019.

49. "Mao Zedong's Talk at the Beidaihe Central Committee Work Conference (Excerpt)," July 18, 1960, Wilson Center Digital Archive.

50. Mike Bird, "When China Opens Markets and Customers Don't Arrive," *Wall Street Journal*, October 6, 2020.

51. Liza Lin and Newley Purnell, "A World with a Billion Cameras Watching You Is Just around the Corner," *Wall Street Journal*, December 6, 2019.

52. Evelyn Cheng, "China Is Building a 'Comprehensive System' for Tracking Companies' Activities, Report Says," CNBC, September 3, 2019.

53. Edward Wong, "Xi Jinping's News Alert: Chinese Media Must Serve the Party," *New York Times*, February 22, 2016.

54. "[Fu Ying on the Law for Management of Foreign Nongovernmental Organizations: Against Preventing Their Beneficial and Legal Activities in China]," *China News*, March 4, 2016, http://www.chinanews.com/gn/2016/03-04 /7784292.shtml; China NGO Project, "Registered Foreign NGO Representative Offices Interactive Map and Filterable Table," October 28, 2020, https://www .chinafile.com/ngo/registered-foreign-ngo-offices-map-full-screen.

55. Yuen Yuen Ang, "Autocracy with Chinese Characteristics," *Foreign Affairs*, May/June 2018.

56. Suisheng Zhao, "The China Model: Can It Replace the Western Model of Modernization?," *Journal of Contemporary China* 19, no. 65 (April 2010): 419–36.

57. Zhao, "The China Model."

58. William H. Overholt, "Is the China Model a Threat?," *East Asia Forum*, July 7, 2019.

59. World Bank, "GDP Per Capita (Current US$)—China, Korea, Rep.," https:// data.worldbank.org/indicator/NY.GDP.PCAP.CD?locations=CN-KR; "Latest Indicators," National Statistics, Republic of China (Taiwan), https://eng .stat.gov.tw/point.asp?index=1.

60. Chris Buckley, "In Lee Kuan Yew, China Saw a Leader to Emulate," *New York Times*, March 23, 2015.

61. "China Lifting 800 Million People out of Poverty Is Historic: World Bank," *Business Standard*, October 13, 2017.

62. World Bank, "GDP Per Capita (Current US$)—China," https://data.worldbank .org/indicator/NY.GDP.PCAP.CD?locations=CN.

63. Li Lei, "Challenge Remains as Nation Tries to Scrap Absolute Poverty," *China Daily*, June 10, 2020, http://global.chinadaily.com.cn/a/202006/10 /WS5ee02eafa310834817251f8b.html.

64. Sonali Jain-Chandra, "Chart of the Week: Inequality in China," International Monetary Fund, September 20, 2018.

65. Thomas Piketty, Li Yang, and Gabriel Zucman, "Income Inequality Is Growing Fast in China and Making It Look More Like the US," LSE US Centre, April 6, 2019, https://blogs.lse.ac.uk/usappblog/2019/04/06/income-inequality -is-growing-fast-in-china-and-making-it-look-more-like-the-us.

66. Jin Han, Qingxia Zhao, and Mengnan Zhang, "China's Income Inequality in the Global Context," *Perspectives in Science* 7 (March 2016): 24–29.

67. Sidney Leng, "China Confirms More Than 40 Per Cent of Population Survived on Just US$141 Per Month in 2019," *South China Morning Post*, June 15, 2020, https://www.scmp.com/economy/china-economy/article/3089128/china -confirms-more-40-cent-population-survived-just-us141.

68. OECD iLibrary, "Education at a Glance 2020," Organisation of Economic Co-operation and Development, 2020, https://www.oecd-ilibrary.org/education /education-at-a-glance-2020_69096873-en.

69. Environmental Performance Index, "2020 EPI Results," September, 11, 2020, https://epi.yale.edu/epi-results/2020/component/epi.

70. Chao Deng and Jonathan Cheng, "Some Economists Question Strength of China's Labor Market," *Wall Street Journal*, June 7, 2020. Organisation for Economic Co-operation and Development, "Employment Database— Unemployment Indicators," May 2020, http://www.oecd.org/employment/emp /employmentdatabase-unemployment.htm; Department of Statistics Malaysia Official Portal, "Key Indicator," August 20, 2020, https://www.dosm.gov.my/v1.

71. National Institute of Statistics and Censuses of Argentina, "Mercado de trabajo. Tasas e indicadores socioeconómicos [Labor market. Socioeconomic rates and in-dicators]," September 2020, https://www.indec.gob.ar/uploads/informesdeprensa /mercado_trabajo_eph_2trim20929E519161.pdf.

72. He Yafei, "Will China and US Enter a New 'Cold War'?," *China Daily*, July 9, 2018, http://usa.chinadaily.com.cn/a/201807/09/WS5b42a4f8a3103349141e16d7.html.

73. He Li, "The Chinese Model of Development and Its Implications," *World Journal of Social Science Research* 2, no. 2 (December 2015): 129.

8

How Freedom Is Caught between Socialism and Capitalism in the Indo-Pacific

Michael R. Auslin

Since 2020, Hong Kong has been undergoing a stark experiment of whether an authoritarian state can take over a free society and keep it economically flourishing while individual rights are increasingly extinguished. If that sounds like a paradox, it is, given that the historical record includes no examples of such a transition to authoritarianism where, ultimately, economic growth and development continued while freedom languished. Indeed, despite appearances to the contrary, there is little evidence that wealthy or free countries are eager to adopt the repressive systems of illiberal powers for supposed economic gain at the cost of their political liberty. Despite this, the People's Republic of China (PRC) is relentlessly pushing its laboratory experiment on Hong Kong, where the Chinese Communist Party (CCP) in 2020 passed a draconian national security law, repudiating its promises to ensure the former colony's freedoms.[1]

The organs of CCP control have been established in Hong Kong, and the new law already has led to numerous prosecutions of any activities that Beijing considers to be secessionist, subversive, or terrorist. Pro-democracy activists have already been arrested under the new law, including several attempting to escape to Taiwan; democracy leaders such as Jimmy Lai have been charged, chilling free expression. Offenses considered serious enough will be taken out of the Hong Kong legal system entirely and prosecuted under mainland law after transferal of the accused to Beijing. Student democracy organizations have disbanded; tighter controls on foreign media and organizations are reducing the free flow of information in the territory; and Hong Kong libraries have been stripped of books by authors the Communist regime in Beijing considers threatening.

How will the disappearance of Hong Kong's traditional freedoms, and the imposition of an authoritarian system of control, affect the territory's economic activity? How long will foreign business remain in an increasingly repressive environment? What will remain of civil society in Hong Kong once the law is being fully executed? In short, will Hong Kong retain any of the qualities of free life that marked it for so many decades?

These are not academic questions, though as the world watches the disappearance of a free Hong Kong, they lead us to the broader issue of which socioeconomic system provides the best way of life: socialism or capitalism? Once discarded as a relic of the Cold War, presumed no longer to matter at the "end of history," the question of socialism versus capitalism has returned with a vengeance, due almost solely to the PRC's rise.[2]

The extraordinary growth of the PRC since the "reform and opening up" era was launched by then paramount leader Deng Xiaoping in 1979 has been taken as the counterpart to the so-called Washington Consensus.[3] This neoliberal argument assumed that free-market capitalism and globalization provide the most successful pathway to economic prosperity and individual freedom; its heyday was during the Reagan and Clinton administrations in the 1980s and 1990s. In contrast, the PRC's supporters claim that an illiberal political system can foster a more dynamic economic environment, leading to a better life for its citizens. Particularly since the 2008 global financial crisis—and more recently after the COVID-19 global pandemic that began in Wuhan, China— Beijing has touted the superiority of its approach, boasting that it avoided the meltdown after the collapse of America's subprime mortgage market and, in 2020, that it was better able to control the coronavirus outbreak and correspondingly suffered less social and economic disruption.

Until the coronavirus pandemic, the world was increasingly torn between the Western, liberal model and the Chinese centralized Leninist model.

The PRC's seemingly unstoppable rise from 1980 through 2015, the year when its stock market faltered and macroeconomic growth began to level off, led many to assume that it indeed had found a better means of ensuring economic growth and social development than had the West. Within the space of a generation, China went through several stages of development, starting from near-subsistence level (especially in the countryside) to middle-income status around 2010.[4] The 1980s and 1990s, in particular, witnessed an expansion of market-oriented mechanisms, starting in coastal special economic zones and expanding to major inland urban centers.

Since the PRC's political system was indelibly connected with the economic model, development also strengthened the state, especially once the CCP began to reassert Leninist-style control after the 2008 global financial crisis.[5] Government stimulus packages and increased government control over the economy led to arguments that political freedom and free-market capitalism were not necessary for robust economic growth. Rather, Chinese officials asserted that a less representative political structure run by trained technocrats would avoid the messiness inherent in democratic polities, achieving superior standards of living, not to mention better educational and scientific outcomes, as well as greater social stability. This last point was reiterated by Beijing in light of the civil disturbances that broke out across the United States in summer 2020.

Such claims oversimplify the complicated patchwork that represents socioeconomic development in China, America, and the rest of the world. There are very few pure political and economic regimes, outside of academic theory. In the Indo-Pacific region in particular, just about every type of political and economic system coexists, making a complex tapestry that continues to evolve as states respond to internal needs and external conditions.

Democratic nations such as Japan and India adopted a form of state capitalism in the 1950s that gave a powerful role to national government in establishing a sphere of economic activity that lies somewhere between socialism and free-market capitalism, yet the results have been very different in each. In Japan, a focus on export industries and manufacturing allowed it to become the world's second-largest economy for decades;

India, however, found its neo-socialist and autarkic economy falling further behind the rest of the world, until near collapse forced the adoption of economic reform in the early 1990s.

Other Asian nations, such as South Korea, moved fitfully along the road of both political and economic liberalization simultaneously in the 1980s, rapidly increasing per capita GDP while giving birth to a freewheeling political system; Taiwan largely followed this route as well during the 1990s. The PRC, as is well known, opened up its southern coastal regions as special economic zones starting in the late 1970s, giving them freedoms and access to the global economy that other, interior regions did not share. In short, there was and remains a spectrum of socioeconomic models throughout the Indo-Pacific, and most nations there occupy positions somewhere short of either pure free-market capitalism or socialism. Even North Korea, run by the despotic Kim family, has attempted to stabilize its economy by allowing private markets to operate.[6]

The broader question that this academic debate addresses is, what is the best balance of political freedom and economic openness? The Western modernization model, apotheosized in the Washington Consensus, presumes that political and economic liberalization go hand in hand. In particular, the post–World War II experience led policy makers in America and Europe to assume that economic liberalization and globalization would create increasingly strong middle classes that would demand political representation, thereby assuring ongoing political liberalization. A robust civil society would ensue, once civil rights and individual freedom were protected by democratic regimes. Human prosperity would be best ensured by this virtuous cycle, resulting in a balanced liberalization among politics, economics, and civil society.

China's growth over the past three decades has fundamentally challenged the West's modernization thesis, yet its own experience shows the dangers in assuming that political repression can coexist beside economic vitality. As Richard McGregor points out in *The Party*, many of the dazzling Shanghai and Beijing skyscrapers that observers point to as proof that China has a market economy were actually built with state support.[7] Conversely, state-owned enterprises (SOEs) in China make up a majority of the economy but account for the minority of profit. Skewed incentives are pervasive throughout the Chinese system, leading to mal-investment and its reverberations, such as massive ghost cities dotting the landscape or zombie SOEs that are protected by the CCP instead of being allowed to wither away.

Just as damaging is the political intervention into the economic sphere. The incompatibility of economic liberalism with authoritarian rule is illustrated by Beijing's 2017 National Intelligence Law, which mandates that private companies (along with citizens) must provide any information, digital records, and the like demanded by the state in the name of national security.[8] Similarly, a crackdown starting in late 2020 on China's tech sector has dramatically increased regulation and control over leading Chinese companies, including the Ant Group, Tencent, and Alibaba, likely threatening future innovation. Even the high-flying tech sector has found itself in the crosshairs because of political fears over its potential strength independent of the party.[9]

To many observers, however, such state control and economic inefficiencies are unimportant compared to the dramatic change in Chinese standards of living over the past generation.[10] Once a developing nation of hundreds of millions of bicycle riders housed in squalid conditions, today's PRC appears to foreigners the exemplar of a modern society, with gleaming buildings, conspicuous displays of wealth, digital commerce, and a cosmopolitan lifestyle. Yet such surface manifestations of development cannot capture the enormous disparities in income that divide Chinese society, especially between the coastal and interior regions, nor do they account for the baneful effects of corruption and abuse of power by party officials, leading intelligentsia, and favored economic elites.

Perhaps most importantly, measurements of Chinese wealth, as imperfect as they are, ignore the question of individual rights and civil society. As noted by historian Frank Dikötter, the CCP has never been interested in sharing power with the people, even at the height of the reform era; sanguinary proof of this was provided by the 1989 Tiananmen Square massacre.[11] Although some level of civil society was allowed to develop after the death of PRC founder Mao Zedong, particularly during the

Deng Xiaoping and Jiang Zemin eras of the 1980s and 1990s, it was always tightly controlled, stunting the ways in which Chinese citizens of the post-Mao period could develop their personal interests or contacts with the outer world. Worse, since 2009, even the small sphere of personal and civic freedom allowed by the CCP has been eroded, especially after current general secretary Xi Jinping came to power in late 2012. Beijing's development of an authoritarian surveillance state, underpinned by ubiquitous facial recognition technology and the so-called social credit system, gives the bureaucracy enormous leverage over the populace. The CCP is back in full control of Chinese society and state today, emphasizing Leninist ideology, and the country is under greater repression than at any time since Mao's reign of terror (excepting the brief, brutal suppression of the 1989 democracy movement). The most recent law, passed in November 2021, makes it a crime to mock the PRC's national heroes, all in a bid to forestall any criticism of the CCP.

As Chinese society turns inward at the orders of the CCP, and as the world watches it wither Hong Kong's democracy, the poverty of life under authoritarian rule is becoming more evident. Not only is China's economy continuing to slow down, but the lives of its people are becoming narrower and more brittle. Rampant nationalism in China cannot detract from the manifest domestic dissatisfaction with the CCP and uncertainty over China's future. The widely reported fact that most of China's elite hold foreign passports and own property abroad, along with the massive capital outflow since 2015, is a harbinger of a more unstable future.[12] And although the CCP has ensured that a much wider section of the population has benefited from economic growth than the Soviet population did under the Communist Party of the Soviet Union, rising expectations for continued wealth production and commensurate freedom to pursue economic interests mean that continued sluggishness in the economy will lead to social friction, if not backlash. It is precisely to forestall such reaction that the CCP has reemphasized socialist ideology and clamped down on civil society (while trying to root out corruption, at least by those opposed to Xi Jinping and his circle). Thus, a vicious circle ensues, further impoverishing both pocketbook and soul.

The nations of the Indo-Pacific, as well as those around the world, are warily watching both China's travails and the equally serious troubles in the West, particularly the United States. Asia is suffering a democracy recession, as argued by Larry Diamond, especially in Thailand and the Philippines, and there is little likelihood of either democracy or free-market capitalism being adopted in Laos and Cambodia; communist Vietnam struggles with opening up its society to the global economy while maintaining strict control at home.[13] Bangladesh, to take another example, has an uneasy mixed-market economy and is ranked as "partly free" by Freedom House, owing to its restrictions on the press and human rights issues. Myanmar (Burma), once a beacon of hope for the transition from military authoritarianism to representative democracy, has been mired in a reactionary turn under power broker (and Nobel Peace Prize winner) Aung San Suu Kyi, and the bloody crackdown on democracy protesters continues. Other nations, such as Malaysia and Indonesia, are democracies grappling with growing Islamic fundamentalism. Singapore, an increasingly important financial center, given the travails of Hong Kong, passed a new "anti-foreign interference" law in October 2021 that many fear will stifle freedom of expression. Most of these same Asian countries fear Beijing's growing power and aggression, and at the same time covet the aid and trade that has made China so powerful over the past few decades.

Yet despite the examples above, it is also the case that few countries are rushing to embrace the type of socialist authoritarianism offered by the CCP. Moreover, democracy is firmly rooted in Australia, India, Japan, South Korea, and Taiwan. Rather than seeing the Chinese way as the only path forward, all nations in the region are searching for sustainable ways of achieving prosperity that preserve their autonomy and, for many, their hard-won domestic freedoms.

Perhaps an anecdote can help bring life to some of the more abstract issues under discussion. Over nearly a third of a century of regular travel to the Indo-Pacific, including some four years living in Japan, I never heard Asians, whether scholars, journalists, business leaders, or the like, talk about the PRC as their role model. They envied its economic growth, of course, and warily respected its increasing power, but none ever talked about wanting their country to become more like China. Rather, almost all wanted their country to become like Japan. They understood that Japan's democracy could be sclerotic and that it had lost its commanding economic position after the 1990s, but they also hungered for its stable society, its undeniable developed economy, its excellent schools, and its green public spaces (which, to an American, seemed meager). Some few, like the Singaporeans, were quite content with their own free-market capitalist system, even if it was married to a more controlled democracy. But the majority were far more interested in pursuing the Japanese model, even fully aware of the country's shortcomings.

Prosperity and its connection to socioeconomic and political systems are perhaps far better understood in the Indo-Pacific region, given its recent history of decolonization, war, and nationalist movements, than in the United States, where no other alternative political or economic system has ever held sway. Perhaps more than Americans, Asians are sensitive to the limitations of grandiose schemes of utopian social planning and have only to remember Mao's Cultural Revolution or Pol Pot's genocide to shrink from the type of radicalism that is popular elsewhere. Whether informed by Buddhist compassion or Confucian humanism, much philosophizing in Asia is quite realistic and hardheaded. Few have discovered the golden mean between individual freedom and social order, and most are comfortable with some level of socioeconomic restriction and political control in exchange for social stability and sustainable growth.[14] Not all Asian nations have achieved such a balance, but their citizens understand that fragile are the conditions that create prosperity, and what seems like the golden egg of authoritarian control and economic well-being is at best a double-edged sword and, at worst, a short-lived mirage.

NOTES

1. "Hong Kong National Security Law Full Text," *South China Morning Post*, July 2, 2020.

2. For "the end of history," see Francis Fukuyama, "The End of History," *National Interest* 16 (Summer 1989): 3–18, https://www.jstor.org/stable/24027184?seq =1#metadata_info_tab_contents.

3. John Williamson, "The National Consensus as Policy Prescription for Development" (lecture in the series *Practitioners of Development* delivered at the World Bank on January 13, 2004).

4. Dominic Barton, "The Rise of the Middle Class in China and Its Impact on the Chinese and World Economies," in *US-China 2022: Economic Relations in the Next 10 Years: Towards Deeper Engagement and Mutual Benefit*, China-United States Exchange Foundation, 2013.

5. David Shambaugh, "Contemplating China's Future," *Washington Quarterly* 39, no. 3 (October 2016): 121–30.

6. See Travis Jeppesen, "Shopping in Pyongyang, and Other Adventures in North Korean Capitalism," *New York Times Magazine*, February 14, 2019; and Victor Cha and Lisa Collins, "The Markets: Private Economy and Capitalism in North Korea?," *Beyond Parallel*, August 26, 2018.

7. Richard McGregor, *The Party* (London: Allen Lane, 2010).

8. Murray Scot Tanner, "Beijing's New National Intelligence Law: From Defense to Offense," *Lawfare*, July 20, 2017.

9. Kai von Carnap and Valarie Tan, "Tech Regulation in China Brings in Sweeping Changes," Mercator Institute for Chinese Studies, November 3, 2021.

10. For an example from a Western perspective, see Ray Dalio, "Understanding China's Recent Moves in Its Capital Markets," *Caixin Global*, August 2, 2021. A popular treatment is Martin Jacques, *When China Rules the World: The End of the Western World and the Birth of a New Global Order* (New York: Penguin Press, 2012).

11. Frank Dikötter, "The People's Republic of China Was Born in Chains," *Foreign Policy*, October 1, 2019.

12. On Chinese-owned passports, see Adina-Laura Achim, "The Ultimate Luxury in China? A Second Passport," *Jing Daily*, August 26, 2019; and Ben Bland, "Foreign Passports Offer Little Protection for China's Elite," *Financial Times*, February 13, 2017.

13. Larry Diamond, "Facing Up to the Democratic Recession," *Journal of Democracy* 26, no. 1 (January 2015): 14–55.

14. For a discussion of Japan, see Michael R. Auslin, *Asia's New Geopolitics: Essays on Reshaping the Indo-Pacific* (Stanford: Hoover Institution Press, 2020), chap. 5.

III

The Contemporary Revival of Socialism and Its Prospects

9

Capitalism, Socialism, and Nationalism

Lessons from History

Niall Ferguson

The Pessimism of Joseph Schumpeter

Joseph Schumpeter was pessimistic. "Can capitalism survive?" he asked in his book *Capitalism, Socialism and Democracy* (1942). His answer was stark: "No. I do not think it can." He then posed and answered a second question: "Can socialism work? Of course it can."[1]

Perhaps the Austrian-born economist's pessimism was simply the effect of teaching at Harvard. By temperament a conservative who was hostile to the New Deal and allergic to Keynesianism, Schumpeter gradually tired of the "cocoon" on the banks of the Charles and came very close to moving to Yale on the eve of World War II.[2] Yet Schumpeter offered four plausible reasons for believing that socialism's prospects would be brighter than capitalism's in the second half of the twentieth century, even if he signaled his strong preference for capitalism in his ironical discussion of socialism.

First, he suggested, capitalism's greatest strength—its propensity for "creative destruction"—is also a source of weakness. Disruption may be the process that clears out the obsolescent and fosters the advent of the new, but precisely for that reason it can never be universally loved. Second, capitalism itself tends toward oligopoly, not perfect competition. The more concentrated economic power becomes, the harder it is to legitimize the

195

system, especially in America, where "big business" tends to get confused with "monopoly." Third, capitalism "creates, educates and subsidizes a vested interest in social unrest"—namely, intellectuals. (Here was the influence of Harvard; Schumpeter knew whereof he spoke.) Finally, Schumpeter noted, socialism is politically irresistible to bureaucrats and democratic politicians.[3]

The idea that socialism would ultimately prevail over capitalism was quite a widespread view—especially in Cambridge, Massachusetts. It persisted throughout the Cold War. "The Soviet economy is proof that, contrary to what many skeptics had earlier believed, a socialist command economy can function and even thrive," wrote Paul Samuelson, Schumpeter's pupil, in the 1961 edition of his economics textbook—a sentence that still appeared in the 1989 edition. In successive editions, Samuelson's hugely influential book carried a chart projecting that the gross national product of the Soviet Union would exceed that of the United States at some point between 1984 and 1997 (see figure 9.1). The 1967 edition suggested that the great overtaking could happen as early as 1977. By the 1980 edition, the time frame had been moved forward to 2002–12. The graph was quietly dropped after the 1980 edition.[4]

Samuelson was by no means the only American scholar to make this mistake. Other economists in the 1960s and 1970s—notably Campbell McConnell and George Bach—were "so over-confident about Soviet economic growth that evidence of model failure was repeatedly blamed on events outside the model's control," such as "bad weather." Curiously, McConnell's textbook more or less consistently estimated US GNP to be double that of the USSR between its 1960 and 1990 editions, despite also insisting in the same period that the Soviet economy had a growth rate roughly double the American.[5] Yet it was Lorie Tarshis whose textbook drew the most damaging fire (from William F. Buckley among others) for its sympathetic treatment of economic planning, despite the fact that Tarshis was more realistic in his assessment of Soviet growth.[6] The uncritical use of the simplistic "production possibility frontier" framework—in which all economies essentially make a choice between guns and butter—was a key reason for the tendency to overrate Soviet performance.[7] For

America leads Russia, but will the gap narrow?

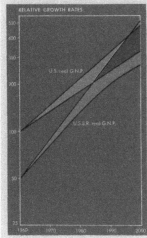

Fig. 1. The range of estimates shown here can make no pretense to accuracy, but they do portray the nature of the Soviet challenge. (Note: All indexes are based upon U.S. real GNP for 1960 = 100 and U.S.S.R. real GNP for 1960 = 50.)

Economic graphs throw light on future growth prospects:

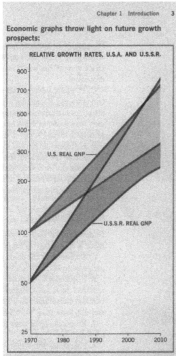

FIG. 1-1. The art of judgment, as well as scientific analysis, is involved in determining reasonable projections of growth rates free of either wishful or paranoid thinking. Not only are Americans and Russians concerned with the outcome of this economic sweepstakes, but so are Asians and Africans interested in choosing that form of economic organization which will move them most rapidly along the road of development. (Source: Fig. 42-1.)

Figure 9.1. Paul Samuelson's Projections of US and USSR GNP, 1961 and 1970. *Source:* Paul A. Samuelson, *Economics: An Introductory Analysis*, 5th ed. and 8th ed. (New York: McGraw-Hill, 1961 and 1970).

Figure 9.2. USSR Gross Domestic Product as a Percentage of US Total (purchasing power parity basis, 1990 international dollars), 1928–91. *Source:* Angus Maddison, "Historical Statistics of the World Economy: 1–2008 AD," spreadsheet, http://www.ggdc.net/maddison/Historical _Statistics/vertical-file_02-2010.xls.

example, as late as 1984 John Kenneth Galbraith could still insist that "the Russian system succeeds because, in contrast with the Western industrial economies, it makes full use of its manpower." Economists who discerned the miserable realities of the planned economy, such as G. Warren Nutter of the University of Virginia, were few and far between—almost as rare as historians, such as Robert Conquest, who grasped the enormity of the Soviet system's crimes against its own citizens.[8]

The majority view exemplified by Samuelson and Galbraith was of course wrong. Despite Schumpeter's pessimism, capitalism survived precisely because socialism did not work. After 1945, according to Angus Maddison's estimates, the Soviet economy was never more than 44 percent the size of that of the United States (see figure 9.2). By 1991, Soviet

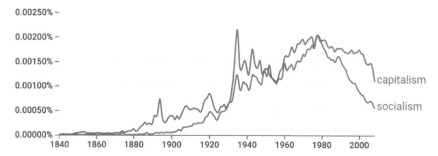

Figure 9.3. Appearance of the Terms "Capitalism" and "Socialism" in English-Language Publications, 1840–2008. *Source:* Google Books Ngram Viewer, https://books.google.com/ngrams.

GDP was less than a third of US GDP. The tendency of American intelligence experts was to exaggerate the extent of Soviet success. But those who visited the Soviet Union could hardly miss its inferiority. Henry Kissinger noted the almost naïve desire of Soviet leader Leonid Brezhnev to impress his American guests when he played host to an American diplomatic delegation at Zavidovo, the Politburo hunting preserve northeast of Moscow, in May 1973. Brezhnev invited Kissinger and his colleagues to dinner at his villa, which, in Kissinger's words, "he first showed off with all the pride of a self-made entrepreneur. He asked me how much such an establishment would cost in the United States. I guessed tactlessly and mistakenly at four hundred thousand dollars. Brezhnev's face fell. My associate Helmut Sonnenfeldt was psychologically more adept: Two million, he corrected—probably much closer to the truth. Brezhnev, vastly reassured, beamed."[9]

Moreover, beginning around 1979, the very term "socialism" went into a decline, at least in the English-speaking world (see figure 9.3). Use of "capitalism" also declined—as the two terms were in some senses interdependent, often appearing on the same page—but not as much. This was a humiliating reversal of fortune. Socialism had led from the second half of the nineteenth century until the mid-1920s, and again in the 1960s and 1970s.

The Origins of Socialism and Capitalism

The terms "capitalism" and "socialism" had their origins in the British Industrial Revolution. As the Chicago economist Thorstein Veblen argued, nineteenth-century capitalism was an authentically Darwinian system, characterized by seemingly random mutation, occasional speciation, and differential survival.[10] Yet precisely the volatility of the more or less unregulated markets created by the Industrial Revolution caused consternation among many contemporaries. Until there were significant breakthroughs in public health, mortality rates in industrial cities were markedly worse than in the countryside. Moreover, the advent of a new and far-from-regular "business cycle," marked by periodic crises of industrial overinvestment and financial panic, generally made a stronger impression on people than the gradual increase in the economy's average growth rate. Although the Industrial Revolution manifestly improved life over the long run, in the short run it seemed to make things worse.

Intellectuals, as Schumpeter observed, were not slow to draw attention to this shadow side. One of William Blake's illustrations for his preface to *Milton* featured, among other somber images, a dark-skinned figure holding up a blood-soaked length of cotton yarn. For the composer Richard Wagner, London was "Alberich's dream come true—Nibelheim, world dominion, activity, work, everywhere the oppressive feeling of steam and fog." Hellish images of the British factory inspired his depiction of the dwarf's underground realm in *Das Rheingold* as well as one of the great leitmotifs of the entire *Ring* cycle, the insistent, staccato rhythm of multiple hammers.

Steeped in German literature and philosophy, the Scottish philosopher Thomas Carlyle was the first writer to identify what seemed the fatal flaw of the industrial economy: that it reduced all social relations to what he called, in his great essay *Past and Present*, "the cash nexus":

> The world has been rushing on with such fiery animation to get work and ever more work done, it has had no time to think of dividing the wages; and has merely left them to be scrambled for by the

Law of the Stronger, law of Supply-and-demand, law of Laissez-faire, and other idle Laws and Un-laws. We call it a Society; and go about professing openly the totalest separation, isolation. Our life is not a mutual helpfulness; but rather, cloaked under due laws-of-war, named "fair competition" and so forth, it is a mutual hostility. We have profoundly forgotten everywhere that *Cash-payment* is not the sole relation of human beings. . . . [It] is not the sole nexus of man with man,—how far from it! Deep, far deeper than Supply-and-demand, are Laws, Obligations sacred as Man's Life itself.[11]

That phrase—the "cash nexus"—so much pleased the son of an apostate Jewish lawyer from the Rhineland that he and his coauthor, the heir of a Wuppertal cotton mill owner, purloined it for the outrageous "manifesto" they published on the eve of the 1848 revolutions.

The founders of communism, Karl Marx and Friedrich Engels, were just two of many radical critics of the industrial society. But it was their achievement to devise the first internally consistent blueprint for an alternative social order. A mixture of Georg Wilhelm Friedrich Hegel's philosophy, which represented the historical process as dialectical, and the political economy of David Ricardo, which posited diminishing returns for capital and an "iron" law of wages, Marxism took Carlyle's revulsion against the industrial economy and substituted a utopia for nostalgia.

Marx himself was an odious individual. An unkempt scrounger and a savage polemicist, he liked to boast that his wife was "née Baroness von Westphalen" but was not above siring an illegitimate son by their maidservant. On the sole occasion when he applied for a job (as a railway clerk) he was rejected because his handwriting was so atrocious. He sought to play the stock market but was hopeless at it. For most of his life he therefore depended on handouts from Engels, for whom socialism was an evening hobby, along with foxhunting and womanizing; his day job was running one of his father's cotton factories in Manchester (the patent product of which was known as Diamond Thread). No man in history has bitten the hand that fed him with greater gusto than Marx bit the hand of King Cotton.

The essence of Marxism was the belief that the industrial economy was doomed to produce an intolerably unequal society divided between the bourgeoisie, the owners of capital, and a property-less proletariat. Capitalism inexorably demanded the concentration of capital in ever fewer hands and the reduction of everyone else to wage slavery, which meant being paid only "that quantum of the means of subsistence which is absolutely requisite to keep the laborer in bare existence as a laborer." In chapter 32 of the first tome of *Capital* (1867), Marx prophesied the inevitable denouement:

> Along with the constant decrease of the number of capitalist magnates, who usurp and monopolize all the advantages of this process of transformation, the mass of misery, oppression, slavery, degradation and exploitation grows; but with this there also grows the revolt of the working class. . . .
>
> The centralization of the means of production and the socialization of labor reach a point at which they become incompatible with their capitalist integument. This integument is burst asunder. The knell of capitalist private property sounds. The expropriators are *expropriated*.

It is no coincidence that this passage has a Wagnerian quality, part *Götterdämmerung*, part *Parsifal*. But by the time the book was published the great composer had left the spirit of 1848 far behind. Instead it was Eugène Pottier's song "The Internationale" that became the anthem of Marxism. Set to music by Pierre De Geyter, it urged the "servile masses" to put aside their religious "superstitions" and national allegiances and to make war on the "thieves" and their accomplices, the tyrants, generals, princes, and peers.

Before identifying why they were wrong, we need to acknowledge what Marx and his disciples were right about. Inequality did increase as a result of the Industrial Revolution. Between 1780 and 1830 output per laborer in the United Kingdom grew over 25 percent but wages rose barely 5 percent. The proportion of national income going to the top percentile of the population rose from 25 percent in 1801 to 35 percent in 1848. In Paris in 1820, around 9 percent of the population was classified as "proprietors and *rentiers*" (living from their investments) and owned 41 percent of recorded wealth. By 1911 their share had risen to 52 percent. In Prussia, the share of income going to the top 5 percent rose from 21 percent in 1854 to 27 percent in 1896 and to 43 percent in 1913.[12] Industrial societies, it seems clear, grew more unequal over the course of the nineteenth century. This had predictable consequences. In the Hamburg cholera epidemic of 1892, for example, the mortality rate for individuals with an income of less than eight hundred marks a year was thirteen times higher than that for individuals earning over fifty thousand marks.[13]

It was not necessary to be an intellectual to be dismayed by the inequality of industrial society. The Welsh-born factory owner Robert Owen envisaged an alternative economic model based on cooperative production and utopian villages like the ones he founded at Orbiston in Scotland and New Harmony, Indiana.[14] It was in a letter to Owen, written by Edward Cowper in 1822, that the word "socialism" in its modern sense first appears. An unidentified woman was, Cowper thought, "well adapted to become what my friend Jo. Applegath calls a Socialist." Five years later, Owen himself argued that "the chief question . . . between the modern . . . Political Economists, and the Communionists or Socialists, is whether it is more beneficial that this capital should be individual or in common."[15] The term "capitalism" made its debut in April 1833 in an English periodical—the London newspaper the *Standard*—in the phrase "tyranny of capitalism," part of an article on "the ill consequences of that greatest curse that can exist amongst men, too much money-power in too few hands."[16] Fifteen years later, the *Caledonian Mercury* referred with similar aversion to "that sweeping tide of capitalism and money-loving which threatens our country with the horrors of a plutocracy."[17]

Yet the revolution eagerly anticipated by Marx never materialized—at least, not where it was supposed to, in the advanced industrial countries. The great bouleversements of 1830 and 1848 were the results of short-run spikes in food prices and financial crises more than of social polarization.[18]

As agricultural productivity improved in Europe, as industrial employment increased, and as the amplitude of the business cycle diminished, the risk of revolution declined. Instead of coalescing into an impoverished mass, the proletariat subdivided into "labor aristocracies" with skills and a *Lumpenproletariat* with vices. The former favored strikes and collective bargaining over revolution and thereby secured higher real wages. The latter favored gin. The respectable working class had its trade unions and working men's clubs.[19] The ruffians had the music hall and street fights.

The prescriptions of *The Communist Manifesto* were in any case singularly unappealing to the industrial workers they were aimed at. Marx and Engels called for the abolition of private property; the abolition of inheritance; the centralization of credit and communications; the state ownership of all factories and instruments of production; the creation of "industrial armies for agriculture"; the abolition of the distinction between town and country; the abolition of the family; "community of women" (wife swapping); and the abolition of all nationalities. By contrast, mid-nineteenth-century liberals wanted constitutional government; the freedoms of speech, press, and assembly; wider political representation through electoral reform; free trade; and, where it was lacking, national self-determination ("home rule"). In the half century after the upheaval of 1848 they got a great many of these things—enough, at any rate, to make the desperate remedies of Marx and Engels seem de trop. In 1850 only France, Greece, and Switzerland had franchises in which more than a fifth of the population got to vote. By 1900 ten European countries did, and Britain's and Sweden's were not far below that threshold. Broader representation led to legislation that benefited lower-income groups. Free trade in Britain meant cheaper bread, and cheaper bread plus rising nominal wages thanks to union pressure meant a significant gain in real terms for workers. Building laborers' day wages in London doubled in real terms between 1848 and 1913. Broader representation also led to more progressive taxation. Britain led the way in 1842 when Sir Robert Peel introduced a peacetime income tax; by 1913 the standard rate was fourteen pence in the pound. Before 1842 nearly all British tax revenue had come from the indirect taxation of consumption via customs and excise duties, regressive taxes that take a proportionately smaller amount of your income the richer you are. By 1913 a third of revenue was coming from direct taxes on the relatively rich. In 1842 the central government had spent virtually nothing on education and the arts and sciences. In 1913 those items accounted for 10 percent of expenditures. By that time, Britain had followed Germany in introducing a state pension for the elderly.

Marx and Engels were wrong on two scores, then. First, their iron law of wages did not exist. Wealth did indeed become highly concentrated under capitalism, and it stayed that way into the second quarter of the twentieth century, but income differentials began to narrow as real wages rose and taxation became less regressive. Capitalists understood what Marx missed: that workers were also consumers. It therefore made no sense to try to grind their wages down to subsistence levels. On the contrary, as the case of the United States was making increasingly clear, there was no bigger potential market for capitalist enterprises than their own employees. Far from condemning the masses to immiseration, the mechanization of textile production created growing employment opportunities for Western workers—albeit at the expense of Indian spinners and weavers—and the decline in the prices of cotton and other goods meant that Western workers could buy more with their weekly wages. The impact is best captured by the exploding differential between Western and non-Western wages and living standards in this period. Even within the West the gap between the industrialized vanguard and the rural laggards widened dramatically. In early-seventeenth-century London, an unskilled worker's real wages were not so different from what his counterpart earned in Milan. From the 1750s until the 1850s, however, Londoners pulled far ahead. At the peak of the great divergence within Europe, London real wages were six times those in Milan. With the industrialization of northern Italy in the second half of the nineteenth century, the gap began to close, so that by the eve of World War I it was closer to a ratio of 3:1. German and Dutch workers also benefited from industrialization, though even in 1913 they still lagged behind their English counterparts.[20]

Chinese workers, by contrast, did no so such catching up. Where wages were highest, in the big cities of Beijing and Canton, building workers received the equivalent of around three grams of silver per day, with no upward movement in the eighteenth century and only a slight improvement in the nineteenth and early twentieth centuries (to around five to six grams). There was some improvement for workers in Canton after 1900, but it was minimal; workers in Sichuan stayed dirt-poor. London workers meanwhile saw their silver-equivalent wages rise from around eighteen grams between 1800 and 1870 to seventy grams between 1900 and 1913. Allowing for the cost of maintaining a family, the standard of living of the average Chinese worker fell throughout the nineteenth century. True, subsistence was cheaper in China than in northwestern Europe. It should also be remembered that Londoners and Berliners by that time enjoyed a far more variegated diet of bread, dairy products, and meat, washed down with copious amounts of alcohol, whereas most East Asians were subsisting on milled rice and small grains. Nevertheless, it seems clear that by the second decade of the twentieth century the gap in living standards between London and Beijing was around six to one, compared with two to one in the eighteenth century.[21]

The second mistake Marx and Engels made was to underestimate the adaptive quality of the nineteenth-century state—particularly when it could legitimize itself as a *nation*-state. In his *Contribution to the Critique of Hegel's Philosophy of Right*, Marx famously called religion the "opium of the masses." If so, then nationalism was the cocaine of the middle classes.

Nationalism had its manifestos too. Giuseppe Mazzini was perhaps the nearest thing to a theoretician that nationalism produced. As he shrewdly observed in 1852, the revolution "has assumed two forms; the question which all have agreed to call social, and the question of nationalities." The Italian nationalists of the Risorgimento

> struggled … as do Poland, Germany, and Hungary, for country and liberty; for a word inscribed upon a banner, proclaiming to the

world that they also live, think, love, and labor for the benefit of all. They speak the same language, they bear about them the impress of consanguinity, they kneel beside the same tombs, they glory in the same tradition; and they demand to associate freely, without obstacles, without foreign domination.[22]

For Mazzini it was simple: "The map of Europe has to be remade." In the future, he argued, it would be neatly reordered as eleven nation-states. This was much easier said than done, however, which was why the preferred modes of nationalism were artistic or gymnastic rather than programmatic. Nationalism worked best in the demotic poetry of writers like the Greek Rigas Feraios ("It's better to have an hour as a free man than forty years as a slave") or in the stirring songs of the German student fraternities ("The sentry on the Rhine stands firm and true"), or even on the sports field, where Scotland played England on St. Andrew's Day, 1872, in the world's first international soccer match (result: 0–0). It was more problematic when political borders, linguistic borders, and religious borders failed to coincide, as they did most obviously in the fatal triangle of territory between the Baltic, the Balkans, and the Black Sea. Between 1830 and 1905, eight nation-states achieved either independence or unity: Greece (1830), Belgium (1830–39), Romania (1856), Italy (1859–71), Germany (1864–71), Bulgaria (1878), Serbia (1867–78), and Norway (1905). But the American Southerners failed in their bids for statehood, as did the Armenians, the Croats, the Czechs, the Irish, the Poles, the Slovaks, the Slovenes, and the Ukrainians. The Hungarians, like the Scots, made do with the role of junior partners in dual monarchies with empires they helped to run. As for such ethno-linguistically distinct peoples as the Roma, Sinti, Kashubes, Sorbs, Wends, Vlachs, Székelys, Carpatho-Rusyns, and Ladins, no one seriously thought them capable of political autonomy.

Success or failure in the nation-building game was ultimately about realpolitik. It suited Camillo Benso, count of Cavour, to turn the rest of Italy into a colonial appendage of Piedmont-Sardinia, just as it suited

Otto Eduard Leopold von Bismarck, count of Bismarck-Schönhausen, to preserve the prerogatives of the Prussian monarchy by making it the most powerful institution in a federal German *Reich*. The most famous line in Giuseppe Tomasi di Lampedusa's 1958 historical novel *The Leopard*—"If we want everything to stay as it is, everything will have to change"—is frequently cited to sum up the covertly conservative character of Italian unification. But the new nation-states were about more than just preserving the cherished privileges of Europe's beleaguered landowning elites. Entities like Italy and Germany, composites of multiple statelets, offered all their citizens a host of benefits: economies of scale, network externalities, reduced transaction costs, and the more efficient provision of key public goods such as law and order, infrastructure, and health. The new states could make Europe's big industrial cities, the breeding grounds of both cholera and revolution, finally safe. Slum clearance, boulevards too wide to barricade, bigger churches, leafy parks, sports stadiums, and, above all, more policemen—all these things transformed the great capitals of Europe, not least Paris, which Georges-Eugène Haussmann completely recast for Napoleon III. All the new states had imposing façades; even defeated Austria lost little time in reinventing itself as "imperial-royal" Austria-Hungary, its architectural identity set in stone around Vienna's Ringstrasse.[23] But behind the façades there was real substance. Schools were built, the better to drum standardized national languages into young heads. Barracks were erected, the better to train the high school graduates to defend their fatherland. And railways were constructed in places where their profitability looked doubtful, the better to transport the troops to the border, should the need arise. Peasants became Frenchmen—or Germans, or Italians, or Serbs, depending on where they happened to be born.

So effective was the system of nation-building that when the European governments resolved to go to war over two arcane issues—the sovereignty of Bosnia-Herzegovina and the neutrality of Belgium—they were able, over more than four years, to mobilize in excess of seventy million men as soldiers or sailors. In France and Germany around a fifth of the prewar population—close to 80 percent of adult males—ended up in uniform. When the leaders of European socialism met in Brussels at the end of July 1914, they could do little more than admit their own impotence. A general strike could not halt a world war.

The Turning of the Tide

What gave socialism a shot was that the hypertrophic nationalism of the first half of the twentieth century plunged the world into not just one but two world wars. Without these catastrophes, it is inconceivable that so many devotees of Marx would have come to power in the seventy years after 1917. The world wars made the case for socialism in multiple ways. First, they seemed to confirm the destructive tendencies of "imperialism, the highest form of capitalism," in Vladimir Lenin's words. Second, they greatly expanded the role of the state, which became the principal purchaser of goods and services in most combatant countries, creating precisely the kind of state-controlled economy that socialist theory claimed would perform better than free markets. Third, the wars acted as a great leveler, imposing very high marginal rates of taxation, wage controls, and price controls in ways that tended to reduce wealth and income disparities. Fourth, in 1917 the German government financed the Bolshevik coup in Russia that brought Lenin to power.

The tragedy was that those who promised utopia generally delivered hell on earth. According to the estimates in the *Black Book of Communism*, the "grand total of victims of Communism was between 85 and 100 million" for the twentieth century as a whole.[24] The lowest estimate for the total number of Soviet citizens who lost their lives as a direct result of Stalin's policies was more than twenty million, a quarter of them in the years after World War II.[25] Mao alone, as Frank Dikötter has shown, accounted for tens of millions: two million between 1949 and 1951, another three million by the end of the 1950s, a staggering forty-five million in the man-made famine known as the Great Leap Forward, yet more in the mayhem of the Cultural Revolution.[26] Even the less bloodthirsty regimes of Eastern Europe killed and imprisoned their citizens on a shocking scale.[27] In the Soviet Union, 2.75 million people were in the Gulag at Stalin's death. The numbers were greatly reduced thereafter, but until the very end of the Soviet system its inhabitants lived in the knowledge that there was nothing but their own guile to protect them from an arbitrary and corrupt state. Other communist regimes around the world, including the very durable dictatorships in North Korea and Cuba, were strikingly similar in the miseries they inflicted on their own citizens.

The various socialist regimes could not even justify their murderous behavior by providing those they spared with higher living standards than their counterparts living under capitalism. On the contrary, they were economically disastrous. The collectivization of agriculture invariably reduced farming productivity. A substantial proportion of the victims of communism lost their lives because of the famines that resulted from collectivization in the Soviet Union and China. North Korea had a similarly disastrous experience. Central planning was a miserable failure for reasons long ago identified by Ludwig von Mises, Friedrich Hayek, and János Kornai, among others. Indeed, the economic performance of strictly socialist countries got worse over time because of rigidities and perverse incentives institutionalized by planning.[28]

Moreover, the evidence is clear that as countries moved away from socialist policies of state ownership and toward a greater reliance on market forces, they did better economically. The most striking example—but one of many—is that of China, which achieved a true great leap forward in economic output only after beginning to dismantle restrictions on private initiative in 1978. After the collapse of "real existing socialism" in Central and Eastern Europe in 1989 and the dissolution of the Soviet Union in 1991, there was widespread recognition (the "Washington Consensus") that all countries would benefit from reducing state ownership of the economy through privatization and from lowering marginal tax rates. As figure 9.4 shows, the highest marginal personal income tax rate was reduced in nearly all Organisation for Economic Co-operation and Development (OECD) countries between the mid-1970s and mid-2000s.

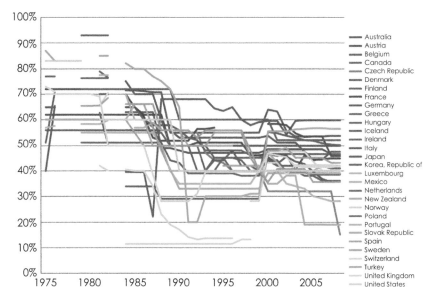

Figure 9.4. Top Marginal Personal Income Tax Rates, OECD, 1975–2008.
Source: Organisation for Economic Co-operation and Development,
https://stats.oecd.org/index.aspx?DataSetCode=TABLE_I7.

The Strange Rebirth of Socialism

By 2007, socialism seemed dead almost everywhere. Only the most ardently blind believers could look at Cuba or Venezuela—much less North Korea—as models offering a better life than capitalism. Even when the era of globalization and deregulation ended in the disarray of the global financial crisis, socialism did not initially show much sign of making a comeback. In most countries, the financial crisis of 2008–9 was more politically beneficial to the populists of the right, illustrating that, as in the nineteenth century, national identity tended to trump class consciousness whenever the two came into conflict.

Why, then, has socialism come back into vogue in our time—and in America, of all places?

To answer this question, it is helpful to turn back to Schumpeter. It will be remembered that he argued, first, that capitalism's propensity for "creative destruction" was also a source of weakness; second, that capitalism tends toward oligopoly, not perfect competition; third, that capitalism "creates, educates and subsidizes a vested interest in social unrest," namely intellectuals; and, finally, that socialism is politically attractive to bureaucrats and (many) democratic politicians. All four tendencies are visible in the United States today. Although policy makers have been successful in reducing the volatility of output and the rate of unemployment since the financial crisis—and very successful in raising the prices of financial assets above their precrisis level—the relative losers of the past decade have been succumbing in alarming numbers to what Anne Case and Angus Deaton have called "deaths of despair."[29] A number of authors have noted the decline in competition that has afflicted the United States in the recent past, most obviously—but by no means only—in the information technology sector, which has come to be dominated by a handful of network platforms.[30] The American academy is now skewed much further to the left than it was in Schumpeter's time. And, just as Schumpeter might have anticipated, a new generation of "progressive" politicians has come forward with the familiar promises to soak the rich to fund new and bureaucratic entitlement programs. It is noteworthy that younger Americans—nine out of ten of whom now pass through the country's left-leaning college system—are disproportionately receptive to these promises.

A fear that Hayek raised in *The Constitution of Liberty* was that of future generational conflict. "Most of those who will retire at the end of the century," he wrote, "will be dependent on the charity of the younger generation. And ultimately not morals but the fact that the young supply the police and the army will decide the issue: concentration camps for the aged unable to maintain themselves are likely to be the fate of an old generation whose income is entirely dependent on coercing the young."[31] Things have not quite worked out that way. A significant portion of older Americans are well provided for with substantial shares of total household wealth—much larger shares than younger generations seem likely to accumulate in the prime of life. Nor do the police and army look likely to be agents of generational warfare. Nevertheless, the recent intergenerational divergence of attitudes toward economic policy suggests that Hayek may have been right to worry about the young.[32]

New York representative Alexandria Ocasio-Cortez is often portrayed as an extremist for the democratic socialist views that she espouses. However, survey data show that her views are close to the median for her generation. The Millennials and Generation Z—that is, Americans ages eighteen to thirty-eight—are burdened by student loans and credit card debt. Millennials' early working lives were blighted by the financial crisis and the sluggish growth that followed. In later life, absent major changes in fiscal policy, they seem unlikely to enjoy the same kind of entitlements enjoyed by current retirees. Under different circumstances, the under-thirty-nines might conceivably have been attracted to the entitlement-cutting ideas of the Republican Tea Party (especially if those ideas had been adhered to). Instead, we have witnessed a shift to the political left by young voters on nearly every policy issue, economic and cultural alike. As figure 9.5 shows, it is the youngest voters in America who are most attracted to socialism, to the extent that those under forty almost prefer it to capitalism. This must be a matter of serious concern for Republicans, as ten years from now, if current population trends hold, Millennials and Gen Z together will make up a majority of the American voting-age population. Twenty years from now, they will represent 62 percent of all eligible voters.

Of course, it depends what is meant by "capitalism." According to a 2018 Gallup poll, just 56 percent of all Americans have a positive view of capitalism. However, 92 percent have a positive view of "small business," 86 percent have a positive view of "entrepreneurs," and 79 percent have a positive view of "free enterprise."[33] It also depends what is meant by "socialism." Asked by Gallup to define socialism, a quarter of Democrats (and Republicans) said it meant equality; 13 percent of Democrats saw it as government services, such as free health care; around the same proportion thought that socialism implied government ownership. (About 6 percent believed that socialism meant being social, including activity on social media.)[34]

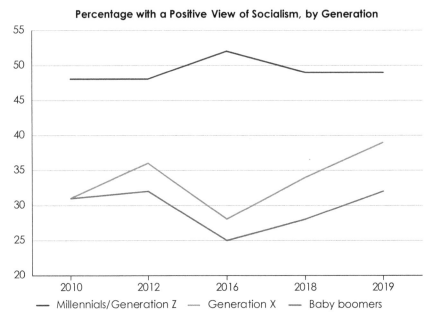

Percentage with a Positive View of Socialism, by Generation

— Millennials/Generation Z   — Generation X   — Baby boomers

Figure 9.5. Attitudes toward Socialism by Age Cohort, United States, 2010–19. *Source:* Lydia Saad, "Socialism as Popular as Capitalism Among Young Adults in U.S.," Gallup, November 25, 2019, https://news .gallup.com/poll/268766/socialism-popular-capitalism-among-young -adults.aspx.

Asked by television journalist Anderson Cooper to define socialism, Ocasio-Cortez replied: "What we have in mind and what my policies most closely resemble are what we see in the UK, in Norway, in Finland, in Sweden."[35] But just how socialist is Sweden today? The country is ninth in the World Economic Forum's competitiveness ranking, twelfth in the World Bank's Ease of Doing Business table, and nineteenth in the Heritage Foundation's Economic Freedom ladder. Many young Americans seem to have in mind the 1970s, rather than the present, when they wax lyrical about Swedish socialism.

So what does American socialism amount to? According to a 2018 Harvard poll, 67 percent of likely voters aged 18 to 29 support single-payer health care. Slightly fewer (62 percent) support making public colleges and universities tuition-free. A similar share (63 percent) supports

Gini Coefficients, Working-Age Population, 2014 or Latest Available Year

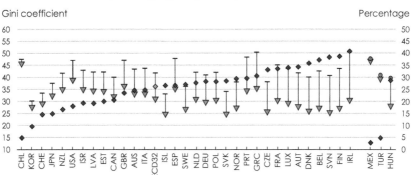

Figure 9.6. Gini Coefficients and Effects of Fiscal Policy, OECD Countries, ca. 2014. *Source:* Orsetta Causa and Mikkel Hermansen, "Income Redistribution through Taxes and Transfers across OECD Countries," VoxEU, March 23, 2018, https://voxeu.org/article/income-redistribution-through -taxes-and-transfers.

Ocasio-Cortez's proposal to create a federal jobs guarantee. Many Gen Z voters are not yet in the workforce, but more than a third (36 percent) support a "militant and powerful labor movement."[36] Although wary of government in the abstract, young Americans nevertheless embrace it as the solution to the problems they perceive. Among members of Gen Z, a 2019 Pew survey found seven in ten believe that the government "should do more to solve problems."[37]

These polling results strongly suggest that what young Americans mean by "socialism" is nothing of the kind. What they have in mind is not the state taking over ownership of the means of production, which is the true meaning of socialism. They merely aspire to policies on health care and education that imply a more European system of fiscal redistribution, with higher progressive taxation paying for cheaper or free health care and higher education. As figure 9.6 shows, OECD countries vary widely in the extent to which they reduce inequality by means of taxes and transfers. At one extreme is Chile, which only minimally reduces its Gini coefficient through its fiscal system; at the other is Ireland, which would be even less egalitarian than Chile without taxes and transfers but which reduces inequality by more than any other OECD country through the various levers of fiscal policy. American voters may one day opt for an Irish level of egalitarianism, but it would be a mistake to regard this as a triumph for socialism. So long as it is a large private sector that is being taxed to pay for the benefits being disbursed to lower-income groups, socialism is not le mot juste.

A final cause of confusion that remains to be resolved is what to make of "socialism with Chinese characteristics." According to *The Economist*, "The non-state sector contributes close to two-thirds of China's GDP growth and eight-tenths of all new jobs."[38] Clearly, the most dynamic Chinese corporations—Alibaba and Tencent, for example—are not state-owned enterprises (SOEs). The state sector has shrunk in relative terms significantly since the beginning of economic reform in the late 1970s. A common conclusion drawn by many Western visitors is that China is now socialist in name only; functionally it is a capitalist economy.

One objection to that conclusion is that since the accession to power of Xi Jinping, there has been a deliberate revival of the state sector. In 2012, for example, private-sector companies received 52 percent of new loans issued by the official bank sector, compared with 32 percent to SOEs. But in 2016 private companies received just 11 percent of new loans, while more than 80 percent flowed to SOEs. The balance has shifted back in the other direction in more recent years, but the central government retains an option to direct credit in this discriminatory way, just as it re-lies on capital controls to prevent Chinese investors from sending more of their money abroad and on anticorruption procedures to confiscate the property of officials and businessmen deemed to have transgressed. Recent developments in China—notably the trimming of the wings of Alibaba founder Jack Ma and the tech sector generally and the promo-tion of the old egalitarian slogan of "common prosperity"—make it clear that the direction of travel in Beijing is away from the market economy.

Schumpeter largely omitted from his analysis an important variable that helps explain why socialism did not prevail in most countries in the second half of the twentieth century—namely, the rule of law. Because

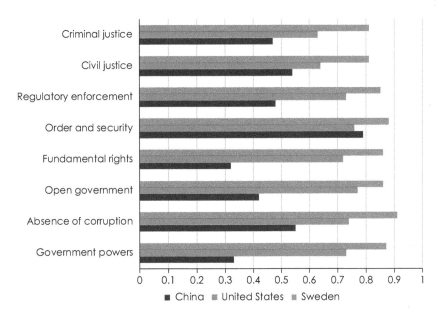

Figure 9.7. World Justice Index Scores for Sweden, the United States, and China, 2019. *Source:* World Justice Project, *WJP Rule of Law Index 2019,* https://worldjusticeproject.org/our-work/research-and-data/wjp-rule-law -index-2019.

socialism at root means a violation of private property rights—the forced acquisition of assets by the state, with or without compensation—the most effective barrier to its spread is in fact an independent judiciary and a legal tradition that protects property owners from arbitrary confiscation. A common error made in the wake of the 1989 revolutions that ended communism in Central and Eastern Europe was to argue that it was capitalism and democracy that were interdependent, whereas in reality it is capitalism and the rule of law. On this basis, it is striking not only that China is so much inferior to the United States by most measures in the World Justice Project Rule of Law Index but also that Sweden is some way ahead of the United States (see figure 9.7).

The defining characteristic of socialist states is not their lack of democracy but their lack of law. So long as China does not introduce a meaningful reform of the law—creating an independent judiciary and a truly free legal profession—all property rights in that country are contingent on the

Table 9.1. Carbon Dioxide Emissions, 2007–2018

	Million tons of carbon dioxide		Share of total emissions (%)	Percentage change (%)	Share of increase (%)
	2007	2018	2018	2007–2018	2007–2018
Canada	551	550	1.6	−0.2	0.0
Mexico	429	462	1.4	7.8	0.09
US	5,861	5,145	15.2	−12.2	0.0
Total North America	6,841	6,158	18.2	−10.0	0.0
Brazil	351	442	1.3	26.0	2.4
Total S. & Cent. America	1,103	1,287	3.8	16.7	4.8
Europe	5,008	4,248	12.5	−15.2	0.0
Total CIS	1,963	2,100	6.2	7.0	3.6
Total Middle East	1,511	2,119	6.3	40.2	15.8
Total Africa	958	1,235	3.6	28.8	7.2
China	7,240	9,429	27.8	30.2	56.9
India	1,366	2,479	7.3	81.5	29.0
Indonesia	387	543	1.6	40.5	4.1
Total Asia Pacific	12,663	16,744	49.4	32.2	106.2

Source: BP plc, BP Energy Outlook, 2019 edition (London, 2019).

will of the Communist Party. It is perhaps worth adding that precisely because property rights in a socialist state are so constrained, there is almost no limit to the negative externalities that can be foisted on citizens and neighboring countries by polluting state enterprises (see table 9.1).

Nearly eighty years ago, Schumpeter was right to identify the inbuilt weaknesses of capitalism and the strengths of socialism and to perceive that democracy alone would not necessarily uphold the free-market system. He correctly identified the enemies within, which would turn against capitalism even in its most propitious habitat, the United States. He did not, however, spend enough time thinking about what institutions might be counted on to defend capitalism against socialism. In a characteristically sarcastic passage setting out the supposed benefits of socialism, Schumpeter notes:

A considerable part of the total work done by lawyers goes into the struggle of business with the state and its organs. It is immaterial whether we call this vicious obstruction of the common good or defense of the common good against vicious obstruction. In any case the fact remains that in socialist society there would be neither need nor room for this part of legal activity. The resulting saving is not satisfactorily measured by the fees of the lawyers who are thus engaged. That is inconsiderable. But not inconsiderable is the social loss from such unproductive employment of many of the best brains. Considering how terribly rare good brains are, their shifting to other employments might be of more than infinitesimal importance.[39]

Conspicuously, Schumpeter did not subsequently acknowledge that defending business against the state is in fact an economically beneficial activity, insofar as it upholds the rights of private property and makes it difficult to violate them. Perhaps he did not feel that he needed to state something so obvious. Yet sometimes it is the responsibility of a public intellectual to do just that.

What makes socialism pernicious is not so much the inefficiency that invariably attends state ownership of any asset as the erosion of property rights that tends inevitably to be associated with the state's acquisition of private assets. Where—as in Sweden in the 1950s and 1960s—socialists acquired a dominant political position without overthrowing property rights in pursuit of direct state ownership, it proved possible to roll socialism back, once the inefficiencies of state control became apparent.[40] But where—as in China or Venezuela—the rule of law has essentially ceased to exist, such self-correction becomes almost impossible. The socialist economy can then go down only one of two possible paths: toward authoritarianism, to rein in the oligarchs and carpetbaggers, or toward anarchy. This is a lesson that young Americans might have been taught at college. It is unfortunate that, as Schumpeter predicted, the modern American university is about the last place one would choose to visit if one wished to learn the truth about the history of socialism.

NOTES

1. Joseph Schumpeter, *Capitalism, Socialism and Democracy* (London: Routledge, 2003), 61, 167; first published in 1942 by Harper & Brothers (New York).
2. Thomas K. McCraw, *Prophet of Innovation: Joseph Schumpeter and Creative Destruction* (Cambridge, MA: Belknap Press, 2007), 307ff., 317.
3. McCraw, *Prophet of Innovation*, 350ff.
4. David M. Levy and Sandra J. Peart, "The Fragility of a Discipline When a Model Has Monopoly Status," *Review of Austrian Economics* 19, no. 2 (2006): 131–35.
5. David M. Levy and Sandra J. Peart, *Soviet Growth & American Textbooks*, SSRN, December 3, 2009, https://ssrn.com/sol3/papers.cfm?abstract_id=1517983.
6. Johanna Bockman, *Markets in the Name of Socialism: The Left-Wing Origins of Neoliberalism* (Stanford, CA: Stanford University Press, 2011).
7. Bockman, *Markets in the Name of Socialism*.
8. On Nutter, see Phillip W. Magness, "The Soviet Economy Was Not Growing; It Was Dying," American Institute for Economic Research, January 10, 2020. Nutter had the distinction of being the first of Milton Friedman's doctoral students to embark on an academic career.
9. Henry A. Kissinger, *Years of Upheaval* (Boston: Little, Brown, 1982), 229.
10. Niall Ferguson, "An Evolutionary Approach to Financial History," *Cold Spring Harbor Symposia on Quantitative Biology* 74 (January 2009): 449–54.
11. Thomas Carlyle, *Past and Present*, book 1, chaps. 1–4; book 4, chaps. 4, 8 (London, 1843).
12. Hartmut Kaelble, *Industrialization and Social Inequality in 19th-Century Europe*, trans. Bruce Little (New York: St. Martin's Press, 1986).
13. Richard J. Evans, *Death in Hamburg: Society and Politics in the Cholera Years, 1830–1910* (Oxford: Oxford University, 1987).
14. A. C. Grayling, *Toward the Light of Liberty: The Struggles for Freedom and Rights That Made the Western World* (New York: Walker & Co., 2007), 189–93.
15. Nan Sloane, *The Women in the Room: Labour's Forgotten History* (London: Bloomsbury Publishing, 2018), 37.
16. *The Standard*, April 23, 1933.
17. *Oxford English Dictionary* online edition.
18. Helge Berger and Mark Spoerer, "Economic Crises and the European Revolution of 1848," *Journal of Economic History* 61, no. 2 (2001): 293–326.

19. See, e.g., Alan Fowler, *Lancashire Cotton Operatives and Work, 1900–1950: A Social History of Lancashire Cotton Operatives in the Twentieth Century* (Aldershot, UK: Ashgate, 2003).

20. Robert C. Allen, "The Great Divergence in European Wages and Prices from the Middle Ages to the First World War," *Explorations in Economic History* 38 (2001): 411–47.

21. Robert C. Allen, Jean-Pascal Bassino, Debin Ma, Christine Moll-Murata, and Jan Luiten van Zanden, "Wages, Prices, and Living Standards in China, Japan, and Europe, 1738–1925," working paper, 2005.

22. Giuseppe Mazzini, "To the Italians," in *The Duties of Man and Other Essays*, trans. Thomas Jones (Charleston, SC: Nabu Press, 2010).

23. Carl E. Schorske, *Fin-de-Siècle Vienna: Politics and Culture* (New York: Random House, 1979).

24. Stéphane Courtois et al., *The Black Book of Communism: Crimes, Terror, Repression*, trans. Jonathan Murphy and Mark Kramer (Cambridge, MA: Harvard University Press, 1999).

25. Rudolph R. Rummel, *Lethal Politics: Soviet Genocide and Mass Murder since 1917* (Piscataway, NJ: Transaction Publishers, 1990).

26. Frank Dikötter, *The Tragedy of Liberation: A History of the Chinese Revolution, 1945–1957* (London: Bloomsbury Publishing, 2013); Dikötter, *Mao's Great Famine: The History of China's Most Devastating Catastrophe, 1958–1962* (New York: Walker & Co.).

27. Anne Applebaum, *Iron Curtain: The Crushing of Eastern Europe, 1944–1956* (London: Allen Lane, 2012).

28. *Economic Report of the President*, with *The Annual Report of the Council of Economic Advisers* (Washington, DC: US Government Printing Office, 2009), 381–426.

29. Anne Case and Angus Deaton, *Mortality and Morbidity in the 21st Century*, Brookings Papers on Economic Activity (Washington, DC: Brookings Institution, Spring 2017), 397–476.

30. Jonathan Tepper, with Denise Hearn, *The Myth of Capitalism: Monopolies and the Death of Competition* (New York: Wiley, 2018).

31. Friedrich Hayek, *The Constitution of Liberty* (London: Routledge, 2014), 258; first published in 1960 by the University of Chicago Press.

32. Niall Ferguson and Eyck Freymann, "The Coming Generation War," *The Atlantic*, May 6, 2019.

33. Frank Newport, "Democrats More Positive About Socialism Than Capitalism," Gallup, August 13, 2018, https://news.gallup.com/poll/240725/democrats-positive -socialism-capitalism.aspx.

34. Newport, "The Meaning of 'Socialism' to Americans Today," Gallup, October 4, 2018, https://news.gallup.com/opinion/polling-matters/243362/meaning-socialism -americans-today.aspx.

35. Anderson Cooper, "Alexandria Ocasio-Cortez: The Rookie Congresswoman Challenging the Democratic Establishment," *CBS News*, January 6, 2019, https:// www.cbsnews.com/news/alexandria-ocasio-cortez-the-rookie-congresswoman -challenging-the-democratic-establishment-60-minutes-interview-full-transcript -2019-01-06.

36. "Harvard IOP Youth Poll Finds Democrats Maintaining Heightened Levels of Interest as Republican Engagement Grows, Preference for Democratic Control of Congress Narrowed Slightly Since Spring," Harvard Kennedy School Institute of Politics, Fall 2018 National Youth Poll, https://iop.harvard.edu/fall -2018-national-youth-poll.

37. Ferguson and Freymann, "The Coming Generation War." See Kim Parker, Nikki Graf, and Ruth Igielnik, "Generation Z Looks a Lot Like Millennials on Key Social and Political Issues," Pew Research Center, January 17, 2019, https://www.pewresearch.org/social-trends/2019/01/17/generation-z-looks-a -lot-like-millennials-on-key-social-and-political-issues.

38. "China's Private Sector Faces an Advance by the State," *The Economist*, December 6, 2018, https://www.economist.com/business/2018/12/08/chinas -private-sector-faces-an-advance-by-the-state.

39. Schumpeter, *Capitalism, Socialism and Democracy*, 198.

40. Magnus Henrekson and Ulf Jakobsson, "Where Schumpeter Was Nearly Right—The Swedish Model and Capitalism, Socialism and Democracy," *Journal of Evolutionary Economics* 11, no. 3 (2001): 331–58.

10

Socialism and the Constitution

Michael W. McConnell

You say you want a revolution
Well, you know
We all want to change the world . . .
You say you'll change the Constitution
Well, you know . . .
You'd better free your mind instead.

—"Revolution," the Beatles (1968)

We don't hear quite as much about "revolution" today as at the time of the Beatles. But we hear lots from young people about "socialism" and the need to "change the Constitution." Yes, we still "all want to change the world." That aspiration never grows old. Contrary to popular memory, however, the Beatles were *not* celebrating revolution in their famous lyrics, let alone a radical revision of the Constitution. No, their message to young people in the 1960s was "you'd better free your mind instead." Which leads to the question: What, exactly, *is* the connection between the drive to socialism and the Constitution?

Justice Oliver Wendell Holmes famously described the US Constitution as "made for people of fundamentally differing views" (*Lochner v. New*

York dissent).[1] By that, he meant that the Constitution does not commit the nation to any particular ideological or economic theory, including laissez-faire capitalism. Instead it leaves decisions about national policy to the democratic process, subject to the constraints of the Bill of Rights. Within the range of ordinary politics, Holmes was correct: Americans can decide, through their elected representatives, to have high taxes or low, generous welfare payments or a basic social safety net, government-owned enterprises or privatization, heavy-handed or light-touch regulation. That is the difference between democratic socialism and a largely free-enterprise economy. As practiced (more in the past than today) in the Scandinavian countries, "democratic socialism" has meant a capitalist, private-profit-driven market economy, with high rates of taxation and economic redistribution. In its postwar British incarnation, "democratic socialism" added government ownership of major industry. (This was abandoned mostly for the pragmatic reason that government is not a good manager of economic enterprise.) None of this is forbidden by the US Constitution. Congress can set taxes as high as it wishes and can devote the proceeds to redistributionist policies. Governments can, if they wish, use the power of eminent domain to seize ownership of the means of production (provided that owners are compensated for the value of property taken), and they have owned and run large enterprises like the Tennessee Valley Authority. Regulation of some sectors of the economy can be so extensive that the companies are rendered "private" in name only. Most policies that go by the label "democratic socialism" are thus permitted under the Constitution, so long as these objectives are pursued peacefully, democratically, and in accordance with law.

But the Constitution is not completely indifferent to the nature of the socioeconomic regime. It does not commit the nation to any one set of policies, but it stands as a barrier to revolutionary absolutism, it rests on a philosophy of individual rights that is most consistent with liberal democracy and private property, and it contains a number of safeguards designed to foster a free and prosperous economy.

Would a Socialist Revolution Require Us to Change the Constitution?

The Beatles were right: a socialist revolution inspired by "pictures of Chairman Mao" (or T-shirts of Che Guevara) would indeed have to "change the Constitution." Revolutions entail violence undisciplined by law or orderly process; the Constitution requires due process of law, enshrines the right of habeas corpus, forbids arbitrary confinement, and interposes a jury of one's peers between the accused and his accusers. Revolutions displace elected government with self-appointed leaders purporting to speak in the name of the People; the Constitution reserves governing power to republican institutions, with regular elections at specified intervals. Revolutions seize control over the media for dissemination of news and opinion; the First Amendment insists that these be under decentralized private control, allowing dissenting voices to be heard—even voices deemed by the dominant group to be retrograde or pernicious. A socialist revolution along Marxist or Maoist lines would bring an end to private property and the market ordering of society through private contract, while the Constitution explicitly protects private property and the obligation of contract.

Of course, this presupposes that at a time of revolutionary upheaval the guardrails of the Constitution would be respected. That is far from certain. It might even seem improbable; revolutionaries do not typically respect the niceties of written constitutions. But the structural features of the Constitution—its division of power among a large number of independently chosen and controlled entities—are designed to make it as difficult as possible for mass movements to impose their will on the nation as a whole, without the time for reflection and resistance. Power is divided among three branches at the national level, fifty different states, and thousands of municipalities, and coercive authority is further divided among police, militia, and military (a point that has come to public attention recently, in connection with the disputed use of federal troops and agents to enforce order in the cities over the objection of local officials). A faction pushing radical change cannot simply seize the levers of power at one central location. It has to build support in diverse places like California and Texas, Chicago and Pensacola. Although the "influence of factious leaders may kindle a flame within their particular States," James Madison wrote, the diffusion of political authority will make them "unable to spread a general conflagration through the other States" (*Federalist No. 10*).[2]

Even apart from actual revolution, the checks and balances built into American government make it difficult to anyone, whatever their ideology, to achieve rapid and transformative change. Both Barack Obama and Donald Trump swept into office with the support of both houses of Congress (Obama with a filibuster-proof majority in the Senate), but both presidents committed the political sin of overreach, both had their agendas delayed by a judiciary that was largely named by the other party, and both lost their majority in the House of Representatives in just two years. Our Constitution allows democratic change, but the checks and balances in the system are designed to slow things down, to give the American people time to reflect on whether the change being pressed by their representatives is really desirable. The Founders attempted to mold public democratic institutions in such a way as to protect "the rights of the minor party" from the "superior force of an interested and overbearing majority" (*Federalist No. 10*).[3] The constitutional system might thus be described as "small-c conservative": not right wing but resistant to rapid and convulsive change from either the right or the left.

The Constitution's principal mechanism for taming and controlling the power of majority factions was what today we would call diversity, which the Founders called "multiplicity of factions." In a relatively homogeneous district or jurisdiction, a particular group—whether ideological, economic, religious, racial, or based on some other common characteristic—can dominate and sweep all before it, without need for compromise or for consideration of the concerns and interests of dissenters. When the majority is "united by a common interest, the rights of the minority will be insecure" (*Federalist No. 51*).[4] The all-white districts of the Jim Crow South provide a familiar historical example: political leaders in such districts had no political need to heed the interests of the African American minority disadvantaged by their policies. But the point can be generalized. Modern social science research has confirmed Madison's intuition that the presence of dissenting voices within deliberative bodies has the effect of reducing polarization and moderating their views. Diversity of ideas thus mitigates the dangers of ideological faction. That is why multimember legislative bodies, elected from a variety of heterogeneous districts, are less susceptible to extremes than social movements or the executive branch, and why the Framers intended Congress to be the central institution for national policy making.

To be sure, this system slows the pace of change, but the Founders regarded this as a plus. It is not possible for people to order their affairs and plan for the future without a certain confidence that the rules will not change in the middle of the game. As Madison explained in *Federalist No. 62*, "It will be of little avail to the people, that the laws are made by men of their own choice, if the laws be ... repealed or revised before they are promulgated, or undergo such incessant changes that no man, who knows what the law is to-day, can guess what it will be to-morrow." Not only does uncertainty about the law "[poison] the blessings of liberty itself," but it dampens the incentive for socially productive economic endeavor. "What prudent merchant will hazard his fortunes in any new branch of commerce when he knows not but that his plans may be rendered unlawful before they can be executed?" Stability and predictability of law is essential to "the success or profit" of "every useful undertaking."[5]

The Philosophy of the Constitution

Although democratic socialism is not "unconstitutional" if achieved through democratic means, the Constitution has a certain philosophical content, which impresses itself subtly and powerfully on the national ethos. The Constitution was written against a backdrop of natural rights theory, in which the predominant purpose of government is to protect the life, liberty, and property of each person. The Founders understood that government of this sort would not only "secure the blessings of liberty" but also establish the preconditions for long-lasting national prosperity. The Constitution did not bind future generations to any particular ideology, but it did presuppose the importance of individual rights, and it laid the groundwork for the most productive economy the world has ever seen.

The writings of English philosopher John Locke are a good place to start. In his *Second Treatise on Government* (1689), Locke reasoned that by nature, all human beings are "free, equal, and independent." This freedom, equality, and independence is the foundation of the rights to personal security and property. As Locke put the point: "Every man has a property in his own person: this no body has any right to but himself. The labour of his body, and the work of his hands, we may say, are properly his."

But while all people have rightful ownership of themselves and the products of their labors, those rights are insecure in the absence of civil society and the protections it can confer. You might spend years cultivating a farm or building a store, only to have everything taken away or destroyed by brigands, mobs, or warlords. Without civil society and the rule of law, no one is safe. Locke called this condition of lawlessness the "state of nature." This term causes some to think that he was speaking of an imaginary period of human history, before recorded history. But the state of nature is not located in a mythical past. It is an ever-present possibility when civil authority breaks down. Think of Iraq after the fall of Saddam Hussein, of Bosnia or Northern Ireland during their troubles, of gangland Chicago, or even of American cities during times of violent unrest. Like weeds in an untended garden, the state of nature breaks out afresh whenever the forces of civil society weaken or retreat.

It bears emphasis that the biggest victims of lawlessness are not the rich and powerful, who can find or buy alternative private forms of protection, but the poor and vulnerable, who cannot. In our society, the victims are all too often minority or recent immigrant communities. The (presumably temporary) retreat of the police from active enforcement of the law in many of our cities leaves these vulnerable people subject to the highest death tolls and destruction of property.

Not only do people in the state of nature live in fear for their personal security, but this insecurity of rights removes the incentive to invest labor and resources in long-term projects of wealth creation. If the fruits of their labors are insecure, no one will make the short-term sacrifice that is necessary to create jobs and prosperity for all. People might wish to use their brains, their muscles, and their savings to cultivate farms, start shops, and create wealth, but who would do so if the profits may be smashed, stolen, or regulated away? The rule of law is a key ingredient of prosperity as well as of freedom and security.

As Locke and the American Founders understood, government itself can be as dangerous to the rule of law as private wrongdoers and can be just as much a threat to property and personal security. The American Revolution was sparked by a British soldier shooting an innocent Bostonian during a protest. An uncontrolled government is not much less dangerous than a mob and may be more so. That is why the recent police brutality and misconduct associated with the killing of George Floyd tapped so deeply into the shared American consciousness. Persons armed with the coercive power of the state must be bound by the rule of law, no less than private malefactors. The rule of law must prevail in police stations as well as on the streets. As James Madison wrote, "In framing a government which is to be administered by men over men, . . . you must first enable the government to control the governed; and in the next place to oblige it to control itself" (*Federalist No. 51*).[6]

What about Slavery?

Some readers are undoubtedly thinking: "What about slavery?" If all human beings are "free, equal, and independent"—if all are entitled to due process of law and protection against the depredations of others—then how could the Constitution permit, and even protect, the institution of slavery? The answer is that it was an ugly compromise without which there would have been no Constitution and no Union. The first step in John Locke's logic was that "every man has a property in his own person: this no body has any right to but himself. The labour of his body, and the work of his hands, we may say, are properly his."[7] It is not logically possible to begin with this premise and end up embracing slavery. Recent efforts such as the *New York Times*'s 1619 Project to portray slavery as foundational to the American ethos have it backward: from the beginning, slavery was in blatant contradiction to the governing philosophy of the new nation, and it had to be eliminated before America could be true to itself.

At the Constitutional Convention, no one doubted that the protections for slavery were a brutal and (for most of the delegates) distasteful compromise. According to Madison's Notes on the Federal Convention, Rufus King of Massachusetts called the treatment of slavery "a most grating circumstance to his mind, and he believed would be so to a great part of the people of America." Gouverneur Morris of Pennsylvania called domestic slavery "a nefarious institution" and "the curse of heaven on the States where it prevailed." Even slaveholders at the Constitutional Convention recognized the horrific character of the institution. George Mason of Virginia, who exercised ownership over hundreds of souls on his plantation on the Potomac, told his fellow delegates that slavery brings "the judgment of heaven on a Country" and that "every master of slavers is born a petty tyrant." Southern delegates typically refrained even from attempting a moral defense. John Rutledge of South Carolina defensively declared that "religion and humanity had nothing to do with [it.] ... The true question at present is whether the Southern States shall or shall not be parties to the Union." His fellow South Carolinian Charles Pinckney feebly suggested that if the region were left to its own devices, South Carolina "may perhaps by degrees do of herself what is wished." Most strikingly, the Framers carefully refrained from employing the terms "slave" or "slavery" in the Constitution, instead using euphemisms such as "persons held to service or labor." One delegate explained why: they were "ashamed to use the term 'slaves.'"[8]

Interestingly, the most determined opponents of slavery tended to be the advocates of a commercial (as opposed to agrarian) republic; capitalism was understood to be the alternative to a slave-labor economy. Later, "Free soil, free labor, free men" became the slogan of the abolitionists and pro-capitalist Republicans. Freedom from bondage was part and parcel of a free economy.

Eventually, the Constitution was amended in the wake of the Civil War to correct the most obvious constitutional flaws stemming from the slavery compromise and attendant racism. First, the Thirteenth Amendment put an end to slavery and involuntary servitude, thus removing the most obvious exception to the natural rights principles of the Constitution. Second, the Fourteenth Amendment extended the rights of citizenship to formerly enslaved people, and indeed to all persons born in the United States (with minor exceptions). These "privileges and immunities of citizens of the United States" include the basic rights to participate in civil society: to own, sell, and use property; to make and enforce contracts; and to equal application of criminal law and protections for personal security, among others. Locke would recognize all of these as fundamental rights. Third, all persons were guaranteed the "equal protection of the laws," thus for the first time enshrining the principle of equality under the law into the Constitution and striking a blow against the evil of racial discrimination. Fourth, the protection of due process of law was extended to acts of the states as well as the federal government. The original Framers assumed that state governments, being closer to the people, would be less dangerous to their rights than the more distant and less accountable national government, which is why the Bill of Rights applied only at the national level. The experience of antebellum slavery, which entailed assaults on almost every fundamental freedom, showed that was an error. And finally, the Fifteenth Amendment forbade voting discrimination on the basis of race—the first of a series of constitutional amendments expanding the right to vote.

To be sure, effective enforcement of these equality protections took a century or more to accomplish and even now remains incompletely fulfilled. But with the adoption of the Thirteenth, Fourteenth, and Fifteenth Amendments, the Lockean promise of respect to all persons as "free, equal, and independent," entitled to protection of both person and property, at last had its place in the fundamental charter of the United States. Subsequent amendments and civil rights statutes further advanced these principles. Adherence to those principles is the most promising means ever devised for achieving both personal liberty and social prosperity.

Legal Safeguards of Liberty

The Framers of the Constitution of 1788 relied primarily on structural safeguards—federalism, separation of powers, enumerated (thus limited) powers, regular elections, and an independent judiciary—to protect natural rights. Thus, the initial Constitution, signed by the delegates in 1787 and ratified by the people of eleven states in 1788, did not even have a Bill of Rights. The leading Framers thought a bill of rights unnecessary because, as Alexander Hamilton put the point, "the Constitution is itself, in every rational sense, and to every useful purpose, a Bill of Rights" (*Federalist No. 84*).[9] This was a political miscalculation: the absence of a bill of rights was the most potent argument against ratification of the new system. Thus, when the First Congress convened in 1790, one of the first orders of business was to amend the Constitution by adding protections for basic natural rights. This is not the occasion for a summary of all the first ten amendments; whole courses and treatises are devoted to nearly every one of them. But two sets of protections are the most significant.

First are the protections for freedoms of conscience and communication: speech and press, assembly and petition, and religion. These freedoms protect the ability of all persons to think for themselves, to say what they think publicly and try to persuade others, and to put their most fundamental beliefs into practice, so long as this is consistent with the equal rights of others and of the public peace. The point of these freedoms is not simply the psychological value of self-actualization, but the formation of a diverse culture in which different ideas can flourish and interact.[10] The First Amendment reflects the same high regard for diversity of views we have already seen in Madison's structural arguments for the multiplicity of factions. A society with a wide variety of views, freely expressed, would of necessity be more tolerant of difference, more open to self-criticism, and less prone to fanaticism. Anyone who has experienced an ideologically homogeneous environment—like many modern universities—can testify to the basic truth of that insight. Importantly, although the legal protections of the First Amendment apply only to the government ("state action")—and originally applied only to the federal government—the philosophical commitment behind those protections served powerfully to shape the American character. Indeed, without public commitment to dissent and diversity, it would not much matter that the government itself is prohibited from acting as the censor. The most significant free speech disputes today take place not in lawsuits against governments but in private arenas such as social media, universities, workplaces, and the press.

Second are the protections for life, liberty, and property through the guarantee of the rule of law. These protections, embodied most clearly in the Due Process Clauses, are the very heart of the Lockean natural rights theory with which this essay began. The Due Process Clauses (referred to here in the plural because there are two Due Process Clauses, one applicable to the federal government and one to the states) do not set any particular standard for liberty or property. Rather, they provide security for the liberty and property people already enjoy under prior law. This is clear from their words: "No person . . . shall be *deprived* of life, liberty, or property without due process of law." To say that a person may not be "deprived" of something presupposes that they had that thing in the first place. Moreover, the requirement that any deprivation be effectuated only with "due process of law" was understood to have the three components of a known, settled law; an objective judge in the case of disputes; and a firm and faithful execution.

The opposite of due process, as the Founders understood it, was arbitrary government: government in which the rights of individuals are dependent on, and vulnerable to, the transient will of those in power. As Locke put it in his *Second Treatise of Government*, all people must have the freedom to order their actions and dispose of their possessions and persons as they think fit, within the bounds of the law, "without asking leave or depending upon the will of any other man." This concept must not be confused with political libertarianism. The rule of law is compatible with extensive regulation in the common interest; how extensive is a matter of democratic choice. But whatever the extent of regulation, it must be achieved in the form of neutral laws, known in advance and applicable on a neutral basis to all.

Prosperity and the Constitution

After the delegates to the Constitutional Convention took their final vote and thirty-nine of them affixed their signatures, the Convention sent the document to the Congress, then sitting in New York, with a letter explaining what they hoped to accomplish. According to the letter, the Constitution would serve what "appears to us the greatest interest of every true American," namely "our prosperity, felicity, safety, perhaps our national existence." Most of the constitutional deliberations had to do with creating the institutions for workable republican government. But as the letter indicates, the delegates sought to promote the "prosperity, felicity, and safety" of the new nation as well. For many of them, that meant creating the prerequisites for a commercial republic.

What were those prerequisites? Let us list the most significant:

- A stable coinage and money supply
- A common market in which Americans could trade freely throughout the thirteen states, with no hindrance from local protectionism
- Exclusive national authority over foreign commerce, to enable the United States to negotiate mutually beneficial trade deals with foreign countries
- A national court system that would protect property and contract rights without the local biases of populist juries
- Sufficient resources and taxing power to finance national expenditures and reduce the national debt
- Guarantees that laws affecting liberty and property would be prospective and general in nature
- National control over the instrumentalities of national commerce, to prevent self-interested local interference with economic activity
- Provision for uniform bankruptcy laws and protections for patents and trademarks "to promote the Progress of Science and useful Arts"
- Prohibition of export taxes at either the state or the national level

None of these provisions could *guarantee* prosperity, but they gave the nation's fledgling government the tools needed to create a free economy. As the first secretary of the Treasury, the farsighted Alexander Hamilton took full advantage of these authorities and charted a course that would make the United States an unparalleled land of opportunity and magnet for immigration and investment from all over the world. To a very great extent, we still benefit from those early steps, but we must never grow complacent or forget the foundations of our success. The Constitution was written for "people of fundamentally different views," and it leaves basic policy choices to the determination of our elected representatives. The Constitution may protect against violent revolution, but it cannot protect against improvident democratic choices. Only an electorate informed about the nature of rights and the rule of law can do that.

Our Present Discontents

After the multiple crises we have experienced in the last few years, the Constitution's safeguards against oppressive majority factions seem to be losing some of their force. Instead of a multiplicity of factions, American politics appears to be hardening into just two, with a winner-take-all attitude and winners determined primarily by turnout rather than appeals to the middle. Congress has become largely reactive and dysfunctional, and the national policy focus has shifted to an overly powerful executive branch. This effectively replaces the constitutional system of checks and balances with what amounts to a plebiscitary democracy. Moreover, the rapidity and national scope of twenty-first-century communication, especially with the advent of social media, makes it easier than ever before for people to "kindle the flames of faction" (Madison's words) into a "general conflagration." The engines of this conflagration may be the populist right, the radical left, or something else entirely.

The Madisonian system relied on the idea that public-spirited leaders representing a multiplicity of factions would have sufficient time and independence to deliberate in good faith with representatives of contrary interests and views and act on the basis of the long-term interests of the nation as a whole. The results of this deliberation, he thought, would be more consonant with protecting "both the common good and the rights of other citizens" (*Federalist No. 10*).[11] Leaders would vote for policies they think wise and would face the voters several years later on the basis of how well those policies work. Today, by contrast, political and opinion leaders are often subservient to the hair-trigger reactions of Twitter-mobilized factions, which have no patience for compromise, little interest in long-term consequences, and a seeming delight in making life miserable for their opponents. Politics in the age of social media is less a search for broad-based solutions than a zero-sum struggle for dominance, with deliberation and compromise signaling weakness.

The greatest challenge of our day is not the receptivity of young people to the siren song of socialism, however troubling that may be. It is the susceptibility of our political culture to demagoguery and division on a scale unprecedented in recent American history. We are fortunate that America's constitutional institutions are as strong and resilient as they are. The stresses on the system from irresponsible leaders egged on by "the demon of faction" (as Hamilton called it) have been formidable. It would be tempting to hope that electing a better class of leaders would get us out of this predicament. But that is a futile hope, for as Madison warned, "enlightened statesmen will not always be at the helm." The excesses on one side only serve to fuel new excesses among its opponents. Real solutions will require a revitalization of stabilizing institutions such as responsible political parties, a credible press, civic education, a larger role for legislative deliberation, and an administrative state governed by the rule of law. Perhaps when the current interlocking crises subside, the American people will be more willing to turn again in that direction. If they do, they will find in the Constitution what Madison called "a republican remedy for the diseases most incident to republican government" (*Federalist No. 10*).[12]

NOTES

1. Lochner v. New York 198 U.S. 45 (1905).
2. Alexander Hamilton, James Madison, and John Jay, *The Federalist Papers*, ed. Clinton Rossiter (New York: Signet Classics, 1999).
3. Hamilton, Madison, and Jay, *Federalist Papers*.
4. Hamilton, Madison, and Jay, *Federalist Papers*.
5. Hamilton, Madison, and Jay, *Federalist Papers*.
6. Hamilton, Madison, and Jay, *Federalist Papers*.
7. Locke acknowledged this logical inconsistency in a backhanded way: he offered justification for a narrow class of servitude for persons captured for fighting an unjust war—conditions obviously inapplicable to the oppressed people held in bondage on American plantations.
8. Max Ferrand, ed., *The Records of the Federal Convention of 1787* (New Haven, CT: Yale University Press, 1966).
9. Hamilton, Madison, and Jay, *Federalist Papers*.
10. Jonathan Rauch's recent book *The Constitution of Knowledge: A Defense of Truth* (Washington, DC: Brookings Institution Press, 2021) is an extended reflection on this point and its relevance for current discourse.
11. Hamilton, Madison, and Jay, *Federalist Papers*.
12. Hamilton, Madison, and Jay, *Federalist Papers*.

11

Socialism versus the American Constitutional Structure

The Advantages of Decentralization and Federalism

John Yoo

Socialism in the United States

Socialism is finally getting its American honeymoon. But federalism's division of power between a national government and fifty sovereign states makes difficult, if not impossible, the unified economic planning necessary to supplant capitalism. Decentralization of power, the Constitution's Framers expected, would promote government effectiveness. But more importantly, they also hoped it would protect individual liberty by encouraging Washington and the states to check each other.

Our Constitution's fundamental decentralization of power does not prevent many Americans from wishing for socialism. A 2019 Gallup poll found that 43 percent of adults believed socialism to be "a good thing" and 47 percent even reported that they could vote for a socialist candidate for president.[1] Although a bare majority still opposes socialism, that view loses popularity among the young. Since 2010, their attitude toward capitalism has deteriorated to the point that Millennials view both capitalism and socialism with equal favor. That contrasts with baby boomers, who support capitalism over socialism by 68–32 percent, and Gen Xers, whose support is 61–39 percent.[2]

Socialism may be finding new popularity because of its ambiguity. The same Gallup poll reported that 6 percent supported socialism because they believed the concept meant being "social," as in friendly and talkative. An even larger proportion (83 percent) of the Millennials told pollsters that they held a positive view of "free enterprise," though 46 percent disliked "big business." Younger Americans went through the Great Recession of 2008–09 and the massive corporate bailout—and witnessed even worse with the COVID-19 lockdowns. They may simply equate "capitalism" with "big business." Others seem to believe that "socialism" means a desire for social justice or equality.

The near majority who view socialism positively may associate it with the welfare state, a safety net, or even environmental protection. They may believe it means the generous welfare systems of the Scandinavian nations, where public-sector spending reaches about half of GDP, compared with about one-third for the United States (which also has a much larger defense budget). Or they may believe that socialism refers to support for "economic and human rights," as Senator Bernie Sanders has defined it. Among those rights were not life, liberty, and the pursuit of happiness but instead "a decent job, affordable housing, health care, education, and, by the way, a clean environment." Socialism seemed to refer to nothing more than the welfare state combined with democracy.

By defining his platform this way, Sanders rendered democratic socialism more appealing. He came close to winning the Democratic presidential primary twice. But by describing socialism as a series of positive rights, to be provided by the public, rather than as negative limits on government as our Constitution does, Sanders gives the game away. He supported a Green New Deal, in which the federal government would seek to end certain sectors of the economy such as airlines or oil and gas production, and would promote other, more environmentally conscious forms of economic activity. He proposed a Medicare for All program that would have done away with all private insurance and made the government the sole payer for health care in the nation.

The massive government intervention necessary to carry out federal management of all energy production and health care in the national economy reveals socialism's true nature. As Peter Berkowitz writes in an earlier chapter in this book, "top-down management of economic life" is "the hallmark of socialism."[3] Under socialism "the state makes the major decisions about production, distribution, and consumption." It also "retains a direct say about who gets what property and how it is employed." Under capitalism, by contrast, "private individuals make the major decisions about production, distribution, and consumption." With a rule of law, the government "protects a far-reaching right to private property." In a capitalist system, private individuals own most capital; under socialism, it is owned mostly by the state.

The large governments needed to successfully operate socialism have led to its many twentieth-century failures. As Friedrich Hayek famously argued in *The Road to Serfdom*, government bureaucracies did not have the intelligence, computational power, or information to decide exactly how much to produce to satisfy the desires of a population. But that did not prevent nations from Russia and China to even the United Kingdom, France, and Italy from trying. The socialist experiment, as Niall Ferguson reminds us in his chapter in this book, did not produce utopia but instead "generally delivered hell on earth."[4] As Ferguson observes, communism cost the lives of between eighty-five million and one hundred million people in the twentieth century. Communist regimes could not even show higher living standards or economic progress as the result of all this tragedy; their centralization instead produced agricultural and industrial disasters. Government planners produced rigid, ossified, state-run systems that destroyed the economies of China, Russia, and Eastern Europe. Socialism today need not run hand in hand with brutal dictatorships, as the Scandinavian nations show. But the authoritarian governments of China, Russia, and Eastern Europe revealed the extremes of state power on which socialism depends.

While the Old World struggled through two world wars, the Great Depression, and the socialist disasters that followed, the United States enjoyed significant immunity. Admittedly, the federal government greatly expanded its size and reach during the New Deal of the 1930s and the Great Society of the late 1960s. The United States, however, never experienced a competitive socialist political party (Eugene Debs set the high watermark with 6 percent of the vote for president in 1912) or the widespread nationalization of industry that occurred in Western Europe. The size of the federal government in terms of the number of employees or as a percentage of the economy still pales in comparison to that of European governments. Compared to our advanced industrial peers, the United States still enjoys a significant decentralization among federal, state, and local governments, which strong institutions of private civil society (such as schools, churches, charities, and civic groups) further cabin.

The failure of socialism throughout American history has given rise to a cottage industry of debate over, as German sociologist Werner Sombart asked as early as 1906, "Why Is There No Socialism in the United States?"[5] Karl Marx and Friedrich Engels, as Ferguson reminds us, expected communist revolutions to break out in the advanced industrial countries, not the economically backward nations of Imperial Russia and Qing China. Socialism, with its prediction of ever greater concentrations of economic power in capital and declining wages for a vast proletariat, should have found a home in the United States at the turn of the twentieth century. But it did not.

Answers for this American exceptionalism have run the gamut. In his classic *Democracy in America*, Alexis de Tocqueville suggested that the United States would not fall prey to the political upheavals of Europe because America never carried the Old World's baggage of feudalism, aristocracy, and an oppressive state. Louis Hartz offered perhaps the most well-known thesis. He argued that Americans have an individualistic society and culture, rooted in a Lockean understanding of the world, that resists the power of the state.[6] Another important school of thought suggests that socialism failed in the United States because capitalism rewarded increasingly productive workers with higher wages and a general level of affluence that rendered socialism unattractive and revolution unlikely. Others argue that America's very diversity makes the class solidarity required for socialism impossible. Americans identify less with economic class than with ethnic, cultural, geographic, religious, and social groups. As Seymour Martin Lipset summarized in 2000, these factors made Americans "born conservatives" who enjoy economic prosperity and social mobility in a land without an aristocratic, centralized state.[7]

These explanations overlook another unique element of the American experiment: our constitutional structure. The United States Constitution originally established a radically decentralized system of government. Dividing power between a single federal government and fifty state governments makes it difficult to achieve the unified economic planning required by socialism. Unlike some European nations such as France, the fifty state governments are not just convenient administrative subdivisions of the national government. Instead, the states retain significant aspects of sovereignty in both their operations and their regulatory reach. The massive government intervention required by socialism would have to overcome not just this division of authority but also the possibility that the states would provide a political forum for opposition to any centralization of power in Washington, DC. The next section will discuss the original Constitution's understanding of federalism and why it adopts a decentralized approach to government power in the United States.

Why Federalism?

As the historical evidence from the Constitutional Convention and the ratification debates demonstrates, the Founders recognized that the states would remain a permanent feature of the national political system. As Chief Justice Salmon Chase declared after the Civil War in *Texas v. White*, the United States is "an indestructible Union, composed of indestructible States."[8] States exist not just out of political convenience, however, but to implement the will of the people and to protect lives, liberty, and property. As James Madison wrote in *Federalist No. 46*, "The federal and state governments are in fact but different agents and trustees of the people, instituted with different powers, and designated for different purposes."[9]

In creating this federal system with its two levels of sovereigns, the Founders explicitly chose decentralization as the guiding principle of our politics. They created a national government of limited, enumerated powers and reserved authority over all other matters to the states. As Madison wrote in *Federalist No. 45*, "The powers delegated by the proposed constitution to the federal government, are few and defined. Those which are to remain in the state governments, are numerous and indefinite."[10] Two years later, the Framers enshrined this principle in the Bill of Rights. As the Tenth Amendment declares: "The powers not delegated to the United States by the Constitution, nor prohibited by it to the States, are reserved to the States respectively, or to the people." The Tenth Amendment merely clarifies the principle behind the Constitution's grant of limited, specialized powers to the federal government, which recognizes the authority of the states over every other subject.

Of course, the Founders replaced the Articles of Confederation because it had become too decentralized for effective government. It is important to understand which powers they sought to place at the national level. Under the Articles, Congress had lacked the power to effectively conduct diplomacy, live up to treaties, and protect the national security. During this critical period, the states could not solve their collective action problems. National defense is the textbook example of a function that the central government must provide because it is non-rivalrous, in that each state benefits equally from it without reducing its availability to others, and it is nonexclusive, in that no state could exclude the others from it and thus force them to pay their fair share.

As a result, the Constitution granted the national government exclusive authority over foreign relations and national security. The Constitution vests the president with the commander-in-chief role and Congress with the power to declare war and raise the military. It grants the president, with the advice and consent of the Senate, the authority to make treaties. It allows Congress to impose economic sanctions on foreign countries and implicitly assumes that the president will conduct diplomacy. And the Constitution specifically prohibits states from engaging in armed conflicts or making agreements with foreign nations. We can view many of the other powers granted to the federal government, most notably the Commerce Clause, as solutions to other collective action problems.[11]

The states retained primary jurisdiction over almost all other domestic matters, such as law and order, property and contracts, and most social and moral legislation. Anti-Federalists attacked the Constitution on the grounds that the Necessary and Proper Clause gave the central government unlimited powers. Madison replied that federal powers "will be exercised principally on external objects, as war, peace, negotiation, and foreign commerce."[12] In contrast, state power would "extend to all objects, which, in the ordinary course of affairs, concern the lives, liberties and properties of the people; and the internal order, improvement, and prosperity of the State." Alexander Hamilton chimed in that the "administration of private justice between the citizens of the same State, the supervision of agriculture, and of other concerns of a similar nature" would remain outside federal power.[13] During the ratification debates, other Federalists declared that the national government could not invade state authority to establish the common-law rules governing property, contracts, trusts and estates, criminal law, and other local matters.

Scholars have argued that this division of authority bears several consequential benefits for public policy. First, states serve as the "laboratories of democracy," as Justice Louis Brandeis wrote.[14] They allow the nation to experiment with a variety of policies to solve pressing national problems, which limits the effects of poor choices to a single state while demonstrating good ideas that can spread. In the 1970s and 1980s, the United States experienced rising levels of violent crime. Federalism allowed states to experiment with a variety of anticrime strategies. Under Mayors Rudy Giuliani and Mike Bloomberg, New York City applied policing methods that produced extraordinary reductions in murder and other crime. If New York's policies had failed, the harmful effects would have remained in New York. If New York City's methods worked, as they did, other cities and states could borrow and adapt them.

Second, federalism allows for the tailoring of government programs to local conditions and different communities.[15] Environmental policy need not impose the same mandates in a state that does not suffer from certain weather conditions as it does in another state. Air pollution standards, for example, should not be the same for a dense, car-centric culture such as California and a low-population prairie state such as Nebraska.

Third, smaller governments may better handle certain subjects—such as crime and family policy—both to promote responsive government closer to the people and to divide authority efficiently between the nation and the states. Economists have found that under certain conditions, smaller governments can provide a more efficient allocation of resources that maximizes the well-being of their citizens.

Fourth, federalism promotes competition between the states. States can offer packages of regulation and taxes that strike different trade-offs of policy. California, for example, can tilt in favor of strict environmental protection but at the cost of regulations that retard industrial growth. It can impose high income taxes in exchange for generous public welfare and spending policies. Texas, of course, can do the exact opposite. Much as the market creates efficiency by forcing producers to compete to win the business of consumers, federalism encourages states to compete over public policy. Individuals benefit because they can choose to live in the states that match their preferences.

Fifth, federalism creates a risk-averse approach to government. It assumes that human knowledge does not necessarily give us the means to solve public-policy problems quickly or perfectly. Federalism creates a dispersed system for policy that allows for trial and error before the nation as a whole need adopt a solution. If the national government errs in crime policy, for example, the states can adopt a different approach. If the states fail to handle a public health outbreak, Washington, DC, can step in with personnel, money and resources, and technical expertise. Decentralization enhances resilience in government such that paralysis or failure at one level does not incapacitate the nation as a whole.

But federalism does more than enhance efficiency in the execution of public policy. It also protects individual liberty. Decentralization does this in several ways. First, federalism protects freedom by dispersing public power. Creating fifty sovereign governments makes it more difficult for any group to implement oppressive policies throughout the land. The Framers clearly anticipated the possibility that organized factions would seek to use the legislative process to the detriment of the public good. In his famous *Federalist No. 10*, James Madison responded to Montesquieu's claim, repeated by the Anti-Federalists, that democracy could survive only in a small nation and that larger territories would eventually collapse into tyranny. Madison argued that the great threat to liberty came from factions. To Madison, "the most common and durable source of factions has been the various and unequal distribution of property," which itself was due to the "diversity in the faculties of men."[16]

Madison's solution did not reject a national government in favor of small, fully autonomous sovereign states—in other words, the Articles of Confederation. Instead, Madison argued that liberty would find better protection in a large republic, where "clashing interests" would cancel each other out. The larger the nation, the more factions that would arise. The larger the nation, the more difficult for these many interests to combine and capture the government. Because the states would retain jurisdiction over most areas of everyday life, any interest that wished to infringe on individual liberty would have to persuade many state legislatures to agree—a difficult task, which is why interest groups will prefer to lobby Washington, DC, for a single national rule instead of seeking change in all fifty state legislatures.

Second, states exert a check on a national government that the Framers worried could become despotic. Today, we think of the protection of individual rights as the responsibility of written constitutional guarantees enforced by courts. If the government violates a protester's right to freedom of speech, he can go to federal court for an order blocking official action. But the original Constitution did not grant to the courts the exclusive protection of liberty. Rather, the Framers included structural limitations on government throughout the document. They wrote the Bill of Rights itself as negative restrictions on the federal government, for example, rather than as positive definitions of individual liberty. Only upon the ratification of the Fourteenth Amendment in the wake of the Civil War did the Bill of Rights become applicable to the federal and state governments. Its protection for privileges or immunities of citizens, for equal protection of the laws, and for due process allowed the Supreme Court to protect individual liberties against the states.

The original understanding of the Bill of Rights sought to preserve mediating institutions as much as, or perhaps more than, individual rights. The First Amendment does not itself define a freedom of speech and religion but instead says that "Congress shall make no law respecting" speech and religion. The Free Exercise and Establishment Clauses preserve religious groups, which themselves can check government. The Second Amendment protects "the right of the people to keep and bear Arms," not just the right of an individual to own a firearm. It protects the existence of the militia, another institution of eighteenth-century self-governance. The Fourth Amendment again protects the "right of the people," not of an individual, to be free from "unreasonable searches and seizures." The Sixth and Seventh Amendments preserve juries, which could check overzealous law enforcement.

The Bill of Rights often uses the rights of "the people" rather than of a "person," because the first ten amendments sought just as much to protect the people from an oppressive federal government as to protect the individual from the majority. The Ninth and Tenth Amendments expressly limit the government rather than define rights at all. The Ninth Amendment declares that "the enumeration in the Constitution of certain rights shall not be construed to deny or disparage others retained by the people." The Tenth Amendment states that "the powers not delegated to the United States by the Constitution, nor prohibited by it to the States, are reserved to the States respectively, or to the people." Even the Constitution's greatest advancement of individual rights, the Bill of Rights, devotes much of its efforts toward preserving decentralized government.

Liberty depends on state-based decentralization as one of its critical means of protection. We assume today that courts have a unique responsibility to protect individual rights. The Framers, however, would not have shared that view because they would not have immediately agreed that courts had the power of judicial review. The power of courts to set aside federal legislation appears nowhere in the constitutional text, and it is only from fine traces left behind in the document, and the greater structure it creates, that John Marshall could deduce the power of judicial review in *Marbury v. Madison*. Instead of just the courts, the original design expected other institutions—primarily the states—to protect individual liberty. Madison made this clear when he introduced his draft of the Bill of Rights in the first federal Congress. "Individual tribunals of justice will consider themselves in a peculiar manner the guardian of those rights," Madison began. "Besides this security, there is a great probability that such a declaration in the federal system would be enforced; because the State Legislatures will jealously and closely watch the operations in this Government." States, Madison predicted, will "be able to resist with more effect every assumption of power, than any other power on earth can do; and the greatest opponents to a Federal Government admit the State Legislatures to be sure guardians of the people's liberty."[17]

States would play two roles in protecting liberty. First, states would bear responsibility for defining and enforcing individual rights. The Framers did not expect the Bill of Rights to exhaust the list of individual rights; indeed, the Ninth Amendment says as much. "The powers reserved to the several States will extend to all the objects," Madison reminded the delegates to the state ratifying conventions, "which, in the ordinary course of affairs, concern the lives, liberties, and properties of the people."[18] Justice William J. Brennan similarly argued that states should play a creative role in defining individual rights more broadly than the federal government.[19]

Second, states would defend those rights when the federal government exceeded its powers. "[T]he state Legislature," Hamilton predicted in *Federalist No. 26*, "will always be not only vigilant but suspicious and jealous guardians of the rights of the citizens, against Encroachments from the federal government."[20] States could limit national invasions of individual rights by exercising their influence over the federal government through the Senate, their House delegations, and even the Electoral College. This idea uses the same mechanism as the political safeguards of federalism. If the states can protect themselves from federal expansions of power, they can use that same influence over the national government to protect individual rights too. The Constitution allows states to protect themselves from the federal government because it expects a certain amount of power in the former to protect individual rights from the latter.[21] If national authorities continued to infringe liberty, the Framers would have looked to the states to organize external resistance. States perform this function not only by acting as a trip wire to detect illegal federal action but also by acting as the organizers of resistance. Hamilton argued in *Federalist No. 28* that states "can at once adopt a regular plan of opposition, in which they can combine all the resources of the community. They can readily communicate with each other in the different states; and unite their common forces for the protection of their common liberty."[22]

The Framers believed that the chief role for federalism would be the protection of the people's liberty. Although limiting the power of the federal government might produce inefficiencies, this cost was necessary in order to guard against potential tyranny by a federal government filled with self-interested, ambitious politicians. Federalism brought important advantages not solely by diffusing power. To be sure, creating different power centers and merely decentralizing authority are not the same thing. We might attribute many of the instrumental benefits of federalism to decentralization of power, which would occur if states had no sovereignty but served only as convenient administrative divisions. But as separate political units, states can oppose the exercise of power by the national government, even if the national government and the people believe that the centralization of power at that moment is good public policy.

By allowing, or even encouraging, the federal and state governments to check each other, the Framers' Constitution seeks to create an area of liberty that cannot be regulated by either government. Dividing political power between the two levels of government appears even more effective considering the presence of a separation of powers in both governments. As James Madison wrote in *Federalist No. 51*, "In the compound republic of America, the power surrendered by the people, is first divided between two distinct and separate departments," here the federal and state governments, "and then the portion allotted to each, subdivided among distinct and separate departments," in other words, the legislative, executive, and judicial branches. "Hence a double security arises to the rights of the people. The different governments will controul each other; at the same time that each will be controuled by itself."[23]

Competition between the federal and state governments was not the only way that federalism would protect liberty. Freedom also would arise from the inefficiencies that the Framers built into the federal system itself. The nation's governments simply would not be able to regulate all the issues of life because, even if they could overcome the internal checks created by their separation of powers, their external powers would come into conflict and cancel each other out. This conclusion is at odds with an instrumental approach to federalism, which seeks to maximize social welfare through efficiency in the making and enforcement of policy. Federalism at times can prevent Washington, DC, from enacting policies that produce nationwide benefits. Nevertheless, the Framers believed this deliberate inefficiency to be necessary in order to protect liberty.

The Framers' Constitution raises several barriers to socialism. It creates a decentralized system of government in which the fifty states bear the primary responsibility for regulating most areas of life while Washington supplies national public goods. This division of authority inhibits the concentration of public power necessary for the unified economic planning demanded by socialism. Instead, the Constitution's federalism and separation of powers establish a checking dynamic between the federal and the state. Governments will compete for the support of their citizens by opposing the excesses of the other. This balancing act would create a space—an absence of government power—where individual freedom could continue to flourish. The next section will review the fate of federalism in the courts.

The Erosion of Federalism

American history shows that federalism initially went too far in its protection of states. Slavery made plain the most obvious flaw in the Constitution's original design—it failed to provide a minimum level of individual rights against states as well as the federal government. Slavery deprived a specific race, brought to the United States from Africa, of the same rights enjoyed by other Americans. The Constitution even gave slave states a political advantage with the rule that slaves counted as three-fifths of a person for purposes of allocating House seats. The Civil War ended slavery, and the Fourteenth Amendment's guarantee of privileges and immunities, equal protection, and due process against the states codified a new birth of freedom.

It would take, however, another century for the civil rights movement to force the United States to live up to the promise of the Reconstruction Amendments. To end the era of Jim Crow, Congress passed the 1964 Civil Rights Act, which prohibited racial discrimination in employment and education, and the 1965 Voting Rights Act, which barred racial discrimination in voting. The civil rights acts greatly extended the reach of federal power at the expense of the states. States could no longer use their police powers to engage in discrimination on the basis of race. But they also furthered federalism's original purpose in forcing the national and state governments to compete to expand individual liberty.

In the area of economic regulation, however, the national government so expanded its power that it undermined the decentralizing elements of federalism. Unlike the end of slavery, the broadening of federal power did not produce any corresponding expansion in individual freedoms. The Great Depression prompted the United States to experiment with socialist-type government. The economy had contracted by about 27 percent and unemployment reached a quarter of the workforce. Upon the inauguration of Franklin D. Roosevelt in 1933, Congress enacted a series of laws—the National Industrial Recovery Act (NIRA) and the Agricultural Adjustment Act (AAA) chief among them—that granted the president extraordinary powers to manage the economy. Under the NIRA, for example, federal agencies issued industry-wide codes of conduct to govern production and employment levels. The AAA gave the administration the power to dictate the crops that farmers could plant. Using these laws, the Roosevelt administration sought to reverse falling prices by setting prices, limiting production, and reducing competition.

Initially, the Supreme Court enforced the historical limits on national power. It invalidated the early New Deal as beyond Congress's powers under the Commerce Clause, which gives Congress the authority to "regulate Commerce . . . among the several States." Federal laws controlling all aspects of economic production violated Supreme Court precedents that held that Congress could not reach manufacturing or agriculture that occurred within a single state.[24] The court matched these limits on the reach of federal regulatory power with a robust protection for economic rights. Until the Great Depression, the court had held that neither the federal nor state governments could override contracts or regulate business in a way that infringed on the rights of free labor. *Lochner v. New York* had struck down minimum wage and maximum hour laws as violations of these individual economic rights.[25] The court similarly greeted early New Deal laws and struck the NIRA and the AAA down.[26]

President Roosevelt responded with his doomed court-packing proposal to add six additional justices to the Supreme Court. Although his plan went down to defeat, his threat ended the judiciary's resistance to the New Deal and opened the floodgates to federal control of the economy. In *West Coast Hotel Co. v. Parrish* (1937), a 5–4 court upheld a state minimum wage law.[27] In *NLRB v. Jones & Laughlin Steel Corp.* (1937), the same 5–4 majority upheld the National Labor Relations Act's national regulation of labor management relations.[28] After the "switch in time that saved nine," the Supreme Court would not invalidate a federal law as beyond the reach of the Commerce Clause for the next six decades. The ultimate expression of federal control over the economy came in *Wickard v. Filburn* (1942), in which a unanimous court of FDR appointees upheld a federal law that barred a farmer from growing wheat on his own farm for his own personal consumption.[29]

With virtually no limit on the Commerce Clause, Congress used its economic regulatory power to steadily concentrate power in Washington, DC. It enacted a series of laws governing workplace conditions, employment terms, and labor-management relations. It created regulatory agencies to govern entire industries, such as the Federal Communications Commission, and markets, such as the Securities and Exchange Commission. But Congress did not stop at economic regulation. In the 1960s and 1970s, it turned the Commerce Clause to social regulation. It enacted a host of civil rights laws, federal crimes, and environmental protections. By the end of the twentieth century, the court suggested that there were limits: the

Commerce Clause could not reach purely noncommercial activity, such as violent crime. But in 2005, it still turned away a challenge to the federal prohibition on the sale of marijuana, even when grown in a backyard and given as a gift between friends.[30]

Despite the potential extent of the Commerce Clause, Congress has shied away from direct control of many traditional local matters, such as education and welfare. States still exercise primary authority over the laws that regulate most matters of everyday life, such as the rules of property and contract, accidents, family, and crime. State governments still operate their own independent executive, legislative, and judicial branches, and they collectively far outstrip the federal government in numbers of law enforcement officers and resources. The New York Police Department, for example, has more sworn officers than the Federal Bureau of Investigation has employees. Even when the federal government has exclusive authority over a subject, such as immigration, it must depend on the cooperation of state officials to fully execute national policy.

Because the Framers hardwired decentralization into the constitutional system, the federal government has had to resort to financial enticement to expand its influence into areas of state control. The Spending Clause, which gives Congress the power "to provide for the common Defence and general Welfare of the United States," poses one of the greatest contemporary threats to federalism. Thanks to the great financial resources made available to the federal government by the Sixteenth Amendment income tax, Congress can offer states large sums of money—but with strings attached. The federal government offers states matching health care funds, but only if states follow the Medicare and Medicaid guidelines; it makes education grants to schools, but only if they obey federal mandates; it supports state welfare programs, but only those that comply with federal regulations. Although the Constitution's decentralized framework remains, the federal government has sought to overcome it with the "sinews of power"—money.

These expansions of the national government through direct regulation under the Commerce Clause or by the indirect influence of federal dollars threaten a concentration of power that could make socialism possible. This vast federal expansion discards the benefits of local, decentralized government and undermines the checking function of the states. It makes the effort of the Supreme Court to stop the Affordable Care Act, popularly known as Obamacare, of particular interest. Obamacare took a major step toward the socialization of health care, which accounts for more than 18 percent of the American economy, with Medicare and Medicaid constituting about 40 percent of the total. Critics challenged several elements of the law, such as its requirement that all adults purchase health insurance or pay a penalty, and its denial of Medicaid funds to states that refused to expand their health care programs in line with Obamacare requirements. In *Sebelius v. NFIB* (2012), the court held that the Commerce Clause did not give the government the power to force unwilling individuals to purchase products.[31] It also found that the federal government could not offer so much funding that the states were "coerced" into participating in federal programs. But it also found that the federal government could use its power of taxation to sanction individuals who refused to purchase insurance.

Sebelius, when combined with other, less prominent cases shoring up the sovereignty of state governments, shows that the current Supreme Court wants to restore some balance to federalism. As legal scholars have argued, other elements of the federal government share this interest in defending state interests, most obviously the Senate with its equal representation by state.[32] But even other, more popular elements of the federal government will pay due attention to federalism. The Electoral College process for selecting the president gives a slight advantage to federalism by giving each state electoral votes equal to its number of senators and members of the House rather than using direct popular election. As the 2000 and 2016 presidential races demonstrated, the state practice of awarding all electoral votes to the winner of its election gives candidates the political incentive to assemble a coalition of states, rather than just campaign in the most populous cities. The Constitution even creates the most popularly accountable branch of the federal government, the House of Representatives, by awarding seats by state, rather than proportionally by national political party support.

The United States of the twenty-first century does not enjoy the decentralized government envisioned in 1788. Centralization may have become inevitable with the nationalization of the economy, the rise of the United States in world affairs, and subsequent globalization. But we can still see the benefits of decentralization in federalism's instrumental advantages of experimentation, diversity, and competition in government. Decentralization still remains in the independent existence of the state governments and their advantages in resources and closeness to the people. What may suffer, as the Commerce and Spending Clauses steadily advance, is the dynamic between the national and state governments. That system of mutual checks and balances, the Framers believed, would constrain government and result in freedom and liberty. History does not suggest that the further centralization of government power would benefit the American people or their experiment in self-government.

NOTES

1. Mohamed Younis, "Four in 10 Americans Embrace Some Form of Socialism," Gallup, May 20, 2019.
2. Lydia Saad, "Socialism as Popular as Capitalism Among Young Adults in the U.S.," Gallup, November 25, 2019.
3. Peter Berkowitz, chapter 1 of this volume.
4. Niall Ferguson, chapter 9 of this volume.
5. The question was first posed in Werner Sombart, "Why Is There No Socialism in the United States?," which was republished in *Failure of a Dream?: Essays in the History of American Socialism*, ed. John Laslett and Seymour Martin Lipset (Garden City, NY: Doubleday, 1974).
6. Louis Hartz, *The Liberal Tradition in America: An Interpretation of American Political Thought Since the Revolution* (New York: Harcourt, Brace, 1955).
7. Gary Marks and Seymour Martin Lipset, *It Didn't Happen Here: Why Socialism Failed in the United States* (New York: W. W. Norton, 2000).
8. 74 U.S. (7 Wall.) 700 (1868).
9. James Madison, *Federalist No. 46*, in *The Federalist (The Gideon Edition)*, ed. George W. Carey and James McClellan (Indianapolis: Liberty Fund, 2001), 243.

10. James Madison, *Federalist No. 45*, in *The Federalist*, 241.
11. See Robert D. Cooter and Neil S. Siegel, "Collective Action Federalism," *Stanford Law Review* 63, no. 1 (2010): 115.
12. James Madison, *Federalist No. 45*, in *The Federalist*, 241.
13. Alexander Hamilton, *Federalist No. 17*, in *The Federalist*, 80–81.
14. New State Ice Co. v. Liebmann, 285 U.S. 262 (1932).
15. See Michael W. McConnell, "Federalism: Evaluating the Founders' Design," *University of Chicago Law Review* 54, no. 4 (1987): 1484, 1493–1500.
16. James Madison, *Federalist No. 10*, in *The Federalist*, 43–44.
17. James Madison, Remarks to the House of Representatives (June 8, 1789), in Bernard Schwartz, *The Bill of Rights: A Documentary History*, vol. 2 (New York: Chelsea House Publishers with McGraw-Hill, 1971): 1031–32. (1971).
18. James Madison, *Federalist No. 45*, in *The Federalist*, 241.
19. William J. Brennan Jr., "State Constitutions and the Protection of Individual Rights," *Harvard Law Review* 90, no. 3 (1977): 489.
20. Alexander Hamilton, *Federalist No. 26*, in *The Federalist*, 130.
21. John Yoo, "The Judicial Safeguards of Federalism," *Southern California Law Review* 70 (1997): 1311.
22. Alexander Hamilton, *Federalist No. 28*, in *The Federalist*, 139.
23. James Madison, *Federalist No. 51*, in *The Federalist*, 270.
24. Hammer v. Dagenhart, 247 U.S. 251 (1918).
25. 198 U.S. 45 (1905).
26. See, for example, A.L.A. Schechter Poultry Corp. v. United States, 293 U.S. 495 (1935).
27. 300 U.S. 379 (1937).
28. 301 U.S. 1 (1937).
29. 317 U.S. 111 (1942).
30. Gonzales v. Raich, 545 U.S. 1 (2005).
31. 567 U.S. 519 (2012).
32. Herbert Wechsler, "The Political Safeguards of Federalism: The Role of the States in the Composition and Selection of the National Government," *Columbia Law Review* 54, no. 4 (1954): 543; Jesse H. Choper, *Judicial Review and the National Political Process* (Chicago: University of Chicago Press, 1980).

IV

Social Democracy and Current Policy Debates

12

The Effect of Economic Freedom on Labor Market Efficiency and Performance

Lee E. Ohanian

The labor market is the centerpiece of every economy. It determines how society's human resources are utilized, both over time and across individuals, and how much workers are compensated for their labor services. In all countries, the labor market is the largest market in the economy: workers receive roughly 60 percent or more of the total income that is generated by market production.

An equally important issue is how well the labor market functions. The difference between a poorly functioning labor market and a well-functioning labor market can mean millions of lost jobs and billions of dollars in lost incomes.

Government policies and institutions have important effects on the efficiency of the labor market. In some economies, such as the United States, labor markets are not heavily regulated, tax rates are fairly low, and economic freedom is relatively high. In some other countries, labor markets are heavily regulated, tax rates are high, and consequently there is less economic freedom.

This paper summarizes research on how government policies that affect freedom of choice within the labor market influence its performance and efficiency. These policies include taxation, minimum wages, unionization, and occupational licensing requirements.

This review shows that freer labor markets, which have lower tax rates, less regulation, and more competition, are much more efficient and dynamic and are associated with higher employee compensation and greater employment.

These findings have important implications for economic policy making. They indicate that policies that enhance the free and efficient operation of the labor market significantly expand opportunities and increase prosperity. Moreover, they suggest that economic policy reforms can substantially improve economic performance in countries with heavily regulated labor markets and high tax rates.

As the United States and the rest of the world continue to address the health, economic, and social challenges presented by the novel coronavirus, sound labor market policies that respect the principles of economic and personal freedom will be central to restoring economic growth, while at the same time promoting public safety.

The US Labor Market: Stability Enhances Economic Growth

This section presents employment, hours worked, and employee compensation data to summarize the performance of the US labor market. These data will show that the United States has a very dynamic labor market that absorbs the large number of new workers constantly entering the labor force and that also reallocates workers across sectors in response to the enormous changes observed in economic and social conditions that have occurred since 1960.

This section will also show that American worker compensation has increased over time at nearly the same rate as productivity and that the shares of income paid to labor and capital have been roughly constant over time after adjusting for capital depreciation.

Figure 12.1 shows the total number of market hours worked in the United States relative to the US working-age population: those between the ages of sixteen and sixty-four. This is the most complete measure of

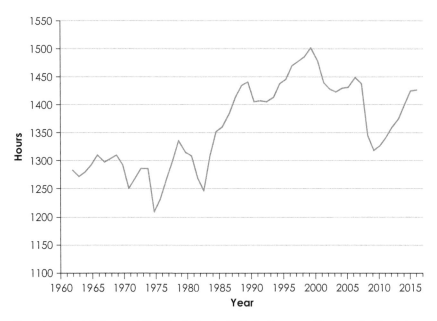

Figure 12.1. US Annual Hours of Market Work. *Source:* Simona E. Cociuba, Edward C. Prescott, and Alexander Ueberfeldt, "US Hours at Work," *Economics Letters* 169 (2018): 87–90.

market work because it combines employment data with the number of hours per worker. This ratio is naturally interpreted as the average annual number of market hours worked per US adult from 1960 to 2019. The data are compiled by Simona Cociuba, Edward Prescott, and Alexander Ueberfeldt.[1]

Standard economic principles indicate that hours worked per adult should be relatively stable in a well-functioning market economy. These data are largely consistent with this view. The average annual hours worked per adult per year in these data are about 1,360, with a standard deviation of just seventy-six hours per adult per year, which is about 6 percent of the mean.

The stability of US hours worked per adult is associated with enormous employment growth. Figure 12.2 shows the number of full-time equivalent US employees between 1960 and 2019. These data, which are constructed

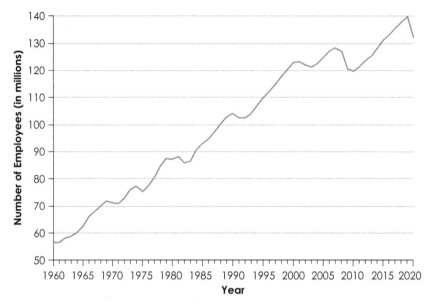

Figure 12.2. US Full-Time Equivalent Employees (millions). *Source:* US Department of Commerce, Bureau of Economic Analysis, "National Data: National Income and Product Accounts," table 6.5D, July 30, 2021, apps.bea.gov.

by the Bureau of Labor Statistics, highlight the dynamism of the American economy. Full-time employment grew smoothly from about 56.5 million full-time equivalent workers in 1960 to about 127.5 million in 2018. This is a gain of about 142 percent.

Although there are some fluctuations from trend growth, particularly around the recessions of the early 1980s, 2000–1, and 2008–9, the otherwise fairly smooth operation of the US labor market is striking. Looking at these graphs, one would be hard-pressed to identify many of the large economic and social changes that occurred over this period and that could have significantly affected the labor market's ability to absorb and allocate workers through 2019.

One such factor is the cohort of thirty-eight million baby boomers that entered the labor market between the late 1960s and the early 1980s. This large influx of young workers did not disrupt the US labor market.

Rather, the graph shows that the labor market readily absorbed this massive increase in the supply of new workers.

Another major factor affecting the labor market has been an ongoing shift from a goods-producing economy to a services-producing economy, in which manufacturing's share of employment declined from more than 25 percent in 1960 to less than 10 percent today.

The substantial increase in labor force participation by women has been another key factor impacting the labor market. Women's participation rose from just 35 percent in the mid-1950s to about 60 percent by the mid-1990s.

Other significant factors have affected the US labor market since 1960. These include the enormous increase in globalization of production, investment, and trade and the development of information and communications technologies, which in turn gave rise to transformational businesses, including Microsoft, Apple, Google, and Amazon. These businesses not only have completely changed several major sectors of the economy but also have created enormous cultural and social change.

All these developments were permanent, game-changing events in the history of the US economy. Yet the US labor market responded to these changes by efficiently absorbing new workers and also reallocating workers across firms, industries, and sectors.

The rapid reallocation of labor is particularly striking in the United States. About 4 percent of US employment turns over every month as workers leave existing positions and move to new positions. A current employment level of about 152 million workers means the equivalent of about seventy-five million job changes in the United States each year.

This remarkable level of job reallocation highlights a rapidly evolving and growing economy in which the labor market quickly moves workers from slower-growing firms and industries to more rapidly growing firms and industries.

The impact of COVID-19 on the US labor market is not seen in these annual data, which end in 2019. Figure 12.3 clearly shows the impact of COVID-19 on the monthly US unemployment rate, combined with federal, state, and local government policy responses on the labor market. These

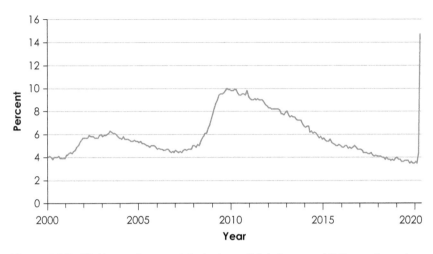

Figure 12.3. US Unemployment Rate (monthly). *Source:* US Department of Labor, Bureau of Labor Statistics.

include shelter-at-home orders, social distancing, and restrictions on large gatherings, among others. Retail, hospitality and leisure, and the travel sectors have been hit particularly hard, as the US unemployment rate increased to over 14 percent in April 2020, a level not seen since the Great Depression.

Now that safe and effective treatments and vaccines ultimately have become available, this paper assumes that COVID-19 will not present the same economic challenges in the long run. The paper presents a policy discussion about how to safely restore work over the next few months before new treatments and vaccines are widely available. This is discussed just before the conclusion.

Figures 12.4 and 12.5 present data on average worker compensation, which is the price of labor. These two figures clarify two commonly held but misunderstood views about worker compensation and the distribution of income. One misunderstood view is that inflation-adjusted compensation has grown very little over time. The other is that the distribution of net income has substantially shifted from workers to capital.

In a competitive, well-functioning labor market, worker compensation grows with worker productivity. Higher productivity means higher value

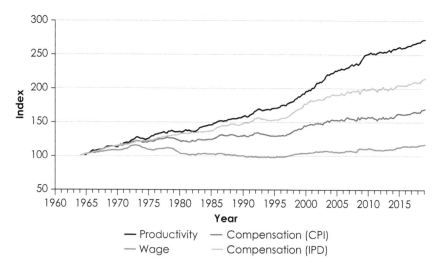

Figure 12.4. Productivity, Hourly Wage, and Total Compensation, Inflation-Adjusted with CPI and GDP Deflator. *Source:* US Department of Commerce, Bureau of Economic Analysis, "National Data: National Income and Product Accounts," apps.bea.gov.

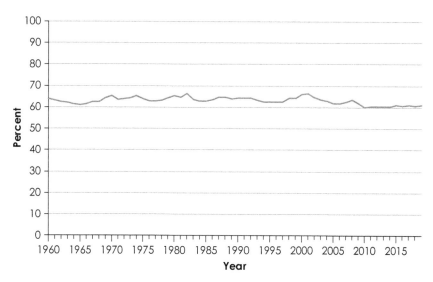

Figure 12.5. Labor Share of Net Income in Nonfarm Business Sector. *Source:* US Department of Commerce, Bureau of Economic Analysis, "National Data: National Income and Product Accounts," apps.bea.gov.

added, and growing worker productivity leads businesses to bid up compensation as they compete for workers.

Figure 12.4 shows real GDP per worker, which is the most common measure of economy-wide labor productivity, along with three different measures of inflation-adjusted compensation, two of which are commonly used but are plagued by significant conceptual and measurement flaws. Taken together, these three series show why some commentators claim that compensation has grown very little over time and that it has not nearly kept up with productivity increases—and why these views are mistaken.

The brown line shows worker wages divided by the consumer price index (CPI). This measure is frequently cited by commentators who argue that workers have not received any significant, inflation-adjusted salary increase for decades, even though their productivity has increased.[2]

Two key problems with this frequently used measure make it inappropriate for inferring compensation growth and for comparing compensation to worker productivity. One is that nonwage benefits, which include employer-provided health plans and vacation among other compensation, have become an increasingly large fraction of total compensation.

In the 1960s, nonwage benefits accounted for only about 6 percent of employee compensation. Today, they have grown to about one-third of total compensation as the value of employer-provided health plans has grown substantially. This large component of compensation is omitted by those who focus just on wages. Moreover, this indicates that although wages may have been a reasonably accurate measure of compensation sixty years ago, they are not today and should not be used as a proxy measure of employee compensation now.

The second problem with this measure arises when comparing it to productivity. This is because the GDP deflator is used to construct worker productivity, but the CPI is used to deflate the wage. Comparing worker compensation to productivity requires that the same price index be used to deflate both measures. The appropriate price index for making this comparison is the GDP deflator because it is by far the broadest price index available, covering all market goods and services.

It is well known that the CPI overstates economy-wide inflation. This means that wages deflated by the CPI will be biased downward not only because of omitted nonwage compensation but also because the CPI grows considerably faster than the GDP deflator.

To see how much the errors of (1) using wages rather than total compensation and (2) using the CPI instead of the GDP deflator matter for these issues, figure 12.4 shows two additional measures: total compensation deflated by the CPI and the appropriate measure for comparing to productivity (total compensation divided by the GDP deflator).

The figure shows that total compensation deflated by the CPI grows over time, in contrast to wages. These two measures show the difference between using the appropriate measure of total compensation and using wages. They also highlight the large quantitative error induced by using just wages as a measure of living standards.

Total compensation divided by the GDP deflator is the third measure presented in the figure. This measure shows very strong growth over time. There is some divergence between productivity growth and compensation growth after 2000. Economists are studying potential factors accounting for this divergence. Although it remains an open question, this divergence has not been caused by a shift of net income from workers to capital, which is another widely held perception.

Rather, this view about labor's share of the economic pie is largely based on a conceptual error. Figure 12.5 shows the distribution of income between labor and capital, net of capital depreciation. The data exclude the self-employed, for whom income attribution between labor and profits is ambiguous. The figure shows a relatively constant share of income paid to labor at about 66 percent. These data stand in sharp contrast to the view that owners of capital are receiving a considerably larger share of net income at the expense of workers.

Rising capital depreciation rates are the reason why labor's share of income net of depreciation has remained constant, even if its share of gross income has declined. The US Bureau of Economic Analysis has changed the definition of capital investments to now include what are known as intangible investments that previously had been expensed items, such as computer software.

These newly classified investments tend to have very high depreciation rates. In addition to expenditures that are now being classified as capital investments, there is a greater share of business investment in previously existing, high-depreciation categories, such as computer equipment, which depreciates much faster than other investments, such as office buildings and factories.

Higher depreciation means a higher gross payment to capital, all else equal. This is because investors require a specific rate of return, net of depreciation, in order to bear capital risk as well as postpone consumption. This rate of return must allow for depreciated capital that must be replaced. After higher depreciation is accounted for, it is striking that the net payments to capital and labor have not changed in any quantitatively important way over time.

Taken together, these data indicate that the US labor market has functioned efficiently over most of the last sixty years in terms of absorbing new workers; reallocating workers across firms, industries, and sectors; and providing compensation that grows roughly with worker productivity and whose share of net income has not changed over time.

American labor market efficiency coincides with a significant amount of economic freedom and lack of economic policy distortions. The next section compares measures of US labor market freedoms with those in some other countries.

Comparing Labor Market Freedom and Policies across Developed Countries

The efficient operation of the US labor market in absorbing new workers has been the exception more than the rule when compared to other developed countries. Today, several major economies with far fewer young workers than the United States, such as France, Italy, and Spain, currently have youth unemployment rates of at least 20 percent, even ten years after the global financial crisis. This compares to a youth unemployment rate of about 8 percent in the United States.[3]

This section provides international perspectives on labor market freedom across countries. The comparison is informative because different countries have adopted very different labor market policies, which in turn have had large effects on the incentives and opportunities within the labor market. It will show that the US labor market is much freer than labor markets in most other countries.

The Heritage Foundation and the Organisation for Economic Co-operation and Development systematically rank countries on labor market freedom and flexibility.[4] Both these rankings have been conducted for many years, and they are widely cited and used in making comparisons across countries and analyzing labor market outcomes.

The Heritage Foundation ranks the United States as having the most labor market freedom among all countries.[5] The ranking is based on six factors: (1) the minimum wage relative to average value added per worker, (2) the cost of hiring new workers, (3) the cost of adjusting worker hours, (4) the cost of dismissing redundant employees, (5) the length of term of mandated notice of dismissal, and (6) the extent and size of mandatory severance pay. Each of these factors in the Heritage Foundation index has important economic implications for the efficient and free operation of the labor market.

The minimum wage relative to average worker productivity gauges how many workers may be negatively affected by the minimum wage because their employment cost exceeds the value of their production. Specifically, if the minimum wage is higher than a worker's productivity, then the worker will not be hired because the hiring organization will take a loss on that worker. Instead, it will focus hiring efforts on workers whose productivity exceeds the minimum wage.

In a free labor market, inexperienced workers would have many more opportunities because employers would not be restricted to paying them a wage exceeding the value of their production. Instead, workers would be paid according to their productivity. Although inexperienced workers may be paid relatively low wages, their pay would rise as their skills increased with experience and job training.

Those who may be priced out of the market due to a high minimum wage include workers who have not yet acquired sufficient skills to realistically compete for higher-wage jobs, such as young workers, immigrants, and workers who have been out of the labor force for a considerable period, such as parents who left the labor force to raise children and workers recovering from long-term disabilities.

The remaining Heritage Foundation measures of labor market freedom are the expenses associated with adjusting and managing a company's workforce. In an efficient and free labor market, these costs should be relatively small on a per-worker basis. However, these costs can be significant and may materially affect firms' human resource decisions when regulations substantially affect these choices.

These adjustment and management costs include overtime premiums and the costs of dismissing redundant workers, including the amount of severance pay and the mandated notification period of dismissal notice, as well as litigation costs and penalties for noncompliance.

As these costs rise, they tend to reduce employment and economic activity because they raise the cost of employing a worker without increasing worker productivity. Over time, higher employment costs resulting from regulations will tend to reduce wages.

The OECD's ranking focuses on what economists refer to as "labor market flexibility."[6] The OECD measures the extent of regulations on individual and collective job dismissal across countries. These regulations make it more expensive to dismiss workers, which in turn reduce employment by raising employee costs. High dismissal costs also impede resource reallocation across different sectors of the economy, and this also slows economic growth. The United States is ranked first in the OECD's index.

The Heritage Foundation and OECD measures of labor market freedom and flexibility summarize factors that directly affect business's demand for labor by affecting the cost of labor. Labor supply, which is the other side of the labor market, is directly affected by other policies.

Table 12.1. Combined 2015 Tax Rate on Labor Income and
Consumption, in Percent

Austria	Belgium	Canada	France	Germany	Italy	Netherlands	Spain	UK	US
63.1	58.2	38.7	64.8	55.8	61.5	58.1	47.4	42.7	28.7

Source: Cara McDaniel, "Forces Shaping Hours Worked in OECD, 1960–2004," *American Economic Journal: Macroeconomics* 3, no. 4 (October 2011): 27–52.

Some of the most important policies that affect labor supply are tax rates. Tax rates change the incentives to work either by reducing a worker's take-home pay (labor income taxes) or by making consumption goods more expensive (sales taxes or value-added taxes).

In the standard model of labor supply, an individual weighs the costs and benefits of working and chooses how much to work at the point where the incremental cost of working, which tends to rise with hours worked, is equated to the incremental benefit of working, which tends to decrease with hours worked. Higher taxes reduce the benefit of working, which means that taxes induce workers to reduce their labor supply and work less, all else equal.

Cara McDaniel has constructed panel data covering fifteen OECD countries beginning in 1950.[7] These data have been updated to 2015. They show that there have been enormous changes over time and across countries in the labor and consumption tax rates that affect labor supply.

Since labor income taxes and consumption taxes have similar effects on labor supply, I have combined McDaniel's data on labor income taxes and consumption taxes into a single composite tax rate by adding them together.[8]

Table 12.1 shows this composite tax rate for selected countries, including several European countries where these tax rates are particularly high. The data are for 2015, which is the most recent year that the data are available, and include national as well as state and local rates.

The table shows that the United States by far has the lowest composite tax rate at 28.7 percent. The composite tax rate for the European countries is much higher, ranging from 42.7 percent (United Kingdom) to 64.8 percent (France).

Table 12.2. Percentage Point Change in Tax Rates, 1950–2015

Austria	Belgium	Canada	France	Germany	Italy	Netherlands	Spain	UK	US
36.7	31.0	19.5	26.1	26.5	36.6	27.9	31.9	17.8	11.6

Source: McDaniel, "Forces Shaping Hours Worked in OECD, 1960–2004."

European tax rates were not always so high. In the 1950s, some European tax rates were lower than the American tax rate. These tax rates rose substantially in the 1970s and early 1980s as many European countries expanded the size and scope of government during that period. Table 12.2 shows how these tax rates have changed between 1950 and 2015. The table also shows the difference between each country's 2015 tax rate and its 1950 tax rate in percentage points.

In Europe, these tax rate increases range from 26.1 percentage points (France) to 36.7 percentage points (Austria). The mean tax rate increase among the continental European countries is 31 percentage points. In contrast, the US tax rate increased by only 11.6 percentage points. The next section summarizes research that uses tax rate data to analyze how tax rates have affected labor supply in the OECD countries.

How Tax Rates and Other Policies Affect Labor Markets across Countries

Figure 12.6 shows hours worked per adult for the United States and for three major European countries: France, Germany, and Italy. The most striking feature of these data is the large drop in the number of market hours of work in the European countries, which are the countries with the largest increase in tax rates.

Hours of market work per adult in France fall from about 1,600 in 1950 to about 1,000 in 2015. Similarly, hours of market work per adult in Germany fall from about 1,550 to about 1,100, and from about 1,450 to about 1,050 in Italy. These are enormous declines. In contrast, US hours worked change little, rising from about 1,250 to about 1,300.

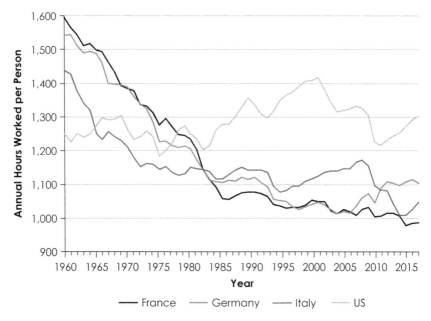

Figure 12.6. Annual Hours of Market Work: France, Germany, Italy, and the United States. *Source:* Lee Ohanian, Andrea Raffo, and Richard Rogerson, "Long-term Changes in Labor Supply and Taxes: Evidence from OECD Countries, 1956–2004," *Journal of Monetary Economics* 55, no. 8 (November 2008): 1353–62.

These very different patterns in hours worked coincide quite closely with changes in the tax rate reported in the previous section. In particular, the composite tax rate increases by about 30 percentage points on average in the three European countries. Hours worked in those same countries decline by about 31 percent. US tax rates rise modestly and US hours worked are unchanged.

Several studies have found that a standard model of labor supply that includes taxation accounts quite closely for these very different changes in hours worked.

Prescott studied how changes in tax rates affected hours worked per adult in Canada, Germany, France, Italy, Japan, the United Kingdom, and the United States.[9] He used national income account data to construct tax rates and then used a standard economic model to predict

Table 12.3. Actual and Predicted Percentage Change in Hours Worked, 1950–2015

Country	Austria	Belgium	Canada	France	Germany	Italy	Netherlands	Spain	UK	US
Actual	-36	-34	8	-38	-40	-29	-21	-13	-22	4
Predicted	-31	-31	-11	-21	-34	-43	-21	-41	-16	-9

Source: Ohanian, Raffo, and Rogerson, "Long-term Changes in Labor Supply and Taxes."

how observed tax rate changes between 1970–74 and 1993–96 changed hours worked. He found that changes in tax rates accounted for almost all the changes in hours worked across these countries. He summarizes his main findings: "In this article, I determine the importance of tax rates in accounting for these differences in labor supply for the major advanced industrial countries and find that tax rates alone account for most of them."

Lee Ohanian, Andrea Raffo, and Richard Rogerson also employ a standard model of labor supply and analyze a larger panel of countries, covering fifteen OECD countries, and over a longer period, from 1956 to 2004.[10] They use the McDaniel (2007, 2011) tax rate series, which was not available at the time of Prescott's analysis.[11]

Table 12.3 summarizes their findings. The model predicts the significant decreases in labor supply for Austria, Belgium, Germany, the Netherlands, and the United Kingdom. The model's prediction error is large for Spain, although that is understandable. Despite higher taxes, Spain implemented many pro-market economic reforms and a shift to more democratic government after Francisco Franco left power. Those factors, which positively affect labor supply, likely attenuated the impact of higher taxes.

The Netherlands is a particularly interesting case. After suffering a nearly one-third drop in hours worked per adult, the nation implemented lower taxes in the 1980s. Following this tax reform, hours subsequently rose by about 12 percent. The model accurately generates the very large drop from the 1950s to the 1980s and the partial recovery in hours worked afterward.

In the twelve countries that experienced at least a 15 percent decline in hours worked, tax changes account for about 85 percent of the overall drop.[12]

Unlike the economists cited thus far, some economists have argued that taxes play a smaller role. For example, Olivier Blanchard and Alberto Alesina, Edward Glaeser, and Bruce Sacerdote argue that cultural differences between Europe and the United States may explain why Europeans work so much less today than Americans.[13] But there are some shortcomings with these different views. One is that these economists are silent on why Europeans worked so much more than Americans in the 1950s or on why European immigrants to the United States do not appear to work systematically less than other American workers. Moreover, these studies do not measure these potential cultural differences, which precludes a formal analysis of this alternative view.

Economists have studied how other policies have affected labor market performance, particularly unemployment. As discussed above, Europe has adopted political institutions and economic policies that have increased labor market rigidity and reduced economic freedom within the labor market.

Blanchard and Justin Wolfers analyzed panel data from European countries to study how the level of unemployment benefits, the duration of benefits, unionization, and employment protection laws affected European unemployment over time and across countries.[14]

Economists have focused on European data because unemployment in many European countries has been much higher than in the United States. Since 1985, French unemployment has averaged around 9 percent per year and German unemployment has averaged around 8 percent per year.

Blanchard and Wolfers found that labor market policies that have increased labor market rigidity and reduced economic freedom have had very large effects on unemployment. They find that the maximum benefit rate, which is the average unemployment benefit measured as a percent of the average wage, has increased European unemployment on average by 1.3 percentage points. They find that the duration of benefits, which has been very high in Europe, increased unemployment by about .75 percentage points. Employment protection policies, which raise the cost of dismissing redundant workers, raised unemployment by about 1 percentage point and unionization raised unemployment by about .6 percentage points.

Taken together, the findings of Blanchard and Wolfers indicate that observed policies could have potentially increased European unemployment by as much as 4.6 percentage points per year. Note that this is the difference between a very healthy labor market and one that is perpetually in a severe recession.

In another influential study, Lars Ljungqvist and Thomas Sargent assess how labor market policies affect European unemployment with a focus on long-term unemployment, which is very prevalent in Europe.[15] They hypothesize that European policies tend to increase long-term unemployment because worker skills deteriorate as unemployment duration rises. In particular, their hypothesis is that some workers ultimately become chronically unemployed as their skills deteriorate so much that unemployment benefits, which have been quite high in Europe, become higher than their market wage. They find that well-intentioned policies account for much of the rise in long-term European unemployment and long-lasting benefits trap European workers in a persistent cycle of unemployment.

These findings have been confirmed for emerging economies. Lorenzo Bernal-Verdugo, Davide Furceri, and Dominique Guillaume study a panel of eighty-five countries, many of which are developing countries, and find that "after controlling for other macroeconomic and demographic variables, increases in the flexibility of labor market regulations and institutions have a statistically significant negative impact both on the level and the change of unemployment outcomes (i.e., total, youth, and long-term unemployment). Among the different labor market flexibility indicators analyzed, hiring and firing regulations and hiring costs are found to have the strongest effect."[16]

Juan Botero et al. report similar findings from an eighty-five-country study. They find that highly regulated labor markets reduce labor force participation and raise unemployment, particularly for young workers.[17]

Minimum Wages: Theory and Evidence

At one time, there was nearly universal agreement among economists and policy makers that high minimum wages depressed employment, particularly for young people who were still in the process of accumulating skills and experience.

The economic logic behind this once-standard view is simple: fixing the price of any good or service above its market price will result in lower demand. In the labor market, this means that any worker who does not deliver enough value to offset an artificially high minimum wage will be unemployed.

Youth unemployment statistics highlight the impact of minimum wages. In mid-2012, more than two years after the end of the last recession, teenage unemployment (ages sixteen to nineteen) was 25 percent, compared to a 6.7 percent unemployment rate for prime-age workers (ages twenty-five to fifty-four). Even in 2019, with the strongest job market in the last fifty years, teenage unemployment was 12.6 percent, compared to a prime-age worker unemployment rate of 2.9 percent.[18]

Despite the simple economic logic described above, and the observed large difference in unemployment rates by age, some commentators today hold the view that raising the minimum wage will have little, if any, effect on unemployment and instead will substantially raise the standard of living among nearly all low-wage workers.

Perhaps the major factor driving this change in opinion was research by David Card and Alan Krueger.[19] In their influential 1994 paper, Card and Krueger compared changes in employment in fast-food restaurants between New Jersey, which increased its hourly wage from $4.25 to $5.05 in 1992, and Pennsylvania, which kept its minimum wage at $4.25. They surveyed about four hundred fast-food restaurants near the New Jersey–eastern Pennsylvania border by phone and asked restaurant managers about employment levels before and after the New Jersey minimum-wage change.

They reported that the New Jersey restaurants had expanded employment by nearly three full-time equivalent workers relative to the Pennsylvania restaurants. This result was extremely surprising, as it defies the most basic economic argument that artificially raising wages of low-skilled labor depresses the demand for that labor.

However, there are problems with Card and Krueger's analysis, including data collection and their research design. In terms of data collection, they relied on telephone surveys with the restaurants. Subsequent research based on better data collection showed very different results.[20]

In a series of papers and a book, David Neumark and William Wascher review many minimum-wage studies, including that of Card and Krueger.[21] In contrast to Card and Krueger, Neumark and Wascher redo the New Jersey and Pennsylvania fast-food restaurant study by using administrative payroll data from fast-food restaurants rather than telephone interviews. Payroll data are more reliable than the telephone interview responses obtained by Card and Krueger because restaurants have a legal obligation to report taxable income and costs.[22]

In contrast to the Card and Krueger study, Neumark and Wascher found that the higher minimum wage in New Jersey had reduced New Jersey employment by about 4 percent relative to Pennsylvania, where the minimum wage was not changed. This finding is in line with standard economic logic and with the majority of previous empirical estimates of the impact of a minimum wage.

Neumark's most recent review of many short-run minimum-wage studies concludes as follows: "The preponderance of evidence indicates that minimum wages reduce employment of the least-skilled workers. Earlier estimates suggested an 'elasticity' of about −0.1 to −0.2. Many estimates are still in this range. . . . More definitively, though, it is indisputable that there *is* a body of evidence pointing to job losses from higher minimum wages. Characterizations of the literature as providing no evidence of job loss are simply inaccurate."[23]

More recently, economists have begun to study the long-run effects of minimum wages on employment. This is important, as the short-run responses to a higher minimum wage, which are the focus of much of the literature, may be very different from long-run responses. This is because it takes time for employers to make adjustments in response to minimum-wage changes, including installation of new capital investments and adoption of new technologies, both of which can substitute for workers.

Research by Isaac Sorkin shows that the difference between the short-run and long-run effects of minimum-wage legislation can be enormous. Sorkin measures the responsiveness of employment to a wage change using the economic concept of demand elasticity, which is the percentage change in labor demand in response to a given percentage change in the wage.[24]

He shows that the contemporaneous elasticity of labor demand can be virtually zero upon impact of a minimum-wage change, in which he estimates that a 10 percent change in the wage generates an immediate .02 percent drop in employment. However, he finds that this sensitivity rises to -.252, meaning that a 10 percent change in the wage generates a 2.5 percent drop in employment after six years, which is roughly one hundred times larger than the immediate effect.

This large difference reflects the fact that as labor costs rise, businesses economize on labor by substituting capital and new technologies for workers and also by offshoring some tasks to lower-cost providers of labor services. This large difference between short- and long-run effects is incredibly important but rarely is documented by empirical studies.

Minimum-wage research has important implications for current policy discussions. In particular, there are a number of proposals to raise the federal minimum wage from its current level of $7.25 per hour to $15 per hour.

At its current level, the minimum wage affects very few workers, just 1.2 percent of the labor force. According to the Labor Department, almost half of minimum-wage workers are younger than twenty-five and account for only about 20 percent of the overall labor force.[25] However, if the minimum wage were raised to $15 per hour, then it would affect over 40 percent of American workers.[26] Krueger, one of the authors of the New Jersey–eastern Pennsylvania study cited above and a former economic adviser to President Obama, warned of job loss if the minimum wage were raised to $15 per hour.[27]

An important risk of a $15 federal minimum wage is that low earners in relatively poor states would be particularly hard hit. For example, the average hourly wage in Mississippi is under $15 per hour.[28]

There are policies that will improve the efficiency of the labor market while promoting compensation growth for those who may be adversely affected by the minimum wage. These policies include expanding the earned income tax credit, increasing the scope and scale of enterprise zones that incentivize businesses to locate in poor neighborhoods, improving our K–12 education system, and expanding preschool programs.

The Impact of Unions on Labor Market Performance

This section summarizes how unions have historically affected labor market efficiency and opportunities. In the late nineteenth and early twentieth centuries, unions focused on increasing worker safety, protecting worker civil rights, supporting education, and limiting the use of child labor.[29]

These efforts were important because labor markets were much less competitive at that time than they are now. In the nineteenth and early twentieth centuries, there were often just a few large employers in a community, which gave employers much more market power than employers have today.

Because worker safety, human rights, and child labor regulations are now well established at the federal, state, and local levels, unions have shifted their focus to increasing compensation and increasing employment, the latter through a process known as featherbedding. A large body of research finds that these aspects of unionization have benefited union members, particularly in the short run, but at the expense of others by depressing economic growth, particularly in heavily unionized industries. Moreover, research shows that unions depress long-run compensation for their members by reducing firm innovation and investments.

Unions have considerable market power in collective bargaining agreements since they are the sole supplier of labor services to the firm. There are hundreds of studies estimating union wage premia. H. Gregg Lewis's survey finds estimated premia around 15–20 percent, meaning that union market power drives up compensation by 15–20 percent over the estimated free market compensation level.[30] More recently, Henry Farber et al., with many references, also report similar union premia estimates.[31]

One way this wage premium depresses economic activity is by raising employer costs. This in turn raises prices and reduces customer demand. Moreover, some of the methods by which unions have generated wage premia, which include strikes, independently depress economic activity. This is because a strike is a tax on investment. By idling a firm's capital stock, a strike, or even the threat of a strike, lowers the expected return to investment, which in turn lowers investment, innovation, and productivity growth. This has very negative consequences for the long-run health of the firm and, ironically, for the long-run health of the union.

Simeon Alder, David Lagakos, and Ohanian analyze the impact of strike behavior and provide both theoretical arguments and empirical evidence that the frequent use of strikes and strike threats in major Rust Belt industries, such as autos and steel, is the main factor responsible for the Rust Belt's long-run economic decline.[32]

The Rust Belt is typically defined as states bordering the Great Lakes, including Ohio, Pennsylvania, Michigan, Illinois, and New York. It accounted for more than 50 percent of the nation's manufacturing employment in 1950. That share declined chronically throughout the 1950s, 1960s, and 1970s, falling to about 38 percent by 1980. This decline preceded the large shift to globalization that began around the mid-1980s and that is widely believed to have negatively affected US manufacturing. However, Alder, Lagakos, and Ohanian find that the historical use of the strike threat by Rust Belt unions accounts for about two-thirds of the decline of the Rust Belt's manufacturing employment share. They also find that the strike threat accounts for much of the Rust Belt's failure to innovate at the same rate as non–Rust Belt producers.[33]

Their most striking conclusion is that in the absence of labor market conflict with unions, the Rust Belt's manufacturing employment share would have held steady at about 51 percent, even with stronger foreign competition. This is because globalization doesn't just replace domestic sales with imports but provides opportunities for competitive domestic producers to sell abroad, thus creating new markets.

José Galdón-Sánchez and James Schmitz study how union work rules that severely limit the tasks that employees can perform in order to increase employment can depress worker productivity by 50 percent or more.[34] These work rules can be as restrictive as not allowing a worker to perform minor maintenance on a machine or change a lightbulb. They show that when iron-ore producers were subjected to increased competition, union work rules were reformed to permit workers to perform more tasks, which doubled worker productivity.

Similarly, Thomas Holmes studies job creation and economic performance right at state borders, where one state is relatively heavily unionized and the state just across the border is a "right-to-work" state that outlaws the union shop.[35] He finds that employment growth over time is much higher in manufacturing plants in the right-to-work states very close to the border than in manufacturing plants that are close to the border in the heavily unionized states.

Union representation among private-sector workers has declined from a high of about 35 percent in the early 1950s to only around 6 percent today. This likely reflects several economic shifts since World War II that have led today's workers to find union representation less attractive.

Perhaps the most important reason is changes in competition. As described above, yesteryear's unions imposed significant economic inefficiencies within bargaining at a time when many American producers faced little competition, either domestically or internationally. But in today's increasingly competitive marketplace, any form of inefficiency threatens firm survival. The fact that public-sector unions have fared much more successfully than private-sector unions supports this competition view. In the public sector, there rarely is any competition among producers and providers of government services. Not surprisingly, union membership among public-sector workers is about 45 percent among local government employees.[36]

A second reason why union organization is much less popular today is that collective bargaining agreements invariably offer a "one-size-fits-all" compensation package for its members. But as workers have become increasingly skilled, and as job responsibilities have become much more specialized, collective bargaining has become outdated.

That private-sector workers are not choosing union representation is the strongest evidence in supporting the view that the union model of yesteryear is not sufficiently valued by today's private-sector workers. This is also reflected in the fact that former union stronghold states, including Indiana, Michigan, and Wisconsin, have voted to become right-to-work states in the last few years.

Private-sector unions have responded to these long-run trends driven by substantially changing bargaining practices to focus on forming cooperative relationships with management and enhancing firm efficiency and performance to increase competitiveness. As an example of this change in union practices, former United Auto Workers (UAW) president Robert King summarized the very significant changes in UAW practices this way: "The 20th-century UAW fell into a pattern with our employers where we saw each other as adversaries rather than partners. Mistrust became embedded in our relations ... [which] hindered the full use of the talents of our members and promoted a litigious and time-consuming grievance culture."[37]

These long-run changes in private-sector unionization density and bargaining practices are natural reactions to increasingly competitive markets, and they are generally improving labor market function by reducing inefficiencies.

The Inefficiency of Occupational Licensing

Licensing occupational practices by a professional bureau has been employed for many years in skilled professions where there is potential for substantial consumer harm. These practices include medicine, law, and dentistry. Licensing is intended to protect consumers by providing objective, third-party confirmation that a provider is professionally qualified to perform a trade.

More recently, professional licensing has spread to many other occupations, particularly occupations where potential consumer damage is extremely modest, such as tour guides, cashiers, card dealers, florists, interior decorators, and hair shampooers. Licensing even extends to professions that are as much or more about providing entertainment as providing a service, such as Maryland, which requires licenses for fortune tellers, and Arizona, which requires licenses for rainmakers.[38]

Today, 29 percent of workers require a professional license, up from 18 percent in 2000 and about 5 percent in the 1950s. Put differently, this means that nearly one of every three workers must have government approval to work in his or her chosen profession.

Most research analyzing occupational licensing has concluded that much of this licensing is not in the interest of protecting consumers but rather exists to insulate incumbent producers from competition at the expense of consumers.

Licensing limits entry of new professionals, which in turn reduces competition in the industry. Licensing fees also raise the cost of doing business. Both these factors drive up prices, thus reducing demand and harming consumers. Morris Kleiner finds wage premia as high as 30 percent due to restricting entry.[39]

Ironically, licensing can also harm incumbent licensees once political and social pressure builds to force regulators to allow reforms. For example, in New York, livery drivers, particularly taxi drivers, are required to purchase a taxi medallion, which simply gives a driver the legal right to operate.[40] Before the popularity of ride-sharing, including Uber and Lyft, the market price of these medallions was as high as $1 million.

However, this price has now fallen to about $100,000, given the introduction of competition from Uber and Lyft. This decline in the price of medallions has led to the loss of virtually all the wealth of some drivers who purchased their medallions at very high prices.

Occupational licensing has also been found to negatively impact historically disadvantaged groups by imposing long training or internship periods.[41] For example, more than 1,700 hours of training are required to become a licensed cosmetologist in California while 4,000 hours of training are required to work with electrical signs in Michigan. Note that this latter requirement may exceed the number of hours used by law students in taking classes, studying, and preparing for the bar exam.

The negative impacts of occupational licensing led then president Obama to commission a special study of this issue by his Council of Economic Advisers and the Treasury Department. They concluded:

> The current licensing regime in the United States also creates substantial costs, and often the requirements for obtaining a license are not in sync with the skills needed for the job. There is evidence that licensing requirements raise the price of goods and services, restrict employment opportunities, and make it more difficult for workers to take their skills across State lines. Too often, policymakers do not carefully weigh these costs and benefits when making decisions about whether or how to regulate a profession through licensing.[42]

Policies to Safely Restore Work during the COVID-19 Crisis

Without safe and effective vaccines available, all economies will need to contend with the novel coronavirus for the near term. Policies should be focused on incentivizing low-risk workers—those who are young and middle-aged and without the risk factors of significant hypertension, diabetes, and cardiopulmonary disease—to return to work.

One policy shift is to convert existing unemployment benefits to unconditional cash transfers. We want low-risk workers to return to work and we do not want social support to be tied to their remaining unemployed. We also can directly subsidize health insurance for workers who do not receive insurance from their employers. Businesses should be incentivized to take precautions to protect their workers from the virus. They could receive tax credits if few of their workers test positive after returning to work. This is in the same spirit as unemployment insurance ratings for businesses, in which the insurance premium paid by a business depends on the frequency that its workers are laid off. This is needed because workers need to feel safe when returning to their places of employment.

Summary and Conclusion

This study has summarized research on how economic freedom affects the labor market. Research shows that high tax rates, high regulations (including occupational licensing), inefficient unionization bargaining practices, and high minimum wages depress the efficient functioning of the labor market. It also shows that many of these policies have benefits for very few while imposing significant costs on the rest of society.

The research cited here has important implications for economic policies. It shows that policy reforms that reduce tax rates, eliminate burdensome regulations, and enhance competition can significantly increase economic growth and job creation. Moreover, the increased economic growth would dwarf the costs to those who currently benefit from the inefficient policies. This means that those who would lose from such reforms could in principle be easily compensated for their losses.

NOTES

1. Simona E. Cociuba, Edward C. Prescott, and Alexander Ueberfeldt, "US Hours at Work," *Economics Letters* 169 (August 2018): 87–90.
2. Chris Nichols, "Tom Steyer Claimed '90% of Americans Have Not Had a Raise for 40 Years.' Is He Right?," *PolitiFact*, October 16, 2019.
3. Organisation for Economic Co-operation and Development (OECD), "Youth Unemployment Rate" (indicator), https://data.oecd.org/unemp/youth -unemployment-rate.htm.
4. Heritage Foundation, "Index of Economic Freedom," 2020, https://www.heritage .org/index/ranking; OECD, "Strictness of Employment Protection—Individual

and Collective Dismissals (Regular Contracts)," 2019, https://stats.oecd.org /Index.aspx?DataSetCode=EPL_OV.

5. Heritage Foundation, "Index of Economic Freedom."

6. OECD, "Strictness of Employment Protection."

7. Cara McDaniel, "Average Tax Rates on Consumption, Investment, Labor and Capital in the OECD 1950–2003," 2007, unpublished manuscript; McDaniel, "Forces Shaping Hours Worked in the OECD, 1960–2004," *American Economic Journal: Macroeconomics* 3, no. 4 (October 2011): 27–52.

8. Labor income taxes and sales taxes on consumption have fairly similar effects on labor supply, as labor taxes reduce take-home pay, which reduces the amount of consumption workers can purchase, while consumption taxes raise the cost of the goods, which also reduces the amount of consumption workers can purchase.

9. Edward C. Prescott, "Why Do Americans Work So Much More Than Europeans?," National Bureau of Economic Research Working Paper 10316, 2004.

10. Lee Ohanian, Andrea Raffo, and Richard Rogerson, "Long-term Changes in Labor Supply and Taxes: Evidence from OECD Countries, 1956–2004," *Journal of Monetary Economics* 55, no. 8 (November 2008): 1353–62.

11. McDaniel, "Average Tax Rates on Consumption" and "Forces Shaping Hours Worked."

12. Canada, New Zealand, and Australia were the other countries in the dataset that had small changes in tax rates. All had relatively constant labor supplies. These countries are omitted from table 12.3 because of space considerations.

13. Olivier Blanchard, "The Economic Future of Europe," *Journal of Economic Perspectives* 18, no. 4 (Fall 2004): 3–26; Alberto Alesina, Edward Glaeser, and Bruce Sacerdote, "Work and Leisure in the US and Europe: Why So Different?," *NBER Macroeconomics Annual*, 2005.

14. Olivier Blanchard and Justin Wolfers, "The Role of Shocks and Institutions in the Rise of European Unemployment: The Aggregate Evidence," *Economic Journal* 110, no. 462 (March 2000): C1–33.

15. Lars Ljungqvist and Thomas Sargent, "The European Unemployment Dilemma," *Journal of Political Economy* 106, no. 3 (June 1998): 514–50.

16. Lorenzo E. Bernal-Verdugo, Davide Furceri, and Dominque Guillaume, "Labor Market Flexibility and Unemployment: New Empirical Evidence of Static and Dynamic Effects," *Comparative Economic Studies* 54, no. 2 (May 2012): 251–73.

17. Juan C. Botero, Simeon Djankov, Rafael La Porta, Florencio Lopez-de-Silanes, and Andrei Shleifer, "The Regulation of Labor," *Quarterly Journal of Economics* 119, no. 4 (November 2004): 1339–82.

18. US Department of Labor, Bureau of Labor Statistics, "Unemployment Rate: 16 to 19 Yrs.," Federal Reserve Bank of St. Louis, January 9, 2020, https://fred.stlouisfed .org/series/LNS14000012; Bureau of Labor Statistics, "Unemployment Rate: 25 to 54 Yrs.," Federal Reserve Bank of St. Louis, January 9, 2020, https://fred.stlouisfed .org/series/LNU04000060.

19. David Card and Alan B. Krueger, "Minimum Wages and Employment: A Case Study of the Fast-Food Industry in New Jersey and Pennsylvania," *American Economic Review* 84, no. 4 (September 1994): 772–93; Card and Krueger, *Myth and Measurement: The New Economics of the Minimum Wage*, 20th anniversary ed. (Princeton, NJ: Princeton University Press, 2015).

20. Card and Krueger, "Minimum Wages and Employment."

21. David Neumark and William L. Wascher, "2000 Minimum Wages and Employment: A Case Study of the Fast-Food Industry in New Jersey and Pennsylvania: Comment," *American Economic Review* 90, no. 5 (December 2000): 1362–96; Neumark and Wascher, *Minimum Wages* (Cambridge, MA: MIT Press, 2008); Card and Krueger, "Minimum Wages and Employment."

22. Card and Krueger, "Minimum Wages and Employment."

23. David Neumark, "The Econometrics and Economics of the Employment Effects of Minimum Wages: Getting from Known Unknowns to Known Knowns," *German Economic Review* 20, no. 3 (August 2019): 321.

24. Isaac Sorkin, "Are There Long-Run Effects of the Minimum Wage?," *Review of Economic Dynamics* 18, no. 2 (April 2015): 306–33.

25. US Department of Labor, Bureau of Labor Statistics, "Characteristics of Minimum Wage Workers, 2018," March 2019, https://www.bls.gov/opub /reports/minimum-wage/2018/pdf/home.pdf.

26. William M. Rodgers III and Amanda Novello, "Making the Economic Case for a $15 Minimum Wage," Century Foundation, January 28, 2019.

27. Alan B. Krueger, "The Minimum Wage: How Much Is Too Much?," *New York Times*, October 9, 2015.

28. PayScale, "Average Hourly Rate for State: Mississippi," https://www.payscale.com /research/US/State=Mississippi/Salary.

29. Lee E. Ohanian, "What—or Who—Started the Great Depression?," *Journal of Economic Theory* 144, no. 6 (November 2009): 2310–35.

30. H. Gregg Lewis, "Union Relative Wage Effects," in *Handbook of Labor Economics*, vol. 2, ed. Richard Layard and Orley Ashenfelter (Amsterdam: Elsevier/North-Holland, 1986), 1139–81.

31. Henry S. Farber, Daniel Herbst, Ilyana Kuziemko, and Suresh Naidu, "Unions and Inequality over the Twentieth Century: New Evidence from Survey Data," National Bureau of Economic Research Working Paper 24587, 2018.

32. Simeon Alder, David Lagakos, and Lee Ohanian, "Competitive Pressure and the Decline of the Rust Belt: A Macroeconomic Analysis," National Bureau of Economic Research Working Paper 20538, 2014.

33. Alder, Lagakos, and Ohanian, "Competitive Pressure and the Decline of the Rust Belt."

34. José E. Galdón-Sánchez and James Schmitz Jr., "Competitive Pressure and Labor Productivity: World Iron-Ore Markets in the 1980's," *American Economic Review* 92, no. 4 (September 2002): 1222–35; Schmitz, "What Determines Productivity? Lessons from the Dramatic Recovery of the US and Canadian Iron Ore Industries Following Their Early 1980s Crisis," *Journal of Political Economy* 113, no. 3 (June 2005): 582–625.

35. Thomas J. Holmes, "The Effect of State Policies on the Location of Manufacturing: Evidence from State Borders," *Journal of Political Economy* 106, no. 4 (August 1998): 667–705.

36. Lee E. Ohanian, "America's Public Sector Union Dilemma," American Enterprise Institute, November 26, 2011.

37. David Walsh, "UAW's Bob King Offers Up Auto Workers as Fodder for Exploitation," World Socialist Web Site, August 4, 2010.

38. Morris M. Kleiner, "Occupational Licensing," *Journal of Economic Perspectives* 14, no. 4 (Fall 2000): 189–202.

39. Kleiner, "Occupational Licensing."

40. Zach Williams, "What Is a Taxi Medallion Worth?," *City & State New York*, August 27, 2019.

41. Maury Gittleman, Mark A. Klee, and Morris N. Kleiner, "Analyzing the Labor Market Outcomes of Occupational Licensing," *Industrial Relations* 57, no. 1 (January 2018): 57–100.

42. US Department of the Treasury, *Occupational Licensing: A Framework for Policymakers*, July 2015.

13

The Costs of Regulation and Centralization in Health Care

Scott W. Atlas, MD

The overall goal of US health care reform is to broaden access for all Americans to high-quality medical care at lower cost. In response to a large uninsured population and increasing health care costs, the Affordable Care Act (ACA, or "Obamacare") aimed first and foremost to increase the percentage of Americans with health insurance. It did so by broadening government insurance eligibility, adding extensive regulations and subsidies to health care delivery and payment, and imposing dozens of new taxes. The ACA was projected to spend approximately $2 trillion over the first decade on its two central components: expanding government insurance and subsidizing heavily regulated private insurance.

Insurance coverage increased under the ACA, but much of that was through an expansion of eligibility for government Medicaid insurance. Through its extensive regulations on private insurance, including coverage mandates, payout requirements, co-payment limits, premium subsidies, and restrictions on medical savings accounts, the ACA counterproductively encouraged more widespread adoption of bloated private insurance and furthered the construct that insurance should minimize out-of-pocket payment for all medical care. Patients in such plans do not perceive themselves as paying for these services, and neither do physicians and other providers. Because patients have little incentive to consider value, prices as well as quality indicators, such as doctor qualifications or hospital experience, remain invisible, and providers do not need to compete. The natural results are overuse of health care services and unrestrained costs.

In response to the failures of the ACA, superimposed on decades of misguided incentives in the system and the considerable health care challenges facing the country, Americans have been presented with two fundamentally different visions of health care reform. On one hand, the goal is a predominantly government-centralized system, by way of either a significant expansion of Medicaid and Medicare or a more direct transition to a "Medicare for All" system. These represent extreme models of government regulation and authority over health care and insurance, which are intended to broaden health care availability to everyone while eliminating patient concern for price. The alternative vision is a competitive, consumer-driven system based on removing regulations that shield patients from considering price, increasing competition among providers, and empowering patients with control of the money. This model is intended to incentivize patients to consider price and value, in order to reduce the costs of medical care while enhancing its value, thereby providing broader availability of high-quality care.

Outside a discussion of the role of private versus public health insurance are two realities. First, America's main government insurance programs, Medicare and Medicaid, are already unsustainable without reforms. The 2019 Medicare Trustees report projects that the Hospitalization Insurance Trust Fund will face depletion in 2026.[1] Most hospitals, nursing facilities, and in-home providers lose money per Medicare patient.[2] Dire warnings about the closure of hospitals and care provider practices are already projected by the Centers for Medicare and Medicaid Services due to the continued payment for services by government insurance below the cost of delivery of those services. Regardless of trust fund depletion, Medicare and Medicaid must compete with other spending in the federal budget. America's national health expenditures now total more than $3.8 trillion per year, or 17.8 percent of gross domestic product (GDP), and they are projected to reach 19.4 percent of GDP by 2027.

In 1965, at the start of Medicare, workers paying taxes for the program numbered 4.6 per beneficiary; that number will decline to 2.3 in 2030 with the aging of the baby boomer generation. Unless the current system is reformed, federal expenditures for health care and social security are projected to consume all federal revenues by 2049, eliminating the capacity for national defense, interest on the national debt, or any other domestic program.[3]

Second, trends in demographics mean that Americans will require medical care at an unprecedented level. America's aging population means more heart disease, cancer, stroke, and dementia—diseases that depend most on specialists, complex technology, and innovative drugs for diagnosis and treatment. Beyond aging alone, the growing burden from lifestyle-induced diseases,[4] including obesity[5] and smoking, are undeniable and enormous. The unique vulnerability of Americans was exposed during the COVID-19 pandemic, which particularly affected the elderly and others with risk factors like obesity and diabetes, disorders that are especially more prevalent in the United States than in other nations. The current trajectory of the system is fiscally unsustainable; meanwhile, millions are already excluded from the excellence of America's medical care.[6]

The Impact of Affordable Care Act Regulations

As a direct result of the ACA's new regulations on insurance pricing and its new mandates on coverage, millions of Americans lost their existing private health plans. The Congressional Budget Office (CBO) projected that about ten million Americans would have been forced off their chosen employer-based health insurance by 2021—a tenfold increase in the number that was initially projected back in 2011.[7] Meanwhile, private insurance premiums have greatly increased under ACA regulations on insurance, most notably those rules approximating modified community rating for premiums and approaching guaranteed issue of coverage. In its first four years, ACA private insurance premiums for individuals doubled and for families increased by 140 percent; this occurred even though

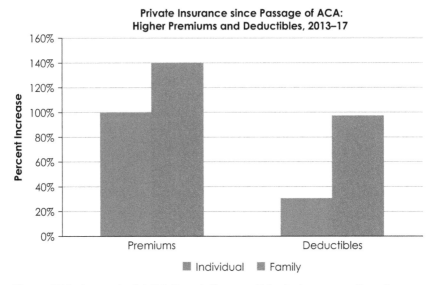

Figure 13.1. Impact of ACA Regulations on Private Insurance Premiums and Deductibles, First Four Years. *Source:* eHealth, "Average Individual Health Insurance Premiums Increased 99% Since 2013, the Year Before Obamacare, & Family Premiums Increased 140%, According to eHealth .com Shopping Data," January 23, 2017.

insurance deductibles (the amount that must be paid before services are covered by the plan) increased by over 30 percent for individuals and by over 97 percent for families (figure 13.1).[8] As time passed, insurance options and prices on ACA exchanges continued to worsen, according to the Department of Health and Human Services (HHS).[9] Many exchange enrollees continued to face large year-on-year premium increases in 2018, according to Kaiser Family Foundation analysis, even in the face of markedly higher deductibles.[10]

The shift into government insurance itself also increases private insurance premiums. Because government reimbursement for health care is below cost, costs are shifted back to the privately insured, pushing up premiums. In some calculations, the underpayment by government insurance adds $1,800 per year to every family of four with private insurance.[11] Nationally, the gap between private insurance payment and government underpayment has become the widest in twenty years, doubling since the initiation of Obamacare.[12]

Choices of private insurance and covered providers under them are dwindling as well, disproving the theory that the law would increase insurance choices and competition. According to a December 2014 study, the exchanges were offering 21 percent fewer plans than did the pre-Obamacare individual market, a decrease to 310 plans nationally in 2015 from 395 plans in the individual market in 2013, the last year before the implementation of Obamacare.[13] For 2018, only one exchange insurer offered coverage in approximately one-half of US counties. As the CBO stated, "Insurance premiums are lower in markets with more insurers, because insurers have stronger incentives to keep premiums low."[14] This rise will affect not only the individual paying the premiums but also taxpayers, because taxpayers subsidize those increasing premiums under Obamacare. Note that the federal government (i.e., federal taxpayers) subsidizes most private premiums—directly or indirectly—at a cost of roughly $300 billion in fiscal year 2016.

For middle-income Americans dependent on subsidized private insurance through government exchanges, the ACA eliminated access to many of the best specialists and best hospitals. Soon after ACA regulations were fully implemented, McKinsey reported that 68 percent of those policies covered only narrow or very narrow provider networks, double that of the previous year.[15] The majority of America's best hospitals in the National Comprehensive Cancer Network were not covered in most of their states' exchange plans. And since late 2014, under Obamacare insurance plans, we have been experiencing a severe shortage of the specialists essential to diagnose and treat stroke, one of the most disabling and lethal diseases in the United States (in some cities, the number of specialists is actually down to zero). Almost 75 percent of ACA private plans became "highly restrictive,"[16] with far fewer hospitals, primary care doctors, and specialists accepting that insurance.[17]

The ACA regulatory environment has encouraged a record pace of consolidation across the health care sector, including mergers of doctor practices and hospitals.[18] The last period of hospital mergers increased medical care prices substantially, at times by over 20 percent, according to a Robert Wood Johnson Foundation report.[19] James Robinson and Kelly Miller reported that when hospitals owned doctor groups, per patient expenditures were 10 to 20 percent higher, or an extra $1,200–$1,700 per patient per year.[20] Cory Capps, David Dranove, and Christopher Ody found that physician prices increased on average by 14 percent for medical groups acquired by hospitals; specialist prices increased by 34 percent after joining a health system.[21] In the wake of the ACA, overall health care expenditures continue to increase—for individuals, for employers, and for taxpayer-funded government programs.

Single-Payer Health Care: The Data on Performance

Single-payer health care is a term that encompasses a variety of health systems in which government insurance, funded by taxes, is the principal payer for all medical care services for its citizens, thereby controlling access to medical care. This arrangement may or may not be associated with legal, alternative private insurance options. Single-payer health care is often misunderstood as a simple system, because one central administrative authority replaces an otherwise more fragmented system. However, its overriding position as the single payer dominates or wholly restricts the delivery of health care goods and services, eliminating market alternatives and ultimately controlling the access and quality of virtually all medical care.

Demographic and fiscal concerns in the wake of the ACA have prompted new calls for single-payer health care. The notion that single-payer health care represents a compelling goal for reform of the US health system is mainly driven by the intuitive attractiveness of a simple concept: the government explicitly "guarantees" medical care. Indeed, many nations claim to "guarantee" health care; many further insist that such health care is provided "free of charge." For instance, England's National Health Service (NHS) Constitution explicitly states, "You have the right to receive NHS services free of charge." Yet the National Health Service taxes citizens about £125 billion per year, roughly equivalent to US$160 billion per year. Canada's "free" health care costs the average family about C$13,311 per year for government health insurance; families among the top 10 percent of income earners in Canada pay C$39,486.[22] Note that beyond direct expenditures for health care, Canada's "free" health care also costs billions of dollars to the overall economy and to individuals in forgone wages. For instance, Stokes and Somerville found that the total lost economic output from waiting longer than medically recommended for treatment for total joint replacement surgery, cataract surgery, coronary artery bypass graft surgery, and magnetic resonance imaging (MRI) scans in 2007 was an estimated $14.8 billion.[23]

Funding the costs of single-payer health care by involuntary taxation is often cited as the main objection to its implementation, and there is no question that a nationalized single-payer system would require massive new taxes on workers. The California State Senate's 2017 analysis by the Appropriations Committee estimated that the single-payer health care proposed for California alone, SB 562, the Healthy California Act, would cost about $400 billion per year, more than double the state's entire annual budget. Senator Bernie Sanders's bill to establish single-payer health insurance in the United States, the Medicare for All Act, sometimes called M4A, has been estimated to cost over $32 trillion in its first decade.[24] Doubling all currently projected federal individual and corporate income tax collections would be insufficient to finance the *added* federal costs of the plan. On the other hand, overall direct health care expenditures in nationalized single-payer systems are lower than in the United States. Single-payer systems universally hold down health care expenditures by limiting availability of doctors, treatments, medications, and technology through their power over patients and doctors as the only direct payer.

An evaluation of single-payer health care must examine its well-documented half-century record in providing timely, quality medical care. Single-payer systems in countries with decades of experience have proved to be inferior to the United States system in important objective measures of both access to care and quality. The truth is that single-payer systems, including those in Canada and in the United Kingdom, Sweden, and numerous other European and Nordic countries, impose extremely long wait times for doctor appointments, diagnostic procedures, drugs, and surgery, specifically as a means to contain expenditures. And that failure to deliver timely medical care has serious costs, including pain, suffering, and death; worse medical outcomes; permanent disability; lack of patient choice about health care; and tremendous societal costs. Moreover, those countries with decades of single-payer experience are now reducing their broadest regulatory constraints by overtly using taxpayer money to shift the patient to *private* health care to solve their failures, in many cases even outside their own borders.

Delays and Waiting Lists for Medical Care

In those countries with the longest experience of single-payer health care, published government data demonstrate massive waiting lists and delays that are virtually never found in the United States. In England alone, according to UK government statistics, a record-setting 4.4 million patients are on NHS waiting lists as of late 2019; 95,252 have been waiting more than six months for treatment; and more than 3,400 patients have waited more than one full year as of July 2018—all *after* already receiving initial diagnosis and referral.[25] As recently as 2013, NHS England felt it necessary to proclaim "zero tolerance" of waits for treatment of more than 52 weeks—*a full year*—after diagnosis.[26]

According to Statistics Canada, the national organization in charge of producing official statistics for the government of Canada, "waiting time has been identified as a key measure of access" and is "the major barrier among those who experienced difficulties obtaining care."[27] In Canada's single-payer system, the 2019 median wait from general practitioner (GP) appointment to specialist appointment—before the SARS pandemic—was 10.1 weeks; when added to the median wait of 10.8 weeks from specialist to first treatment, the median wait after seeing a doctor to start treatment was 21 weeks, or about five months.[28] An average wait for a Canadian cardiology patient was 4.9 weeks for the cardiologist appointment after seeing

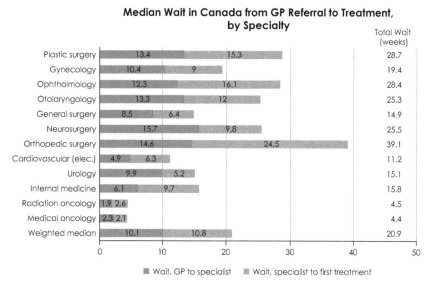

Figure 13.2. Canadians Face Long Wait Times between Seeing Their GP and Receiving Treatment from a Specialist. *Source:* Adapted from Bacchus Barua and Mackenzie Moir, *Waiting Your Turn: Wait Times for Health Care in Canada, 2019 Report*, Fraser Institute.

the GP and another 6.3 weeks to start treatment, which means 11.2 weeks from GP appointment to first treatment. The average Canadian woman waits 10.4 weeks after seeing the GP to see the gynecologist and another 9 weeks for first treatment, or 19.4 weeks total from GP visit to treatment. For simply an appointment with the qualified specialist after already waiting and seeing the GP, Canadians wait another 12.3 weeks (three months) for an ophthalmologist; they wait another 15.7 weeks (four months) to see a neurosurgeon; and they endure their bone and joint pain for 14.6 weeks (three and one-half months) while waiting to see an orthopedist for further evaluation before another 24.5 weeks for treatment (figure 13.2). Bacchus Barua and David Jacques estimated that the purely monetary costs of waiting in Canada exceeded C\$6.3 billion during 2018, or about C\$5,860 per person, without considering medical costs, such as increased risk of mortality or adverse events that result directly from long delays for treatment.[29] Indeed, the Supreme Court of

Canada, in the 2005 *Chaoulli v. Quebec* decision, famously stated, "Access to a waiting list is not access to health care."

Despite the clear importance of the availability of medical care when it is needed, prolonged wait times for care are commonly found in health systems with government-controlled nationalized health insurance—not just as a consequence of limitations and imbalances in supply and demand but specifically as a means of restricting access.[30] In fact, "waiting lists are the most commonly used means of limiting demand" in these health systems.[31] In many countries that otherwise rely on free-market economics, the health care sector stands out as being subjected to far more regulation and centralization akin to programs under socialism.

Long waits are a defining characteristic of hyper-regulated single-payer systems as a means of cost containment, but they stand in stark contrast to US health care. While the world still grapples with important health care issues due to the SARS2 coronavirus pandemic, one unnoticed consequence specifically plaguing single-payer systems is the massive wait lists for postponed or skipped medical care other than COVID-19 during the pandemic. In the UK, NHS waiting lists have bloated to record numbers: more than 5.45 million patients are waiting for care to begin for their diagnosed illnesses. As just one example of the problem, Parth Patel and Chris Thomas, in their 2021 report "Building Back Cancer Services in England" for the UK's Institute for Public Policy Research, projected it will take seven years for missed cancer chemotherapy and twelve years for missed radiation therapy backlogs to clear. For patients with cancer, the significance of that delay cannot be overstated. In 2021, Canada's already scandalous waits for specialist medical care exploded to reach a median 25.6 weeks after referral from the general practitioner—the longest ever recorded—according to the 2021 report by Moir and Barua from the Fraser Institute, with almost a full year wait for orthopedic or neurosurgery treatment.

Aside from organ transplants, "waiting lists are not a feature in the United States," as stated by the OECD and verified by numerous studies.[32] For instance, John Ayanian and Thomas Quinn note that "in contrast to England, most United States patients face little or no wait for elective cardiac care."[33] Low-risk patients in the United States "sometimes have to wait all day or even be rescheduled for another day," according to the Agency for Healthcare Research and Quality's *Technology Assessment: Cardiac Catheterization in Freestanding Clinics* (September 2005)—that is, a wait of even one day was considered notable. Ironically, US media reporting of wait times was widespread and cited as a wake-up call for whole-system reform when 2009 data showed that time to appointment for Americans averaged *20.5 days* for five common specialties (note that in 2017, after the implementation of the ACA, wait times had increased by 30 percent compared with 2014).[34] That reporting failed to note that those US waits were for healthy checkups in almost all cases, by definition the lowest medical priority. Even for low-priority checkups and purely elective, routine appointments, US wait times are far shorter than for seriously ill patients in countries with single-payer health care.

Although an exhaustive study of access to every medical or surgical treatment is impossible to perform and beyond the scope of this paper, it is enlightening to look at access to care for two common diseases: cancer, representing a life-threatening disease, where timely diagnosis and treatment are critical to outcome; and cataracts, a disease causing severe disability that prevents independent living and is associated with numerous other secondary medical problems. We will then consider access to prescription drugs, medical technology, and critical care. Specific examples of health care outcomes from some of the most significant illnesses are also discussed.

Cancer

Delay in initiation of treatment for cancer, the world's number one or two leading cause of death, is associated with worse survival.[35] In the United Kingdom's single-payer NHS, more than 22 percent of cancer patients referred for "urgent treatment" currently wait more than *two months* for their first treatment after receiving the diagnosis in England (NHS wait time statistics in Q4 2019)—a number that has been increasing despite

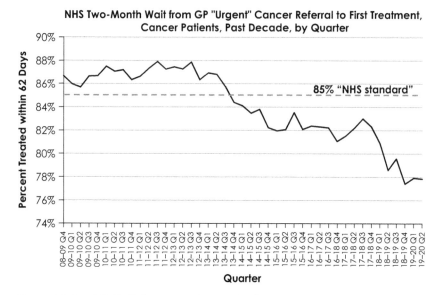

Figure 13.3. NHS Statistics on Patient Waits for Treatment after GP "Urgent Referral for Cancer," Past Decade through Q2 2019–20. *Source:* 2020 NHS England statistics.

government efforts and that exceeds even its own arbitrarily set "standard," which declared that it would be acceptable for 15 percent of cancer patients to wait two full months for first treatment (figure 13.3).

In the United Kingdom, 9.6 percent of breast cancer patients received first treatment within the two-month period after specialist diagnosis, but 30 percent of colorectal cancer patients, 28.2 percent of lung cancer patients, and 29.2 percent of urological cancer patients waited more than two months after "urgent referral" to start therapy. Similarly, 21 percent of brain surgery patients in England wait more than four months after diagnosis to be treated. In Canada's single-payer system, the most recent data revealed a median wait for neurosurgery, after patients have already seen the doctor, of 32.9 weeks—about eight months.

One study of 3.67 million US patients with breast, prostate, lung, colorectal, renal, and pancreas cancer from 2004 to 2013 showed a median wait of twenty-seven days.[36] All cancer treatment began in less than two months, except for prostate cancer, generally a more indolent tumor (up to eighty-seven days). Note that timely access to treatment of cancer reveals significantly longer waits (24 percent to 91 percent longer) from initial diagnosis to treatment in the US single-payer Veterans Affairs system than in other hospital settings.[37]

Cataract Surgery

Cataract, a degenerated, opacified lens in the eye, is the world's leading cause of blindness, affecting more than 24.4 million Americans ages forty and older. By age seventy-five, approximately half of all Americans have cataracts, according to National Eye Institute statistics. Surgical removal of the lens is the only treatment, without which patients often have severely limited vision even approaching blindness. Intraocular lens replacement has been universally established as the treatment of choice. The visual impairments in elderly patients can be severe enough to prevent independence, and the time waiting for cataract surgery can represent a large proportion of their remaining lives. Brown calculated quality-of-life impact from the SHARE data of ten European nations that given a 3.3-month average wait for surgery and an additional twelve months from a patient noting disabling vision loss means 15.3 months between disability and treatment.[38] She calculated that this wait for cataract surgery had the equivalent negative impact as having limb amputation or significant coronary artery disease.

In a study of ten European nations, the average patient waited more than three months for cataract surgery, and 31.6 percent of patients overall waited longer than three months.[39] This does not include the wait of up to one full year to see the ophthalmologist. More recent OECD data show the following waits (table 13.1) for cataract surgery after referral by a specialist.[40]

For their vision-restoring surgery, most recent data show that Canadians with cataracts waited a median time of 20.2 weeks. In contrast, there is almost no waiting for cataract surgery in the United States beyond

Table 13.1. Waiting Times for Cataract Surgery, after Appointment with Specialist Physician, in Selected OECD Nations

Country	Waiting Time (days)
Austria	30.0
Denmark	63.0
Finland	103.0
Israel	132.0
Netherlands	58.8
New Zealand	75.0
Norway	129.0
Spain	105.0
Sweden	57.0
Portugal	133.3
United Kingdom	78.3

Sources: Stefania M. Mojon-Azzi and Daniel S. Mojon, "Waiting Times for Cataract Surgery in Ten European Countries: An Analysis Using Data from the SHARE Survey," British Journal of Ophthalmology 91, no. 3 (March 2007): 282–86; and other sources.

patient-chosen deferral. In fact, thousands of people from other countries commonly seek their cataract surgery in the United States every year.

Prescription Drugs

The regulations of single-payer systems prevent patient access to the newest drugs for cancer and serious diseases, sometimes for years, unlike US regulations. Even though pharmaceuticals are perhaps the most heavily regulated technology in the nation, requiring staggering costs and time until approval for use, the United States has been by far the most frequent location for launching new drugs of virtually all types. The United States is the most frequent originator of new cancer drugs—by a factor of at least four—surpassing any country studied in the previous decade, including Germany, Japan, Switzerland, France, Canada, Italy, and the United Kingdom, according to *Annals of Oncology*.[41] Two-thirds of the "novel drugs" approved in 2015 (twenty-nine of forty-five, or 64 percent) were approved in the United States before any other country.[42] Women in single-payer Canada and in the United Kingdom even had far fewer choices of hormonal contraceptive drugs (62 percent and 54 percent, respectively) than American women, who had access to twenty-six contraceptive drugs over a fifteen-year period, as reported in the Canadian medical literature in 2016.[43]

Cancer drugs, generally making up the largest proportion of all new drugs, deserve special consideration, because time is of the essence for treating these life-threatening diseases. The OECD showed that survival is strongly associated with the system's availability of new cancer drugs, and specifically more so than the provision of drugs free of charge.[44] Of all newly approved cancer drugs from 2009 to 2014, single-payer systems of the United Kingdom, Australia, France, and Canada had approved only 30–60 percent of those approved in the United States by June 30, 2014.[45] Of the world's fifty-four new cancer drugs launched from 2013 to 2017 and available within two years, fifty-one (94 percent) were available within two years in the United States (figure 13.4).[46] For Brits with cancer, only thirty-eight of fifty-four (70 percent) were available; for Canada's cancer patients, only twenty-nine of fifty-four (53 percent) were available; cancer patients in France had access to only twenty-three of fifty-four (43 percent); and Australian cancer patients had access to fifteen of fifty-four (28 percent).

And yet, in 2017, single-payer NHS England introduced a new regulation, the "budget impact test," to cap drug prices specifically based on system expenditures rather than medical efficacy.[47] This regulation will further restrict drug access, even though cancer patients could be forced to wait years for life-saving drugs, some already available in the United States. As just one important projection under that single-payer NHS rule, a dementia drug for Alzheimer's disease would be required to cost only £29.60 per year, less than US$4 per month, or it would be unavailable to patients (as calculated by the Alzheimer's Society), ironically restricted due to overall cost to the system specifically because so many patients need it.[48]

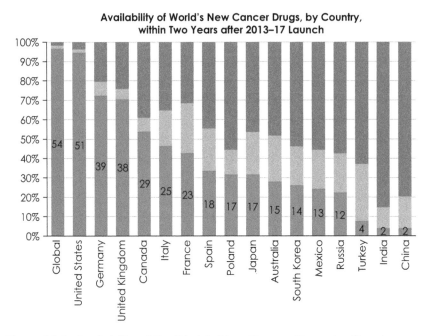

Availability of World's New Cancer Drugs, by Country, within Two Years after 2013–17 Launch

Figure 13.4. Availability of the World's New Cancer Drugs, by Country, within Two Years after 2013–17 Launch (as of December 2018). Exact number of drugs available in each country of the world's total of 54 total is noted; green shaded column in chart indicates percentage of the 54 total. *Sources:* IQVIA Institute, *Global Oncology Trends 2019: Therapeutics, Clinical Development and Health System Implications,* 2019; data from Statista, https://www.statista.com/statistics/696020 /availability-of-new-oncology-drugs-by-country.

Medical Imaging Technology

Sophisticated imaging technology, including magnetic resonance imaging (MRI) and computed tomography (CT) scanning, has revolutionized diagnosis and treatment. Today, imaging is central to the diagnosis and treatment of most of the world's most serious disorders, including cancer,[49] stroke,[50] and heart disease, and it has long been proven cost-effective.[51] Moreover, numerous studies have proved that the availability of CT and MRI scanners is highly correlated with better outcomes in diseases with the most mortality and morbidity.[52] Access to state-of-the-art imaging is a foundation of twenty-first-century medical care.

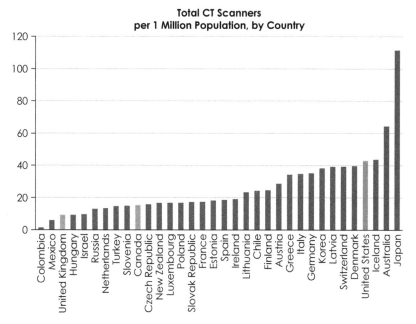

Figure 13.5. CT Scanners by Country, Most Recent Data Available. *Source:* Organisation for Economic Co-operation and Development (OECD), "Computed Tomography (CT) Scanners" (indicator), 2020, https://doi.org/10.1787/bedece12-en.

All governments impose heavy regulatory burdens on manufacturers of medical devices, including diagnostic imaging technology, for proof of safety and efficacy prior to and during use in the clinical setting. Separately, notwithstanding the importance of diagnostic scanners in medical care, highly centralized health systems more broadly regulate the purchase and utilization of these expensive scanners, specifically to limit the outlays for their use. Single-payer, centralized health systems, particularly those of Canada and the United Kingdom, are notorious for their low numbers of CT and MRI scanners (figures 13.5 and 13.6).[53] Overall, the United States employs far lighter regulatory restrictions on the availability and utilization of advanced technology devices such as CT and MRI scanners. However, regulatory certificate-of-need (CON) requirements in thirty-four states, Puerto Rico, and the District of Columbia still limit approvals of competitive medical technology.[54] The original intent of CON laws was to support

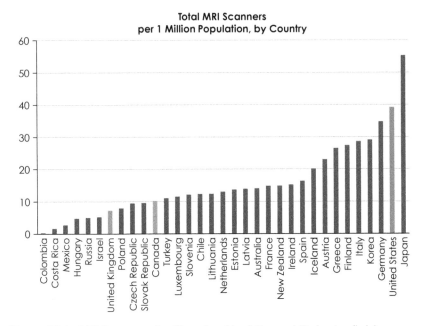

Figure 13.6. MRI Scanners by Country, Most Recent Data Available.
Source: OECD, "Magnetic Resonance Imaging (MRI) Units" (indicator), 2020, https://doi.org/10.1787/1a72e7d1-en.

indigent care by limiting overinvestment in unnecessary equipment and facilities. CON regulations fail to increase the level of indigent care but do restrict the supply of regulated medical services in those states: fewer beds per person and fewer MRI and CT scanners per person.[55] Availability of imaging is specifically reduced in nonhospital settings, driving patients to seek MRI, CT, and PET (positron emission tomography) scanning either out of state or in hospitals, likely increasing costs.[56]

ICU and Critical Care

Concerns about the lack of capacity of medical systems and hospitals to deal with intensive-care-unit (ICU) and critical-care needs became a top issue in 2020, as the world grappled with the COVID-19 pandemic. No country can realistically have instant availability of unlimited emergency medical care, whether doctors, drugs, or technology. Preparedness can without question be improved, though, and all systems will now focus on preventing future shortcomings. In the context of this manuscript, the evidence in peer-reviewed medical journals is clear on two facts: (1) the United States has the most well-equipped system in the world for these patients, and (2) the United States has the best outcomes from severe respiratory disease requiring ICU treatment.

Medical care for the sickest patients requires ICU access, technology, medications, and highly skilled, specialist physicians. Despite some variations in terminology, the availability of ICU beds in the United States dwarfs the availability in single-payer systems. According to a Columbia University study, the United States has 20–31 beds per one hundred thousand people, more than all other countries in that study, including Canada's 13.5, Denmark's 6.7–8.9, Australia's 8.0–8.9, Sweden's 5.8–8.7, Japan's 7.9, the United Kingdom's 3.5–7.4, and New Zealand's 4.8–5.5.[57] Statista cited data from the National Center for Biotechnology Information, and the journals *Intensive Care Medicine* and *Critical Care Medicine* noted that the United States had 34.7 critical care beds per one hundred thousand, leading Germany (29.2), Italy (12.5), France (11.6), South Korea (10.6), Spain (9.7), Japan (7.3), the United Kingdom (6.6), China (3.6), and India (2.3).[58] Adjusting these numbers as a proportion of each nation's specific elderly population,[59] data show that the United States exceeds every other country in available critical-care beds per one hundred thousand of its sixty-five-plus population (figure 13.7), those most at risk for needing an ICU: United States (239.31), Germany (136.13), South Korea (83.73), France (64.62), Italy (58.82), Spain (52.98), India (38.33), the United Kingdom (38.24), China (32.73), and Japan (29.13). Ironically, as we hear critics of the US system now bemoaning an alleged shortage of ICU beds, some critics recently pushed for more regulation to constrain the increasing number of ICU beds through certificate-of-need laws.[60] However, the United States has shifted even further toward more ICU beds as a percentage of total hospital beds.[61]

Outcomes in severely ill patients cared for in ICUs are also reported as superior in the United States. The journal *Lancet Infectious Diseases* reported a study of more than twenty-five thousand ICU patients with sepsis, a severe illness due to infection typically requiring ICU care, in which

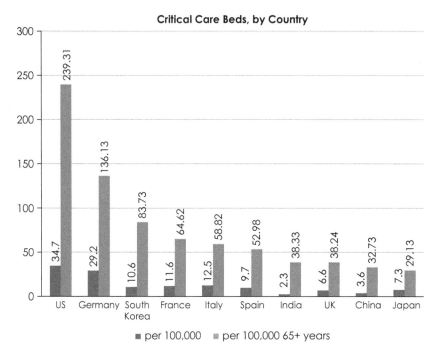

Figure 13.7. Available Critical Care Beds, per One Hundred Thousand and per One Hundred Thousand Ages Sixty-Five Years and Older, by Country. *Sources:* Niall McCarthy, "The Countries with the Most Critical Care Beds per Capita," *Forbes*, March 12, 2020; World Bank staff estimates based on age/sex distributions of United Nations Population Division's *World Population Prospects: 2019 Revision.*

the odds of hospital death were between 51 percent and 65 percent higher in Europe than in the United States.[62] Although their reported "adjusted" odds for death were only 5 percent to 19 percent higher in Europe than in the United States, those researchers asked, Is the higher mortality rate in Europe than in the USA due to a lower number of ICU beds available in Europe? Other analyses have shown that there is a strong correlation between ICU beds and hospital death in ICU patients, including in patients specifically with sepsis and severe respiratory illnesses, many of whom need mechanical ventilators for assisted breathing.[63]

Numerous studies have consistently demonstrated mortality rates from severe sepsis in Western Europe and Japan to be significantly higher than in the United States.[64] In one global study of 1,794 patients in sixty-two countries with severe sepsis in which 1,545 (86 percent) were admitted to the ICU, the overall hospital mortality was 28.4 percent. Among regions with more than one hundred patients, North America (98 percent were US patients) had the lowest hospital death rate (24.2 percent).[65] Acute respiratory distress syndrome (ARDS), another life-threatening condition that depends on mechanical ventilators as the mainstay of patient management, comprises 10 percent of all ICU admissions. ARDS has a high global mortality rate of 35 percent to 46 percent.[66] Although it is difficult to find international comparison data, the American fatality rate was at the lowest end of that range, 34.8 percent, in one 2011 study of 435 ARDS patients.[67] A 2017 study in *Lancet Respiratory Medicine* compared ARDS outcomes in "high-income European countries" (over 90 percent of cases from the United Kingdom [1,441], France [1,312], Spain [1,030], Italy [752], the Netherlands [412], Sweden [330], Ireland [277], Germany [275], and Portugal [247]) with ARDS outcomes in "high-income rest-of-world countries" (over 90 percent of cases from the United States [1,421], Australia [695], Japan [643], and Canada [380]). The odds of survival in ICUs and in hospitals were significantly higher in the "high-income rest-of-world countries" than in high-income European countries.[68]

Outcomes from Serious Disease

Long waits in single-payer systems for diagnosis, treatment, drugs, and technology have major consequences for patients, as documented throughout the peer-reviewed medical journals. In single-payer systems, patients are often waiting months, even after their doctors recommended urgent treatment for the most life-threatening illnesses. The ultimate consequence of single-payer care's hyper-regulation and restricted access is worse health outcomes compared with the US system for nearly all the most serious diseases—the illnesses that cause the most deaths, as well as the most important chronic diseases that lead to the most disability, including cancer,[69] heart disease,[70] stroke,[71] high blood pressure,[72] and diabetes[73] (figures 13.8–10). As one indicator of outcomes, Bacchus

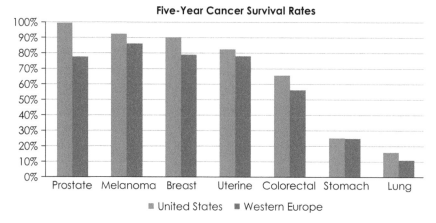

Figure 13.8. Comparison of Five-Year Survival Rate, United States versus Western Europe, 2000–2002, from Seven Common Cancers. The United States has superior survival from all common cancers compared with Western European nations. *Source:* Arduino Verdecchia et al., "Recent Cancer Survival in Europe: A 2000–02 Period Analysis of EUROCARE-4 Data," *Lancet Oncology* 8, no. 9 (September 2007): 784–96.

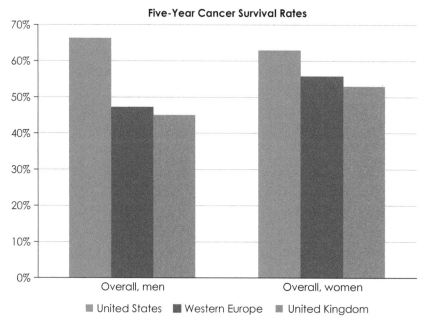

Figure 13.9. Comparison of Five-Year Survival Rates for Men and Women, United States versus Western European Nations. Note the statistically significant increased survival for American men and women compared with the average Western European and especially the United Kingdom. *Source:* Verdecchia et al., "Recent Cancer Survival in Europe."

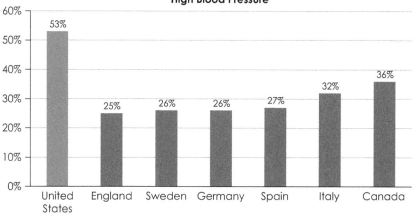

Patients Receiving Treatment, If Diagnosed as High Blood Pressure

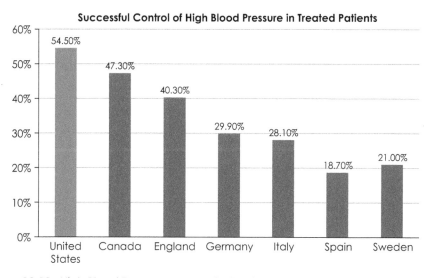

Successful Control of High Blood Pressure in Treated Patients

Figure 13.10. High Blood Pressure: Access to Treatment by Percentage of Diagnosed Patients Receiving Treatment, by Country, Ages Thirty-Five to Sixty-Four Years (top); and Successful Control by Percentage of Treated Patients by Country, Ages Thirty-Five to Sixty-Four Years (bottom). The United States has more effective medical care for high blood pressure compared with other developed countries, including those held as models for single-payer care. *Sources:* Kenneth E. Thorpe et al., "Differences in Disease Prevalence as a Source of the U.S.-European Health Care Spending Gap," *Health Affairs* 26, suppl. 2 (2007): w678–86; Eileen M. Crimmins et al., "Are International Differences in Health Similar to International Differences in Life Expectancy?," in *International Differences in Mortality at Older Ages: Dimensions and Sources* ed. Eileen M. Crimmins et al., Panel on Understanding Divergent Trends in Longevity in High-Income Countries, Committee on Population, Division of Behavioral and Social Sciences and Education, National Research Council (Washington, DC: National Academies Press, 2010); Katharina Wolf-Maier et al., "Hypertension Treatment and Control in Five European Countries, Canada, and the United States," *Hypertension* 43, no. 1 (January 2004): 10–17.

Barua, Nadeem Esmail, and Taylor Jackson calculate that among women in Canada alone over a sixteen-year period, more than forty-four thousand additional patients died due to Canada's wait times for medically necessary nonemergency treatment.[74] Although potentially stressed beyond any foreseeable need, the US system is uniquely prepared to care for patients with life-threatening diseases.

It should be noted that the superior disease outcomes in the United States are generally reported as group data for all affected patients. It is also true that some disease outcomes, as well as broader measures not necessarily reflective of only health care, including life expectancy and infant mortality, are worse for certain populations, including some minorities and lower socioeconomic groups in the United States.[75] This is not unique to the United States.[76] Throughout the developed world, and regardless of health care system, infant mortality rates, as one example, are far worse for minority and lower socioeconomic populations. For instance, racial-ethnic minorities consistently demonstrate significantly higher infant mortality rates, roughly double those of the majority population, in the government-run systems of Canada[77] and the United Kingdom (figure 13.11).[78] While these differences by race are among the most perplexing dilemmas and most serious problems in society, they are likely multifactorial and identifiable even when the effects of other risk factors (maternal age, marital status, parity, and education) are taken into account.

As opposed to the new enthusiasm of some for a move toward single-payer care in the United States, those countries with decades of single-payer experience are now reducing their broadest regulatory constraints by overtly paying for *private* health care to solve their failures. In 2016, the UK government spent more than half of its total budgetary increase from taxpayers on private and other non-NHS providers.[79] Even though England's NHS is projected to hit a £30 billion funding shortfall in 2020–21, one of the very few areas where funding is increasing is to non-NHS providers. Sweden, often heralded as the paradigm of a successful welfare state, increased municipal government spending on private care contracts by 50 percent in the past decade as a deregulatory move to repair its single-payer system. Primary care clinics and nursing facilities are now run by the private sector or receive substantial public funding. Major deregulation in pharmacies to permit private-sector competition has also been introduced into Sweden's previous government monopoly on prescription and nonprescription drugs.[80] In a striking regulation pullback, Denmark's patients using taxpayer-funded single-payer health care can choose a private hospital—even outside the country—if the waiting time for the treatment exceeds one month.[81] The governments of Finland, Ireland, Italy, the United Kingdom, the Netherlands, Norway, Spain, and Sweden, all with single-payer care, also now spend taxpayer money on private care, sometimes even outside their own countries, to solve their failures to deliver adequate care.

Medicare for All: Creating an American Single-Payer System

Single-payer systems hold down health care costs by limiting availability of doctors, treatments, medications, and technology. Our own government's Medicare and Medicaid programs employ similar methods to hold down costs. Data on payments to health care providers show a significant underpayment from both Medicare and Medicaid for health care (figure 13.12).[82] That underpayment—payment for services *below the cost* of administering those services—has increased significantly since the implementation of the ACA.

Underpayment for medical care has consequences beyond shifting costs to those with private insurance. Beyond the limited access to doctors due to below-cost payments by Medicaid, the medical literature demonstrates that disease outcomes under government insurance are worse than those for medically similar patients under private coverage (table 13.2); race and income were not associated with worse outcomes in several of these studies (Medicaid patients are typically using purely government insurance with its restrictive coverage for medical care, without supplemental private insurance).[83]

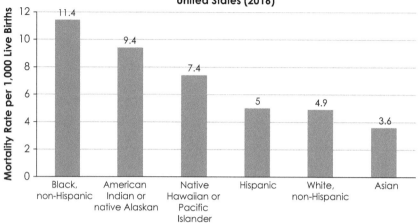

A: Infant Mortality by Race and Ethnicity of Mother, United States (2016)

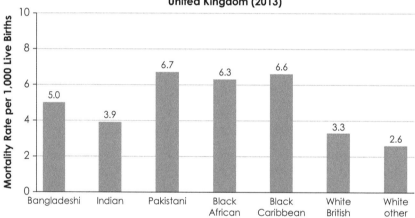

B: Infant Mortality Rate by Race and Ethnicity of Mother, United Kingdom (2013)

Figure 13.11A–D. Infant Mortality Rates of (A) United States, (B) United Kingdom, (C) Quebec, and (D) Canada by Race and Ethnicity of Mother. Note significantly higher infant mortality rates of minority populations in these countries, with or without single-payer health care. *Sources:* Centers for Disease Control and Prevention, *User Guide to the 2016 Period Linked Birth/Infant Death Public Use File*, 80; Office for National Statistics (UK), "Large Differences in Infant Mortality by Ethnic Group," June 24, 2008; Office for National Statistics (UK), "Pregnancy and Ethnic Factors Influencing Births and Infant Mortality: 2013," October 14, 2015; Zhong-Cheng Luo et al., "Birth Outcomes and Infant Mortality among First Nations, Inuit, and non-Indigenous Women by Northern versus Southern Residence, Quebec," *Journal of Epidemiology and Community Health* 66, no. 4 (September 2012): 328–33; Public Health Agency of Canada, *Key Health Inequalities in Canada: A National Portrait*, 2018, 81.

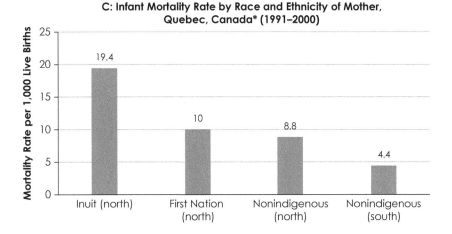

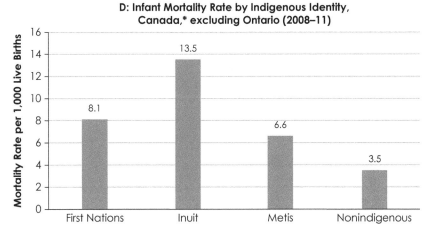

*Canada calculations defined infants as "live birth" for all births 500 grams or larger birth weight.

Figure 13.11A–D. (continued)

Owing to Medicare's below-cost payment for care, access to care is already at risk, and this would undoubtedly worsen if expanded to Medicare for All. The Office of the Actuary of the Centers for Medicare and Medicaid Services (CMS) in 2019 warned of serious limitations in availability of care for Medicare beneficiaries. CMS calculated that most hospitals, skilled nursing facilities, and in-home health care providers already lose money per Medicare patient. It warned that "we expect access to Medicare-participating

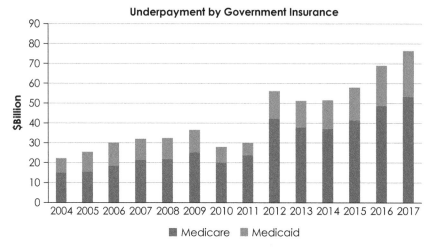

Figure 13.12. Underpayment to Hospitals for Delivered Care, Medicare and Medicaid, 2004–17. Note the significant jump in the deficit to hospitals from payment *below cost* of services by government insurance in 2012, after ACA regulations came into effect. *Source:* Analysis of American Hospital Association Annual Survey data, 2018, community hospitals.

physicians to become a significant issue in the long term under current law" even without moving toward Medicare for All.[84]

A shift to the extreme regulatory milieu of Medicare for All or any similar single-payer system would almost immediately jeopardize access to timely medical care, as documented in the proposals themselves. By eliminating private insurance, Medicare for All imposes large and immediate reductions in payments to doctors and hospitals now treating patients under private insurance, including cuts of more than 40 percent for hospitals and 30 percent for physicians that would grow more severe over time. As Charles Blahous states, we cannot know with certainty the extent to which these cuts would disrupt the supply and timeliness of health care services.[85] It is also noteworthy that more than 70 percent of US seniors rely on private insurance to supplement or replace traditional Medicare, whether Medicare Advantage, Medigap, or employer-sponsored coverage, and that millions more use private drug coverage.[86] Abolishing private insurance, whether overtly by law or by the slower pathway of introducing

Table 13.2. Comparison of Medical Outcomes by Source of Insurance

Medical Disorder	Comparison of Patient Outcomes with Medicaid versus Private Insurance
Major surgery	Need longer hospital care (42% longer), incur more hospital costs (26% more), and are almost two times more likely to die in the hospital than those with private insurance; 13% more likely to die, stay in the hospital 50% longer; and cost of care 20% more than those with no insurance (Damien J. LaPar et al., "Primary Payer Status Affects Mortality for Major Surgical Operations," *Annals of Surgery* 252, no. 3 [September 2010]: 544–51; 893,658 major surgeries)
Cancer of the mouth and throat	50% more likely to die than patients with private health insurance (Joseph Kwok et al., "The Impact of Health Insurance Status on the Survival of Patients With Head and Neck Cancer," *Cancer* 116, no. 2 [2010]: 476–85; 1,231 patients)
Colon cancer	57% more likely to die postoperatively than patients with private insurance, a death rate not significantly different from that of the uninsured (Rachel Rapaport Kelz et al., "Morbidity and Mortality of Colorectal Carcinoma Surgery Differs by Insurance Status," *Cancer* 101, no. 10 [2004]: 2187–94; 13,415 adults)
Heart procedures	More likely to die from strokes and heart attacks than patients with private insurance and suffered the same outcome as those who lacked insurance altogether; more than twice the risk of death, heart attack, or other serious cardiac event within one year of cardiac surgery compared with privately insured patients (Michael A. Gaglia et al., "Effect of Insurance Type on Adverse Cardiac Events after Percutaneous Coronary Intervention," *American Journal of Cardiology* 107, no. 5 [2011]: 675–80; 13,573 patients)
Lung transplants	Die sooner than patients with private insurance undergoing lung transplants for end-stage pulmonary diseases; 8.1% less likely to survive ten years after surgery than privately insured and uninsured patients (Jeremiah Allen et al., "Insurance Status Is an Independent Predictor of Long-Term Survival after Lung Transplantation in the United States," *Journal of Heart and Lung Transplantation* 30, no. 1 [2011]: 45–53; 11,385 patients)

Note: Even after standardizing for medical differences among patients, Medicaid patients fare worse than those under private insurance, sometimes even worse than those with no insurance at all.

a "public option," will radically alter the timely access and high-quality health care that today's Medicare beneficiaries enjoy.

Strategic Deregulation in Health Care

The impact on the price that consumers are paying directly for medical care is illustrated in two cases: (1) medical procedures not covered by insurance and (2) insurance coverage with higher deductibles. Such simpler models of health care purchasing ultimately generate downward pressure on prices from doctors competing for patients. For instance, prices rapidly decreased when patients paid out-of-pocket for LASIK corrective vision surgery and MRI or CT screening. Additional evidence from studies of consumers' use of MRIs and outpatient surgery shows that introducing price transparency and defined-contribution benefits further encourages patients to compare price.[87]

Consumer spending on health care is significantly lower for those using high-deductible coverage,[88] without any consequent increases in emergency room visits or hospitalizations and without the hypothesized harmful impact on low-income families or the chronically ill.[89] Health spending reductions averaged 15 percent annually, and the savings increased with the level of the deductible and when paired with health savings accounts (HSAs). More than one-third of the savings by enrollees resulted from lower costs per health care utilization, that is, value-based decision making by consumers.[90] While especially relevant to patients using high-deductible plans with HSAs, these reforms pressure prices downward for all health care consumers.

The focus of the first years of the Trump administration in health care reform was centered on strategic deregulation to increase competition and reduce prices, intended to improve access to high-quality health care for patients, regardless of source of payment. Although legislative "repeal and replace" efforts aimed at reversing in entirety the regulatory burdens and taxes of the ACA have stalled, several directives and agency-level initiatives have begun. Most can be considered deregulatory in nature, with specific objectives of improving price transparency; reducing barriers to competition among insurers, providers, and sellers; empowering consumers with access to tools and information to assess value; expanding choices; and decentralizing power from the federal government to the states.

Since 2017, specific deregulatory moves focused on health insurance demonstrate the impact of deregulation and included the following: (1) eliminating the individual mandate by setting the regressive tax penalty to zero; (2) permitting lower-cost, reduced-mandate group insurance offerings by broadening availability of Association Health Plans; and (3) reversing a regulatory limitation on lower-cost short-term, limited-duration plans. By expanding lower-cost-coverage choices for consumers and increasing competition among insurers, these deregulatory actions are estimated to save Americans $450 billion over the decade.[91]

Insurance deregulation has also been implemented under Medicare. Nationwide, a record 3,148 private insurance plans now participate in Medicare Advantage (MA), a private coverage alternative to traditional government Medicare insurance selected by about one-third of seniors. After reversing a regulatory cap on MA plans, the average Medicare beneficiary can now choose from twenty-eight plans offered by seven firms in 2020. Nationally, the increase is 15 percent over 2019 and provides the largest number of plans in the history of the program. The continual increase in choices of coverage under MA from nineteen in 2016 to twenty-eight in 2020 reversed the trend of reduced choices under the Obama administration, when thirty-three plans offered in 2010 declined to eighteen in 2015.[92] These private plans provide extra benefits not covered by traditional Medicare. Former HHS secretary Alex Azar announced that average premiums for MA plans will drop by 23 percent compared with 2018—down to the lowest monthly premiums since 2007—likely a result of competition among insurers. This reduction in premiums reversed the increases seen from 2012 through 2015 under the Obama administration's regulatory policies.

The Trump administration had also focused on improving price transparency to reduce the cost of health care. President Trump signed an executive order to require providers paid by Medicare to post prices for a range of procedures. He also introduced a legal requirement barring pharmacy gag clauses under Medicare Part D plans,[93] clauses that had prohibited pharmacists from volunteering that a medication may be less expensive than an insurance co-pay if purchased for cash—as was the case more than 20 percent of the time.[94] Data also reveal that prices vary tremendously between drugstores for the same exact drug. According to a December 2017 study, the national average price for a one-month supply of five common generics ranged by a *factor of twenty* among different retailers for a given drug.[95] Even in a single city, the thirty-day supply price showed a *tenfold to seventeenfold* variation per drug. For the nearly forty million seniors taking five or more medications daily, the savings from price comparison shopping could be hundreds of dollars per month if patients were sufficiently informed and incentivized to consider prices.

Under the Trump administration, the Centers for Medicare and Medicaid Services (CMS) finalized its mandate requiring pharmaceutical manufacturers to disclose the list price of prescription drugs in direct-to-consumer television advertisements. The Trump administration also announced a proposal to do away with complex behind-the-scenes arrangements that generate rebates of $179 billion to pharmacy benefit managers (PBMs), replacing rebates with discounts to beneficiaries (patients) at the point of sale.[96] PBMs are middlemen that control "formularies," the lists of drugs covered by a plan. Rebates from drug companies to PBMs are payments for influence—either to position a drug on the formulary as "exclusive" or to give it preferred status over competitors. PBMs act counter to patient interests while aggravating the lack of price transparency. These complex behind-the-scenes rebates reward inflated list prices, on which patient premiums are often based. This prevents patients from taking account of price. A growing number of tools are now becoming available to compare prices. CMS finalized a rule in 2018 requiring Medicare Part D drug plans to provide electronic tools to doctors that would at least allow discussion with patients regarding out-of-pocket costs for prescription drugs at the time a prescription is written.

High drug prices represent an especially difficult issue in health care, and the current Biden administration is formulating ways to address this. Drugs are probably the most significant reason for the past half century's unprecedented gains against the deadliest, most debilitating diseases. Yet there is a long-standing conundrum: the same policies that are associated with the lower prices seen in other countries—price regulation and weaker patent rights—are also associated with delayed launches and reduced access to drugs.[97] Any regulatory policy must be introduced without suffocating the innovation crucial to new drug development, given the unique need for massive capital investment at extraordinary risk for years until eventual market entry. For example, the Hatch-Waxman Act of 1984 represents an example of successfully combining government regulation with deregulation to generate the desired compromise—continued innovation in safe drug development, alongside increased price competition by generics. While it extended the length of a patent to partially offset the time spent on FDA-required clinical trials, the act simplified and expedited the development and approval processes for generics.[98] Facilitating market entry to enhance competition among drugmakers has been an effective tool to dramatically lower prices (figure 13.13).[99]

The FDA under the Trump administration has also made progress in facilitating drug approvals by streamlining and simplifying approval processes: the year 2017 saw sixty-eight new drugs and biologics approved and a 60 percent increase in generic drug approvals over the previous year.

Over the years 2017 and 2018, average new prescription drug approvals as well as generic drug approvals increased by approximately 71.6 percent relative to 2008–16 under the previous administration. Similarly, average annual generic drug approvals increased by 69.3 percent in 2017 and 2018 relative to 2008–16. *The impact?* The average annual prescription drug inflation (CPI-Rx) was only 2.5 percent, compared with 3.5 percent in 2008–16. That rate was also significantly lower relative to the overall inflation index (CPI) during 2017–18 versus during 2008–16 (.2 percent

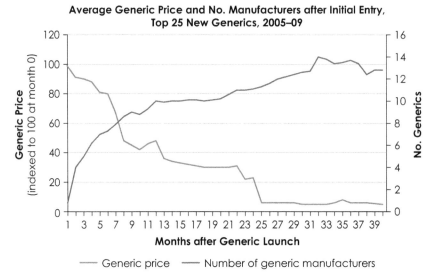

Average Generic Price and No. Manufacturers after Initial Entry, Top 25 New Generics, 2005–09

— Generic price   — Number of generic manufacturers

Figure 13.13. The average generic drug price historically responds to market competition. Prices fall and stabilize to about 6 percent of the drug's initial price two years following its launch, as the number of competing generics entering the market increases. *Source:* Ernst R. Berndt and Murray L. Aitken, "Brand Loyalty, Generic Entry and Price Competition in Pharmaceuticals in the Quarter Century after the 1984 Waxman-Hatch Legislation," *International Journal of the Economics of Business* 18, no. 2 (2011): 177–201. *Source of data:* IMS Health, National Sales Perspective, National Prescription Audit: December 2009.

compared with 1.8 percent). And for the first time in decades, the average price of prescription drugs has declined (figure 13.14).[100]

Conclusion

In most nations, heavy regulation of the supply of health care goods and services care is coupled with marked centralization of payment for medical care. The United States has a far less centralized but still highly regulated system in which health expenditures are roughly equal from public and private insurance. The system is characterized by its unique private

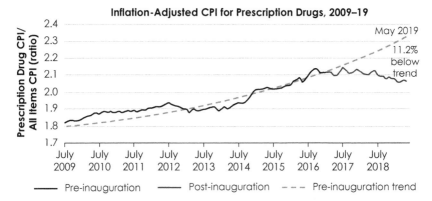

Figure 13.14. The inflation-adjusted prescription drug price index has decreased significantly in 2017–19. The CPI covers retail transactions, which are about three-fourths of all prescription drug sales. Inflation adjustments are calculated using the ratio of the CPI of prescription drugs relative to the CPI-U (Urban) for all items. The pre-inauguration expansion trend in annual growth rates is estimated over a sample period from July 2009 through December 2016; 2017–18 projected levels are then reconstructed from projected growth rates. *Source:* Council of Economic Advisers, *Reforming Biopharmaceutical Pricing at Home and Abroad,* February 2018.

components: more than two hundred million Americans, including most seniors on Medicare, use private insurance. The US system is the world's most effective by literature-based, objective measures of access, quality, and innovation, but US health care demands reform. Health care costs are high and increasing, and the projected demand for medical care by an aging population and the future burden of lifestyle-related disease threaten the sustainability of the system.

Although the regulatory expansion under the Affordable Care Act reduced the uninsured population, it generated increased private insurance premiums, a withdrawal of insurers from the market, and sector-wide consolidation that is historically associated with higher prices and reduced choices of medical care. In its wake, American voters are now presented with two fundamentally different visions for reform that have a diametrically opposed reliance on regulation and centralization: (1) single-payer proposals, including Medicare for All, or public options that generally lead to single-payer care, based on the most extreme level of government regulation and authority over health care and health insurance; or (2) a consumer-driven system that relies on strategic deregulation to increase market-based competition among providers and empowers patients with control of the money. Both pathways are intended to contain overall expenditures on health care and broaden access.

Intuitively, a single-payer model of health care represents a simplification, but the reality is that such centralized systems impose overwhelming restrictions on both demand and supply. Government-centralized single-payer systems actively hold down health care expenditures mainly by sweeping restrictions on the utilization and payment for medical procedures, drugs, and technology under the single authority of the central government. The overall costs of this false simplification are enormous, creating societal costs that extend beyond calculated tax payments that are required to support such a system.

The alternative approach involves rule elimination and decentralization, that is, strategic deregulation, to induce competition for value-seeking patients. Reducing the price of health care by competition, instead of more regulation, generates lower insurance premiums, reduces outlays from government programs, and broadens access to quality care. Broadly available options for cheaper, high-deductible coverage less burdened by regulations; markedly expanded health savings accounts; and tax reforms to unleash consumer power are keys to achieving price sensitivity for health care. Reforms to increase the supply of medical care by breaking down long-standing anticonsumer barriers to competition, such as archaic certificates-of-need for technology, unnecessary state-based licensure of physicians, and overly regulated pathways to drug development, while facilitating transparency of price and quality among doctors and hospitals, would generate further competition and reduce the price of health care. Preliminary results from such deregulatory actions demonstrate promising results and offer an evidence-based context for the broader discussion of the role and reach of government regulation in socialism compared with free-market systems.

NOTES

1. Centers for Medicare and Medicaid Services (CMS), *2019 Annual Report of the Boards of Trustees of the Federal Hospital Insurance and Federal Supplementary Medical Insurance Trust Funds*, April 2019.

2. John D. Shatto and M. Kent Clemens, "Projected Medicare Expenditures under an Illustrative Scenario with Alternative Payment Updates to Medicare Providers," CMS Office of the Actuary, April 22, 2019.

3. National Research Council and National Academy of Public Administration, *Choosing the Nation's Fiscal Future* (Washington, DC: National Academy of Sciences, 2011).

4. Farhad Islami et al., "Proportion and Number of Cancer Cases and Deaths Attributable to Potentially Modifiable Risk Factors in the United States," *CA: A Cancer Journal for Clinicians* 68, no. 1 (January/February 2018): 31–54.

5. Organisation for Economic Co-operation and Development (OECD), *OECD Factbook 2018* (Paris: OECD, 2018).

6. Centers for Medicaid and CHIP Services, "Estimated Medicaid and CHIP Enrollment Data," August 2019, Medicaid.gov; Robin Rudowitz, Elizabeth Hinton, and Larisa Antonisse, "Medicaid Enrollment & Spending Growth: FY 2018 & 2019," Kaiser Family Foundation; CMS, *2019 Annual Report of the Boards of Trustees of the Federal Hospital Insurance and Federal Supplementary Medical Insurance Trust Funds*; National Research Council and National Academy of Public Administration, *Choosing the Nation's Fiscal Future*.

7. Congressional Budget Office, "Insurance Coverage Provisions of the Affordable Care Act—CBO's January 2015 Baseline."

8. eHealth, "Average Individual Health Insurance Premiums Increased 99% Since 2013, the Year Before Obamacare, & Family Premiums Increased 140%, According to eHealth.com Shopping Data," January 23, 2017.

9. CMS, "County by County Analysis of Plan Year 2018 Insurer Participation in Health Insurance Exchanges."

10. Ashley Semanskee, Gary Claxton, and Larry Levitt, "How Premiums Are Changing in 2018," Kaiser Family Foundation, November 29, 2017.

11. Will Fox and John Pickering, *Hospital and Physician Cost Shift: Payment Level Comparison of Medicare, Medicaid, and Commercial Payers*, Milliman Client Report, December 2008.

12. American Hospital Association and Avalere Health, *Trendwatch Chartbook 2014: Trends Affecting Hospitals and Health Systems* (Washington, DC: American Hospital Association, 2014).

13. Alyene Senger, "Measuring Choice and Competition in the Exchanges: Still Worse Than before the ACA," Heritage Foundation Issue Brief 4324 on Health Care, December 22, 2014.

14. Congressional Budget Office, "Private Health Insurance and Federal Policy," February 2016, https://www.cbo.gov/publication/51130.

15. Erica Coe et al., "Hospital Networks: Configurations on the Exchanges and Their Impact on Premiums," McKinsey Center for US Health System Reform, December 2013.

16. Caroline F. Pearson and Elizabeth Carpenter, "Plans with More Restrictive Networks Comprise 73% of Exchange Market," Avalere, November 30, 2017.

17. Chris Sloan and Elizabeth Carpenter, "Exchange Plans Include 34 Percent Fewer Providers than the Average for Commercial Plans," Avalere, July 15, 2015.

18. Leemore Dafny, "Hospital Industry Consolidation: Still More to Come?," *New England Journal of Medicine* 370, no. 3 (January 16, 2014): 198–99.

19. Martin Gaynor and Robert J. Town, "The Impact of Hospital Consolidation," Robert Wood Johnson Foundation Publication/The Synthesis Project, June 1, 2012.

20. James C. Robinson and Kelly Miller, "Total Expenditures per Patient in Hospital-Owned and Physician-Owned Physician Organizations in California," *JAMA* 312, no. 16 (October 22–29, 2014): 1663–69.

21. Cory Capps, David Dranove, and Christopher Ody, "The Effect of Hospital Acquisitions of Physician Practices on Prices and Spending," Institute for Policy Research, Northwestern University, Working Paper Series WP-15-02, February 2015.

22. Bacchus Barua and Sazid Hasan, *The Private Cost of Public Queues for Medically Necessary Care*, 2018, Fraser Institute.

23. Ernie Stokes and Robin Somerville, *The Economic Costs of Wait Times in Canada*, a study commissioned by the British Columbia Medical Association and the Canadian Medical Association (Milton, ON: Centre for Spatial Economics, 2008).

24. John Holahan, Linda J. Blumberg, and Lisa Clemens-Cope, *The Sanders Single-Payer Health Care Plan: The Effect on National Health Expenditures and Federal and Private Spending* (Washington, DC: Urban Institute, 2016); Charles Blahous, "The Costs of a National Single-Payer Healthcare System," Government

Spending Working Papers, Mercatus Center, George Mason University, July 30, 2018.

25. National Health Service, "Statistical Press Notice: NHS Referral to Treatment (RTT) Waiting Times Data, September 2019," NHS press release, November 14, 2019.

26. House of Commons Committee of Public Accounts, *NHS Waiting Times for Elective Care in England*, Fifty-fifth Report of Session 2013–14, April 29, 2014.

27. Gisèle Carrière and Claudia Sanmartin, "Waiting Time for Medical Specialist Consultations in Canada, 2007," Statistics Canada, Catalogue no. 82-003-XPE, *Health Reports* 21, no. 2 (June 2010).

28. Bacchus Barua and Mackenzie Moir, *Waiting Your Turn: Wait Times for Health Care in Canada, 2019 Report*, Fraser Institute.

29. Bacchus Barua and David Jacques, *The Private Cost of Public Queues for Medically Necessary Care, 2019*, Fraser Research Bulletin, March 2019, Fraser Institute.

30. Jeremy Hurst and Luigi Siciliani, "Tackling Excessive Waiting Times for Elective Surgery: A Comparison of Policies in Twelve OECD Countries," OECD Health Working Papers, no. 6, 2003.

31. John G. Cullis, Philip R. Jones, and Carol Propper, "Waiting Lists and Medical Treatment: Analysis and Policies," in *Handbook of Health Economics*, vol. 1B, ed. Anthony J. Culyer and Joseph P. Newhouse (Amsterdam: Elsevier, 2000).

32. Robert J. Blendon et al., "Confronting Competing Demands to Improve Quality: A Five-Country Hospital Survey," *Health Affairs* 23, no. 3 (May/June 2004).

33. John Z. Ayanian and Thomas J. Quinn, "Quality of Care for Coronary Heart Disease in Two Countries," *Health Affairs* 20, no. 3 (May/June 2001): 55–67.

34. Merritt Hawkins, 2009, 2014, and 2017 *Survey of Physician Appointment Wait Times*.

35. Alok A. Khorana et al., "Time to Initial Cancer Treatment in the United States and Association with Survival over Time: An Observational Study," *PLOS ONE* 14, no. 4 (April 2019).

36. Khorana et al., "Time to Initial Cancer Treatment in the United States."

37. Karl Y. Bilimoria et al., "Wait Times for Cancer Surgery in the United States: Trends and Predictors of Delays," *Annals of Surgery* 253, no. 4 (April 2011): 779–85.

38. Melissa M. Brown, "Do Waiting Times Really Matter?," *British Journal of Ophthalmology* 91, no. 3 (March 2007): 270–71.

39. Stefania M. Mojon-Azzi and Daniel S. Mojon, "Waiting Times for Cataract Surgery in Ten European Countries: An Analysis Using Data from the SHARE Survey," *British Journal of Ophthalmology* 91, no. 3 (March 2007): 282–86.

40. OECD, *Health at a Glance 2019: OECD Indicators*, https://doi.org/10.1787 /4dd50c09-en, and other OECD data.

41. Bengt Jönsson and Nils Wilking, "Market Uptake of New Oncology Drugs," *Annals of Oncology* 18, suppl. 3 (June 2007): iii31–iii48.

42. US Food and Drug Administration, Center for Drug Evaluation and Research, *Novel Drugs 2015 Summary*, January 2016.

43. Christine Troskie et al., "Regulatory Approval Time for Hormonal Contraception in Canada, the United States and the United Kingdom, 2000–2015: A Retrospective Data Analysis," *CMAJ Open* 4, no. 4 (October–December 2016): E654–E660.

44. Vladimir Stevanovic and Rie Fujisawa, *Performance of Systems of Cancer Care in OECD Countries: Exploration of the Relation between Resources, Process Quality, Governance, and Survival in Patients with Breast, Cervical, Colorectal, and Lung Cancers*, HCQI Expert Group meeting, Paris, May 27, 2011.

45. Yuting Zhang, Hana Chantel Hueser, and Inmaculada Hernandez, "Comparing the Approval and Coverage Decisions of New Oncology Drugs in the United States and Other Selected Countries," *Journal of Managed Care and Specialty Pharmacy* 23, no. 2 (February 2017): 247–54.

46. IQVIA Institute, *Global Oncology Trends 2019: Therapeutics, Clinical Development and Health System Implications*, 2019; data from Statista, https://www.statista .com/statistics/696020/availability-of-new-oncology-drugs-by-country.

47. National Institute for Health and Care Excellence (NICE) and NHS England, "Changes to NICE Drug Appraisals: What You Need to Know," April 4, 2017.

48. Jane Ogden, "How Will NICE's Budget Impact Test Affect New Drug Availability?," *Prescriber* 28, no. 8 (August 2017): 9–12.

49. MERCURY Study Group, "Diagnostic Accuracy of Preoperative Magnetic Resonance Imaging in Predicting Curative Resection of Rectal Cancer: Prospective Observational Study," *British Medical Journal*, September 25, 2006.

50. Ethan S. Brandler and Nayeem Baksh, "Emergency Management of Stroke in the Era of Mechanical Thrombectomy," *Clinical and Experimental Emergency Medicine* 6, no. 4 (December 2019): 273–87.

51. Joanna M. Wardlaw et al., "Immediate Computed Tomography Scanning of Acute Stroke Is Cost-Effective and Improves Quality of Life," *Stroke* 35, no. 11 (November 2004): 2477–83; Patrick M. Rao et al., "Effect of Computed

Tomography of the Appendix on Treatment of Patients and Use of Hospital Resources," *New England Journal of Medicine* 338, no. 3 (January 15, 1998): 141–46.

52. Arduino Verdecchia et al., "Patient Survival for All Cancers Combined as Indicator of Cancer Control in Europe," *European Journal of Public Health* 18, no. 5 (October 2008): 527–32; Campbell S. D. Roxburgh et al., "Changes in the Multidisciplinary Management of Rectal Cancer from 2009 to 2015 and Associated Improvements in Short-Term Outcomes," *Colorectal Disease* 21, no. 10 (October 2019): 1140–50; Stevanovic and Fujisawa, *Performance of Systems of Cancer Care in OECD Countries.*

53. OECD, "Computed Tomography (CT) Scanners" (indicator), 2020, https://doi .org/10.1787/bedece12-en; and "Magnetic Resonance Imaging (MRI) Units" (indicator), 2020, https://doi.org/10.1787/1a72e7d1-en (both accessed March 13, 2020).

54. National Conference of State Legislatures, "CON-Certificate of Need State Laws—8/25/2016."

55. Thomas Stratmann and Jacob W. Russ, "Do Certificate-of-Need Laws Increase Indigent Care?," Working Paper No. 14-20, Mercatus Center, George Mason University, July 2014.

56. Thomas Stratmann and Matthew C. Baker, "Are Certificate-of-Need Laws Barriers to Entry? How They Affect Access to MRI, CT, and PET Scans," Working Paper, Mercatus Center, George Mason University, January 2016.

57. Meghan Prin and Hannah Wunsch, "International Comparisons of Intensive Care: Informing Outcomes and Improving Standards," *Current Opinion in Critical Care* 18, no. 6 (December 2012): 700–706.

58. Niall McCarthy, "The Countries with the Most Critical Care Beds per Capita," *Forbes*, March 12, 2020.

59. World Bank staff estimates based on age/sex distributions of United Nations Population Division's *World Population Prospects: 2019 Revision.*

60. Rebecca A. Gooch and Jeremy M. Kahn, "ICU Bed Supply, Utilization, and Health Care Spending: An Example of Demand Elasticity," *JAMA* 311, no. 6 (February 12, 2014): 567–68.

61. David J. Wallace et al., "Critical Care Bed Growth in the United States," *American Journal of Respiratory and Critical Care Medicine* 191, no. 4 (February 15, 2015): 410–16.

62. Mitchell M. Levy et al., "Outcomes of the Surviving Sepsis Campaign in Intensive Care Units in the USA and Europe: A Prospective Cohort Study," *Lancet Infectious Diseases* 12, no. 12 (December 2012): 919–24.

63. Hannah Wunsch et al., "Variation in Critical Care Services across North America and Western Europe," *Critical Care Medicine* 36, no. 10 (October 2008): 2787–93.

64. See, for example, SepNet Critical Care Trials Group, "Incidence of Severe Sepsis and Septic Shock in German Intensive Care Units: The Prospective, Multicenter INSEP Study," *Intensive Care Medicine* 42, no. 12 (December 2016): 1980–89; S. H. M. Heublein et al., "Epidemiology of Sepsis in German Hospitals Derived from Administrative Databases," part of "Abstracts—6th International Congress 'Sepsis and Multiorgan Dysfunction,'" *Infection* 41 supp. (August 2013): S71–S72; Levy et al., "Outcomes of the Surviving Sepsis Campaign"; Richard R. K. Beale et al., "Promoting Global Research Excellence in Severe Sepsis (PROGRESS): Lessons from an International Sepsis Registry," *Infection* 37, no. 2 (June 2009): 222–32; Takayuki Ogura et al., "Treatment of Patients with Sepsis in a Closed Intensive Care Unit Is Associated with Improved Survival: A Nationwide Observational Study in Japan," *Journal of Intensive Care* 6 (2018): 57.

65. Andrew Rhodes et al., "The Surviving Sepsis Campaign Bundles and Outcome: Results from the International Multicentre Prevalence Study on Sepsis (the IMPreSS Study)," *Intensive Care Medicine* 41, no. 9 (September 2015): 1620–28, and supplement.

66. Eddy Fan, Daniel Brodie, and Arthur S. Slutsky, "Acute Respiratory Distress Syndrome: Advances in Diagnosis and Treatment," *JAMA* 319, no. 7 (February 20, 2018): 698–710; Giacomo Bellani et al., "Epidemiology, Patterns of Care, and Mortality for Patients with Acute Respiratory Distress Syndrome in Intensive Care Units in 50 Countries," *JAMA* 315, no. 8 (February 23, 2016): 788–800.

67. Guangxi Li et al., "Eight-Year Trend of Acute Respiratory Distress Syndrome: A Population-based Study in Olmsted County, Minnesota," *American Journal of Respiratory and Critical Care Medicine* 183, no. 1 (January 1, 2011): 59–66.

68. John G. Laffey et al., "Geo-economic Variations in Epidemiology, Patterns of Care, and Outcomes in Patients with Acute Respiratory Distress Syndrome: Insights from the LUNG SAFE Prospective Cohort Study," *Lancet Respiratory Medicine* 5, no. 8 (August 2017): 627–38.

69. Arduino Verdecchia et al., "Recent Cancer Survival in Europe: A 2000–02 Period Analysis of EUROCARE-4 Data," *Lancet Oncology* 8, no. 9 (September 2007): 784–96; Concord Working Group, "Cancer Survival in Five Continents: A Worldwide Population-Based Study," *Lancet Oncology* 9, no. 8 (August 2008): 730–56.

70. Padma Kaul et al., "Long-Term Mortality of Patients with Acute Myocardial Infarction in the United States and Canada: Comparison of Patients Enrolled in

Global Utilization of Streptokinase and t-PA for Occluded Coronary Arteries (GUSTO)-I," *Circulation* 110, no. 13 (September 28, 2004): 1754–60.

71. See, for example, Fabio Levi et al., "Trends in Mortality from Cardiovascular and Cerebrovascular Diseases in Europe and Other Areas of the World," *Heart* 88, no. 2 (2002): 119–24; Kaul et al., "Long-Term Mortality"; Melissa L. Martinson, Julien O. Teitler, and Nancy R. Reichman, "Health across the Life Span in the United States and England," *American Journal of Epidemiology* 173, no. 8 (2011): 858–65; Ayanian and Quinn, "Quality of Care for Coronary Heart Disease in Two Countries"; Harinda C. Wijeysundera et al., "Association of Temporal Trends in Risk Factors and Treatment Uptake with Coronary Heart Disease Mortality, 1994–2005," *JAMA* 303, no. 18 (2010): 1841–47; Kenneth E. Thorpe, David H. Howard, and Katya Galactionova, "Differences in Disease Prevalence as a Source of the U.S.-European Health Care Spending Gap," *Health Affairs* 26, suppl. 2 (2007): w678–86.

72. Y. Richard Wang, G. Caleb Alexander, and Randall S. Stafford, "Outpatient Hypertension Treatment, Treatment Intensification, and Control in Western Europe and the United States," *Archives of Internal Medicine* 167, no. 2 (2007): 141–47.

73. See, for example, Katharina Wolf-Maier et al., "Hypertension Treatment and Control in Five European Countries, Canada, and the United States," *Hypertension* 43, no. 1 (2004): 10–17; Wang, Alexander, and Stafford, "Outpatient Hypertension Treatment, Treatment Intensification, and Control in Western Europe and the United States"; Emmanuela Gakidou et al., "Management of Diabetes and Associated Cardiovascular Risk Factors in Seven Countries: A Comparison of Data from National Health Examination Surveys," *Bulletin of the World Health Organization* 89, no. 3 (2011): 172–83.

74. Bacchus Barua, Nadeem Esmail, and Taylor Jackson, *The Effect of Wait Times on Mortality in Canada*, Fraser Institute, 2014.

75. Jiaquan Q. Xu et al., "Deaths: Final Data for 2016," *National Vital Statistics Reports* 67, no. 5 (2018).

76. Centers for Disease Control and Prevention, *User Guide to the 2016 Period Linked Birth/Infant Death Public Use File*, 80.

77. Zhong-Cheng Luo et al., "Birth Outcomes and Infant Mortality among First Nations, Inuit, and non-Indigenous Women by Northern versus Southern Residence, Quebec," *Journal of Epidemiology and Community Health* 66, no. 4 (September 2012): 328–33; Public Health Agency of Canada, *Key Health Inequalities in Canada: A National Portrait*, 2018, 81.

78. Office for National Statistics (UK), "Pregnancy and Ethnic Factors Influencing Births and Infant Mortality: 2013," October 14, 2015.

79. Sarah Neville, "NHS Funds Diverted to Private Sector," *Financial Times*, March 26, 2017.

80. David Landes, "Sweden's Pharmacy Monopoly Finished," *The Local: Sweden's News in English*, July 1, 2009.

81. Karolina Socha and Mikael Bech, "Extended Free Choice of Hospital—Waiting Time," *Health Policy Monitor*, October 2007.

82. Charles Blahous, "How Much Would Medicare for All Cut Doctor and Hospital Reimbursements?," Manhattan Institute for Policy Research, October 10, 2018.

83. Jeremiah G. Allen et al., "Insurance Status Is an Independent Predictor of Long-Term Survival after Lung Transplantation in the United States," *Journal of Heart and Lung Transplantation* 30, no. 1 (2011): 45–53; Joseph Kwok et al., "The Impact of Health Insurance Status on the Survival of Patients With Head and Neck Cancer," *Cancer* 116, no. 2 (2010): 476–85; Rachel Rapaport Kelz et al., "Morbidity and Mortality of Colorectal Carcinoma Surgery Differs by Insurance Status," *Cancer* 101, no. 10 (2004): 2187–94; Michael A. Gaglia et al., "Effect of Insurance Type on Adverse Cardiac Events after Percutaneous Coronary Intervention," *American Journal of Cardiology* 107, no. 5 (2011): 675–80.

84. Shatto and Clemens, "Projected Medicare Expenditures."

85. Blahous, "How Much Would Medicare for All Cut Doctor and Hospital Reimbursements?"

86. Juliette Cubanski et al., "Sources of Supplemental Coverage Among Medicare Beneficiaries in 2016," November 28, 2018, http://kff.org/issue-brief/sources-of-supplemental-coverage-among-medicare-beneficiaries-in-2016; Gretchen Jacobson, Jennifer Huang, and Tricia Neuman, "Medigap Reform: Setting the Context for Understanding Recent Proposals," Medicare, January 13, 2014, http://kff.org/medicare/issue-brief/medigap-reform-setting-the-context.

87. Sze-jung Wu et al., "Price Transparency for MRIs Increased Use of Less Costly Providers and Triggered Provider Competition," *Health Affairs* 33, no. 8 (August 2014): 1391–98; James C. Robinson, Timothy Brown, and Christopher Whaley, "Reference-Based Benefit Design Changes Consumers' Choices and Employers' Payments for Ambulatory Surgery," *Health Affairs* 34, no. 3 (March 2015): 415–22.

88. Amelia Haviland et al., "Do Consumer-Directed Health Plans Bend the Cost Curve over Time?," National Bureau of Economic Research Working Paper 21031, March 2015.

89. Amelia Haviland et al., "How Do Consumer-Directed Health Plans Affect Vulnerable Populations?," *Forum for Health Economics and Policy* 14, no. 2 (2011): 1–12.

90. Amelia Haviland et al., "The Effects of Consumer-Directed Health Plans on Episodes of Health Care," *Forum for Health Economics and Policy* 14, no. 2 (2011): 1–27.

91. Council of Economic Advisers, *Deregulating Health Insurance Markets: Value to Market Participants*, February 2019.

92. Gretchen Jacobson et al., *Medicare Advantage 2020 Spotlight: First Look*, Kaiser Family Foundation, October 2019, http://kff.org/medicare/issue-brief/medicare -advantage-2020-spotlight-first-look, and author's analysis of Kaiser Family Foundation's *CMS Medicare Advantage Landscape and Enrollment Files*, 2010–19.

93. National Community Pharmacists Association, "Pharmacists Survey: Prescription Drug Costs Skewed by Fees on Pharmacies, Patients," June 28, 2016.

94. Karen Van Nuys et al., "Frequency and Magnitude of Co-payments Exceeding Prescription Drug Costs," *JAMA* 319, no. 10 (2018): 1045–47.

95. Lisa L. Gill, "Shop Around for Lower Drug Prices," *Consumer Reports*, April 5, 2018.

96. Credit Suisse, Americas/United States/Europe Equity Research Pharmaceuti- cals & Biotechnology, *Global Pharma and Biotech*, April 18, 2017.

97. Iain M. Cockburn, Jean O. Lanjouw, and Mark Schankerman, "Patents and the Global Diffusion of New Drugs," *American Economic Review* 106, no. 1 (2016): 136–64.

98. Richard A. Epstein and Bruce Kuhlik, "Navigating the Anticommons for Pharmaceutical Patents: Steady the Course on Hatch-Waxman," John M. Olin Program in Law and Economics Working Paper No. 209 (2004).

99. Ernst R. Berndt and Murray L. Aitken, "Brand Loyalty, Generic Entry and Price Competition in Pharmaceuticals in the Quarter Century after the 1984 Waxman-Hatch Legislation," *International Journal of the Economics of Business* 18, no. 2 (2011): 177–201.

100. Council of Economic Advisers, *Reforming Biopharmaceutical Pricing at Home and Abroad*, February 2018.

14

The Economic Impact of a Universal Basic Income

John F. Cogan and Daniel L. Heil

At various times throughout our nation's history, a wave of collectivist sentiment has swept the country. These waves, born out of a deep disenchantment with current circumstances, are often characterized by a fervent, but mistaken, belief that society can be improved by subordinating the interest of the individual to centralized government control. We are experiencing such a collectivist wave today. Riding atop this populist wave is a strong sentiment that government should use its power to tax to redistribute income from rich to poor. A popular policy instrument for this redistribution is the universal basic income (UBI).

In the last few years, interest in the policy has seen a resurgence. Democratic presidential candidate Andrew Yang made it the centerpiece of his campaign. UBI experiments are now being conducted in Sweden, South Korea, the Netherlands, and Kenya. In the United States, Stockton, California, is currently running a pilot project and the cities of Compton, California, and Hudson, New York, are scheduled to begin pilot projects before the end of 2020.[1] A Hill-HarrisX poll in August 2020 found that 55 percent of all surveyed persons, and 69 percent of those ages eighteen to thirty-four, supported a UBI.[2]

Proponents of a national UBI argue that the policy would represent a substantial improvement over the current transfer system. They expect that a UBI will provide an adequate standard of living for all while reducing the stigma attached to existing transfer programs. Moreover, supporters believe that compared with existing assistance programs, a UBI would better target those in need and reduce work disincentives.

In this paper, we consider whether various UBI plans could meet these ambitious goals. Using data from the Current Population Survey (CPS) and TAXSIM, we analyze the impact of various proposed national US UBI plans on aggregate labor supply, the distribution of household income, and the federal budget. Specifically, we examine two types of UBI plans, both of which are designed to eliminate poverty. First, we explore an idealized plan that would replace the entire federal transfer system with a poverty-level UBI benefit to all households regardless of income. Second, we explore a prototype UBI plan that would offer a poverty-level benefit that would phase out as earnings rise. The prototype UBI plan would replace cash and near-cash means-tested federal transfer programs and federal disability programs. Our analysis quantifies the inherent trade-offs in UBI plans with regard to the adequacy of benefits, the degree of work incentives, and the fiscal impact. We find that neither plan would meet the objectives of UBI proponents.

Government expenditures under the idealized plan would be approximately the same as those of the income transfer programs it would replace. The plan would also marginally improve work incentives compared to the current system. However, because the idealized plan does not phase out assistance as earnings rise, it would significantly redistribute government assistance from poor to rich households, precisely the opposite of the goal of UBI proponents. Government assistance to the poorest fifth of US households would be reduced by more than 50 percent. Senior citizens receiving Social Security and Medicare benefits would bear a disproportionate share of this reduction. About three-fourths of the current transfer system's assistance would be shifted to the richest fifth of households. Thus, even if the substantial political hurdles of eliminating Social Security and Medicare could be overcome, the idealized UBI fails to achieve its goal of improving the targeting of government assistance.

In contrast, the prototype UBI plan, which phases out assistance by 50 percent as earnings rise, would better target government assistance to the poor. But the phase-out would worsen work incentives compared with the current system and thereby reduce US aggregate labor supply. Like the change in the distribution of government assistance, the impact of the UBI on aggregate labor supply is modest, a reduction of 2.6 percent. Annual federal government transfer payments under the prototype plan would exceed those of the current system by about $200 billion, necessitating either a permanent increase in taxes or government borrowing, or some combination of the two. Despite the increased outlays, the prototype plan's impact on the transfer system would be surprisingly small. Under the prototype UBI, the share of government assistance to the poorest fifth of US households would increase by only 8 percent compared to the current system.

We explore alternatives to the prototype plans to ascertain the impact of lowering the phase-out rate and reducing the basic income guarantee. This analysis sheds further light on the trade-offs inherent in a UBI. Reducing the prototype plan's phase-out rate to 25 percent actually worsens aggregate work incentives. Although work incentives for prototype plan recipients would improve, the lower phase-out rate would increase the number of workers receiving UBI assistance. Each of these new recipients would face the alternative plan's 25 percent work disincentive. We also consider a deficit-neutral plan that would reduce the guaranteed benefit to 80 percent of the poverty line. Since this plan would cover fewer households than the prototype plan, the aggregate labor supply effects would be smaller. The lower benefit levels, however, would leave some households in poverty.

The paper is organized as follows: We describe how the UBI works and the major conceptual arguments for and against a national UBI. Next we assess the fiscal, economic, and distributional impacts of the idealized UBI plan. Then we describe attempts to enact a UBI during the Nixon and Carter administrations and present empirical estimates of the impact of a proto-typical UBI plan and its variants. We conclude with some thoughts on the viability of a national UBI plan.

What Is a Universal Basic Income?

In its most elemental form, the UBI offers a nationally uniform annual cash grant from the federal government to all individuals. This cash grant serves as a government-guaranteed floor on recipients' income. The grant comes with no strings attached; that is, it is given without requiring recipients to take responsibility for self-support or self-improvement.

The UBI has a long intellectual lineage. Scholars from Thomas Paine in the late 1700s to Milton Friedman, James Tobin, and Robert Theobald in the twentieth century have developed the conceptual rationale for the UBI, enumerated its advantages, and advocated its adoption. Progressives have long believed that all individuals have a basic human right to a decent standard of living in the form of adequate housing, nutrition, and health care. A universal basic income is a means of ensuring this basic right. Furthermore, because aid is available on equal terms to all individuals, there is no stigma and, therefore, no loss of dignity attached to receiving its benefits. Progressives are also attracted by the fact that the UBI allows recipients more flexibility to devote less time to work and more time to activities that enhance their quality of life, including obtaining more education and enjoying cultural or recreational activities. Some advocates go so far as to assert that a UBI will encourage labor market participation, rather than discouraging it as existing welfare programs do.

Conservatives are similarly attracted by the fact that the UBI allows recipients to decide for themselves how much of each of the elements of a decent living standard they prefer. This feature makes the UBI a less paternalistic system by allowing individuals more freedom of choice than a system that provides aid in the form of in-kind benefits. Conservatives are also attracted by the UBI's potential to replace income transfer programs that have large work disincentives.

At this conceptual level, the critique of the UBI centers on three of its misconceptions, two of which are misconceptions of human nature. First, UBI proponents presume that it doesn't matter whether individuals enjoy a level of material well-being through their own efforts or from government-mandated payments from others. This ignores a crucial facet of living a fulfilled life, namely that an individual's efforts and sacrifices to achieve a personal goal are essential to that person's sense of self-worth. It is the striving to reach a personal goal, more than achieving a level of material well-being, that provides life's true rewards.

A second misconception is that unconditional aid will not dampen the natural human desire for self-reliance and self-improvement. In reality, individuals receiving such aid have less reason to provide for themselves by being employed, looking for employment, or improving their skills. This is true regardless of whether or not the UBI has a means test. The degree to which these incentives influence behavior may vary from one person to another, but they operate on all persons, including those with a strong commitment to self-reliance. Recognition of this fundamental fact of human nature is the reason that down through the ages, charities, mutual aid societies, religious organizations, and governments have made requirements for self-improvement a cornerstone of their welfare policies.

A third misconception is that the money to finance the UBI comes from the government. Government is merely a pass-through entity that transfers income from some members of society to UBI recipients. Such transfers, of course, take place in all compassionate societies, but they have invariably been accompanied by requirements that recipients accept corresponding responsibilities. Governmentally conferred welfare rights must necessarily be accompanied by governmentally imposed duties on recipients or other members of society. Under the UBI, the government confers a right to a decent living standard but imposes no corresponding responsibilities on recipients. At the same time, it assumes that others should finance this living standard through their own labor. Such a policy divides a society between payers and recipients, potentially leading to resentment and discontentment. Providing individuals with free access to goods and services produced by other members of the society is a defining attribute of socialism. In this regard, the UBI is part and parcel of socialist policy.

These criticisms notwithstanding, advocates argue that a UBI would still be an improvement over the current income transfer system. They point out that compared with the current system, UBI assistance carries less of a stigma and is less paternalistic; its greater transparency increases the ability of government to redistribute income according to its desires; and since it could be administered by a computer, it is more efficient.

The advocates have a point. Today's federal income transfer system consists of more than a hundred separate federal programs that are spread across more than a dozen separate government agencies, each with its own bureaucracy and administrative costs. Income transfer programs have been added in piecemeal fashion over the past eight decades, each to meet some specific need at a point in time. The result is a complex web of highly inefficient, often overlapping programs that provide a wide variety of uncoordinated cash and in-kind benefits to persons located across the range of the US income distribution. Some programs base eligibility on demographic characteristics, some on income, others also on assets. Some take account of aid received from other programs, others do not. Some federal programs are administered by the federal government, others by state governments, and still others by local governments.

The system includes separate cash assistance programs for retirees, the disabled, low-income families with children, farmers, and low-income veterans; income supplements for low-wage workers and supplemental child-support payments to single mothers; health care assistance for the elderly, the disabled, the homeless, and millions of middle-class individuals; and home ownership subsidies and separate rental and public housing assistance. There are energy subsidies for home heating in the winter, air-conditioning in the summer, and weatherizing homes in all seasons; food assistance for daily groceries, school lunches, breakfasts, and afternoon snacks; job and vocational training and work experience assistance; day care assistance; foster care subsidies; higher education student grants and subsidized loans; rehabilitation assistance for the disabled; and a variety of social services, including legal aid, family planning, recreational support, transportation subsidies, and financial counseling services.

This mind-numbingly complex system transferred about $2.8 trillion from one group in society to another in 2019, most of it without regard to recipients' income. That year, over 60 percent of all US households received cash or in-kind benefits from at least one federal entitlement program; 47 percent received benefits simultaneously from two or more programs; and 21 percent received benefits from three or more programs. Excluding households headed by persons ages sixty-five and older, virtually all of whom receive Social Security or Medicare, 49 percent of US households received benefits from at least one federal entitlement program.

Most assistance has little to do with alleviating poverty.[3] In 2019, nearly 55 percent of assistance went to households in the middle three income quintiles, and over 10 percent went to the top quintile. More than $700 billion was distributed to households in the upper half of the income distribution. In this paternalistic system, slightly over half of all assistance is provided in the form of in-kind benefits.

Numerous studies have documented the large work disincentives that accompany the system's transfers, especially those from its means-tested programs. The Supplemental Nutrition Assistance Program (SNAP, also known as the food stamp program) imposes a 24 percent marginal tax rate, the Temporary Assistance for Needy Families (TANF) program approximately a 50 percent marginal tax rate, and the Supplemental Security Income (SSI) program a 100 percent marginal tax rate. The subsidies for health insurance under the Affordable Care Act (ACA) have a marginal tax rate that ranges from 10 to 15 percent. The Medicaid program has a sudden death provision that terminates eligibility once a family's income or assets exceed a certain threshold. The resulting loss of family health benefits could easily be worth a few thousand dollars per year. Work disincentives are not limited to means-tested programs. Unemployment insurance and Social Security disability benefits also contain large work penalties. The Earned Income Tax Credit (EITC), by supplementing earnings of low-income workers, creates a positive work incentive for some workers. However, because its benefits eventually phase out, the program creates a work disincentive for others. The work disincentives are exacerbated when families receive benefits from more than one program at a time, or when a program such as the EITC provides benefits to families who are also paying federal income and payroll taxes.

The system's work disincentives affect a large portion of the US working-age population. In 2019, seventy-one million persons, constituting nearly 40 percent of the working-age population (ages twenty-one to sixty-four), lived in households that received benefits from at least one means-tested entitlement program. Half of this large group faced a marginal tax rate greater than 33 percent, excluding Medicaid and the ACA. Forty percent faced a marginal tax rate greater than 40 percent. These high marginal tax rates among a significant fraction of prime-age workers are now large enough to lower the US labor force participation rate, aggregate US productivity, and human capital formation, ultimately reducing the nation's economic output.

An Idealized UBI Plan

The existing income transfer system's deficiencies would seem to make a powerful case for a UBI as an alternative. But the power of the case depends on how the UBI is structured and how much of the existing transfer system it would replace. We begin with a consideration of an idealized UBI.

The idealized plan would replace the entire federal system of income transfer programs. In its place, the plan would make an annual basic income available to all persons regardless of their earned income and would not have any phase-down provision. The plan's annual income guarantee would be set in accordance with the ambitious goal of eliminating US poverty. Households would receive an annual cash payment equal to their poverty threshold.[4] These thresholds vary by household size, age of the householder, and the number of children under eighteen.[5] Table 14.1 summarizes the policy parameters of the idealized UBI.

The major programs that the idealized plan would replace and their expenditures in 2019 are presented in table 14.2. The programs are broken down into social insurance programs, which typically do not have a significant phase-down provision, and means-tested programs, which have phase-down provisions. As the bottom line of the table shows, the

Table 14.1. The Idealized UBI

Maximum benefit	100% of poverty line
One-person HH*	$13,300
Four-person HH*	$25,926
Phase-out rate	0%
Programs eliminated	All federal transfer programs

*Households with a head of household under age sixty-five.

Table 14.2. Federal Income Transfer Programs and Expenditures, 2019 (in billions)

Social Insurance Programs	Outlays	Means-Tested Programs	Outlays
SS Retirement (OASI)	$898	Medicaid	$427
SS Disability Insurance (SSDI)	$146	Affordable Care Act (ACA)	$56
Medicare	$651	Veterans benefits (cash and health care)	$200
Unemployment Insurance	$28	SNAP (food stamps)	$63
		Children's nutrition programs	$24
		Housing assistance	$49
		Tax credits	$99
		Supplemental Security Income (SSI)	$56
		TANF and family support	$32
		Other programs	$47
Total	**$1,723**	**Total**	**$1,054**

Notes: OASI is the Old-Age and Survivors Insurance program. Medicaid includes the Children's Health Insurance Program (CHIP). Veterans benefits include all cash and health care benefits. TANF is the Temporary Assistance for Needy Families program. Tax credits include the Earned Income Tax Credit and the Child Tax Credit. Housing assistance includes public housing, Section 8 (the housing choice voucher program), and related federal programs. Other programs include discretionary energy assistance; the Special Supplemental Nutrition Program for Women, Infants, and Children (WIC); training, employment, and social services; and other smaller income security programs. Source: https://www.whitehouse.gov/omb/historical-tables.

federal expenditure savings from eliminating these programs would total almost $2.8 trillion.

Our assessment of the UBI's impact is based on data from the 2020 Annual Social and Economic Supplement of the Current Population Survey.[6] The survey provides detailed economic and demographic information on about sixty thousand US households and serves as the federal government's primary source of information on US household income, poverty, and labor force behavior.[7] Income and work data in the CPS correspond to 2019 annual values. We supplement the CPS data with tax imputations from TAXSIM, the widely used tax model from the National Bureau of Economic Research, to create a nationally representative sample of household incomes, labor supply, income transfer program participation status, and tax rates.[8]

The CPS and TAXSIM also allow us to calculate how each household's income would be affected by a UBI program that replaces existing income transfer programs. Our assessment includes both static and dynamic estimates. The static estimates assume that household members do not respond to the change in work incentives from replacing existing income transfer programs with a UBI. The dynamic estimates assume individuals change their labor supply in response to the changes in income and effective marginal tax rates.[9]

The issue of labor supply responses to changes in wages, nonwage income, and tax rates has been the subject of extensive economic analysis. This rich body of research has produced a strong consensus around a modest range of empirical estimates. A 10 percent decrease in wages, or equivalently a 10 percent increase in a worker's marginal tax rate, reduces a primary worker's hours of work by between 1.5 and 3.5 percent. The same change in the wage or tax rate will reduce a secondary worker's hours of work by between 2.2 percent and 4.2 percent. For both types of workers, a 10 percent increase in income (without any change in wages) reduces hours of work by about .5 percent.[10]

In our dynamic analysis of the idealized UBI plans, the elimination of existing transfer system programs affects labor supply, as a general rule, by lowering the marginal tax rate and nonwage income of household

Table 14.3. The Current Transfer System and an Idealized UBI

	Current System	Idealized UBI
Poverty rate (including in-kind benefits)	3.3%	.1%
Outlays (in billions)	$2,777	$2,797
Share of transfers by quintile		
Bottom quintile	35.0%	16.2%
Middle three quintiles	54.8%	59.4%
Top quintile	10.2%	24.4%

members who are receiving government transfers from these programs.[11] Both of these changes would, all else equal, increase labor supply among these household members. The idealized UBI's income guarantee, however, reduces labor supply by increasing the nonwage income of all households. Thus, the aggregate labor supply impact of the idealized UBI is theoretically ambiguous.

Our dynamic analysis uses the midpoint of the aforementioned ranges to estimate the change in hours of work due to changes in marginal tax rates for primary and secondary workers separately. To capture the guaranteed income's impact, the dynamic analysis uses the aforementioned response to nonwage income.[12] When we turn to analysis of the prototype plan, which contains a phase-down provision that alters marginal tax rates, the same empirical measures are used.[13]

Table 14.3 shows how the idealized UBI compares to the existing federal transfer system. The plan would succeed in virtually eliminating poverty.[14] Throughout this paper, the poverty rate is calculated by including the market value of in-kind benefits as countable income. Since the UBI replaces in-kind benefits with cash, excluding these benefits from the poverty calculation would exaggerate the poverty reduction from the UBI. In table 14.3, the poverty rate declines from 3.3 percent to a negligible fraction of the population.[15] The idealized plan would also be self-financing as total UBI expenditures would be roughly the same as those of the programs it replaces.

As a general rule, a UBI program that replaces the existing transfer system reduces the amount of assistance provided to beneficiaries of current transfer programs. These beneficiaries are usually lower-income households. The UBI spreads the savings across a far larger group of households that are not current recipients of transfer programs and usually have higher incomes. This general tendency is manifested by our idealized UBI plan. Table 14.3 shows the share of government assistance going to households in various quintiles of the income distribution. To show the distributional impact of the idealized plan, households are placed in quintiles according to their income in the absence of any government assistance. The plan shifts the distribution of government assistance sharply away from lower- to higher-income households. The share of government assistance going to households in the bottom quintile would decline from 35 percent in the current system to 16 percent under the idealized UBI, a $530 billion reduction in government assistance. Meanwhile, households in the top quintile would receive 24.4 percent of all federal transfer spending under the UBI compared to only 10 percent in the current system, an increase of $400 billion.[16]

The idealized plan would also shift a substantial amount of government assistance from senior citizens to the rest of the population. At the aggregate level, about $850 billion would be transferred annually from households headed by a senior citizen. Over 85 percent of all senior citizen households would receive less in UBI payments than the value of benefits they receive in the current transfer system. The vast majority of the reduction comes from the loss of Social Security and Medicare benefits. To see this clearly, consider the benefits of a married couple with typical lifetime earnings who begin collecting Social Security benefits in 2019 at age sixty-six. This household receives $44,000 in Social Security benefits per year. They also qualify for Medicare, the annual insurance value of which is about $11,000 per enrollee. In place of this $66,000, the household would receive the idealized UBI plan's poverty-level income guarantee of just $15,453.

As we noted earlier, the impact of the idealized plan on labor supply is theoretically ambiguous. Under our idealized plan, aggregate labor

Table 14.4. Labor Supply Effects of the Idealized UBI

Share of tax units with	
Lower MTRs (marginal tax rates)	22.6%
Higher MTRs	5.3%
Labor supply effects among	
All workers	1.8%
Workers ages 21–64	1.2%
Effect on GDP	1.0%

supply would increase slightly, by 1.8 percent among workers of all ages (see table 14.4). GDP would rise, but only by approximately .2 percent.[17] Given the numerous elasticities employed in our analysis and the large distributional impacts of the policy, a multitude of factors could account for the labor supply increase. But the simplest explanation stems from the fact that the policy is budget neutral. With budget neutrality, the additional payments to some individuals are offset by equal payment reductions to others. Correspondingly, the labor supply responses to these increases and decreases offset one another. This leaves the reduction in marginal tax rates from the elimination of existing transfer programs as the primary driver of changes in labor supply.[18]

The smaller labor supply increase among workers ages twenty-one to sixty-four in table 14.4 implies a larger labor supply response among persons ages sixty-five and older. The underlying labor supply estimates used in our analysis do not distinguish among workers by age, so the elasticity used for seniors is assumed to be the same as that for prime-age workers. Under this assumption, the large relative increase among senior citizens is a consequence of their relatively large reduction in nonwage income due primarily to the loss of Social Security and Medicare benefits. Our estimated labor supply response overstates the change among seniors who are currently out of the workforce if, as is likely, seniors are less responsive to changes in their income than non-seniors.

The prospects for congressional enactment of a UBI plan that shifts more than $500 billion in government aid per year away from the poorest fifth of households to middle- and upper-income households and also reduces aggregate labor supply and GDP are, at best, slim. Additionally, eliminating or replacing any government program has always been an uphill battle. Ronald Reagan once remarked that "a government bureau is the nearest thing to eternal life we'll ever see on this earth." The same could be said about government programs. But the programs to be replaced by the idealized UBI plan are a particularly formidable group. Social Security, the granddaddy of all federal entitlement programs, has long been regarded as "the third rail of American politics." Politicians who tamper with its benefits have done so at their own political peril. Although some may view eliminating Social Security as within the realm of political feasibility, it would be an extraordinary undertaking. Similarly, eliminating Medicare, Medicaid, and the Affordable Care Act, which together provide health care assistance to over 110 million people, and instead providing those people with cash assistance to purchase private insurance seem implausible without a complete overhaul of the US health insurance system.

The adverse impacts of the idealized UBI plan help us understand why no US president has proposed, and why no US Congress has debated, a national UBI plan that would replace the entire US transfer system, despite the fact that UBI plans have been around for a long time and have an impressive intellectual lineage.

The aforementioned drawbacks lead us naturally to a consideration of alternative, scaled-down UBI plans. What would a more practical plan look like? How would the UBI be structured and which federal transfer programs would it replace? Could such a plan correct the deficiencies of the current income transfer system? To provide some guidance, we can look to the historical record.

Previous Attempts to Enact a UBI

There have been two notable attempts in US history to enact national UBI plans. Both President Nixon and President Carter proposed a guaranteed annual income as major presidential initiatives. Initially, both proposals were warmly greeted by Congress and the national press. But once the details of the proposals became clear, support turned into opposition and Congress ultimately rejected both plans. The failure of these proposals contains important lessons for the design of any national universal basic income plan.

A guaranteed annual income was the centerpiece of both presidents' plans to overhaul the existing welfare system. Both presidents viewed the welfare system as a failure. President Nixon charged that "it breaks up homes. It often penalizes work. It robs recipients of dignity. And it grows." President Carter declared that "the welfare system is anti-work, anti-family, inequitable in its treatment of the poor and wasteful of taxpayers' dollars." Both presidents proposed a guaranteed annual income that would phase down as incomes rose to replace this failed system.[19]

The Nixon plan set the annual income guarantee at about 40 percent of the poverty line. The Carter plan set the income floor between 40 percent and 65 percent depending on whether the household head was expected to work or not. Both plans contained an income disregard that allowed households to earn a specified amount before benefits would be reduced. President Carter, having learned from earlier criticism of the work disincentives in the Nixon plan, set the income disregard at a much higher level. Both plans reduced the amount of assistance by 50 percent for each dollar of earned income above the disregard. Assistance phased out completely when a household's income equaled or nearly equaled the poverty line.

Despite the promises to replace existing welfare programs, both presidential plans left the vast majority of the existing system intact. Both plans initially proposed to eliminate only federal cash and near-cash means-tested welfare programs, specifically food stamps (now SNAP), Aid to Families with Dependent Children (now TANF), Old-Age Assistance, Aid to the Blind, and Aid to the Totally and Permanently Disabled (now Supplemental Security Income or SSI). After political opposition, President Nixon reversed course and retained the food stamp program. President Carter's plan also eliminated low-income energy assistance. Neither plan eliminated existing means-tested in-kind benefit programs, such as Medicaid, housing assistance, child and elderly nutrition programs, and college tuition subsidies.[20] Neither plan would replace the vast array of Great Society child and social welfare services for the poor and near poor. Neither plan would eliminate the large social insurance programs, such as Social Security, Medicare, Railroad Retirement, disability and unemployment benefits, and black lung benefits for coal miners. In terms of federal dollars, the Nixon and Carter plans would replace only a small portion of the existing welfare system.

As a result, both plans added their guaranteed annual incomes on top of, rather than in place of, the existing network of income transfer programs. This, more than any other factor, caused the proposals' downfall. Both presidents had staked much of their case for reforms on the grounds that they would improve work incentives and shrink the size of the existing welfare system. But layering the guaranteed income plan on top of existing programs added a 50 percent earnings penalty on top of the existing system's earnings penalties. This increased effective marginal tax rates faced by many families and thereby worsened work incentives. In the Nixon plan, for example, the marginal tax rates were at least 70 percent and could exceed 100 percent for families who received income support from his plan and assistance from at least one other welfare program. These high marginal tax rates led Milton Friedman to drop his support for Nixon's plan, declaring it to be "a striking example of how to spoil a good idea."[21] The Carter plan, despite its large income disregard, imposed similarly high marginal tax rates on recipient households.[22] Additionally, the high income disregard raised the income threshold for households to qualify for assistance payments. The higher threshold added millions of individuals to the ranks of those receiving government aid, thereby creating a new work disincentive for a large additional segment of the working population.

The large work disincentives among persons receiving assistance would cause a sizable reduction in labor supply. This was not a hypothetical idea. The federal government had begun several large negative income tax social experiments in the late 1960s. The results of these experiments were just becoming available when President Nixon introduced his proposal. By the time President Carter introduced his plan, the labor supply impact from these experiments had been widely disseminated. They played an important role in official government assessments of his plan. These experiments, and a large body of evidence from nonexperimental data, showed that high marginal tax rates created a statistically significant and, in most cases, a large negative impact on labor supply. The reduction in work ran counter to central claims by the Nixon and Carter administrations that their plans would improve work incentives.

An additional factor contributed to the Carter plan's defeat. Research results showing that negative income tax programs increased marital instability were the final nail in the coffin containing President Carter's welfare reform plan. These results, which have stood the test of time, are relevant to UBI proposals today.

The experience with the Nixon and Carter proposals provides some lessons for designing a UBI that would constitute all, or part, of a new US income transfer system. Both UBI plans focused solely on reforming the welfare system, as opposed to the entire income transfer system. Thus, neither program contemplated replacing large social insurance programs, such as Social Security, Medicare, disability, and unemployment insurance. Within the welfare system, neither proposal was willing to replace the in-kind benefit programs that provide health care, nutrition, housing, and social services benefits to the poor and near poor. Neither proposal attempted to guarantee an annual income equal to the poverty line. Because the cost of doing so was prohibitive, both plans settled for a goal less ambitious than the eradication of poverty. In both proposals, the 50 percent phase-out rate, on top of the work disincentives of remaining programs, imposed work penalties on many recipients that Congress found unacceptably high.

Analysis of Prototype UBI Plans

The experience with the Nixon and Carter plans shows that designing a workable UBI requires confronting important and inescapable trade-offs between the adequacy of benefits, work incentives, and the number of households that receive government aid. The adequacy of benefits for the poorest members of society is determined largely by the level of the basic income guarantee. Work incentives are determined primarily by the rate at which UBI assistance is phased down as earned income, that is, income from nongovernmental sources, rises.[23] The number of individuals receiving UBI aid and the adequacy of benefits for nonpoor individuals are determined by a combination of the two. Work incentives and the program's level of support for low-wage workers can be improved by more slowly phasing down UBI assistance as earned income rises. But a lower phase-down rate necessarily increases both the number of individuals receiving government assistance and the total cost of assistance. The program's cost to taxpayers can be reduced by lowering the guaranteed benefit, but this reduces the adequacy of benefits, both for the poor and for low-wage workers.

To explore the magnitude of these trade-offs, this section presents an empirical analysis of a prototype UBI plan and modifications to it. As with the idealized UBI plan, the analysis uses data from the 2020 Current Population Survey and TAXSIM to assess the prototype plan's impact on the poverty rate, the number of persons who received government assistance payment and the total cost to taxpayers, the marginal tax rates on recipients, and the impact of these rates on labor supply and GDP.

Like the idealized plan, the prototype plan has an ambitious goal: eliminating poverty. To achieve this goal, the program's basic income guarantee for each household is set at the household's poverty threshold. For a household headed by a single person under age sixty-five, this annual amount is $13,300. For a household of four with two children and no person age sixty-five or older, the annual amount is $25,926. Our prototype plan phases down assistance by 50 cents for each dollar of earned income.[24] Table 14.5 summarizes the prototype UBI's policy parameters.

Following Presidents Nixon and Carter, the plan's objective is to replace most spending on federal means-tested cash and near-cash assistance programs.[25] Although such a plan seems as though it would replace most of the welfare system, it actually would replace only a modest fraction of it, and even less of the entire federal income transfer system. This is because

Table 14.5. The Prototype UBI

Maximum benefit	100% of poverty line
One-person HH*	$13,300
Four-person HH (with two children)*	$25,926
Phase-out rate	50%
Programs eliminated	EITC, Additional Child Tax Credit, SSI, SNAP, SSDI, TANF, and Housing Assistance
2019 outlays of eliminated programs (in billions)	$445

* Household (HH) headed by a person under age sixty-five.

the major social insurance programs account for nearly two-thirds of total federal spending on transfer payments (see table 14.2). Within the remaining one-third that consists of means-tested programs, the major health care programs, Medicaid, and the insurance subsidies under the ACA constitute the lion's share of the total. Expenditures on the programs that would be replaced by the prototype UBI plan, which include Temporary Assistance for Needy Families, Supplemental Security Income, Supplemental Nutrition Assistance Program, the Earned Income Tax Credit, the additional child tax credit, Social Security disability payments, and black lung disability payments, constitute only 16 percent of all federal transfer program spending and 42 percent of total means-tested program spending.

The impact of the prototype plan is summarized in table 14.6. The plan would effectively achieve the stated objective of eliminating poverty.[26] But the poverty reduction would come at a steep cost. Annual prototype UBI assistance payments would total $648 billion, about $200 billion more than the programs it replaces. It would increase total transfer spending by 7 percent. Total federal government transfer payments under the prototype UBI would be only slightly more targeted to lower-income households than they are under the current system. The share of transfer spending going to households in the bottom quintile would rise only slightly, from 35 percent to 38 percent.[27] These estimates are not significantly affected by our dynamic labor supply assumptions (see the appendix).

Table 14.6. Prototype UBI and the Current System

	Current System	Prototype UBI
Poverty rate (including in-kind benefits)	3.3%	.1%
UBI outlays (billions)	—	$648
Total transfer spending (billions)	$2,777	$2,980
Share of HHs receiving UBI	—	38.9%
Share of HHs receiving government assistance	62.0%	66.5%
Share of transfers by quintile		
Bottom quintile	35.0%	37.9%
Middle three quintiles	54.8%	51.7%
Top quintile	10.2%	10.4%

Note: These figures include dynamic effects from the reduction in labor supply after the introduction of the UBI. We discuss the magnitude of these effects below. Estimates without dynamic effects are presented in the appendix.

The prototype UBI would increase the percentage of households that receive federal assistance. Thirty-nine percent of households would receive UBI payments. Another 28 percent of households would not receive UBI payments but would receive assistance from other government programs. The increase occurs primarily because the phase-out income level under the prototype plan is higher than the eligibility thresholds of the programs they replace. Under the prototype plan, UBI assistance phases out at 200 percent of the poverty line, or $51,852 for a household of four with two children. The annualized income eligibility threshold for food stamps is 130 percent of the poverty line, or $33,475 for the same household.[28] The earnings eligibility thresholds for SSI for households are only a fraction of the prototype plan's threshold. For example, in 2020 the earnings threshold for a married couple with a disabled child is $3,257, only one-tenth the prototype plan's threshold.[29] The income cutoff for TANF eligibility and the type of household income that is counted in determining eligibility vary from state to state. All states have maximum allowable earnings thresholds. No state has an earnings threshold that comes even close to the prototype plan's income threshold. For example, in 2016, only three states, Alaska, Hawaii, and Minnesota, had TANF earnings thresholds greater than the poverty line for a single household head with two children.[30] Of the major programs that the prototype plan replaces, only the Earned Income Tax Credit had a higher earnings threshold in 2019: $52,493 for a married household with two children.[31]

Means-tested programs that would be replaced by the prototype UBI typically impose high marginal tax rates on recipients, usually in excess of 50 percent and in some cases 100 percent. So a UBI that has a phase-out rate even as high as 50 percent would substantially lower marginal tax rates for most recipients of means-tested programs. But this group is only a small fraction of UBI recipients. The UBI extends assistance to a larger group of persons who do not qualify for existing welfare programs. For these individuals, the UBI adds 50 percent to their marginal tax rate.

Replacing the EITC program with a prototype UBI plan increases the marginal tax rate substantially for a portion of EITC recipients. The EITC supplements the wages of certain low-wage workers by up to 45 percent.[32] Under a prototype UBI plan, this 45 percent work incentive is replaced by a 50 percent work disincentive, a swing in the recipient's marginal tax rate of 95 percentage points. We estimate that about four million workers have an effective negative marginal tax rate from the EITC.[33] To avoid this large change, the UBI could include an income disregard equal to the income threshold where a tax filer's EITC benefit reaches the maximum level. For workers with incomes less than this disregard, the UBI's marginal tax rate would be zero instead of 50 percent.[34] The disregard, however, would increase UBI participation by over 20 percent and add $232 billion to the annual budgetary cost of the program.

Table 14.7 summarizes the UBI's impact on marginal tax rates and aggregate labor supply. About 9 percent of workers would face lower marginal tax rates. Over three times that number, 31 percent, would face higher marginal tax rates. The increase in marginal tax rates in the latter group would overwhelm the reduction in the former group, and labor supply among all UBI recipients would decline by 22.4 percent. Prototype UBI recipients account for about 15 percent of all hours worked. As a consequence, US aggregate labor supply would decline by 2.6 percent, permanently reducing aggregate GDP by 1.3 percent. This would amount to approximately $270 billion in lost output if the UBI program were

Table 14.7. Labor Supply Effects of the Prototype UBI

Share of tax units with	
Lower MTRs	9.3%
Higher MTRs	31.1%
Labor supply effects among	
UBI recipients	−22.4%
All workers	−2.6%
Workers ages 21–64	−2.9%
Effect on GDP	−1.3%

initiated in 2019. In addition, the UBI plan's excess spending would necessitate an increase in taxes or in government borrowing. Although the effects of these means of financing are not incorporated into our analysis, higher taxes would further reduce the labor supply and GDP.

One might be tempted to conclude that the prototype plan's large work disincentives could be alleviated by lowering the phase-down rate. Column 2 of table 14.8 shows the impact of reducing the prototype plan's phase-out rate from 50 percent to 25 percent. The lower phase-out rate would indeed improve work incentives by lowering each UBI recipient's marginal tax rate. But the lower phase-out rate would extend UBI payments to an additional forty-six million people ages twenty-one to sixty-four. This extension subjects these people to the 25 percent marginal tax rate in addition to their income and payroll tax rates. The net impact would reduce the US aggregate supply of labor relative to the prototype plan with a 50 percent phase-out rate. Additionally, under this more generous alternative plan, annual UBI payments would rise to $1.03 trillion compared to the $450 billion of annual federal spending on programs it replaces.

To address the prototype plan's deficit consequences, the impact of a second alternative is explored in column 3 of table 14.8. This alternative is designed so that UBI expenditures roughly equal the expenditures on the federal programs it replaces. The plan achieves federal budget neutrality by reducing the prototype plan's income guarantee to 80 percent of the poverty line. The budget neutrality, however, comes at the expense of

Table 14.8. Variations of the Prototype UBI

	Prototype Plan	Reduced Phase-Out	Deficit Neutral
Maximum benefit	100% of poverty line	100% of poverty line	80% of poverty line
Phase-out rate	50%	25%	50%
Poverty rate (including in-kind benefits)	.1%	.1%	1.6%
UBI outlays (billions)	$648	$1,030	$437
Share of HH receiving UBI	38.9%	64.5%	32.0%
People receiving UBI (21–64)	57.0 million	102.9 million	46.4 million
Share of transfers by quintile			
Bottom quintile	37.9%	35.3%	38.0%
Middle three quintiles	51.7%	54.9%	51.1%
Top quintile	10.4%	9.8%	10.9%
Share of tax units with			
Lower MTRs	9.3%	12.7%	10.8%
Higher MTRs	31.1%	52.1%	24.6%
Labor supply effects among			
UBI recipients	−22.4%	−8.4%	−22.9%
All workers	−2.6%	−3.3%	−.7%
Workers ages 21–64	−2.9%	−3.5%	−.9%
Effect on GDP	−1.3%	−2.1%	−.4%

reducing poverty. The poverty rate would decline, but 1.6 percent of the population, about five million individuals, would still remain in poverty. This second alternative reduces UBI participation and thus would reduce the adverse labor supply effects. Aggregate labor supply would fall by .7 percent and GDP would decline permanently by .4 percent per year.

Summary and Conclusions

At a conceptual level, the universal basic income represents a radical departure from long-standing US welfare policy. This policy has required recipients to undertake efforts to improve their station in life as a condition of receiving aid. Although such requirements often carry a stigma, they have most often been designed to prevent individuals from becoming dependent. The UBI's provision of unconditional aid departs sharply from this policy. Given the breadth of UBI's assistance, the UBI carries a risk of making large segments of the population dependent.

UBI supporters acknowledge this departure and counter that a UBI will improve work incentives and redistribute income to achieve a more equitable income distribution. Our economic analysis has cast serious doubt on these claims. Although a UBI can improve work incentives among recipients of the transfer programs it replaces, a UBI worsens work incentives among UBI recipients who are not beneficiaries of these programs. In our analysis of a UBI that has no phase-down provision, aggregate labor supply increases slightly. But such a plan dramatically worsens the distribution of income by redistributing government transfer payments from lower- to higher-income households. In our analysis of UBI plans that have phase-down provisions, work incentives are reduced and, as a result, these plans would all significantly reduce aggregate US labor supply and, thereby, US economic output. These plans show little improvement in the distribution of income.

Our economic analysis also finds that while a national UBI plan with a goal of eliminating poverty can be financed within current federal budget expenditures, this can be accomplished only if the UBI replaces all federal income transfer programs, including Social Security, Medicare, and Medicaid. A UBI plan with the same goal that retains these programs will sharply increase federal spending, necessitating a substantial increase in taxes or in government borrowing.

Three additional caveats regarding analyses of UBI plans are warranted. A common mistake in policy analysis is to compare an ideally designed new program with the reality of existing programs. Each existing program is a product of inevitable compromises made in Congress to enact the program and a patchwork of revisions to the initial program made over several years. In the case of the UBI, the inevitable compromises and revisions would invariably entail unintended inequities that would be different, but no less problematic, than those in the system it is replacing. One obvious example would result from regional and urban-rural cost-of-living differences. UBI proponents often regard these differences as minor, an issue to be dealt with later. But unless these cost-of-living differences are taken into account in the plan, significant inequalities among similarly situated people will arise. These differences played a significant role when Congress considered President Nixon's plan. New York representatives objected to the plan's income guarantee as too low for northern industrial states and too lavish for southern rural states. Conceptually, the inequity could be addressed by the adoption of suitable regional and urban-rural cost-of-living indexes. But to date, the United States has not developed such satisfactory indexes despite glaring inequities in tax assessments, the distribution of federal grants, and the distribution of transfer payments across states and regions of the country.

Another potential inequity arises when the UBI replaces only a part of the existing system. Partial replacement can result in individuals who receive UBI enjoying a higher disposable income than individuals who do not receive UBI assistance. This inequity would be particularly pronounced because under the UBI the taxes paid by the latter group finance the assistance provided to the former group. An example of this can be seen in our prototype plan. Since the plan does not replace Medicaid, some UBI recipients would receive health care subsidies that are not available to individuals not receiving UBI aid. For a typical household of four, the Medicaid assistance can easily have a market value of more than $10,000. Ironically, one of the initial motivations for President Nixon's plan was that welfare recipients often had a higher income, factoring in welfare assistance, than the individuals who were paying taxes to finance welfare payments. The Nixon plan foundered partly on its inability to fix this problem.

A second caveat regards the UBI's provision of cash in lieu of in-kind benefits. Many UBI proponents envision the UBI as a replacement for the entire welfare system, including in-kind benefit programs. Since most welfare assistance is provided in the form of in-kind benefits, the savings from eliminating in-kind benefit programs are large. But the structure of these programs is not an accident of history. In-kind assistance has grown steadily since the 1930s, both in absolute terms and relative to cash assistance. Nearly all the federal welfare programs added since the 1950s have provided in-kind benefits: Medicaid, SNAP, Affordable Care Act subsidies, Section 8 housing subsidies, day care assistance, and energy subsidies are just a few examples of the additional in-kind programs. Meanwhile, the only new cash assistance programs have been the Earned Income Tax Credit and refundable child credits. The consistent trend toward in-kind benefits across successive generations of policies reflects an overwhelming paternalism among policy officials and the public. It also reflects the extraordinary lobbying power among in-kind service providers, ranging from physicians, hospitals, and pharmaceutical companies to housing developers, farmers, and school cafeteria workers unions. So a successful effort to replace the entire welfare system with a UBI is likely to be only temporary. More likely than not, pressure will emerge to re-create in-kind benefit programs. If initially UBI income guarantees are set at levels designed to compensate individuals for their forgone in-kind benefits, the subsequent re-creation of these programs could produce an extraordinarily costly system.

A third caveat concerns the inevitable pressure to increase UBI assistance levels once the program has begun. Throughout US history, starting as far back as the early 1800s, Congress has repeatedly and consistently expanded federal entitlement programs by incremental amounts. In previous work, John Cogan has identified and documented the force, termed the "equally worthy claim," that causes this liberalization.[35] The force originates from a well-meaning impulse to treat all similarly situated persons equally under the law. It works as follows: When an entitlement law is first enacted, for policy or fiscal reasons, it usually confines benefits to individuals deemed to be particularly worthy of assistance. As time passes, groups of excluded individuals lay claims that they are no less deserving of aid. Pressure is brought by, or on behalf of, these excluded groups to relax eligibility rules. But the broadening of eligibility rules just brings another group of claimants closer to the eligibility boundary line and the pressure to relax qualifying rules begins over again. The process of liberalization repeats itself until the entitlement program reaches a point where its original goals are no longer recognizable. A UBI is likely to be particularly sensitive to the equally worthy claim. A small reduction in the program's phase-out rate can substantially increase the number of persons receiving assistance. For example, using the CPS data, a 5 percentage point reduction in our prototype UBI plan's phase-out rate would increase UBI participation by over 10 percent.

The Nixon and Carter administrations could not overcome the inherent trade-offs between a UBI plan's generosity, its cost, and its effect on work. Today's UBI supporters face the same challenges that confounded policy makers in the 1970s. By providing income support without imposing any self-improvement requirements on recipients, the UBI represents a dangerous break from the long history of US welfare policy. Its no-strings-attached benefit raises the cost of the federal income transfer system substantially and worsens work incentives, while only marginally improving the targeting of government assistance on low-income households.

Appendix

Table 14.A1. Prototype Plan: Static versus Dynamic Estimates

	Static	Dynamic
Poverty rate (including in-kind benefits)	.1%	.1%
UBI outlays (in billions)	$567	$648
Share of HHs receiving UBI	38.7%	38.9%
Share of transfers by quintile		
Bottom quintile	39.2%	37.9%
Middle three quintiles	50.3%	51.7%
Top quintile	10.5%	10.4%

Table 14.A2. Lower Phase-Out Plan: Static versus Dynamic Estimates

	Static	Dynamic
Poverty rate (including in-kind benefits)	.1%	.1%
UBI outlays (in billions)	$974	$1,030
Share of HHs receiving UBI	64.3%	64.5%
Share of transfers by quintile		
Bottom quintile	36.1%	35.3%
Middle three quintiles	54.1%	54.9%
Top quintile	9.8%	9.8%

Table 14.A3. Deficit-Neutral Plan: Static versus Dynamic Estimates

	Static	Dynamic
Poverty rate (including in-kind benefits)	1.4%	1.6%
UBI outlays (in billions)	$388	$437
Share of HHs receiving UBI	31.7%	32.0%
Share of transfers by quintile		
Bottom quintile	38.9%	38.0%
Middle three quintiles	50.1%	51.1%
Top quintile	11.0%	10.9%

NOTES

The authors thank Michael Boskin, Tom Church, John Raisian, and John Taylor for valuable comments.

1. The Stockton Economic Empowerment Demonstration is currently giving 125 Stockton residents a monthly payment of $500 (https://www.stocktondemon stration.org). The Compton Pledge will provide between $300 and $600 in monthly assistance to eight hundred Compton residents until 2022 (https://comptonpledge .org/). The HudsonUp project will provide $500 monthly to twenty-five Hudson residents until 2025 (https://www.hudsonup.org/).
2. Hill-HarrisX, "Poll: Majority of Voters Now Say the Government Should Have a Universal Basic Income Program," *The Hill*, August 14, 2020.
3. For a comprehensive analysis of the current transfer system and its effects on poverty, see Richard V. Burkhauser et al., "Evaluating the Success of President Johnson's War on Poverty: Revisiting the Historical Record Using a Full-Income Poverty Measure," National Bureau of Economic Research Working Paper 26532, 2019, and Bruce D. Meyer and James X. Sullivan, "Measuring the Well-Being of the Poor Using Income and Consumption," *Journal of Human Services* 38 (2003): 1180–1220.
4. To determine the UBI amount, we treat each tax unit as a separate household. Tax filers who would be claimed as a dependent on their parents' return are not assigned a separate UBI amount.
5. We use the US Census Bureau's poverty thresholds. The thresholds are available at https://www.census.gov/data/tables/time-series/demo/income-poverty /historical-poverty-thresholds.html.
6. An overview of the survey and the public use data files are available at https:// www.census.gov/data/datasets/time-series/demo/cps/cps-asec.html.
7. CPS economic data include income, assets, and hours and weeks of work; participation in major federal and state income transfer programs; and the amounts of income received from each program. The CPS underestimates enrollment and benefits for key federal transfer programs. In programs where the underestimates are particularly large, we impute enrollment and rescale benefits to match administrative data.
8. TAXSIM is available at http://taxsim.nber.org/taxsim32. For an overview of the model, see Daniel Richard Feenberg and Elizabeth Coutts, "An Introduction

to the TAXSIM Model," *Journal of Policy Analysis and Management* 12, no. 1 (1993): 189–94.

9. We focus on the dynamic effects throughout the paper. The static estimates are presented in the appendix.

10. The income and substitution elasticities used to calculate the labor supply changes are from the Congressional Budget Office (CBO), *How the Supply of Labor Responds to Changes in Fiscal Policy*, 2012, https://www.cbo.gov/sites /default/files/cbofiles/attachments/10-25-2012-Labor_Supply_and_Fiscal _Policy.pdf. The assumed substitution elasticities vary by income with a person-weighted mean of .27. The income elasticity for all persons is set at −.05.

11. The Earned Income Tax Credit is an important exception as we discuss in the prototype UBI plan section.

12. For persons with positive hours of work under the current system, the labor supply response to the UBI is calculated directly from these elasticities and the change in marginal tax rates and income (measured by including the market value of in-kind benefits). For persons who are not working under the current system but who would have a greater incentive to work under the UBI, we derived their labor supply from the aforementioned elasticities. Specifically, we converted the elasticities to absolute changes in labor supply by multiplying the elasticities by the average hours of work among persons with positive hours of work.

13. In our computation of dynamic labor supply responses in households with two or more earners, the worker with the largest earnings is assumed to be the primary worker. All other workers are designated secondary workers.

14. Even with the idealized UBI, a small number of households remain below the poverty line. These households reported business income losses, capital losses, or other negative sources of income.

15. The official US poverty rate of 10.5 percent includes only cash in determining household income.

16. The differences between quintiles are due to large differences in household size by quintile. Households in the top quintile have an average of three persons, while households in the bottom quintile average 1.5 persons.

17. The GDP impact is equal to the earning-weighted change in hours worked.

18. Beyond work disincentives, the idealized UBI would also contain a significant marriage penalty. A non-married couple under age sixty-five would each receive $13,300. If they married, their combined benefit would be only $17,196, a loss of $9,404. The marriage penalty could be avoided by assigning benefits

per capita rather than by household. This would require either significantly higher spending or a reduction in the guaranteed income amount, leaving some Americans in poverty.

19. The history of Nixon's and Carter's guaranteed income proposals is explored in John Cogan, *The High Cost of Good Intentions* (Stanford, CA: Stanford University Press, 2018).

20. Under President Carter's plan, assistance to families with children would be further supplemented by an expansion of the Earned Income Tax Credit.

21. Daniel Patrick Moynihan, *The Politics of a Guaranteed Income: The Nixon Administration and the Family Assistance Plan* (New York: Random House, 1973), 370.

22. Under President Carter's plan, assistance was reduced for different forms of income by different percentages. For example, interest income would reduce benefits at a lower rate while veterans benefits would reduce assistance at a higher rate. The earnings disregard also varied by family type and size. For a two-parent family with two children the annual disregard was $3,800. For a family of four with two children, the Earned Income Tax Credit provided a 10 percent credit on annual earnings up to $4,000, the income level at which the family claiming the standard deduction would begin to have a pre-credit income tax liability. For earnings above this level, the credit declined at a 10 percent rate.

23. These trade-offs exist even under a UBI plan that does not contain a phase-down provision and is financed by personal income taxes. The income tax serves the same function, particularly for work incentives, as a phase-down of benefits. Both reduce the net amount an individual receives from the government as earned income increases. This point is especially important in considering a nationwide basic income plan for the United States, since personal income taxes are the primary source of federal revenues. Using other forms of taxation to finance a UBI's cost will have different effects on work incentives. Andrew Yang has, for example, proposed a value-added tax (VAT) as a financing mechanism. A VAT taxes consumption rather than income and, therefore, has less of a work disincentive. However, it is a highly regressive tax that works against the very purpose of a UBI, namely to redistribute income from higher-income to lower-income individuals.

24. For the purpose of computing UBI payments, seniors' Social Security benefits are counted as earned income.

25. To date, advocates of national UBI plans have provided few details on the program's structure and the existing programs that the UBI would replace. Andrew

Yang, to his credit, has offered some details as to the parameters of his UBI and the existing programs his Freedom Dividend plan would replace. His plan, which offers individuals age eighteen or older a choice of either $12,000 per year or their benefits under the current system, would replace between $500 billion and $600 billion in annual expenditures. He is vague about the programmatic makeup of these savings, specifically mentioning only "welfare programs, food stamps, (and) disability." Andrew Yang, "The Freedom Dividend, Defined," 2020, https://www.yang2020.com/what-is-freedom-dividend-faq.

26. Like the idealized plan, a small number of households technically remain below the poverty line due to reported negative income sources.

27. As with the idealized plan, the quintiles are calculated on the basis of household income in the absence of any government assistance.

28. Food stamp eligibility uses the Health and Human Services poverty guidelines. These guidelines differ slightly from the US Census Bureau's poverty thresholds, which we use to calculate a household's UBI benefit.

29. Social Security Administration, Office of Disability and Income Security Programs, *Understanding Supplemental Security Income–2020 Edition*, Publication No. 17-008, September 2020, 25, https://www.ssa.gov/pubs/EN-17-008.pdf.

30. Megan Thompson et al., *State TANF Policies: A Graphical Overview of State TANF Policies as of July 2016*, OPRE Report 2018-55, US Department of Health and Human Services, May 2018, fig. 2, 4, https://www.acf.hhs.gov/sites /default/files/opre/wrd_2016_databook_companion_piece_05_15_18_508.pdf.

31. Internal Revenue Service, "Earned Income Tax Credit Income Limits and Maximum Credit Amounts," updated or reviewed December 7, 2020, https:// www.irs.gov/credits-deductions/individuals/earned-income-tax-credit/earned -income-tax-credit-income-limits-and-maximum-credit-amounts.

32. The amount of the EITC depends on the number of children in the tax filing unit.

33. The additional child tax credit provides a similar work incentive of 15 percent for approximately six million low-income parents. Interactions between the EITC and ACTC mean that some parents have a marginal tax rate of –60 percent. For these workers, the prototype UBI marginal tax rate increase would amount to a 110-percentage-point increase in their marginal rate.

34. In 2019, childless tax filers reached the maximum EITC benefit at $6,920, filers with one child at $10,370, and filers with two or more children at $14,570.

35. Cogan, *The High Cost of Good Intentions*.

15

Taxation, Individual Actions, and Economic Prosperity

A Review

Joshua Rauh and Gregory Kearney

A move toward socialist, government-centered economic systems in the United States, as proposed by the political left, would require a substantial increase in government resources, which could be brought about only through significant increases in tax revenue. According to data from Organisation for Economic Co-operation and Development (OECD) (figure 15.1), the US government spent 38 percent of GDP in 2018, placing it above countries such as Ireland (25 percent), Chile (26 percent), Korea (31 percent), and Switzerland (34 percent) but significantly below most OECD nations. The countries that top the list are France (56 percent), Finland (53 percent), and Belgium (52 percent).

Although increases in government expenditures can temporarily be financed through public-sector borrowing, eventually such borrowing must be repaid through taxation or monetarization of the debt by the central bank. In this piece, we review research on the distortionary effects of taxation to shed light on the likely consequences of attempts to move to a system in which a significantly larger share of the economy consists of government expenditures.

Most current proposals to fund large-scale expansions of government programs, such as Medicare for All or the Green New Deal, rely on progressive income taxation and wealth taxation. That is, the proposals

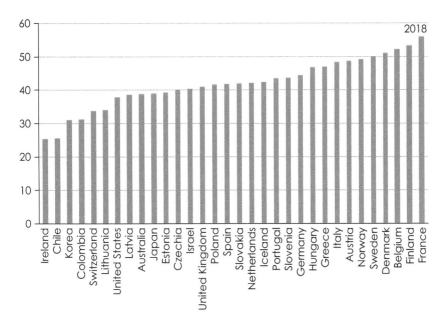

Figure 15.1. General Government Revenue as a Percentage of GDP, 2018; General Government Spending as a Percentage of GDP (%). *Source:* Organisation for Economic Co-Operation and Development, https://data.oecd.org/gga/general-government-spending .htm#indicator-chart.

typically involve raising the top tax rates for high-earning households, lowering the earnings thresholds at which households face those top tax rates, imposing taxes on wealth, or some combination of these measures. Analyses, including those by the Committee for a Responsible Federal Budget, have concluded that the extent of spending in these proposals could not be financed through these channels alone—in fact, it would be mathematically impossible to do so—and the United States would have to resort to other forms of taxation, introducing a national consumption tax, for instance, or value-added taxes, which would be directly paid by a very large share of the population, not just the upper end of the income or wealth distribution.[1]

However, surveys by the Pew Research Center suggest that a large majority of Americans (86 percent) favor the government raising taxes on "the wealthiest Americans," while rather few (12 percent) favor raising taxes on "people like them."[2] Given these preferences, it seems most likely that the first main political movement toward the financing of a substantially expanded government sector would take place through increased income taxation and wealth taxation. In this piece, we therefore focus on income taxation and wealth taxation, the limits to their potential for raising revenue, the impact they have on taxpayer behavior, and the societal costs of such distortions.

The basic principle underlying the study of taxation is that the imposition of taxes will alter the behavior of agents in the economy. In the words of seventeenth-century French minister of finance Jean-Baptiste Colbert, "The art of taxation consists in so plucking the goose as to procure the largest quantity of feathers with the least possible amount of hissing." From the perspective of government authorities aiming to extract maximum value from the economy, the ideal tax is one that does not induce any behavioral response that would reduce the size of the government's take or the overall economic pie that represents the economy. Finding such taxes necessarily implies a starting point of ignoring the distributional features of the tax, including whether the tax at application is progressive or regressive, as the government can redistribute the proceeds of the tax to achieve any distribution it views as equitable.

For the purposes of this piece, we will focus on taxation of individuals, as corporate income taxes remain quantitatively less important for raising revenues—although they may be highly distortionary in terms of both capital allocation and employment.[3]

The simplest individual tax that cannot be avoided through individual behavioral change is a lump-sum tax that applies universally and is unaffected by the taxpayer's actions. Taxes that are levied in equal amount on all taxpayers are known as poll taxes or head taxes.[4] Of course, if individuals can change jurisdictions by moving out of the country or region that imposes such a tax, they can escape this tax as well. A tax on land value, most famously espoused in the nineteenth century by Henry George, has similar or possibly even superior efficiency properties, since if there is an efficient real estate market, there is nothing an individual can do to avoid the land tax: selling the land to leave the jurisdiction would occur at a price that reflected the land's reduced value due to the tax.[5] In the words of Milton Friedman, "The least bad tax is the property tax on the unimproved value of land, the Henry George argument of many, many years ago."[6]

Several other lines of inquiry about taxation stem from a string of early-twentieth-century University of Cambridge economists. One insight of the work of Arthur Pigou in 1920 was that government should tax activities that it would like to encourage less of due to their imposition of negative externalities. These ideas are today manifest in pollution taxes and carbon taxes, among others.[7] A young Cambridge mathematics lecturer, Frank Ramsey, pioneered research in 1927 on the optimal structures of sales and commodity taxes.[8] His main conclusion was that the optimal consumption tax on each good should fall with the representative consumer's demand elasticity. This minimizes the societal economic loss (or "deadweight loss") for any given amount the government must raise through commodity taxation.

Despite the theoretical advantages of lump-sum taxes, land-value taxes, Pigouvian taxes, and consumption taxes on goods with inelastic demand, 70 percent of taxes in the United States are collected in the form of income tax. The challenge of income taxation is that it may discourage productive activities that grow the economy, and it may also lead taxpayers to invest in tax avoidance or tax evasion. In the spirit of Colbert, public-finance economists often view the effect that changes in tax rates have on reported taxable income as a measure of how efficient or inefficient the income tax is, an approach pioneered by Martin Feldstein in the 1990s.[9]

As we discuss later in this paper, there is increasing evidence that the responsiveness of the individual income tax base to taxation is higher than is typically assumed, particularly when one considers the high-income individuals who pay a large share of income taxes. A broader issue that we also address is that the economics profession has paid more attention to government revenue maximization than to overall economic prosperity.

Regarding the approach of directly taxing wealth, history increasingly suggests that wealth taxation is an inefficient means through which to raise tax revenue. For one thing, any taxpayer potentially subject to the wealth tax is strongly incentivized to alter his behavior from economically productive behaviors such as capital investment to inefficient behaviors such as paying lawyers and accountants to avoid the tax altogether, thus lowering tax revenues and effectively compounding the cost of the tax. A number of European countries that once had such tax policies eventually faced this reality and abandoned the measures altogether.

Finally, the distortions and flaws of different approaches to taxation raise questions about the fundamental premise on which most recent taxation proposals rest: that government involvement in the market is more effective in remedying societal problems, such as inequitable distribution of resources, than the private market. This remains the most problematic argument that has undergirded most socialist arguments around wealth or income confiscation throughout history.

Income Taxation

In the implementation of income tax policy, a fundamental distinction that must be understood is the difference between marginal tax rates and average tax rates. Under a progressive tax regime, marginal tax rates increase with higher levels of income, which is the main reason, together with their higher incomes, that high-income individuals pay a greater share of the tax burden (figure 15.2).

Although a given taxpayer's income may place him or her in a particular tax bracket with a corresponding marginal tax rate, the *average tax rate* at which taxpayers pay the entirety of their taxes is usually much lower. This is because only the portion of a taxpayer's taxable income that falls within a given bracket is subject to that corresponding marginal tax rate. Therefore, after an individual claims deductions and pays the taxes owed at the proper rates of different brackets, the overall percentage of income that is paid will be less than the top marginal rate. As income rises, the average tax rate approaches the top-bracket marginal tax rate.

It is an underappreciated fact that the US income tax system is one of the most progressive among OECD countries (figure 15.3). Furthermore,

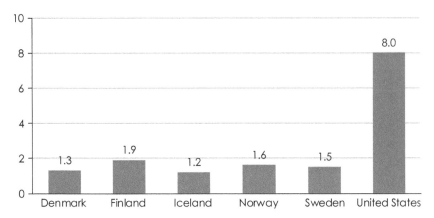

Figure 15.2. The Progressivity of Personal Income Tax Structures in the Nordic Countries and the United States; Top Tax Rate Threshold as a Multiple of the Average Wage. *Note:* For example, if the US threshold as a multiple of the average wage was lowered to Denmark's, the top marginal tax rate would apply to filers earning just $68,802. Simulations assume a single taxpayer and married taxpayers with two dependents living in California. *Sources:* Council of Economic Advisers, Organisation for Economic Co-operation and Development.

this has been trending in a more pronounced direction over the last forty years. In that time frame, the share of federal taxes paid by households in the highest quintile increased from 55 percent in 1979 to 69 percent in 2017.[10] This outpaces the United Kingdom, Germany, Sweden, and even France.[11] That is in part due to the differences between the tax rates at lower income levels across these countries. For example, in France the marginal tax rate is 30 percent for people who reach the income level of $33,000. The federal marginal rate at this same income level in the United States is a mere 12 percent. Therefore, in order to make the United States tax regime even *more progressive*, the higher rates at which high-income individuals are already taxed would need to be increased to an even more extreme degree.

Owing to the lack of uniformity in states' approaches to taxation, the United States provides an interesting experiment on the effects of progressive tax systems. According to the Illinois Policy Institute, immigration trends over the past decade show that four out of the five states with

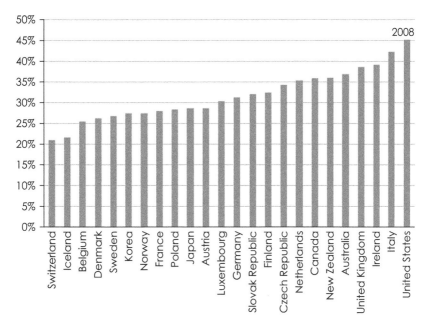

Figure 15.3. Share of Taxes of Richest Decile, 2008; Share of Taxes Paid by Richest Decile (%). *Source:* Organisation for Economic Co-operation and Development, *Growing Unequal? Income Distribution and Poverty in OECD Countries* (Paris: OECD Publishing, 2008).

the worst trends in net population growth had progressive income tax regimes.[12] Conversely, the states that experienced the greatest population growth over the same period had a flat tax or no state income taxes. A poll of individuals leaving Illinois—the state with the most negative change in population numbers in raw terms and second to worst in percentage (−1.3 percent)—showed that the top reason for leaving was in fact taxes.[13] Thus, although making taxes higher may seem to be an effective approach to raising revenues, one must consider the potential revenue loss generated as a result of a behavioral response to these measures.

The modern tradition of serious economic modeling of optimal income tax rates goes back to yet another economist from the United Kingdom, James Mirrlees. In a noted 1971 paper, he introduced endogenous labor income to the classical utilitarian model and derived revenue-maximizing marginal tax rates that *decline* with income, seeming to provide theoretical evidence against progressive income taxation.[14] In this framework, individuals with an ability to earn high incomes can choose to work less and produce at lower income levels, thus paying less tax. In theory, if there is a single top earner in an economy with positive marginal tax rates at that earner's income level, the marginal tax rate on income above that earner's income should be set to zero—the government would collect no less income tax and the individual might produce more.[15] However, the public-economics profession has spent the intervening decades modifying and revising this fundamental result. The "zero tax rate at the top" result is local to the top earner, and the shape of the ability distribution near the top can have large effects on the efficiency-maximizing rate of high earners.[16]

Martin Feldstein emphasized the so-called elasticity of taxable income (ETI) as a measure of the efficiency of a tax system. The ETI is an attempt to measure the impact on tax revenues of changes in tax rates and subsequent behavioral changes. For example, an ETI of 1 means roughly that if an individual's marginal tax rate rises by 1 percent, he will report 1 percent less taxable income to the government. To take the example further, imagine a taxpayer with taxable income of $250,000 facing a 50 percent marginal tax rate. If that tax rate increases to 51 percent, that is a 2 percent increase in the individual's marginal tax rate, so an ETI of 1 would imply that such an increase would lead the individual to report $5,000 less taxable income ($2\% \times 1 \times \$5,000$) after the tax reform.[17]

Many research papers attempt to calculate an "optimal" marginal income tax rate that would maximize government revenue, taking into consideration the fact that higher marginal tax rates will reduce taxable income. Although the mainstream economics profession rarely cites the work of Art Laffer, his famous curve that peaks at a revenue-maximizing tax rate (figure 15.4) is certainly the clearest available exposition of this concept. The revenue-maximizing income tax rate depends on a number of assumptions about economic behavior, first and foremost among them the ETI.

The ETI might not be a perfect measure of the ability of an income tax system to collect revenue without changing economic behavior, but

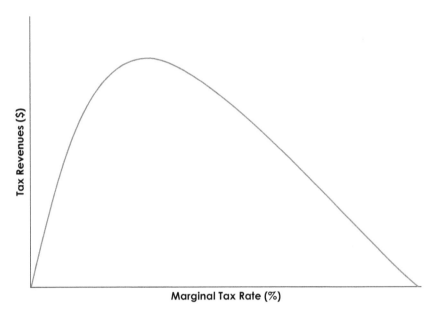

Figure 15.4. Laffer Curve Graphical Representation. *Source:* Authors' representation.

it is close. As pointed out by Raj Chetty, some of the costs of sheltering income are transfers from one economic agent to another, including charitable contributions, trusts for descendants, or even payments to tax attorneys. In this context, Chetty essentially provides an argument that high taxation is not as bad as the behavioral response of taxable income would make it seem, since the welfare of all the beneficiaries of tax evasion may be undervalued by taxpayers.[18]

Of course, this also highlights the fact that tax systems that allow for these types of avoidance effectively favor one activity over another. Furthermore, the nature of this discussion makes obvious that the goal pursued by most of the public-economics research profession as far as income taxation is concerned is quite narrow. If a tax can be collected without changing the activity that generates the tax base too much in a distortionary way, then it is viewed by the profession as a good tax, and as long as the government doesn't actually lose money by raising tax rates, then such tax increases are acceptable.

Perhaps the most widely known recent paper in this literature, by the Nobel Prize–winning economist Peter Diamond and his coauthor Emmanuel Saez, calculates an optimal top tax rate of 73 percent, while another, by Thomas Piketty, Saez, and Stefanie Stantcheva, calculates an optimal top tax rate of 83 percent.[19] Although they do not cite Laffer, in effect their approach is analogous to identifying the top of a Laffer Curve. If the definition of socialism is "a system in which the perceived unjust distribution of income is righted through extensive state intervention and control," these papers sound as though they are advocating a socialist approach to taxation.

These results have been criticized on many grounds. Certainly, by incorporating the possibility of disincentives to invest in human capital and innovation, the long-term revenue-maximizing top tax rate must be lower than those implied by the above papers. The work of many economists, including Joseph Stiglitz, has confirmed the general intuition of the Mirrlees results.[20] In a recent paper from the Hoover Institution, Ken Judd and three coauthors come to similar conclusions as Mirrlees, going as far as supporting negative rates on top income levels. Overall, since the publication of Mirrlees's research and related examples, OECD countries have become less progressive in their tax systems, as the United States has grown increasingly progressive.[21]

Another issue with papers that claim to justify high optimal top tax rates is their assumptions about key behavioral parameters, particularly the ETI, which is set to .20 or .25. Further, recent empirical evidence that considers effects on both extensive margin (out-migration) and intensive margin (tax avoidance by stayers) raises the possibility that the ETI for high earners might be significantly higher.

One issue is that many ETI estimates do not account for taxpayer departures. Two papers—the first by Enrico Moretti and Daniel Wilson, the second by David Agrawal and Dirk Foremny—establish that average tax rates matter significantly as they relate to changes in out-migration trends among high earners, in both intranational and international settings.[22] Moretti and Wilson study star scientists in the United States and write: "Overall, we conclude that state taxes have a significant effect on geographical location of star scientists and possibly other highly skilled workers. While there are many other factors that drive when innovative individuals and innovative companies decide to locate, there are enough firms and workers on the margin that relative taxes matter." These out-migration trends also largely depend on how easily one is able to move between geographical locations. For example, in the United States state-to-state migration is quite easy; however, international migration, or emigration, may spur greater barriers.

Tax avoidance behavior is also important for the high earners who ultimately pay most of the income taxes. A study by Joshua Rauh and Ryan Shyu examines both extensive and intensive margin impacts on expected gains in tax revenues due to Proposition 30 in California in 2012.[23] These impacts together are shown to have eroded 45.2 percent of windfall tax revenues from the reform within the first year and 60.9 percent within two years, but the intensive margin of tax avoidance accounts for 90.5 percent of the total response. With the deductibility of state taxes removed by the 2017 Tax Cut and Jobs Act, California's income tax is likely close to the top of the Laffer Curve.

The finding that high-income taxpayers are more elastic in their behavior than had been previously modeled is a necessary correction to the research in this field. It is perhaps even more important, however, to emphasize how narrow the objective is of studies that claim to derive an optimal top income tax rate.

Their objective is simply to maximize the government's collection of economic resources. That is, the public-economics profession has in large part decided to focus on what tax rate allows the government to redistribute the most economic resources from those whose earnings primarily form the taxable income base to those whom the government chooses. Although the "hissing" metaphor of Colbert has sometimes been given the interpretation of referring to behavioral responses, it might be better applied to overall losses in total economic activity. Seen in this light, it seems that research in public economics has in fact been asking how to pluck the goose so as to procure the largest quantity of feathers, regardless of the amount of hissing. This would be the top of the Laffer Curve.

An objective grounded in prosperity would begin by asking what system and size of government would maximize the total long-term productive output of a society, subject to some constraints involving distributional outcomes, not what income tax rate maximizes government revenue. This is of course a more challenging enterprise, and preferences as to the distributional outcomes and how to specify them will naturally vary. Yet it would be better to go in this direction than to implicitly accept the notion that the optimal tax rate is at the top of the Laffer Curve—at the point where the government literally cannot squeeze another dime out of a given tax base by raising its rate.

Wealth Taxation

In January 2019, Senator Elizabeth Warren proposed the "Ultra-Millionaire Tax," which sought to place a 2 percent annual rate on those with a household net worth exceeding $50 million and a 3 percent rate on those with a household net worth of $1 billion. Senator Bernie Sanders in September of that year provided his own version of the wealth tax, with a greater number of wealth brackets, ultimately culminating in an 8 percent tax rate on taxpayers with a net worth over $10 billion.

These would not be unprecedented measures when one considers tax policy from an international perspective. In 1990, twelve OECD countries had their own versions of a wealth tax; however, today this number stands at four (Spain, Switzerland, Norway, and Belgium). Why the fall in popularity? Wealth taxes have proved difficult to administer due to the avoidance measures taken by the targeted taxpayers. As a result, the taxes never yielded the anticipated revenue.[24] Worse, the impact due to the outward flow of wealth in some instances proved to compound the problem. According to French economist Eric Pichet, France's wealth tax cost the government as much revenue as the total ultimately yielded by the tax.[25]

Saez and his fellow UC Berkeley economist Gabriel Zucman—the primary advisers on the Warren wealth tax plan—aimed to address these risks by including various measures in the proposal, including a "large exit tax" of 40 percent on wealthy taxpayers attempting to evade payment by renouncing their citizenship. Additionally, they would revoke exemptions for certain asset classes that were included in the European plans.[26]

Setting aside questions regarding the precedents this would set as relates to the government's ability to confiscate a citizen's property, these types of measures, as noted by Pichet, incentivize one set of unproductive behaviors over a set of more productive ones. Even the precise value of wealth when tied up in private businesses or other illiquid assets becomes very challenging to ascertain, and despite Saez and Zucman's efforts, high-net-worth taxpayers will still pay a fortune to lawyers and accountants to avoid this tax. The Berkeley economists admit this reality at least in the context of estate taxes when explaining in their wealth tax proposal:

> Estate tax revenue collected in 2017 from wealthy individuals who died in 2016 was only $20 billion. This is only about 0.13% of the $15 trillion net worth that the top 0.1% wealthiest families owned in 2016. This demonstrates quantitatively that the estate fails to take much of a bite on the wealthiest (in spite of a reasonably high 40% nominal tax rate above the $5 million exemption threshold, set to increase to $10 million in 2018). The main factor driving such low tax revenue is tax avoidance.[27]

While the writers of this quote presumably would argue this is evidence of the need to implement wealth taxes that are airtight to all possible evasion or avoidance, they are up against the empirical fact that essentially all major countries that have attempted the wealth tax have failed to achieve this goal.

At the end of the day, even if the targeted taxpayers were somehow unable to shelter their accumulated wealth, such a tax disincentivizes the accumulation of wealth for part of the targeted class of taxpayers, as there is no longer a clear reason to accumulate substantial wealth. Instead, high earners are incentivized to consume as much as they have to in order fall below the threshold that initiates the tax. Again, these types of behaviors come at the cost of more productive behaviors, such as investment in productive new companies or innovations, and those compounding costs must be understood when projecting potential revenue growth as a result of the wealth tax. And under the structure of this tax plan, the embedded incentives encourage an important class of potential investors to avoid investing altogether.[28]

One therefore understandably wonders what possible benefits there could be from a tax that has historically yielded little return in the form of tax revenues and has a costly impact on economic growth. Saez and Zucman in their public writings represent a different public-policy aim than simply trying to raise tax revenues to fund government expenditures. A month prior to the release of the economics of their plan, they articulated this aim in a *New York Times* op-ed, "Alexandria Ocasio-Cortez's Tax Hike Idea Is Not About Soaking the Rich." They explain:

> Just as the point of taxing carbon is not to raise revenue but to reduce carbon emissions, high tax rates for sky-high incomes do not aim at funding Medicare for All. They aim at preventing an oligarchic drift that, if left unaddressed, will continue undermining the social compact and risk killing democracy.[29]

With this statement, the authors reinterpret the wealth tax as a Pigouvian tax against the externality of "oligarchic drift." This is a much different public-policy objective than simply attempting to raise adequate tax revenues for a particular policy initiative that may or may not help poor Americans. Instead, this is a more clearly stated desire to bequeath to the state the ability to confiscate property on the pretext of maintaining democratic norms. This is a separate argument that is more a question about the importance of private property rights. However, what is clear is that this line of reasoning does not constitute a real refutation of the existing evidence that wealth taxation fails as a means in raising tax revenues and in incentivizing productive economic activities.

As a practical and political philosophical matter, private property rights are essential to the maintenance of a functioning free society. As Friedrich Hayek presciently explained in *The Road to Serfdom*:

The system of private property is the most important guarantee of freedom. It is only because the control of the means of production is divided among many people acting independently that we as individuals can decide what to do with ourselves. When all the means of production are vested in a single hand, whether it be nominally that of "society" as a whole or that of a dictator, whoever exercises this control has complete power over us. In the hands of private individuals, what is called economic power can be an instrument coercion, but it is never control over the whole life of a person.[30]

This is not merely a hypothetical consideration, as the countries that have violated the private property rights of private entities throughout history have paid a steep price. As recently as 2012, the Argentinian government decided to take an extraordinary step in nationalizing 51 percent of one foreign shareholder's stake in the country's largest oil and gas company, based on the government's claim that the gas company was not producing a sufficient amount of energy for the country. However, the shareholder pointed out that this was due to the fact that the government had instituted draconian price controls that disincentivized further production and exploration.[31]

Nevertheless, what followed was predictable: Argentina became a far riskier market for foreign investors. The World Bank ranks countries by the ease with which individuals can conduct business there, and between 2011 and 2012, in the aftermath of the nationalization efforts, Argentina fell eight spots in those rankings, from 113th to 121st.[32] In the most recent rankings, from 2019, Argentina reached its all-time low: 126th.[33]

The case of Argentina is typical of the lessons to be gained about the efficacy of central governments' ability to achieve policy goals. Government involvement begets further government involvement, and this ultimately results in economically disadvantageous results for the general population. This begins with the same false presuppositions of the proponents of the wealth tax—that centralized bodies transcend personal interest and therefore can do better than the private market in achieving fairer results. As Adam Smith famously explained regarding this idea, "By pursuing his own interest [the individual laborer or investor] frequently promotes that of the society more effectually than when he really intends to promote it. I have never known much good done by those who affected to trade for the public good."[34]

Between the evidence showing the small proportion of tax revenue captured by the tax as well as the inordinate cost imposed on local economies due to wealth and its owners flowing out to evade it, the imposition of a wealth tax seems likely to lead to reduced economic prosperity overall. Furthermore, even if the tax is intended to achieve more equitable outcomes for the broader society through wealth confiscation, the historical record suggests that these efforts only worsen the economic conditions for the wider population in the name of ameliorating them. Violations of this sort must be considered in the broader context of the historical record and what have proved to be the vital societal preconditions for economic success.

Implications for the Economic Impact of Plans for Higher-Income and Wealth Taxation

Aside from considering the general thrust of the policy prescription coming from the left, it is helpful to examine specific measures. One tax proposal in particular that has garnered significant interest is Senator Sanders's plan to establish a new top marginal rate of 52 percent on incomes above $10 million and a 4 percent income-based premium on households. These two changes would result in a federal top marginal rate of 56 percent on incomes above $10 million, which, combined with FICA taxes and state tax rates, would put top bracket marginal rates above 70 percent.[35]

The Tax Foundation estimates that the overall change in tax revenues *without considering the macroeconomic or behavioral impacts* would be an additional $3.1 trillion in tax revenue between 2020 and 2029. However, when one considers the aforementioned impacts, additional tax revenues ultimately fall to $2.1 trillion in the same time frame. Worse, the United States' gross domestic product and capital stock would fall 2 percent and

2.5 percent, respectively. Consequently, the country would lose approximately 1.5 million jobs.[36]

The pretexts for such heavy-handed measures and the subsequent pain endured as a result are the potential benefits from programs like Medicare for All. However, programs of this sort are never as straightforward as they initially seem. For example, independent analyses from policy think tanks, ranging from the Urban Institute to the Mercatus Center, have concluded that the cost of Medicare for All for just ten years would be $32 trillion to $34 trillion.[37] The annual additional federal costs that would result would therefore be approximately $10,000 per American. Thus, the taxation plan proposed by Sanders would be nowhere near adequate in paying for such a program. An analysis by the Heritage Foundation shows that if the taxation plan were financed through payroll taxes, there would have to be "an additional 21.2 percent tax on every dollar that every American earns," even assuming that there would be no economic responses that would reduce the tax base.[38]

Further concerns surround the availability of health care under such a regime. Sanders's plan aims to reimburse health care providers at rates used by Medicare. However, this is only potentially 60 percent of what private insurers currently pay. Therefore, it is quite likely that access to care would become more strained due to severe cuts to the revenues.[39] The example of Medicare for All is instructive in understanding how large government programs funded through laborious tax regimes ultimately result in worse outcomes for the general population. This is not a new observation. In 1988, a former proponent of socialist policies, Chinese scholar Peter Nolan, described the failures of socialist policies in rural China as follows:

> Errors of all kinds have been made in the socialist countries' rural polices, but . . . none has been so important as the misplaced belief in the virtues of large-scale (in terms of numbers of workers) units of production. Not only are there managerial diseconomies of scale, but a potentially powerful weapon in propelling forward a poor, capital-scarce economy is lost, the dynamism of myriads of "petty commodity producers" struggling to improve their families' situation.[40]

Although food production and health care are obviously much different industries, the fundamental premises on which the logic of the argument rests are the same. Hence, there is reason to be skeptical of legislation that establishes centrally controlled "Rube Goldberg machines" that promise better efficiency and outcomes. Such approaches are increasingly in opposition to the historical and current data-driven analysis of such policies. Therefore, we argue that tax policy must avoid a repeat of the same mistakes of the past and reject higher top-bracket income tax rates and wealth taxes, as these will serve to reduce economic activity and overall prosperity.

Conclusion

Throughout the course of history, movements to increase redistribution have arisen alongside narratives surrounding material imbalance or unfairness. As these movements grow in intensity, it is often the case that a desire to right these perceived wrongs becomes a goal that proponents believe is worth achieving by any means necessary. In such an environment, facts are paramount, and the willingness to express realities must become stronger to counter extreme passion.

To any passing observer, it appears that the United States has reached an inflection point with respect to the country's prospective economic vision. While these debates rage, the mainstream economics profession has converged on certain norms of calibrating economic models to derive revenue-maximizing marginal tax rates. Economists can debate the level of income tax rates that maximizes government revenue, but taxing society at those rates involves forgoing massive amounts of economic output and economic prosperity, as economic activity is reduced or driven abroad and the remaining spending power becomes concentrated in the hands of government. The profession has devoted little effort to measuring that forgone prosperity.[41]

Meanwhile, although much of the economics profession highlights the flaws of capitalism, there have been growing calls for more invasive, socialist policies such as greater progressivity in the United States' tax regime; wealth confiscation; and more nationalized sectors of the economy. These calls come despite a body of evidence showing that the country is already one of the more progressive tax regimes in the world, that wealth confiscation results in worse outcomes for the broader economy, and that nationalizing areas of the economy creates worse outcomes for Americans. However, these policies do provide certain narrow benefits: greater power and control to a select group of insiders at the expense of freedom.

Almost any human being is susceptible to such passion, especially in times of great uncertainty. James Madison and Alexander Hamilton understood this back in 1788. Discussing the best way by which to organize Congress, they wrote in *Federalist No. 55*, "In all very numerous assemblies, of whatever characters composed, passion never fails to wrest the sceptre from reason. Had every Athenian citizen been a Socrates; every Athenian assembly would still have been a mob."[42] This struggle with human nature remains relevant today.

Therefore, before abandoning the economic vision that made the United States a beacon of freedom and opportunity for generations of people from all around the world for a vision misguidedly put forth through weaponizing the envies and passions of a reasonably concerned public, we hope that people heed the words of Edmund Burke when he reflected on the French Revolution,

> I should . . . suspend my congratulations on the new liberty of France, until I was informed how it had been combined with government; with public force; with the discipline and obedience of armies; with the collection of an effective and well-distributed revenue; with morality and religion; with the solidity of property; with peace and order; with civil and social manners.[43]

It is with that same spirit that one must ponder the potential outcome of proposed changes in our tax system, our broader economic system, and most importantly the way in which our government treats our natural rights as Americans.

NOTES

1. Committee for a Responsible Federal Budget, *Choices for Financing Medicare for All,* March 17, 2020, http://www.crfb.org/papers/choices-financing-medicare-all.
2. Pew Research Center, *Most Americans Say There Is Too Much Economic Inequality in the U.S., but Fewer Than Half Call It a Top Priority,* January 9, 2020, https://www.pewsocialtrends.org/2020/01/09/most-americans-say-there-is-too-much-economic-inequality-in-the-u-s-but-fewer-than-half-call-it-a-top-priority.
3. Xavier Giroud and Joshua Rauh, "State Taxation and the Reallocation of Business Activity: Evidence from Establishment Level Data," *Journal of Political Economy* 127, no. 3 (2019): 1262–1316. As with other taxes, the burden of corporate income taxes will be carried most of all by those who cannot alter their behavior to avoid the taxes. Corporations may be particularly adept at tax avoidance, primarily by shifting the location of their capital to other jurisdictions.
4. Oxford Reference, "lump sum tax," https://www.oxfordreference.com/view/10.1093/oi/authority.20110803100118753.
5. Henry George, *Progress and Poverty: An Inquiry into the Cause of Industrial Depressions and of Increase of Want with Increase of Wealth; the Remedy* (1879).
6. "An Interview with Milton Friedman," *Human Events* 38, no. 46 (1978).
7. Arthur Pigou, *The Economics of Welfare* (London: Macmillan, 1920).
8. Frank Ramsey, "A Contribution to the Theory of Taxation," *Economic Journal* 37 (1927): 47–61.
9. Martin Feldstein, "The Effect of Marginal Tax Rates on Taxable Income: A Panel Study of the 1986 Tax Reform Act," *Journal of Political Economy* 103, no. 3 (1995): 55–72; Feldstein, "Tax Avoidance and the Deadweight Loss of the Income Tax," *Review of Economics and Statistics* 81, no. 4 (1999): 674–80.
10. Congressional Budget Office, "The Distribution of Household Income, 2017," October 2020, https://www.cbo.gov/publication/56575.
11. Dylan Matthews, "America's Taxes Are the Most Progressive in the World: Its Government Is Among the Least," *Washington Post* (April 5, 2013).
12. Illinois Policy Institute, "Slowest-Growing States Have Progressive Income Taxes," 2020.
13. Illinois Policy Institute, "Poll: High Taxes Are Top Reason Illinoisians Want to Leave State," 2019.

14. James Mirrlees, "An Exploration of the Theory of Optimum Income Taxation," *Review of Economic Studies* 38, no. 2 (1971): 175–208.

15. The Library of Economics and Liberty, Encyclopedia Biographies, "James Mirrlees: 1938–2018," https://www.econlib.org/library/Enc/bios/Mirrlees.html #IfHendersonCEE2BIO-057_footnote_nt443. The library's website notes that Mirrlees had been an adviser to Britain's Labour Party, which "for decades imposed marginal taxes in excess of 80 percent." Mirrlees wrote: "I must confess that I had expected the rigourous analysis of income taxation in the utilitarian manner to provide arguments for high tax rates. It has not done so."

16. Emmanuel Saez, "Using Elasticities to Derive Optimal Income Tax Rates," *Review of Economic Studies* 68 (2001): 205–29.

17. Often the ETI is measured with respect to the "net-of-tax" rate, or one minus the tax rate.

18. Raj Chetty, "Is Taxable Income Elasticity Sufficient to Calculate Deadweight Loss? The Implications of Evasion and Avoidance," *American Economic Journal: Economic Policy* 1, no. 2 (2009): 31–52.

19. Peter Diamond and Emmanuel Saez, "The Case for a Progressive Tax: From Basic Research to Policy Recommendations," *Journal of Economic Perspectives* 25, no. 4. (2011): 165–90; Thomas Piketty, Emmanuel Saez, and Stefanie Stantcheva, "Optimal Taxation of Top Labor Incomes: A Tale of Three Elasticities," *American Economic Journal: Economic Policy* 6, no. 1 (2014): 230–71.

20. Joseph E. Stiglitz, "Pareto Efficient and Optimal Taxation and the New New Welfare Economics," *Handbook of Public Economics* 2 (1987): 991–1042.

21. Kenneth L. Judd et al., "Optimal Income Taxation with Multidimensional Taxpayer Types," Stanford University Working Paper, 2018; Gregory Mankiw, Matthew Weinzierl, and Danny Yagan, "Optimal Taxation in Theory and Practice," *Journal of Economic Perspectives* 23, no. 4 (2009): 147–74.

22. Enrico Moretti and Daniel J. Wilson, "The Effect of State Taxes on Geographical Location of Top Earners: Evidence from Star Scientists," *American Economic Review* 107, no. 7 (2017): 1858–1903; David R. Agrawal and Dirk Foremny, "Relocation of the Rich: Migration in Response to Top Tax Rate Changes from Spanish Reform," *Review of Economics and Statistics* 101, no. 2 (2019): 214–32.

23. Joshua Rauh and Ryan Shyu, "Behavioral Responses to State Income Taxation of High Earners: Evidence from California," National Bureau of Economic Research Working Paper 26349, 2020.

24. Joseph Zeballos-Roig, "Here's Why Europe Has Mostly Ditched Wealth Taxes over the Last 25 Years—Even as Elizabeth Warren and Bernie Sanders Seek Them for the US," *Business Insider,* November 17, 2019.

25. Eric Pichet, "The Economic Consequences of the French Wealth Tax," *La Revue de Droit Fiscal* 14 (2008): 5.

26. Emmanuel Saez and Gabriel Zucman, "How Would a Progressive Tax Work? Evidence from the Economics Literature," 2019, http://gabriel-zucman.eu/files /saez-zucman-wealthtaxobjections.pdf.

27. Saez and Zucman, "How Would a Progressive Tax Work?," 20.

28. John H. Cochrane, "Wealth and Taxes," Cato Institute, *Tax and Budget Bulletin*, no. 86 (2020).

29. Emmanuel Saez and Gabriel Zucman, "Alexandria Ocasio-Cortez's Tax Hike Idea Is Not About Soaking the Rich," *New York Times* (January 22, 2019).

30. Friedrich Hayek, *The Road to Serfdom* (London: Institute of Economic Affairs, 2005), 41.

31. Simon Romero and Raphael Minder, "Argentina to Seize Control of Oil Company," *New York Times,* April 5, 2013.

32. World Bank, *Doing Business 2011*, 2010); World Bank, *Doing Business 2012*, 2011.

33. World Bank, *Doing Business 2019*, 2018.

34. Adam Smith, *Wealth of Nations,* bk. 4, chap. 2 (London: W. Strahan and T. Cadell, 1776), https://www.econlib.org/library/Smith/smWN.html?chapter_num=27 #book-reader.

35. The plan would also repeal the Section 199A pass-through deduction, which allows a 20 percent deduction for qualified pass-through business income.

36. Erica York and Garrett Watson, "Analysis of Democratic Presidential Candidate Individual Income Tax Proposals," Tax Foundation, 2020.

37. Linda Blumberg et al., *From Incremental to Comprehensive Health Reform: How Various Reform Options Compare on Coverage and Costs*, Urban Institute, 2019; Charles Blahous, "The Costs of a National Single-Payer Healthcare System," Mercatus Working Paper, Mercatus Center, 2018.

38. Marie Fishpaw and Jamie Bryan Hall, "In Charts, How Medicare for All Would Make Most Families Poorer," Heritage Foundation, 2019.

39. Ramesh Ponnuru, "Want Medicare for All? Be Ready to Wait," *Bloomberg Opinion*, October 30, 2019.

40. Peter Nolan, *The Political Economy of Collective Farms: An Analysis of China's Post-Mao Rural Reforms* (New York: Routledge, 1988), 3.

41. Martin Feldstein, "Tax Avoidance and the Deadweight Loss of the Income Tax." This is perhaps the closest estimate in a respected economics journal. In 1999 Feldstein estimated that as of 1993 the deadweight loss of individual income taxation amounted to a full 60 percent of total individual taxable income.

42. James Madison and Alexander Hamilton, "The Federalist No. 55," 1788, https://founders.archives.gov/documents/Hamilton/01-04-02-0204.

43. Edmund Burke, *Reflections on the Revolution in France* (New Haven, CT: Yale University Press, 2003), 8.

V
Afterword

.

16

In an Emerging New World, Choose Economic Freedom

George P. Shultz

The world is on a hinge of history. The future is going to be different from the past in major ways.

At the end of the Second World War, people such as Dean Acheson, George Marshall, and Harry Truman sat atop another hinge of history, though they may not have realized it at the time—you can know something is important without knowing exactly what it is that you are dealing with. But when they looked around at the devastation that had been wrought across the globe, with tens of millions of lives lost and economies of allies and adversaries alike in ruins, they saw how the United States could work with both to help. American economic resources could help to rebuild infrastructure and restart economies. American military resources could help protect those efforts from new conflicts. There wasn't a grandiose plan to do so, but bit by bit sectors and countries from across the world were drawn into a voluntary, shared framework—one in which the United States could do well for itself and that was also appealing to others around the world who could see their own success in it too. I think it's fair to say that when the Cold War came to an end, a security and economic commons had been built in the world, which everybody benefited from.

But that commons is now eroding—and it should be clear that new challenges are coming at us. New communications technologies make speech and information available to anyone, anywhere, simultaneously. This adds new dimensions to the old challenge of effectively governing over diversity. New forms of production, such as advanced automation or additive manufacturing (also known as 3-D printing), reduce the importance of labor costs and make it easier to produce goods closer to where they will be used; along with a shift toward services in advanced economies, this development could upend traditional trade relationships and industrialization patterns. Data science and machine learning promise to transform a host of industries, jobs, and products. That includes new weaponry and ways of war fighting that put destructive power in the hands of more and more actors around the world, with disruptive effects. Major changes in the global demographic picture have set the advanced economies, most of them (save the United States and other immigration countries) with shrinking workforces, on a completely separate path from that of the poorest emerging economies in Africa or South Asia, whose youth populations are set to explode, despite the poor governance and economic opportunities available to them. What happens in these parts of the world, long ignored, will impact us too. And major technical and scientific challenges loom: the environment, energy, climate, pandemics, and health.

How should the United States respond to this complex, emerging new world?

The message I wish to convey is that when navigating these big changes—or even because of the scale of such changes at home and elsewhere—it becomes more important than ever to have common principles to work from so that you steer a good course. And though the institutions and techniques to deliver them may change, the core approaches today are no different from the ones that animated Acheson and Marshall and Truman after the war: personal liberty, ensured through a just and responsive government (and realized through good individual educational foundations), and the market price system, which is really just a way of enabling personal choice and initiative, within a feedback loop, for social benefit.

But history shows that when novel policy challenges arise, it's tempting for governments to abandon such principles in the name of "doing something." Consider the following piece of advice to the president of the United States:

> Why are the old rules not working? . . . Much of our economic think-ing and economic policy has not yet caught up with the changes that have taken place in the structure of our economy. We continue to rely on monetary and fiscal policies that worked reasonably well ten or twenty years ago, unmindful of the profound changes in our eco-nomic environment.

Such words echo today, but this is not a quote from a Senator Sanders stump speech. Rather, it is from a 1971 letter, marked "personal and confi-dential," from Fed chair Arthur Burns to President Richard Nixon—a let-ter that I recently stumbled upon from my own collections in the Hoover Archives. In it, Burns—the widely respected "pope of economics" himself, struggling to respond to public and political panic over inflation—is ad-vocating for an economy-wide system of federally administered wage and price controls, one that would in fact be enacted just two months later. Burns's new approach was initially met with rapturous and bipartisan ap-plause across the country—before leading to a decade of disastrous con-sequences. This experience instilled my own sense that, in the end, even wise people are fallible—and that, even in times of upheaval, it's good economics that leads to good policies, and to good results for the country.

We may think of market principles as defining of the American system, but the challenges we often hear voiced against them today are not novel. Members of the public, alongside intellectuals and political leaders in both parties, have often found cause to abandon them when convenient. In our recent book *Choose Economic Freedom*, John Taylor and I—alongside hon-orary coauthor the late economist and Hoover fellow Milton Friedman, our friend and colleague who supplied many relevant words of wisdom during his lifetime—tell the story of what happens when these principles are abandoned and when they are once again heeded.[1] As we once again look to new policy challenges in this country, I'd like to remind people of those lessons, forged through the crucible of an earlier American age of "democratic distemper" (to borrow Hoover fellow Mo Fiorina's phrase), without having to relive the pain that proved it.[2]

Let's return to that chaotic era in American history by setting the scene.[3] In 1962, I was a faculty member at the University of Chicago. I had read the new and energetic Kennedy administration's President's Council of Economic Advisers annual report, which issued a set of soft guidelines for wage and price changes designed to set the sights of labor and management on wage and price changes in a way that would keep inflation under control.[4] They outlined voluntary, productivity-linked "guideposts" to stabilize wage and price setting in industries they said exercised market power. Their concerns about inflation were underlined by Lyndon Johnson's Vietnam War and Great Society spending.

I worried, though, that these guidelines might be the conceptual precursors of harder, government-directed wage and price controls. Such a move would paralyze the open-market economy that underlies American prosperity. So, in collaboration with my colleague Robert Aliber, we held a conference on the issue, and many heavy hitters attended—top-notch economists of all persuasions, including George Stigler, Allan Meltzer, then CEA chair Gardner Ackley, and future labor secretary John Dunlop. Milton Friedman gave an outstanding address against wage and price guidelines (or guideposts), pointing to the harms they cause—including that it is actually in the business's and the economy's interest to violate such government requests, thereby encouraging a sense of lawlessness—and showing that inflation is instead a "monetary phenomenon" caused by bad fiscal policy. In response, Robert Solow, who like Friedman would also later win a Nobel Prize, offered "The Case against the Case against the Guideposts"—in effect arguing for them, using a technical justification based on the employment level and firms' market power. Although Friedman and Solow disagreed, the conference was a success; the issues were well identified. Aliber and I gathered together the papers and transcripts of the discussions and published them in a book.[5] So the subject was on my mind.

Not long afterward, I became secretary of labor. In this capacity, I was preoccupied with settling major strikes, fighting against discrimination in the workplace, and managing on the president's behalf the desegregation of schools in seven Southern states, sixteen years after the *Brown v. Board of Education* decision of 1954.

By July 1970, however, I became the first director of the Office of Management and Budget (OMB). I sensed, after a time, that wage and price controls were, indeed, in the air, so I gave a speech making the case that we had the budget under control and, with a reasonable monetary policy, inflation would be brought under control. All we needed was the patience to see these orthodox policies through, so the title of my speech was "Steady as You Go." I argued:

> A portion of the battle against inflation is now over; time and the guts to take the time, not additional medicine, are required for the sickness to disappear. We should now follow a noninflationary path back to full employment.[6]

Instead, the pace toward controls picked up. In August 1970, Congress gave the president the authority to impose them. In effect, Congress said, "We have given you the tools; now it's up to you to do the job." Meanwhile, the accelerating growth of dollars in foreign hands posed the threat of a run on the bank (Fort Knox), with inflationary implications.

This was about the time that Burns, as chairman of the Federal Reserve at the time, wrote to President Nixon. In his private letter, dated June 22, 1971, Burns argued that structural changes in the economy made it difficult to control inflation, that sound monetary and fiscal policies—classical policies—would not work as in the past, and that a new approach was needed. He advocated a six-month wage and price freeze. Obviously, he thought that government-directed controls would work, giving the Fed a major assist in taming inflation. He was an expert in the business cycle, with many years conducting research at the National Bureau of Economic Research, so this was a surprising change in his thinking. Burns argued:

> In my judgment, some of us are continuing to interpret the economic world on the model of the 1940s and 1950s. In fact, the structure of the economy has changed profoundly since then.

There was a time when the onset of a business recession was typically followed in a few months by a decline in the price level and in wage rates, or at least by a moderation of the rise. That is no longer the case. The business cycle is still alive, indeed too much so; but its inner response mechanism, which has never stood still, is now very different from what it was even ten or twenty years ago.

Failure to perceive this may be responsible for some shortcomings in our national economic policy. I doubt if we will bring inflation under control, or even get a satisfactory expansion going, without a major shift in economic policy.[7]

I resisted—even making my case at a dramatic, last-moment weekend retreat with the president at Camp David. But the decisions had already been made, and I had lost. On Sunday, August 15, 1971, the president announced a ninety-day wage and price freeze, to be followed by more elaborate controls and a surcharge of 10 percent on imported goods and services. On three television networks, he said, "The time has come for a new economic policy for the United States." Nixon's "shock" was a radical departure from the free-market price system of personal decision making and responsibility upon which our American system was based.

Disaster had struck, I thought. But it didn't look that way. The stock market logged its largest ever one-day increase. In fact, the freeze was hugely popular—with the public, with most businesses (especially given the new tariffs that went along with it), and among politicians from both parties—so much so that I was frightened, as the natural flow and feedback of economic variables in the economy was being stifled. This enthusiastic endorsement of the freeze from Richard Reynolds Jr., president of the Reynolds Metals Company, was typical:

A very good and forceful move at a critical time. . . . The President's program is going to help the economy generally and basic industries, including aluminum, in particular. His action was certainly warranted by the condition of the economy. We don't have the demand.... It is quite clear that the President deserves praise for the scope of this action.[8]

I did have some help. A number of economists, published in the *Wall Street Journal* and in *Newsweek*, argued against the freeze. And Milton Friedman was quoted in *Newsweek* as saying: "[President Nixon] has a tiger by the tail. Reluctant as he was to grasp it, he will find it hard to let go."[9]

At first, the wage-price freeze seemed to work, as it came at a time when inflation was already in the process of declining and commodity prices were soft in the world markets. The "temporary" freeze was inevitably followed up by explicit, compulsory wage and price controls, which turned out to be very intrusive on the economy. People were unable to change wages and prices without the consent of the so-called Price Commission or Pay Board. The seven-member Price Commission and the fifteen-member Pay Board were established with members from labor, business, and the public. The controls were administered with enthusiasm by a Cost of Living Council, headed by John Connally, secretary of the Treasury.

At the conclusion of the ninety-day freeze period, the council enacted Phase II of the controls, which would stay in place through the 1972 election. Under Phase II, corporations were allowed to pass increased costs through to prices but were slowed down by prenotification and profit margin limitation requirements; for example, companies with sales exceeding $100 million had to register price increases thirty days in advance, which could then go ahead, barring rejection from the Price Commission. Price growth was targeted at 2.5 percent. Wages were to be limited to 5.5 percent annual growth. Burns, who had earlier turned down a seat on the Cost of Living Council, was appointed to head the Committee on Interest and Dividends, which stated that corporate dividend growth should be limited to just 4 percent. Burns described the committee as "a new instrument for jawboning." The complexity of administering the controls grew.

In the short term, the consumer price index (CPI), which measures inflation, declined and real GDP rose. All this led to the landslide reelection of President Nixon. But trouble lay ahead. The economy sputtered, and prices were a problem. The Cost of Living Council, the bureaucracy responsible for administering the controls, was intrusive. No wage or price change could take place without approval by the Pay Board or the Price Commission, so the gears of the economy ceased working in the normal and natural ways that produce an efficient system.

On June 12, 1972, I moved from OMB to become Treasury secretary, and the Cost of Living Council control system, now headed by Don Rumsfeld and Dick Cheney, reported to me. Working with Rumsfeld and Cheney, and with the president's support, we designed an effort to ease away from the rigidity of Phase II. On January 11, 1973, the president announced Phase III of the wage and price controls. The idea was to scale back the institutional complexity of the program and to rely more on voluntary cooperation in the private sector. We knew that an initial burst of suppressed inflation was likely to show its head, but following that, we expected a more settled period (at the time, the CPI was growing at an annual rate of 3.6 percent). So the Price Commission and the Pay Board were abolished in favor of "self-administration" by obligated parties: Firms with sales exceeding $250 million had to report quarterly profits and price changes to the council, but advance clearances were no longer required. Annual price growth targets were still set, but firms could petition for exceptions. The complexity in relating all of this today shows just how hard it is to unwind the idea that a centralized command-and-control system is somehow simpler than the natural workings of the market.

One humorous sideline to all this was a discussion in which Herb Stein, chairman of the Council of Economic Advisers, said to the president, referring to the popularity of the earlier wage-price freeze: "Mr. President, you can't walk on water twice," to which President Nixon replied, "You can if it's frozen." It was clear then where policy was once again headed.

When that expected inflation uptick came, Nixon decided to reimpose controls. A new sixty-day price freeze was implemented in June 1973, beginning phase IV of the program—despite the president simultaneously warning the American public against becoming "addicted" to the tool. By that point, I had to say to the president, "This is your call, but it's directly opposed to my advice, and I think you are making a mistake. Under the circumstances, you need to find a new secretary of the Treasury."

Meanwhile, the controls went on. Under Phase IV, the Cost of Living Council's administrative focus was on trying to induce supply expansion despite the price freeze and limits on exports, especially for food items. Wholesale agricultural goods were exempted in a bid to encourage production, while retail food prices were controlled, resulting in shortages. I recall a colleague in my office exclaiming about Washington-area supermarkets: "We've got great prices posted on the shelves for meat—but we've got no meat!" The wholesale price of oil was similarly capped, at $4.25 per barrel, and scheduled to gradually rise over six months toward the world price (a plan disrupted by the Arab oil boycott, which sent up global prices faster than the US domestic oil prices were rising to meet them).

Faced with these disruptions, and poor public reaction, the president ended this second freeze early, after just thirty-five days. Further price controls were gradually scaled back, from covering 44 percent of all CPI basket prices in August 1973 down to 12 percent of CPI basket prices in April 1974.

But the controls—or the threat of their reimposition—never really stopped. Not six months after allowing the Cost of Living Council to dissolve in the spring of 1974, Congress reversed itself in August by granting a request from President Ford to establish a Council on Wage and Price Stability, which lasted until President Reagan took office. Everyone remembers President Carter's gas lines, as price controls in the oil sector led to shortages during the 1979 Iranian Revolution. What you control, you get less of. As Milton Friedman (himself invoking Edmund Burke) said of wage and price controls, "That is one of those 'very plausible schemes . . . with very pleasing commencements [that] have often shameful and lamentable conclusions.'"[10]

So what can we draw from this history of radical public policy? Above all, the main lesson is that orthodox policies, and the accountability of the free-market price system, work well and that selectively deviating from them can lead to trouble.

President Nixon, it might be said, did us a great favor by demonstrating that heavy-handed and open-ended interventions, as exemplified by the wage and price controls, generally do not work. He imposed them on the economy with broad political support and arranged to have them administered by talented people such as John Connally, John Dunlop, Don Rumsfeld, and Dick Cheney, among others. So he gave the country a lesson that even with high talent at the helm and the wind at your back, this approach doesn't work. He also showed that in thick of it, political affiliation does not guarantee a principled defense in this realm.

We also must be careful about the argument, as in the Arthur Burns letter, that the economy is a mess and doesn't work right anymore, so classical methods won't work. When you reach that stage of the argument, you almost inevitably reach for a different and untested lever—in this case, wage and price controls.

As is likely to be the case should it happen again, Burns's and others' prescriptions of drastic policy change proved to be wrong. It took years before Paul Volcker, in his own role as chair of the Federal Reserve, would return to classical but effective monetary policies alongside the freedom of decision making among businesses, workers, and consumers across the broader economy that Burns said would not work.

They did work. It took a while for inflation to come under control, but once it did, the economy took off. By the end of 1982, inflation was substantially reduced and stabilized, and everyone could see it was going to stay that way. The last remnants of the controls were killed off. And this lesson goes well beyond avoiding wage and price guideposts or controls. The same lessons apply to the other market-oriented reforms that began in the 1980s, including tax and regulatory policies. The marginal rate of income taxation, for example, having been reduced by Presidents Kennedy and Johnson from 90 percent to 70 percent, was brought down to 50 percent by President Reagan. Meanwhile, the regulatory burden across a number of sectors of the economy was also lightened. And in 1983, the economy took off like a bird.

So remember, markets generally work (even, or perhaps particularly so, in times of uncertainty), and excessive interventions by government in the operations of the economy or in personal decision making can cause problems, sometimes severe. Watch out for charges that the world has changed, or society has changed, or the economy has changed, as justifications for suddenly abandoning your principles. Arguments to break with "the old rules" will always come; countering those is a continuous process—one that should aim to address new challenges and new public concerns. We do face major changes coming over this hinge of history. So we should observe these new trends, acknowledge them and learn to understand them, and then develop a credible, long-term strategy to confront them—before the urgency of an exigent crisis throws the door open to poor options and poor political choices. By owning up to the face of an emerging new world today, we will be in a better position to succeed in it by building from our shared American principles of individual liberty and prosperity.

NOTES

1. George P. Shultz and John B. Taylor, *Choose Economic Freedom: Enduring Policy Lessons from the 1970s and 1980s* (Stanford, CA: Hoover Institution Press, 2020).

2. Morris Fiorina, "The Democratic Distemper," Project on Governance in an Emerging World, Hoover Institution, May 2019. https://www.hoover.org/research/democratic-distemper.

3. The following text recalling this era is excerpted and adapted from two previous tellings: as published in Shultz and Taylor, *Choose Economic Freedom*, described here, and previously in a September 2017 speech I delivered to a meeting of the Economic History Association in San Jose, titled "Dreams Can Be Nightmares."

4. White House, Council of Economic Advisers, *Economic Report of the President* (Washington, DC: US Government Printing Office, 1962).

5. George P. Shultz and Robert Aliber, *Guidelines, Informal Controls, and the Market Place: Policy Choices in a Full Employment Economy* (Chicago: University of Chicago Press, 1966).

6. George P. Shultz, "Prescription for Economic Policy: 'Steady As You Go'" (speech, meeting of the Economic Club of Chicago, Chicago, April 22, 1971).

7. An original copy of the letter appears in the George P. Shultz collections of the Hoover Instruction Archives. It is reprinted in Shultz and Taylor, *Choose Economic Freedom*.

8. Richard Reynolds Jr. quoted in Walter Stovall, "Banks, Firms Laud Nixon Move," Associated Press, August 17, 1971.

9. Milton Friedman, "Why the Freeze Is a Mistake," *Newsweek*, August 30, 1971.

10. Friedman, "Why the Freeze Is a Mistake."

About the Contributors

TERRY L. ANDERSON has been a senior fellow at the Hoover Institution since 1998 and is currently the John and Jean De Nault Senior Fellow. He is the past president of the Property and Environment Research Center in Bozeman, Montana, and a Professor Emeritus at Montana State University.

SCOTT W. ATLAS, MD, is the Robert Wesson Senior Fellow at the Hoover Institution of Stanford University and a member of Hoover Institution's Working Group on Health Care Policy. Dr. Atlas investigates the impact of government and the private sector on access, quality, pricing, and innovation in health care and is a frequent policy adviser to government and industry leaders in these areas.

MICHAEL R. AUSLIN, PhD, is the Payson J. Treat Distinguished Research Fellow in Contemporary Asia at the Hoover Institution, Stanford University. A historian by training, he specializes in US policy in Asia and geopolitical issues in the Indo-Pacific region. He is the author of *Asia's New Geopolitics* and *The End of the Asian Century*, among other books. Previously an associate professor of history at Yale, he is now the senior adviser for Asia at the Halifax International Security Forum and a senior fellow at the Foreign Policy Research Institute.

PETER BERKOWITZ is the Tad and Dianne Taube Senior Fellow at the Hoover Institution, Stanford University. From 2019 to 2021, he served as director of the Policy Planning Staff at the United States State Department and as the executive secretary of the department's Commission on Unalienable Rights. He is the author of four books and the editor of six. A contributor to *RealClearPolitics*, he has published hundreds of articles on a variety of topics in a diversity of publications. He is a 2017 recipient of The Bradley Prize.

RUSSELL A. BERMAN, the Walter A. Haas Professor in the Humanities at Stanford University, is a senior fellow at the Hoover Institution and director of the Herbert and Jane Dwight Working Group on the Middle East and the Islamic World.

JOHN F. COGAN is the Leonard and Shirley Ely Senior Fellow at the Hoover Institution and a faculty member in the Public Policy Program at Stanford University. Cogan's research is focused on US budget and fiscal policy, federal entitlement programs, and health care. His latest book, *The High Cost of Good Intentions* (2017), is the recipient of the 2018 Hayek Prize.

LARRY DIAMOND is a senior fellow at the Hoover Institution and the Mosbacher Senior Fellow in Global Democracy at the Freeman Spogli Institute for International Studies (FSI) at Stanford University. He is also a Bass University Fellow in Undergraduate Education and professor, by courtesy, of political science and sociology at Stanford.

ELIZABETH ECONOMY is a senior fellow at Stanford University's Hoover Institution. She is the author most recently of *The World According to China* (2021) and *The Third Revolution: Xi Jinping and the New Chinese State* (2018). She is a member of the Aspen Strategy Group and the Board of Managers of Swarthmore College. During 2021–23, she is on leave from Hoover to serve as senior adviser for China to the secretary of commerce. The views expressed in this piece are her own and do not necessarily reflect the views of the US government.

NIALL FERGUSON, MA, DPhil, is the Milbank Family Senior Fellow at the Hoover Institution, Stanford University, and a senior faculty fellow of the Belfer Center for Science and International Affairs at Harvard.

STEPHEN HABER is the Peter and Helen Bing Senior Fellow at the Hoover Institution and the A.A. and Jeanne Welch Milligan Professor in the School of Humanities and Sciences at Stanford University.

DANIEL L. HEIL is a policy fellow at the Hoover Institution whose focus is on the federal budget, tax policy, and federal antipoverty programs. Heil's interests include replacing failed policies with state and federal initiatives that alleviate poverty by encouraging workforce participation and human capital development.

GREGORY KEARNEY is a master's candidate at Princeton University's School of Public and International Affairs, studying economics and public policy. Previously, he worked as a research analyst at the Hoover Institution, as a research economist at the Council of Economic Advisers at the White House, and at Deloitte & Touche as a consultant on the Global Transfer Pricing team in New York.

EDWARD P. LAZEAR (1948–2020) was the Morris Arnold and Nona Jean Cox Senior Fellow at the Hoover Institution and the Davies Family Professor of Economics at Stanford University's Graduate School of Business. Lazear served at the White House from 2006 to 2009, where he was chairman of the President's Council of Economic Advisers. Before arriving at Stanford, he taught at the University of Chicago.

MICHAEL W. MCCONNELL is the Richard and Frances Mallery Professor of Law and the director of the Constitutional Law Center at Stanford Law School and a senior fellow at the Hoover Institution. He served as a federal appellate judge from 2002 to 2009. His most recent book is *The President Who Would Not Be King: Executive Power under the Constitution* (Princeton University Press, 2020).

LEE E. OHANIAN is a senior fellow at the Hoover Institution and a distinguished professor of economics and director of the Ettinger Family Program in Macroeconomic Research at the University of California, Los Angeles (UCLA).

JOSHUA RAUH is a senior fellow at the Hoover Institution and the Ormond Family Professor of Finance at Stanford's Graduate School of Business. He formerly served at the White House, where he was principal chief economist on the President's Council of Economic Advisers, and taught at the University of Chicago's Booth School of Business (2004–09) and the Kellogg School of Management (2009–12).

GEORGE P. SHULTZ (1920–2021) had a distinguished career in government, in academia, and in the world of business. He was one of two individuals to have held four different federal cabinet posts; he taught at three of this country's great universities; and for eight years he was president of a major engineering and construction company.

JOHN YOO is a visiting fellow at the Hoover Institution, Emanuel S. Heller Professor of Law at the University of California–Berkeley School of Law, and a nonresident senior fellow at the American Enterprise Institute.

Index